The Holocaust
in American Life

Other Books by Peter Novick

THE RESISTANCE VERSUS VICHY
The Purge of Collaborators in Liberated France

THAT NOBLE DREAM
*The "Objectivity Question" and the
American Historical Profession*

The Holocaust
in American Life

Peter Novick

HOUGHTON MIFFLIN COMPANY

BOSTON · NEW YORK

1999

For information about permission to reproduce selections from
this book, write to Permissions, Houghton Mifflin Company,
215 Park Avenue South, New York, New York 10003.

Library of Congress Cataloging-in-Publication Data
Novick, Peter, date.
The Holocaust in American life / Peter Novick.
p.   cm.
Includes bibliographical references and index.
ISBN 0-395-84009-0
1. Holocaust, Jewish (1939–1945) — Foreign public opinion,
American. 2. Holocaust, Jewish (1939–1945) — Influence.
3. Holocaust, Jewish (1939–1945) — Historiography.
4. Jews — United States — Attitudes. 5. Public opinion —
United States. I. Title.
D804.45.U55N68   1999
943.53'18 — dc21   99-20074 CIP

Printed in the United States of America

Book design by Robert Overholtzer

QUM 10 9 8 7 6 5 4 3 2 1

For J. K. N.

CONTENTS

Introduction / 1

Introduction

THIS BOOK had its origin in curiosity and skepticism. The curiosity, which engaged me as an historian, had to do with why in 1990s America — fifty years after the fact and thousands of miles from its site — the Holocaust has come to loom so large in our culture. The skepticism, which engaged me as a Jew and as an American, had to do with whether the prominent role the Holocaust has come to play in both American Jewish and general American discourse is as desirable a development as most people seem to think it is. The years I've spent working on this book have helped to satisfy the curiosity, and confirmed the skepticism. In this Introduction I'll be outlining for the reader the approach I've taken to the historical question, to make what I have to say easier to follow. I'll also suggest some of the grounds of my skepticism, so that the reader will know "where I'm coming from."

Part of my puzzlement about how Americans became so "Holocaust conscious" had to do with timing: why now? Generally speaking, historical events are most talked about shortly after their occurrence, then they gradually move to the margin of consciousness. It was in the 1920s and 1930s, not the 1950s and 1960s, that novels, films, and collective consciousness were obsessed with the carnage of Passchendaele and the Somme. By the fifties and sixties — forty years and more after the events of the Great War — they had fallen down a memory hole where only historians scurry around in the dark. The most-viewed films and the best-selling books about the Vietnam War almost all appeared within five or ten years of the end of that conflict, as did the Vietnam Veterans Memorial in Washington. With the Holocaust the rhythm has been very different: hardly talked about for the first twenty years or so after World War II; then, from the 1970s on, becoming ever more central in American public discourse — particularly, of course, among Jews, but also in the culture at large. What accounts for this unusual chronology?

The other part of my puzzlement was: why here? There is nothing surprising about the Holocaust's playing a central role in the consciousness of Germany, the country of the criminals and their descendants. The same might be said of Israel, a country whose population — or much of it — has a special relationship to the victims of the crime. To a somewhat lesser extent, this could be said of nations occupied by Germany during the war which were the scene of the deportation to death (or the actual murder) of their Jewish citizens. In all of these countries the parents or grandparents of the present generation directly confronted — resisted, assisted, in any case witnessed — the crime; in all cases, a fairly close connection. In the case of the United States none of these connections are present. The Holocaust took place thousands of miles from America's shores. Holocaust survivors or their descendants are a small fraction of 1 percent of the American population, and a small fraction of American Jewry as well. Only a handful of perpetrators managed to make it to the United States after the war. Americans, including many American Jews, were largely unaware of what we now call the Holocaust while it was going on; the nation was preoccupied with defeating the Axis. The United States was simply not connected to the Holocaust in the ways in which these other countries are. So, in addition to "why now?" we have to ask "why here?"

Although these questions haven't been looked at systematically by scholars — perhaps because they haven't been looked at systematically — there is something of a tacit consensus on the answer. This answer — sometimes explicitly, always implicitly, Freudian — treats the current centrality of the Holocaust as an inevitable development. "Trauma," according to the standard dictionary of psychoanalysis, is "an event in the subject's life defined by its intensity, by the subject's incapacity to respond adequately to it, and by the upheaval and long-lasting effects that it brings about in the psychical organization." For a time the trauma can be repressed, but "repressed material . . . has a permanent tendency to re-emerge into consciousness."[1] Indeed, in the Freudian canon, "trauma" and "repression" define each other. Trauma is that which is so unbearable that it has to be repressed; repression is the consequence of something too traumatic to be borne; together they inevitably give rise to "the return of the repressed." The Holocaust, according to this influential explanation, had been a traumatic event, certainly for American Jews, more diffusely for all Americans. Earlier silence was a manifestation of repression; the explosion of talk in recent years has been "the return of the repressed."

For all of its elegance, I don't find this schema persuasive in explaining the evolution of Holocaust consciousness in the United States. Its applicability to various European countries, and to Israel, has been treated by other writers, and won't much concern us here. In the United States, in the special case of Holocaust survivors, the succession of trauma, repression, and return of the repressed often seems plausible. (Even here, though, as we'll see, survivors in the late 1940s frequently wanted to talk about their Holocaust experiences and were discouraged from doing so.) And surely there were some American Jews — perhaps even some gentiles — for whom the Holocaust was a traumatic experience. But the available evidence doesn't suggest that, overall, American Jews (let alone American gentiles) were traumatized by the Holocaust, in any worthwhile sense of that term. They were often shocked, dismayed, saddened, but that's not the same thing, certainly not for purposes of setting in train the inexorable progression of repression and the return of the repressed. Characteristically, it is simply assumed that the Holocaust *must* have been traumatic. And if it wasn't talked about, this *must* have been repression.

There is another way to look at the evolution of Holocaust consciousness in the United States, one that doesn't involve conjuring up such dubious entities as a "social unconscious." In the 1920s the French sociologist Maurice Halbwachs began to study what he was one of the first to call "collective memory." Instead of viewing collective memory as the past working its will on the present, Halbwachs explored the ways in which present concerns determine what of the past we remember and how we remember it. (There is a grim appropriateness in adopting Halbwachs's approach to the study of Holocaust memory. When, in occupied France, he protested the arrest of his Jewish father-in-law, Halbwachs was sent to Buchenwald, where he died.)[2]

Collective memory, as Halbwachs used the phrase, is not just historical knowledge shared by a group. Indeed, collective memory is in crucial senses ahistorical, even anti-historical. To understand something historically is to be aware of its complexity, to have sufficient

detachment to see it from multiple perspectives, to accept the ambiguities, including moral ambiguities, of protagonists' motives and behavior. Collective memory simplifies; sees events from a single, committed perspective; is impatient with ambiguities of any kind; reduces
events to mythic archetypes. Historical consciousness, by its nature,
focuses on the *historicity* of events — that they took place then and not
now, that they grew out of circumstances different from those that
now obtain. Memory, by contrast, has no sense of the passage of time;
it denies the "pastness" of its objects and insists on their continuing
presence. Typically a collective memory, at least a significant collective
memory, is understood to express some eternal or essential truth
about the group — usually tragic. A memory, once established, comes
to define that eternal truth, and, along with it, an eternal identity, for
the members of the group. Serbs' central memory, the lost Battle of
Kosovo in 1389, symbolizes the permanent Muslim intention to dominate them. The partitions of Poland in the eighteenth century gave
that country an "essential" identity as "the Christ among nations," cru-
cified and recrucified by foreign oppression. The annual pilgrimage of
French workers to the Mur des Fédérés, site of the slaughter of *com-
munards* in 1871, was a reminder of the eternal enmity between prole-
tariat and bourgeoisie.

Thinking about collective memory in this way helps us to separate
ephemeral and relatively inconsequential memories from those that
endure and shape consciousness. "Remember the Alamo," "Remember
the *Maine*," and "Remember Pearl Harbor" were briefly very resonant,
but were pretty much abandoned when their work was done. There
are "memory spasms" on the occasion of round-numbered anniversa-
ries — the bicentennial of the American Revolution, the quincente-
nary of Columbus's first voyage — but the flurry of commemorations
on such occasions doesn't signify that we're in the presence of important collective memory.

In the Jewish tradition, some memories are very long lasting. The
ritualized remembrance of the Exodus from Egypt and of the destruction of the Temple symbolize the permanence of God's guardian-
ship of the Jews — and of His wrath when they stray. Other Jewish
memories have had a contingent existence, depending on current
needs. The suicide at Masada was absent from Jewish memory for almost two thousand years, though the text describing the event was
readily available. This was not because Masada was a "trauma" that
was "repressed," but because traditional Judaism focused on survival

and holy study rather than on military resistance. The tradition remembered Rabbi Yohanan ben Zakkai and the establishment of the academy at Yavneh, not Eleazar ben Yair and the mass suicide. Zionists in the twentieth century found Masada more relevant to their self-understanding and self-representation, and a new collective memory emerged. Some memories, once functional, become dysfunctional. The concluding chapters of the Book of Esther tell of the queen's soliciting permission to slaughter not just the Jews' armed enemies but the enemies' wives and children — with a final death toll of seventy-five thousand. These "memories" provided gratifying revenge fantasies to the Jews of medieval Europe; in the present era of ecumenism these chapters have simply disappeared from Purim commemoration; most American Jews today are probably unaware that they exist.

If in looking at Holocaust memory in the United States we take Halbwachs's approach, relating memory to current concerns, we're led to look at just what those concerns have been, how they've been defined, and who has defined them. We'll consider how those concerns have, in one period, made Holocaust memory seem inappropriate, useless, or even harmful; in another period, appropriate and desirable. As we examine the changing fortunes of Holocaust memory, we'll be struck by how they relate to changing circumstances and, particularly among American Jews, changing decisions about collective self-understanding and self-representation.

One way of looking at these contrasting notions of the operation of collective memory is to say that Freud treats memory as imposed, while Halbwachs treats it as chosen. But that doesn't get it quite right unless we qualify the word "chosen." People often think of "choice" as implying *free* choice, but the sort of choices we're speaking of are shaped and constrained by circumstances. (The circumstances we'll be looking at include the cold war and the continuing conflict in the Middle East, changing attitudes toward the muting or the parading of ethnic differences, changes in attitudes toward victims, and strategies of communal survival.) Often people take the word "choice" to imply a thoughtful decision arrived at after consideration of all the pros and cons, a calculation of advantages and disadvantages. But while, as we'll see, there are some examples of that sort of choice in matters having to do with Holocaust memory, more often than not we'll find intuitive choices, or tacit choices, made without much thought for their consequences. And we always have to ask ourselves *whose* choices we're talking about. Concerning our collective memories, as in other aspects of collective consciousness, most of us are pretty conformist and take our cues from others. Finally, there is the institutionalization of memory, something that Halbwachs thought particularly important. An accumulation of previous choices, considered and unconsidered, has produced a set of institutions dedicated to Holocaust memory and a substantial cadre of Holocaust-memory professionals. Together, these provide self-perpetuating momentum to the centering of the Holocaust, independent of any further decision-making.

So the story of how the Holocaust was first marginalized, then came to be centered in American life will be a story of choices only in the attenuated sense just described. American Jews will be at the heart of the story, since Jews have taken the initiative in focusing attention on the Holocaust in this country. But it will be far from an exclusively Jewish story. For one thing, American Jews, no less than other Americans, have been shaped by American culture, and even in the construction of their Jewish consciousness have responded to political, social, and cultural changes that have affected all Americans. And though it was Jewish initiative that put the Holocaust on the American agenda, we have to ask what characteristics of late-twentieth-century American society and culture made gentile Americans receptive to that initiative. Some of the influences that have shaped how, and how much, we talk about the Holocaust are well known and can be traced in the printed record; others are more obscure and can be reconstructed only from archival sources. And these influences have interacted in complicated ways. I'll do my best to make the story understandable, but I can't make it straightforward, or free of contradictions.

I said at the outset that besides the "strictly historical" question I've just been discussing, I bring to this project skepticism about the bottom line — about whether all the attention paid to the Holocaust is as desirable as it's usually said to be. In fact, there are two separate balance sheets. One has to do with the consequences for American Jewry of putting the Holocaust at the center of its self-understanding and self-representation; the other with the consequences of heightened awareness of the Holocaust for American society at large.

The meaning for American Jewry of its centering of the Holocaust is inseparable from the context in which that centering has taken place. One of the most important elements of that context has been the decline in America of an integrationist ethos (which focused on what Americans have in common and what unites us) and its replacement by a particularist ethos (which stresses what differentiates and divides us). The leaders of American Jewry, who once upon a time had sought to demonstrate that Jews were "just like everybody else, except more so," now had to establish, for both Jews and gentiles, what there was about Jews that made them different.

What *does* differentiate American Jews from other Americans? On what grounds can a distinctive Jewish identity in the United States be based? These days American Jews can't define their Jewishness on the basis of distinctively Jewish religious beliefs, since most don't have much in the way of distinctively Jewish religious beliefs. They can't define it by distinctively Jewish cultural traits, since most don't have any of these either. American Jews are sometimes said to be united by their Zionism, but if so, it is of a thin and abstract variety: most have never visited Israel; most contribute little to, and know even less about, that country. In any case, in recent years Israeli policies have alternatively outraged the secular and the religious, hawks and doves — a less than satisfactory foundation for unity. What American Jews *do* have in common is the knowledge that but for their parents' or (more often) grandparents' or great-grandparents' immigration, they would have shared the fate of European Jewry. Within an increasingly diverse and divided American Jewry, this became the historical foundation of that endlessly repeated but empirically dubious slogan "We are one."

As I remarked earlier, there is a circular relationship between collective identity and collective memory. We choose to center certain memories because they seem to us to express what is central to our collective identity. Those memories, once brought to the fore, reinforce that form of identity. And so it has been with the Holocaust and American Jewry. The Holocaust, as virtually the only common denominator of American Jewish identity in the late twentieth century, has filled a need for a consensual symbol. And it was a symbol well designed to confront increasing communal anxiety about "Jewish continuity" in the face of declining religiosity, together with increasing assimilation and a sharp rise in intermarriage, all of which threatened demographic catastrophe. The Holocaust as central symbol of Jewishness has furthered in the late twentieth century what German Jews in the early nineteenth century had called *Trotzjudentum*, "Jewishness out of spite": a refusal to disappear, not for any positive reason, but, nowadays, so as not to grant Hitler a "posthumous victory."

Many Jewish commentators have warned that a Holocaust-centered Judaism would not work to ensure Jewish survival — that it would be a turnoff, alienating the young. Whether or not this proves to be true in the long run, so far this hasn't happened. At bar and bat mitzvahs, in a growing number of communities, the child is "twinned" with a young victim of the Holocaust who never lived to have the ceremony, and by all reports the kids like it a lot.[3] Adolescent Jews who go on organized tours to Auschwitz and Treblinka have reported that they were "never so proud to be a Jew" as when, at these sites, they vicariously experienced the Holocaust.[4] Jewish college students oversubscribe courses on the Holocaust, and rush to pin yellow stars to their lapels on Yom Hashoah (Holocaust Remembrance Day). And it's not just the young. Adult Jews flock to Holocaust events as to no others and give millions unstintingly to build yet another Holocaust memorial.

Another, parallel development in contemporary American culture has furthered this development. There has been a change in the attitude toward victimhood from a status all but universally shunned and despised to one often eagerly embraced. On the individual level, the cultural icon of the strong, silent hero is replaced by the vulnerable and verbose antihero. Stoicism is replaced as a prime value by sensitivity. Instead of enduring in silence, one lets it all hang out. The voicing of pain and outrage is alleged to be "empowering" as well as therapeutic.

Transformations on the individual level are mirrored at the level of the group. The historian Charles Maier of Harvard, with perhaps a little exaggeration, has described modern American politics as "a competition for enshrining grievances. Every group claims its share of public honor and public funds by pressing disabilities and injustices. National public life becomes the settlement of a collective malpractice suit in which all citizens are patients and physicians simultaneously."[5] All of this, of course, meshes with the new emphasis on separate group identity rather than on "all-American" identity. In practice, the assertion of the group's historical victimization — on the basis of race, ethnicity, gender, or sexual orientation — is always central to the group's assertion of its distinctive identity.

The growth of a "victim culture" wasn't the cause of American Jewry's focusing on the Holocaust in recent decades, but it has been an important background condition. As we'll see, in the 1940s and 1950s American Jews believed they had more reason than others to shun a victim identity, and this resulted in conscious decisions to downplay the Holocaust. By the 1980s and 1990s many Jews, for various reasons, wanted to establish that they too were members of a "victim community." Their contemporary situation offered little in the way of credentials. American Jews were by far the wealthiest, best-educated, most influential, in-every-way-most-successful group in American society — a group that, compared to most other identifiable minority groups, suffered no measurable discrimination and no disadvantages on account of that minority status. But insofar as Jewish identity could be anchored in the agony of European Jewry, certification as (vicarious) victims could be claimed, with all the moral privilege accompanying such certification.[6]

The grounding of group identity and claims to group recognition in victimhood has produced not just a game of "show and tell," with members of the class waving their arms to be called on to recount their story. In Jewish discourse on the Holocaust we have not just a competition for recognition but a competition for primacy. This takes many forms. Among the most widespread and pervasive is an angry insistence on the uniqueness of the Holocaust. Insistence on its uniqueness (or denial of its uniqueness) is an intellectually empty enterprise for reasons having nothing to do with the Holocaust itself and everything to do with "uniqueness." A moment's reflection makes clear that the notion of uniqueness is quite vacuous. Every historical event, including the Holocaust, in some ways resembles events to which it might be compared and differs from them in some ways. These resemblances and differences are a perfectly proper subject for discussion. But to single out those aspects of the Holocaust that were distinctive (there certainly were such), and to ignore those aspects that it shares with other atrocities, and on the basis of this gerrymandering to declare the Holocaust unique, is intellectual sleight of hand. The assertion that the Holocaust is unique — like the claim that it is singularly incomprehensible or unrepresentable — is, in practice, deeply offensive. What else can all of this possibly mean except "your catastrophe, unlike ours, is ordinary; unlike ours is comprehensible; unlike ours is representable."

Matter-of-fact references by blacks to their "ghetto" (a century-old usage) are condemned as pernicious attempts to steal "our" Holocaust. Let Ted Turner, denouncing what he regards as Rupert Murdoch's autocratic behavior, refer to Murdoch as a "führer," and the Anti-Defamation League (I'm not making this up) sends out a press release demanding an apology for Turner's having demeaned the Holocaust.[7] The greatest victory is to wring an acknowledgment of superior victimization from another contender. Officials of the U.S. Holocaust

Memorial Museum tell, with great satisfaction, a story of black young-sters learning of the Holocaust and saying, "God, we thought *we* had it bad."[8]

Apart from being our ticket of admission to this sordid game, American Jewish centering of the Holocaust has had other practical consequences. For many Jews, though this is much less true now than it was a few years ago, it has mandated an intransigent and self-righteous posture in the Israeli-Palestinian conflict. As the Middle Eastern dispute came to be viewed within a Holocaust paradigm, that tangled imbroglio was endowed with all the black-and-white moral simplicity of the Holocaust. And in this realm the Holocaust frame-work has promoted as well a belligerent stance toward any criticism of Israel: "Who are you, after what you did to us (or allowed to be done to us), to dare to criticize us now?" (I should say here, and will attempt to show later on, that contrary to the convergent claims of anti-Semites and self-congratulatory Jewish publicists, I don't think all the invoca-tions of the Holocaust have had any significant influence on American policy toward Israel. That policy has been based primarily on consid-erations of *Realpolitik*, and to a lesser extent on calculations of Ameri-can Jewish political influence.)

Turning the Holocaust into the emblematic Jewish experience has also, I think, and as I'll try to show, been closely connected to the in-ward and rightward turn of American Jewry in recent decades. If, as Cynthia Ozick has written, "all the world wants the Jews dead," and if the world was, as many have argued, indifferent to Jewish agony, why should Jews concern themselves with others?[9] Once again, we're deal-ing with a complex phenomenon in which cause and effect are all mixed up. But I think the centering of the Holocaust in the minds of American Jews has contributed to the erosion of that larger social con-sciousness that was the hallmark of the American Jewry of my youth — post-Holocaust, but pre–Holocaust-fixation.

In a way, the guarding of the memory of the Holocaust is very much in the Jewish tradition; certainly, forgetting the Holocaust — hardly an option — would be contrary to tradition. As Yosef Yerushalmi has re-minded us, the Hebrew Bible contains the verb "to remember," in its various declensions, 169 times (along with numerous injunctions not to forget).[10] Yet what Jews are enjoined to remember is almost always God's handiwork; secular history, insofar as such a category is even ad-mitted by the tradition, gets short shrift.[11] Mourning and remember-ing the dead are, of course, traditional Jewish obligations. But Judaism has consistently disparaged excessive or overly prolonged mourning. Cremation is forbidden because it would dispose of the body too soon, but also forbidden is embalming, because it would preserve the body too long. Mourn, to be sure, is the message, but then move on: "choose life." One of the things I find most striking about much of recent Jewish Holocaust commemoration is how "un-Jewish" — how *Christian* — it is. I am thinking of the ritual of reverently following the structured pathways of the Holocaust in the major museums, which resembles nothing so much as the Stations of the Cross on the Via Dolorosa; the fetishized objects on display like so many fragments of the True Cross or shin bones of saints; the symbolic representations of the Holocaust — notably in the climax of Elie Wiesel's *Night* — that employ crucifixion imagery. Perhaps most significantly, there is the way that suffering is sacralized and portrayed as the path to wisdom — the cult of the survivor as secular saint. These are themes that have some minor and peripheral precedent in Jewish tradition, but they resonate more powerfully with major themes in Christianity.[12]

Finally, there is the question of how we present ourselves to, how we wish to be thought of by, that vast majority of Americans who are not Jewish. The principal "address" of American Jewry — the representation of Jewishness and the Jewish experience visited by more Americans than any other, and for most the only one they'll ever visit — is the Holocaust museum on the Mall in Washington. There surely isn't going to be a *second* Jewish institution on the Mall, presenting an alternative image of the Jew. And there surely isn't going to be *another* set of legislatively mandated curricula about Jews in American public schools, besides the proliferating Holocaust curricula zealously promoted by Jewish organizations — something to balance the existing curricula, in which, for enormous numbers of gentile children (Jewish ones too, for that matter), the equation Jew-equals-victim is being inscribed.

So I wind up asking a traditional question — a question often mocked but sometimes appropriate. I ask about our centering of the Holocaust in how we understand ourselves and how we invite others to understand us: "Is it good for the Jews?"

Then there's the balance sheet for our nation as a whole. There are many reasons why concern with the Holocaust among the 2 or 3 percent of the American population that is Jewish came to pervade American society. I will mention one important reason here, if only because it is often nervously avoided. We are not just "the people of the book," but the people of the Hollywood film and the television mini-series, of the magazine article and the newspaper column, of the comic book and the academic symposium. When a high level of concern with the Holocaust became widespread in American Jewry, it was, given the important role that Jews play in American media and opinion-making elites, not only natural, but virtually inevitable that it would spread throughout the culture at large.

Whatever its origin, the public rationale for Americans' "confronting" the Holocaust — and I don't doubt that it is sincerely argued and sincerely accepted — is that the Holocaust is the bearer of important lessons that we all ignore at our peril. Where once it was said that the life of Jews would be "a light unto the nations" — the bearer of universal lessons — now it is the "darkness unto the nations" of the death of Jews that is said to carry universal lessons. There is a good deal of confusion, and sometimes acrimonious dispute, over what these lessons are, but that has in no way diminished confidence that the lessons are urgent. Individuals from every point on the political compass can find the lessons they wish in the Holocaust; it has become a moral and ideological Rorschach test.

The right has invoked the Holocaust in support of anti-Communist interventions abroad: the agent of the Holocaust was not Nazi Germany but a generic totalitarianism, embodied after 1945 in the Soviet bloc, with which there could be no compromise. On a philosophical level, the Holocaust has been used by conservatives to demonstrate the sinfulness of man. It has provided confirmation of a tragic worldview, revealing the fatuousness of any transformative — or even seriously meliorative — politics. For other segments of the right, the Holocaust revealed the inevitable consequence of the breakdown of religion and family values in Germany. And, as is well known, the "abortion holocaust" figures prominently in American debate on that question.

For leftists, the claim that American elites abandoned European Jewry during the war has been used to demonstrate the moral bankruptcy of the establishment, including liberal icons like FDR. For liberals, the Holocaust became the locus of "lessons" that teach the evils of immigration restriction and homophobia, of nuclear weapons and the Vietnam War. Holocaust curricula, increasingly mandated in public schools, frequently link the Holocaust to much of the liberal agenda — a source of irritation to American right-wingers, including Jewish right-wingers like the late Lucy Dawidowicz.

For the political center — on some level for all Americans — the Holocaust has become a moral reference point. As, over the past generation, ethical and ideological divergence and disarray in the United States advanced to the point where Americans could agree on nothing else, all could join together in deploring the Holocaust — a low moral consensus, but perhaps better than none at all. (This banal consensus is indeed so broad that, in a backhanded way, it even includes that tiny band of malicious or deluded fruitcakes who deny that the Holocaust took place. "If it happened," they say in effect, "we would deplore it as much as anyone else. But it didn't, so the question doesn't arise.") And in the United States the Holocaust is explicitly used for the purpose of national self-congratulation: the "Americanization" of the Holocaust has involved using it to demonstrate the difference between the Old World and the New, and to celebrate, by showing its negation, the American way of life.

The idea of "lessons of the Holocaust" seems to me dubious on several grounds, of which I'll here mention only two. One might be called, for lack of a better word, pedagogic. If there are, in fact, lessons to be drawn from history, the Holocaust would seem an unlikely source, not because of its alleged uniqueness, but because of its extremity. Lessons for dealing with the sorts of issues that confront us in ordinary life, public or private, or not likely to be found in this most extraordinary of events. There are, in my view, more important lessons about how easily we become victimizers to be drawn from the behavior of normal Americans in normal times than from the behavior of the SS in wartime. In any case, the typical "confrontation" with the Holocaust for visitors to American Holocaust museums, and in burgeoning curricula, does not incline us toward thinking of ourselves as potential victimizers — rather the opposite. It is an article of faith in these encounters that one should "identify with the victims," thus acquiring the warm glow of virtue that such a vicarious identification brings. (Handing out "victim identity cards" to museum visitors is the most dramatic example of this, but not the only one.) And it is accepted as a matter of faith, beyond discussion, that the mere act of walking through a Holocaust museum, or viewing a Holocaust movie, is going to be morally therapeutic, that multiplying such encounters will make one a better person. The notion that lessons derived from such encounters are likely to have any effect on everyday personal or political conduct seems to me extremely dubious on pedagogic grounds. We appear to be following the principle Thomas de

Quincey advanced in 1839: "If once a man indulges himself in murder, very soon he comes to think little of robbing, and from robbing he comes next to drinking and Sabbath-breaking, and from that to incivility and procrastination."[13]

Another ground on which I find the idea of lessons of the Holocaust questionable can be called pragmatic: what is the payoff? The principal lesson of the Holocaust, it is frequently said, is not that it provides a set of maxims, or a rule book for conduct, but rather that it sensitizes us to oppression and atrocity. In principle it might, and I don't doubt that sometimes it does. But making it the benchmark of oppression and atrocity works in precisely the opposite direction, trivializing crimes of lesser magnitude. It does this not just in principle, but in practice. American debate on the bloody Bosnian conflict of the 1990s focused on whether what was going on was "truly holocaustal or merely genocidal"; "truly genocidal or merely atrocious." A truly disgusting and not a merely distasteful mode of speaking and of decision-making, but one we are led to when the Holocaust becomes the touchstone of moral and political discourse.

The problem transcends the Bosnian tragedy, which is simply its most dramatic illustration. It is connected to the axiom of the uniqueness of the Holocaust and its corollary, that comparing anything to the Holocaust is illegitimate, indeed indecent. I have suggested that the very notion of uniqueness is vacuous, but rhetorically — for ideological or other purposes — the claim of uniqueness (or its denial) can be powerful. Whatever its success, the intention of talking in Germany of the uniqueness and incomparability of the Holocaust is to prevent Germans from evading confrontation with that which is most difficult, painful, and therefore probably most useful to confront. Let us remember the context in which many Germans — decent Germans — objected to the so-called relativization of the Holocaust in recent years. The context included the insistence of Chancellor Helmut Kohl's party that as a price for supporting a law against denying the Holocaust, the law had to include a provision making it illegal to deny the suffering of Germans expelled from the East after 1945. In this German context — and context, as always, is decisive — "relativization" meant equating crimes *against* Germans to crimes *by* Germans. Which, of course, many Germans wished to do. Those Germans who insisted on the uniqueness of the Holocaust, who condemned its relativization, did so to block what they correctly regarded as a move to evade confrontation with a painful national past, evade the implications of such a confrontation for the present and future.[14]

The identical talk of uniqueness and incomparability surrounding the Holocaust in the United States performs the opposite function: it promotes *evasion* of moral and historical responsibility. The repeated assertion that whatever the United States has done to blacks, Native Americans, Vietnamese, or others pales in comparison to the Holocaust is true — and evasive. And whereas a serious and sustained encounter with the history of hundreds of years of enslavement and oppression of blacks might imply costly demands on Americans to redress the wrongs of the past, contemplating the Holocaust is virtually cost-free: a few cheap tears.

So, in the end, it seems to me that the pretense that the Holocaust is an American memory — that Americans, either diffusely, as part of Western civilization, or specifically, as complicit bystanders, share responsibility for the Holocaust — works to devalue the notion of historical responsibility. It leads to the shirking of those responsibilities that *do* belong to Americans as they confront their past, their present, and their future.

In this introduction I've sketched the historical approach and the moral concerns that inform the chapters that follow. I'm sure almost every reader will have at least some quarrels with the historical account; I can't imagine that there is any reader who will share all of my evaluations. My aim in writing this book — at once modest and grandiose — is to provoke discussion about the questions it raises: how we got to where we are concerning the memory of the Holocaust, and whether where we are is where we want to be.

Part One

THE WAR YEARS

[1]

"We Knew in a General Way"

WE BEGIN at the beginning, with the response of American gentiles and Jews to the Holocaust while the killing was going on. Though we'll be concerned mostly with how the Holocaust was talked about after 1945, the wartime years are the appropriate starting point. They were the point of departure for subsequent framing and representing, centering or marginalizing, and using for various purposes the story of the destruction of European Jewry.

At the same time, America's wartime response to the Holocaust is what a great deal of later Holocaust discourse in the United States has been about. The most common version tells of the culpable, sometimes willed obliviousness of American gentiles to the murder of European Jews; the indifference to their brethren's fate by a timid and self-absorbed American Jewry; the "abandonment of the Jews" by the Roosevelt administration — a refusal to seize opportunities for rescue, which made the United States a passive accomplice in the crime.

By the 1970s and 1980s the Holocaust had become a shocking, massive, and distinctive *thing*: clearly marked off, qualitatively and quantitatively, from other Nazi atrocities and from previous Jewish persecutions, singular in its scope, its symbolism, and its world-historical significance. This way of looking at it is nowadays regarded as both proper and natural, the "normal human response." But this was not the response of most Americans, even of American Jews, while the Holocaust was being carried out. Not only did the Holocaust have nowhere near the centrality in consciousness that it had from the 1970s on, but for the overwhelming majority of Americans — and, once again, this included a great many Jews as well — it barely existed as a singular event in its own right. The murderous actions of the Nazi regime, which killed between five and six million European Jews, were all too real. But "the Holocaust," as we speak of it today, was largely a retrospective construction, something that would not have been recognizable to most people at the time. To speak of "the Holocaust" as a distinct entity, which Americans responded to (or failed to respond to) in various ways, is to introduce an anachronism that stands in the way of understanding contemporary responses.

The sheer number of victims of the Holocaust continues to inspire awe: between five and six million. But the Holocaust took place — we know this, of course, but we don't often think of its implications — in the midst of a global war that eventually killed between fifty and sixty million people. There are those for whom any such contextualization is a trivializing of the Holocaust, a tacit denial of the special circumstances surrounding the destruction of European Jewry. Certainly such contextualization can be used for these purposes, as when the French rightist Jean-Marie Le Pen dismisses the Holocaust as a mere "detail" of the history of the Second World War. But it was the overall course of the war that dominated the minds of Americans in the early forties. Unless we keep that in mind, we will never understand how the Holocaust came to be swallowed up in the larger carnage surrounding it. By itself, the fact that during the war, and for some time thereafter, there was no agreed-upon word for the murder of Europe's Jews is not all that significant. What is perhaps of some importance is that insofar as the word "holocaust" (lowercase) was employed during the war, as it occasionally was, it was almost always applied to the totality of the destruction wrought by the Axis, not to the special fate of the Jews. This usage is emblematic of wartime perceptions of what we now single out as "the Holocaust."

There are many different dimensions to the wartime marginality of the Holocaust in the American mind: what one knew, and what one believed; how to frame what one knew or believed; devising an appropriate response. In principle these questions are separable; in practice they were inextricably entwined. In this chapter we'll look at the perceptions and responses of the American people as a whole; in Chapter 2, at American Jews; in Chapter 3, at the American government.

Although no one could imagine its end result, all Americans — Jews and gentiles alike — were well aware of Nazi anti-Semitism from the regime's beginning in 1933, if not earlier. Prewar Nazi actions against

Jews, from early discriminatory measures to the enactment of the Nuremberg Laws in 1935 and culminating in Kristallnacht in 1938, were widely reported in the American press and repeatedly denounced at all levels of American society.[1] No one doubted that Jews were high on the list of actual and potential victims of Nazism, but it was a long list, and Jews, by some measures, were not at the top. Despite Nazi attempts to keep secret what went on in concentration camps in the thirties, their horrors were known in the West, and were the main symbol of Nazi brutality. But until late 1938 there were few Jews, as Jews, among those imprisoned, tortured, and murdered in the camps. The victims were overwhelmingly Communists, socialists, trade unionists, and other political opponents of the Hitler regime. And it was to be another four years before the special fate that Hitler had reserved for the Jews of Europe became known in the West.

The point should be underlined: from early 1933 to late 1942 — more than three quarters of the twelve years of Hitler's Thousand-Year Reich — Jews were, quite reasonably, seen as among but by no means as the singled-out victims of the Nazi regime. This was the all-but-universal perception of American gentiles; it was the perception of many American Jews as well. By the time the news of the mass murder of Jews emerged in the middle of the war, those who had been following the crimes of the Nazis for ten years readily and naturally assimilated it to the already-existing framework.

Only in the aftermath of Kristallnacht were large numbers of Jews added to the camp populations, and even then for the most part briefly, as part of a German policy of pressuring Jews to emigrate. Up to that point, German Jewish deaths were a tiny fraction of those inflicted on Jews by murderous bands of Ukrainian anti-Soviet forces twenty years earlier. Though American Jews responded with deeper dismay and horror to prewar Nazi anti-Semitism than did gentile Americans, their reaction was not unmixed with a certain weary fatalism: such periods had recurred over the centuries; they would pass; in the meantime one did what one could and waited for better days.

In the West, the onset of the war resulted in less rather than more attention being paid to the fate of the Jews. The beginning of the military struggle — and dramatic dispatches from the battlefronts — drove Jewish persecution from the front pages and from public consciousness. Kristallnacht, in which dozens of Jews were killed, had been on the front page of the *New York Times* for more than a week; as the wartime Jewish death toll passed through thousands and into millions, it was never again featured so prominently.[2]

From the autumn of 1939 to the autumn of 1941 everyone's attention was riveted on military events: the war at sea, the fall of France, the Battle of Britain, the German invasion of the Soviet Union. As Americans confronted what appeared to be the imminent prospect of unchallenged Nazi dominion over the entire European continent, it was hardly surprising that except for some Jews, few paid much attention to what was happening to Europe's Jewish population under Nazi rule. That the ghettoization of Polish Jewry and the deportation of German and Austrian Jews to Polish ghettos had brought enormous suffering no one doubted. Beyond this, little was known with any certainty, and the fragmentary reports reaching the West were often contradictory. Thus in December 1939 a press agency first estimated that a quarter of a million Jews had been killed; two weeks later the agency reported that losses were about one tenth that number.[3] (Similar wildly differing estimates recurred throughout the war, no doubt leading many to suspend judgment on the facts and suspect exaggeration. In March 1943 *The Nation* wrote of seven thousand Jews being massacred each week, while *The New Republic* used the same figure as a conservative daily estimate.)[4]

In the course of 1940, 1941, and 1942 reports of atrocities against Jews began to accumulate. But these, like the numbers cited, were often contradictory. In the nature of the situation, there were no first-hand reports from Western journalists. Rather, they came from a handful of Jews who had escaped, from underground sources, from anonymous German informants, and, perhaps most unreliable of all, from the Soviet government. If, as many suspected, the Soviets were lying about the Katyn Forest massacre, why not preserve a healthy skepticism when they spoke of Nazi atrocities against Soviet Jews? Thus, after the Soviet recapture of Kiev, the *New York Times* correspondent traveling with the Red Army underlined that while Soviet officials claimed that tens of thousands of Jews had been killed at Babi Yar, "no witnesses to the shooting . . . talked with the correspondents"; "it is impossible for this correspondent to judge the truth or falsity of the story told to us"; "there is little evidence in the ravine to prove or disprove the story."[5]

The most important single report on the Holocaust that reached the West came from a then-anonymous German businessman, and was passed on in mid-1942 by Gerhard Riegner, representative of the

World Jewish Congress in Switzerland. But Riegner forwarded the report "with due reserve" concerning its truth. Though the main outlines of the mass-murder campaign reported by Riegner were all too true, his informant also claimed to have "personal knowledge" of the rendering of Jewish corpses into soap — a grisly symbol of Nazi atrocity now dismissed as without foundation by historians of the Holocaust. By the fall of 1943, more than a year after Riegner's information was transmitted, an internal U.S. State Department memorandum concluded that the reports were "essentially correct." But it was hard to quarrel with the accompanying observation that the 1942 reports were "at times confused and contradictory" and that they "incorporated stories which were obviously left over from the horror tales of the last war."[6]

Such embellishments as the soap story furthered a will to disbelieve that was common among Jews and gentiles — an understandable attitude. Who, after all, would *want* to think that such things were true? Who would not welcome an opportunity to believe that while terrible things were happening, their scale was being exaggerated; that much of what was being said was war propaganda that the prudent reader should discount? One British diplomat, skeptical of the Soviet story about Babi Yar, observed that "we ourselves put out rumours of atrocities and horrors for various purposes, and I have no doubt this game is widely played."[7] Indeed, officials of both the U.S. Office of War Information and the British Ministry of Information ultimately concluded that though the facts of the Holocaust appeared to be confirmed, they were so likely to be *thought* exaggerated that the agencies would lose credibility by disseminating them.[8]

If American newspapers published relatively little about the ongoing Holocaust, it was in part because there was little hard news about it to present — only secondhand and thirdhand reports of problematic authenticity. News is event-, not process-oriented: bombing raids, invasions, and naval battles are the stuff of news, not delayed, often hearsay accounts of the wheels of the murder machine grinding relentlessly on. And for senior news editors the experience of having been bamboozled by propaganda during the First World War was not something they'd read about in history books; they had themselves been made to appear foolish by gullibly swallowing fake atrocity stories, and they weren't going to let it happen again.

Perhaps another reason for limited press attention to the continuing murder of European Jewry was that, in a sense, it didn't seem interesting. This is not a decadent aestheticism but is in the very nature of "the interesting": something that violates our expectations. We are interested in the televangelist caught with the bimbo, the gangster who is devout in his religious observance: vice where we expect virtue, virtue where we expect vice; that which shatters our preconceptions. To a generation that was not witness to the apparently limitless depravity of the Nazi regime, the Holocaust may tell us something about what mankind is capable of. But Americans in the early forties took it for granted that Nazism was the embodiment of absolute evil, even if the sheer scale of its crimes was not appreciated. The repetition of examples was not, as a result, "interesting." (For some dedicated anti-Communists, including a number of Jewish intellectuals writing for *Partisan Review* and *The New Leader*, it was Soviet iniquity, played down in the press during the wartime Russian-American honeymoon, that was more interesting, and more in need of exposure.)

Throughout the war few Americans were aware of the scale of the European Jewish catastrophe. By late 1944 three quarters of the American population believed that the Germans had "murdered many people in concentration camps," but of those willing to estimate how many had been killed, most thought it was 100,000 or fewer. By May 1945, at the end of the war in Europe, most people guessed that about a million (including, it should be noted, both Jews and non-Jews) had been killed in the camps.[9] That the man in the street was ill informed about the Holocaust, as about so much else, is hardly shocking. But lack of awareness was common among the highly placed and generally knowledgeable as well: only at the very end of the war did ignorance dissipate. William Casey, later the director of the Central Intelligence Agency, was head of secret intelligence in the European theater for the Office of Strategic Services, the predecessor of the CIA.

> The most devastating experience of the war for most of us was the first visit to a concentration camp. . . . We knew in a general way that Jews were being persecuted, that they were being rounded up . . . and that brutality and murder took place at these camps. But few if any comprehended the appalling magnitude of it. It wasn't sufficiently real to stand out from the general brutality and slaughter which is war.[10]

William L. Shirer, the best-selling author of *Berlin Diary*, who during the war was a European correspondent for CBS, reported that it was only at the end of 1945 that he learned "for sure" about the Holocaust; the news burst upon him "like a thunderbolt."[11]

How many Americans had knowledge of the Holocaust while it was going on is as much a semantic as a quantitative question. It calls for distinctions among varieties of awareness, consciousness, belief, attention. There was an inclination on the part of many to avert their eyes from things too painful to contemplate. *Life* magazine, in 1945, printed a letter from a distressed reader:

> Why, oh why, did you have to print that picture? The truth of the atrocity is there and can never be erased from the minds of the American people, but why can't we be spared some of it? The stories are awful enough but I think the picture should be retained for records and not shown to the public.[12]

The picture in question was not of Jewish bodies stacked like cordwood at a liberated concentration camp, but of a captured American airman on his knees, being beheaded by a Japanese officer. (Inundated as we have been in recent decades by images of violence — oceans of blood, in vivid color, brought by television into our living rooms — it is easy to forget how much less hardened sensibilities were in the forties.) War doesn't put concern for civilians — especially civilians who are not one's own citizens — anywhere on the agenda. War is about killing the enemy, and in World War II this included killing unprecedented numbers of enemy civilians. War isn't about softening one's heart, but about hardening it. A much-decorated veteran of the Eighth Air Force:

> You drop a load of bombs and, if you're cursed with any imagination at all you have at least one quick horrid glimpse of a child lying in bed with a whole ton of masonry tumbling down on top of him; or a three-year-old girl wailing for *Mutter . . . Mutter . . .* because she has been burned. Then you have to turn away from the picture if you intend to retain your sanity. And also if you intend to keep on doing the work your Nation expects of you.[13]

It has often been said that when the full story of the ongoing Holocaust reached the West, beginning in 1942, it was disbelieved because the sheer magnitude of the Nazi plan of mass murder made it, literally, incredible — beyond belief. There is surely a good deal to this, but perhaps at least as often, the gradually emerging and gradually worsening news from Europe produced a kind of immunity to shock. A final point on disbelief. Accounts of the persecution of Jews between the fall of 1939 and the summer of 1941 often spoke of "extermination" and "annihilation." This was not prescience but hyperbole, and prudent listeners took it as such. By the following years, when such words were all too accurate, they had been somewhat debased by premature invocation.

Probably more important than "knowledge" in the narrow sense is how knowledge is framed. We have already seen how prewar experience — indeed, experience down through 1942 — placed Jews among but not as the singled-out victims of Nazism. (As of the spring of 1942, the Germans had murdered more Soviet prisoners of war than Jews.)[14] This kind of preexisting framework lasted for most Americans through the remainder of the war. But there were other reasons why the particularly savage and systematic program of murdering European Jewry tended to be lost amid the overall carnage of war.

For most Americans, the Pacific conflict was a matter of much greater concern than the war in Europe. Working fourteen hours a day in the Brooklyn Navy Yard, the future playwright Arthur Miller observed "the near absence among the men I worked with . . . of any comprehension of what Nazism meant — we were fighting Germany essentially because she had allied herself with the Japanese who had attacked us at Pearl Harbor."[15] American soldiers and sailors were continuously engaged in combat with the Japanese from the beginning to the end of the war — first retreating, then advancing across the islands of the Pacific. It was not until the last year of the war, after the Normandy invasion, that there was equal attention given to the European theater. Certainly in popular representations of the war, especially in the movies, it was the Japanese who were America's leading enemy. "Axis atrocities" summoned up images of American victims of the Bataan Death March — not of Europeans, Jewish or gentile, under the Nazi heel.

When wartime attention did turn to Nazi barbarism, there were many reasons for not highlighting Jewish suffering. One was sheer ignorance — the lack of awareness until late 1942 of the special fate of Jews in Hitler's Europe. The Nazi concentration camp was the most common symbol of the enemy regime, and its archetypal inmate was usually represented as a political oppositionist or member of the resistance. Probably one of the reasons for this was that the seemingly natural framework for the war was one of actively contending forces: the dramatically satisfying victim of Nazism was the heroic and principled oppositionist. By contrast, Jews killed by the Nazis were widely perceived, less inspirationally, as passive victims, though sometimes they were portrayed as opponents of Nazism to fit the script. Thus the editor of the *Detroit Free Press* explained that the Nazi prisoners he saw liberated had been in the camps because "they refused to accept the political philosophy of the Nazi party.... First Jews and anti-Nazi Germans, then other brave souls who refused to conform."[16]

In the Hollywood version of the camps, which perhaps reached more Americans than any other, it was the dissident or *résistant* who was the exemplary victim. One of the few wartime Hollywood films that depicted Jewish victimhood *and* resistance was *None Shall Escape*, which concludes with a rabbi exhorting his people to resist the Nazis — which they do, "dying on their feet" and taking some German troops with them. The rabbi's speech included a line about "tak[ing] our place along with all other oppressed peoples," and the rebellion ended beneath a cruciform signpost on a railroad platform, the rabbi and his people dying at the foot of a cross.[17]

If some of the reasons for deemphasizing special Jewish victimhood were more or less spontaneous, others were calculated. In the case of Germany — unlike Japan — there was no offense against Americans to be avenged, no equivalent of "Remember Pearl Harbor." The task of American wartime propagandists was to portray Nazi Germany as the mortal enemy of "free men everywhere." That the Nazis were the enemy of the Jews was well known; there was no rhetorical advantage in continuing to underline the fact. The challenge was to show that they were *everyone's* enemy, to broaden rather than narrow the range of Nazi victims. In meeting this challenge, the Office of War Information resisted suggestions for a focus on Jewish victimhood. Leo Rosten, head of the OWI's "Nature of the Enemy" department and a popular Jewish writer, responding to a suggestion that atrocities against Jews be highlighted, said that "according to [our] experience, the impression on the average American is much stronger if the question is not exclusively Jewish."[18] Indeed, it was stronger among one segment of the population engaged in fighting the Nazis. In November 1944 the army magazine *Yank* decided not to run a story of Nazi atrocities against Jews on the grounds — as related to the man who wrote the story — that "because of latent anti-Semitism in the Army, he ought, if possible, to get something with a less Semitic slant."[19]

There was another reason for not emphasizing Hitler's "war against the Jews": to sidestep the claim that America's struggle with Germany was a war *for* the Jews.[20] The claim that American Jews were dragging the country into a war on behalf of their brethren in Europe was a staple of prewar isolationist discourse. The *America First Bulletin* had spoken of "numerous groups which fight for America's entry into the war — foreign and racial groups which have special and just grievances against Hitler." This view was endorsed by Charles Lindbergh in a notorious speech.[21] Public assertions of this kind ceased with Pearl Harbor, but they had a lively underground existence thereafter. In 1943 former ambassador William Bullitt was telling people that "the Roosevelt administration's emphasis on the European war as opposed to the Asian one was the result of Jewish influence."[22]

The charge of Jewish warmongering had often focused on Hollywood. Shortly before Pearl Harbor, Senator Gerald Nye of North Dakota held hearings on the subject, summoning for interrogation those with "Jewish-sounding" names.[23] The Nye hearings were called off after the war began, but there was continued sensitivity on this score in Hollywood. And it was reinforced by Washington. A June 1942 *Government Information Manual for the Motion Pictures* feared that "there are still groups in this country who are thinking only in terms of their particular group. Some citizens have not been aware of the fact that this is a people's war, not a group war."[24] Hollywood executives probably didn't need prodding on this score. Responding to a 1943 suggestion that a film be made about Hitler's treatment of the Jews, studio heads who were polled replied that it would be better to consider a film "covering various groups that have been subject to the Nazi treatment [which] of course would take in the Jews."[25]

Along with the minimizing of particular Jewish victimhood was the development of formulas stressing Nazi "godlessness," which exaggerated Nazi animus toward Christian denominations. Wartime discourse was filled with references to the "Protestant, Catholic, and Jewish" victims of Nazism. (It was during the Hitler years that American philo-Semites invented the "Judeo-Christian tradition" to combat innocent, or not so innocent, language that spoke of a totalitarian assault on "Christian civilization.")[26] A variant of this theme acknowledged the present Jewish priority in victimhood but held that, once finished with Jews, Hitler would turn on others.[27]

For all of these reasons, in all media and in almost all public pronouncements, there was throughout the war not much awareness of the special fate of the Jews of Europe. Sometimes this was simply due to a lack of information, sometimes the result of spontaneous and "well-meaning" categories of thought and speech. When downplaying Jewish victimhood was conscious and deliberate, the purposes were hardly vicious: to emphasize that the Nazis were the enemy of all mankind, in order both to broaden support for the anti-Nazi struggle and to combat the charge that World War II was a war fought for the Jews. Among those who minimized special Jewish suffering there were surely some with less high-minded motives, but there is little reason to believe they had much influence. In any event, the result was that for the overwhelming majority of Americans, throughout the war (and, as we will see, for some time thereafter) what we now call the Holocaust was neither a distinct entity nor particularly salient. The murder of European Jewry, insofar as it was understood or acknowledged, was just one among the countless dimensions of a conflict that was consuming the lives of tens of millions around the globe. It was not "the Holocaust"; it was simply the (underestimated) Jewish fraction of the holocaust then engulfing the world.

[2]

"If Our Brothers Had
Shown More Compassion"

BUT WHAT OF American Jews? Their contemporary response to the Holocaust has been the topic of a lot of discussion in recent years. Virtually all writers on the subject, mixing sadness and anger in varying proportions, deplore what they describe as the woefully thin and inadequate nature of that response. Of the two book-length treatments of the subject, one is entitled *The Deafening Silence;* the other asks rhetorically, *Were We Our Brothers' Keepers?* — and returns the expected answer.[1] Weighing heavily in the evaluation is the voice of the survivors. Elie Wiesel:

> While Mordecai Anielewicz and his comrades fought their lonely battle in the blazing ghetto under siege . . . a large New York synagogue invited its members to a banquet featuring a well-known comedian. . . . The factories of Treblinka, Belzec, Maidanek and Auschwitz were operating at top capacity, while on the other side, Jewish social and intellectual life was flourishing. Jewish leaders met, threw up their arms in gestures of helplessness, shed a pious tear or two and went on with their lives: speeches, travels, quarrels, banquets, toasts, honors. . . .
>
> If our brothers had shown more compassion, more initiative, more daring . . . if a million Jews had demonstrated in front of the White House . . . if Jewish notables had started a hunger strike. . . . Who knows, the enemy might have desisted.[2]

One book concludes by observing that "the Final Solution may have been *unstoppable* by American Jewry, but it should have been *unbearable* for them. And it wasn't."[3]

This way of framing the issue points to the existence of two separate though related questions, both highly charged. First, in the realm of feeling, did American Jewry display an unnatural disengagement or indifference in the face of the catastrophe facing Europe's Jews? Second, in the realm of action, did American Jewry, as a result of fear, timidity, or self-absorption, fail to press energetically for potentially effective strategies of rescue?

To speak of an entity — "American Jewry" — is to go awry at the outset. It is even more misleading to speak, as many do, apropos those years, of the "American Jewish community." The use of the word "community" has become standard in recent decades, but it is a term of art — of aspiration or of exhortation, not of description. From the late 1960s one could speak of the overwhelming majority of American Jews being united in support of Israel, and this has produced, if not "community," at least some tenuous approximation of unity. But as of the early 1940s no common beliefs united an "American Jewry," which was, besides, considerably more socially diverse than it later became. There was the transfer of old-country divisions: Jews of German origin versus *Ostjuden*, and among the latter, a somewhat attenuated split between *Litvaks* and *Galitzianers*. For the Orthodox (themselves divided into warring camps), Reform Jews were not much better than apostates; for Reform Jews, the Orthodox were relics of a superstitious past they had put behind them. Secularists, who included most of the Jewish intelligentsia, called down a plague on all their houses. In New York, there were few shared values between the uptown Republican bankers of the American Jewish Committee and leftist trade unionists from the Lower East Side. Within the Jewish working class there was no love lost — or sense of solidarity — among socialists, Communists, and labor Zionists. In other immigrant groups, class struggles and ethnic struggles had often merged, producing increased communal solidarity — Catholic workers battling Protestant employers. But it was Jewish bosses who hired Jewish gangsters to terrorize Jewish workers in the garment industry (and sometimes vice versa). None of this is to deny the existence of some tenuous bonds of solidarity that transcended divisions, but there had been little in the American Jewish experience to strengthen such bonds, and much to weaken them.

This was even more true of the bonds that connected (or didn't connect) American Jews to the Jews of Europe — the extent to which worldwide ties of "peoplehood" were a felt reality and the basis of effective claims for international Jewish solidarity. Such ties are *made* — unmade, remade — not *found*, which is obscured by the everyday fashion of speaking of them as "recognized" or "acknowledged." To say that they are made is not to say that they are any less real than if they are found. The Bill of Rights, which was made, is no less real than the Grand Canyon, which was found. When peoplehood is strongly felt, and acted upon, it is real; when it isn't, it isn't. A sense of Jewish peoplehood arose and flourished in response to historical circumstances: shared (traditional) religious observance, shared (Yiddish, Hebrew, Ladino) language, shared (pervasive, near-universal) exclusion from and persecution by dominant majorities, shared (distinctive) customs and traditions. When all of these ceased to be shared by much of American Jewry, a sense of peoplehood inevitably thinned and became a less widely shared element of consciousness. It is often said that real (primal) ties of Jewish peoplehood were replaced with an empty (vacuous) universalism. One can, to be sure, find examples of this — one can find examples of anything. But for the vast majority of American Jews for whom international ties of Jewish peoplehood atrophied, they were not replaced by loyalty to any universalist doctrines, but by loyalty to America.[4]

By World War II, the peak of mass immigration was forty years in the past, and of course many families had come even earlier. There were few fond memories of the old country, no *Fiddler on the Roof* idylls. Philip Roth is one among many who reports the "willful amnesia" he encountered when he tried to find out about life in Europe from his grandparents: "They'd left because life was awful, so awful, in fact, so menacing or impoverished or hopelessly obstructed, that it was best forgotten."[5] The *Landsmanschaften*, hometown associations that had preserved a sense of connection with Europe, were rapidly declining, as were institutions that kept a common language alive. The circulation of Yiddish newspapers kept dropping; Yiddish theaters were closing. Shortly before the war, Abraham Cahan, the editor of the *Jewish Daily Forward*, America's leading Yiddish newspaper, resignedly remarked that "the children are becoming Americanized, and it is only natural; they live in this country and it treats them as its own."[6] There was a gradual but steady drift from the consciousness in which one would be described — would think of oneself — as a Jew who happens to live in America, to the consciousness in which, to use a standard phrase of the time, one was an American who "happens to be Jewish."

With Hitler's rise to power, and especially during the war, empathy with the Jews of Europe did indeed produce, among many American Jews, a greater sense of Jewish identification. But years of American acculturation had worked to limit the depth of that identification. The impact of those years on the young American Jew was summed up by Shlomo Katz in 1940:

> The concept of the Jewish people throughout the world as a unit may not be strange to him ideologically [but] personally he has already lost the feeling of unity with the larger whole. . . . Only the slimmest cultural and psychic ties bind him to Jews of Poland, Palestine, Germany or Russia. . . . The immensity of the tragedy appalls him . . . but not sufficiently to make him a living part of the drama. Between him and the European scene there lie years . . . of life in America. These years, with all the cultural baggage that was accumulated in them, he does not share with Europe's Jews; and they stand between him and them.[7]

In the very year that Hitler was extruding Jews from the German state apparatus, President Roosevelt was welcoming them to Washington. "Dig me up fifteen or twenty youthful Abraham Lincolns from Manhattan and the Bronx," he said to a friend.[8] The very visible presence of so many Jews among Roosevelt's closest aides led anti-Semites to call his administration the "Jew Deal." With the coming of the war, opportunities for full Jewish participation in American society, both substantively and symbolically, increased much further. If Colin Kelly, a pilot killed after sinking a Japanese ship, was one of the first American war heroes, the press also noted that his bombardier, Meyer Levin, had died with him. There were the celebrated "Four Chaplains" (two Protestants, a Catholic, and a Jew) who went down with the USS *Dorchester* after giving their life vests to sailors who had none. A popular wartime song looked forward to the day "when those little Yellow Bellies meet the Cohens and the Kellys." There was the all-but-obligatory inclusion of Jews in Hollywood platoon rosters: a Feingold in *Bataan*, a Weinberg in *Air Force*, a Diamond in *Pride of the Marines*, a Jacobs in *Objective, Burma!*, an Abraham in *Action in the North Atlantic*, and a Greenbaum in *The Purple Heart*.

Jewish participation in the American war effort was not, of course, limited to celluloid: more than a half million young Jews served in the armed forces, and naturally concern for their safety had first claim on

their families and friends. Jewish American GIs were expected —
always in principle and sometimes in practice — to crawl out under
enemy fire to bring in wounded Irish Americans or Italian Americans,
as the latter were expected to do for them. Members of the older immigrant generation surely tested much higher for feelings of international Jewish peoplehood. At the same time, and not unconnected
with this, they were closer to a tradition that made it in principle impermissible to violate the laws of Sabbath observance to save the life of
a gentile, let alone risk one's own life. The point is not that deep
American loyalty and strongly felt ties of Jewish peoplehood are in-
compatible; whatever the difficulties of reconciliation in principle,
they are rarely a problem in practice. But there was a certain psychological and rhetorical tension between the two, particularly in the
cauldron of war.

In recent years it has become not just permissible but in some circles laudable for American Jews to assert the primacy of Jewish over
American loyalty. "We are Jews first and whatever else second," says
Rabbi Haskel Lookstein, the author of a searing indictment of American Jews' reaction to the Holocaust.[9] But in the early forties such assertions weren't just (publicly) unsayable; they were, except for some
members of the immigrant generation, unthinkable for most American Jews.

There was another important factor working in these years to make
American Jews, especially of the younger generation, think of themselves more as Americans and less as Jews. If since the 1960s there has
been a revival of ethnic identity in American culture, this followed on
a period in which ethnicity as a basis of identity seemed of dubious legitimacy. Indeed, the very word hardly existed: people spoke of "racial
groups" or "race feeling." The only cognate to "ethnic" in common usage was "ethnocentric," which enlightened opinion, since the 1920s,
had been insisting was a bad thing. Identity was properly based not on
"blood" but on the values, habits, and animating vision of the culture
in which you were raised. And that, for most American Jews except
older members of the immigrant generation, was American culture.
The revulsion against identity (and politics) based on "blood" or tribal
loyalties was, of course, powerfully reinforced after 1933 when such notions came to be embodied in *Der Stürmer*. To the counterassertion
"*You* may think you're an American, but Hitler knows you're a Jew," a
plausible reply was "Thank you, but I prefer to go to other sources for
my anthropology."[10]

There was an enormous range of responses to the Holocaust among American Jews: on the one hand, instances of psychic devastation verging on derangement; on the other, indifference verging on obliviousness. Trying to make any generalization about half-century-old feelings, privately expressed and seldom recorded, is, to put it mildly, not easy. It is particularly difficult in this case because the refiguring of memory has been pushed in two opposite directions. The insistence that American Jews must have been shattered by the news of the Holocaust works toward retrospective inflation of the depth of contemporary feelings. But there has also developed a ritualized discourse of guilt and repentance, which tends toward minimizing one's original reaction in order to play the repentant "bad son." Memoirs of the period abound with examples of both.

The one thing that can be said with reasonable certainty is that, on the whole, recency of immigration — which meant stronger family connections to Europe — was closely tied to the depth of feeling the Holocaust evoked among American Jews. Baldly stated, it was the difference between contemplating that abstraction "European Jewry" being destroyed and imagining Aunt Minnie at Treblinka. Everything we know about differences in the responses of various segments of American Jewry suggests that this was the case. The Yiddish-language press had much greater coverage of the events of the Holocaust than the Anglo-Jewish press. It was in immigrant centers like the Lower East Side of Manhattan and the Williamsburg section of Brooklyn that wartime memorial activity was concentrated.

There is some truth to the assertion that defining oneself more as an American and less as a Jew served to diminish one's reaction to the Holocaust. Young Jews, particularly the better-educated, were not only farther from their roots but were more likely to be influenced by the pervasive downgrading of "racial" ties. But there is one great difficulty with explanations of the thin contemporary American Jewish response to the Holocaust which emphasize excessive Americanization and its corollary, decreased Jewish identity. The difficulty is that the same marginalization of the Holocaust in consciousness took place in the Yishuv — the Jewish community of Palestine — more than half of whose members had left Europe since 1933.

The *Palestine Post,* on November 25, 1942, carried a report from the Polish government-in-exile of an alleged order by Heinrich Himmler to kill all Polish Jews by the end of 1942. It got four brief paragraphs, with much more space and more prominence given to "Soviet Army

Scores Smashing Victory" (at Stalingrad) and "Allies Advance on Tunis, Bizerta." Even the Pacific war news got bigger play than the Himmler order. On March 30 of the following year, "Premier of Bengal Dismissed" was given more space in the *Post* than the bottom-corner story "Half Million Jews Killed in Warsaw," which reported — falsely as of this date — that all of Warsaw's Jews had been killed. Yehuda Bauer, a leading Israeli Holocaust scholar, writes that the wartime Palestinian press would "go into ecstasies about some local party-political affair, while the murder of the Jews of Europe is reported only in the inside pages."[11] Dina Porat, in her study of the Yishuv and the Holocaust, observes that "the extermination ceased to command special attention once the details had become familiar." A month of mourning proclaimed when the scale of the ongoing catastrophe became clear in late 1942 "proved to be too great a burden on the public": only the first of weekly days of prayer was observed; movie houses that were to be closed for the month were reopened after their owners protested that their livelihoods were threatened. Overall, she concludes, "in Palestine daily life continued scarcely affected by the war," except for increased prosperity as a result of purchases by the British army, and spending by its soldiers.[12]

The comparison between Jews in the United States and in Palestine is relevant to the assertion that it was "excessive assimilation" that limited the American Jewish response to the Holocaust. It is equally interesting to see how closely the response of many American Jews paralleled that of non-Jewish Americans — a reminder that it is a mistake to think of two discrete populations. If American gentiles drastically underestimated the size of the Jewish death toll in Europe, so did many Jews. Shortly after the war, at a time when the figure of six million had been widely publicized, a young sociologist polled Chicago Jews about the Holocaust. Half of those surveyed seriously underestimated the extent of Jewish losses. A bookkeeper: "Does it run in the millions? No, it doesn't run into the millions. Well, maybe it's close to a million. No, it couldn't be that many." The wife of a garment manufacturer: "Hundreds of thousands, I'm sure of it. Of course they do say millions, but so many people we thought were gone have been accounted for, so who knows?"[13]

There were "very Jewish" Jews who, like so many gentiles, remained ignorant of the Holocaust until the end of the war. Eli Ginzberg, the son of a professor at the Jewish Theological Seminary and himself active in Jewish affairs before Pearl Harbor, worked in the Pentagon during the war. He rejected what he was told about concentration camps as "gross exaggerations." "The conception of mass genocide was beyond my imagination and it was not until the camps had been overrun by the U.S. forces that I realized that the impossible had indeed occurred."[14] Lieutenant Colonel Lewis Weinstein, also involved in Jewish communal activity, was a member of General Eisenhower's staff. In the spring of 1945 he was puzzled by a reference on a map to a "death camp." Inquiring of a colleague, he was told that "a million, perhaps two million Jews had been murdered at Auschwitz." Weinstein later wrote: "I was stunned. I had never heard such numbers. I had not known of the bestiality of systematic, scientific, high priority Nazi mass murder. . . . I had heard of murders in the hundreds, in the thousands — but millions of murders!? The information was shattering."[15]

While, overall and on average, American Jews knew more about the Holocaust than their non-Jewish neighbors, such instances of wartime ignorance abound. If the mainstream press contained little about the Holocaust while it was going on, the same was true of much of the Jewish press. Indeed, many Jewish periodicals have had a good deal more coverage of the Holocaust in 1973, 1983, and 1993 than they had in 1943. Sometimes — there is no way to know how often — this downplaying of the Holocaust may have been deliberate, a way to keep up morale. It is said (the matter is in dispute) that at the Theresienstadt concentration camp Rabbi Leo Baeck deliberately kept from his fellow prisoners his knowledge that deportation to Poland meant death: there was nothing they could do about it, and it would cause needless distress. Something like this calculation was made by the editor of the Jewish Publication Society. Early in the war he worried about the psychological effect of too much bad news on American Jews, and turned down manuscripts that dealt with the camps. "I think the time has come when a responsible organization like ours must call a halt to terrorizing the Jewish population in this country — the last Jewish population which still retains its self-confidence."[16]

Perhaps most striking is the extent to which, even among committed Jews, the Jewish dimension of Nazi criminality did not necessarily seem the most important, particularly for members of the younger generation. Shad Polier was the son-in-law of Rabbi Stephen S. Wise, head of the American Jewish Congress. (After the war, Polier, with Wise's daughter Justine, headed the Congress for some years.) Writing to his wife in the immediate aftermath of Kristallnacht, Polier expressed satisfaction with President Roosevelt's recall of the American ambassador to Berlin as a gesture of protest against the Nazi-sponsored pogrom. But what really mattered, he told Justine, was what Roosevelt was going to do with respect to the embargo on arms to the Republicans in the Spanish Civil War, and on this score he was far from confident.[17]

After the war began, and after the main outlines of the Holocaust had become known, it was common for Jewish writers to interpret Nazi atrocities in a universalist fashion — stressing that Jews were far from the only victims. A writer in the Zionist *Jewish Frontier* warned in 1944 against forgetting "what was done to the Czechs, the Poles, the Jews, the Russians."[18] An American Jewish Committee staff memorandum urged emphasis on "the new spirit of Poland under the heel of the Nazis, the new spirit of kinship and camaraderie among all sections of the Polish population — Catholics, Protestants, Jews. . . . It should always be pointed out that Nazi tyranny does not discriminate between Jew and Pole."[19] The editor of the *Menorah Journal* noted that "the sufferings of the Jews, inordinate and compounded as they are, constitute but parts of the suffering of all the victims of savagery today."[20] Similarly, Rabbi Wise repeatedly reminded people that "as Jews we have borne the heaviest burden." But, he continued, consistent with the approved representation of the war as an ideological struggle, "Jews have become the victims of the Fascist terrorism because they are the unbowed protagonists of freedom, faith, democracy."[21]

One can't, of course, infer grassroots Jewish framings of the Holocaust from the statements of Jewish organizational spokesmen or from journalists who wrote for the Jewish press. Such people are unrepresentative of American Jewry as a whole, being simultaneously more Jewish and less Jewish than those for whom they claimed to speak. They are "more Jewish" in the obvious sense that most Jews don't have their degree of full-time commitment to Jewishness. And they are "less Jewish" in that their public role, the fact that they know what they say is being listened to by a gentile audience, may make their utterances less frank, less expressive of spontaneous feelings, more "correct," than conversation around the kitchen table.[22]

Overall, the framing of many, perhaps most, American Jews paralleled that of non-Jewish Americans in one crucial respect. In a close examination of the Jews of Rochester, New York, during the war, Abraham Karp concluded that they knew a great deal about torture and mass murder; they had read about atrocity after atrocity, "each new one dissipating to some degree the impact and immediacy of the earlier"; but they did not know about "the Holocaust." "That was a perception . . . which came years later."[23]

More highly charged than the question of American Jews' contemporary emotional response to the Holocaust, or how they framed it, is the question of their practical response. The commonly accepted view within American Jewry in recent years has been that American Jews were unforgivably delinquent in not continually and energetically pressing for rescue. This is not a merely historical observation; it became the foundation of a powerful mobilizing discourse of expiation.

In campaigns on behalf of Soviet Jewry in the 1970s, the slogan "Never again" was spelled out as meaning "Never again, as in the early forties, shall American Jews abandon threatened brethren abroad. This time we must do the right thing." The most systematic invocation of the theme of expiation has been in calls for total American Jewish solidarity with an embattled Israel. In a 1991 speech Israeli Prime Minister Yitzhak Shamir said that the memory of inaction during World War II was "heavy on the conscience" of American Jews and motivated their activism on behalf of Israel. "Let us hope that they will find the strength to correct what they missed fifty years ago."[24] Jonathan Pollard from his prison cell: "So what was I supposed to do? Let Israel fend for herself? If you think that this is what I should have done, then how can we condemn all those smug, self-righteous 'American' Jews during the Second World War who consciously participated in the abandonment of European Jewry?"[25]

How much *did* organized American Jewry do to press for rescue efforts? There were a number of specially focused efforts. Orthodox Jewish groups worked tirelessly to save endangered rabbis and yeshiva students, who, by traditional religious criteria, should have priority. The Jewish Labor Committee did what it could for Jewish trade unionists and socialists (but not Communists) who were in peril. Academic organizations tried to assist threatened scholars. Zionists in both the United States and Palestine gave priority to saving their European comrades over those who had turned to Eretz Yisrael only when they were themselves in danger. And, of course, all who could do so exerted themselves on behalf of members of their own families — which is, in a sense, what the above-named groups were doing.

But in general, rescue was not a high-priority item for major American Jewish organizations, or their leaders, during the war. The archives of the American Jewish Committee and the American Jewish Congress show scant attention to the question. (The Anti-Defamation League of B'nai B'rith in these years concerned itself exclusively with domestic matters.) The largest wartime effort to unite American Jewry — the American Jewish Conference of 1943 — did not originally include rescue on the agenda, and when it did come up, it got short shrift. There were a few mass meetings demanding "action," but usually without any clear notion of what form that action might take, and seeming to function more for catharsis than for serious mobilization. (The composer Kurt Weill said of the wartime pageant *We Will Never Die*, on which he collaborated, that it had "accomplished nothing. . . . All we have done is make a lot of Jews cry, which is not a unique accomplishment.")[26] There were some private approaches to the Roosevelt administration by representatives of individual organizations and by joint delegations, but they were not assiduously pursued. The leading Jewish organizations boycotted and sought to discredit the one group that worked most energetically for rescue, the Emergency Committee to Save the Jewish People of Europe, founded by Peter Bergson, a representative of the "Zionist-revisionist" Irgun in the United States.

Why was this the case? Various, usually accusatory explanations have been offered. Many of these describe the failure to press for rescue as simply a corollary of American Jewish indifference. Beyond this, one prevalent explanation is that inaction was the result of the general timidity of American Jewry, and, in particular, its fear that agitation for rescue would exacerbate domestic anti-Semitism.[27] There's no doubt that there often was reluctance among Jews to push Jewish issues in public. Paul Jacobs has described, from his childhood, a sensibility common among the older generation: "A Jew did not 'make rishis.' "

To "make rishis" was to stir up a fuss of some kind, and it was a cardinal sin, for it supposedly made Jews vulnerable to the potential wrath of the

Christian world. This world was conceived of as something like a potentially evil sleeping giant who, if awakened by a loud noise, might, and
probably would, turn on the disturber of his peace and do him harm.[28]

American Jews, and particularly Jewish organizations, were clearly
worried about anti-Semitism in the wartime United States. Immediately after Pearl Harbor, the director of the Anti-Defamation League,
noting an increase in anti-Semitism in recent years, warned his
colleagues that it could be expected to increase further. "There will
be hundreds of thousands of bereaved families, a substantial part
of whom have been conditioned to the belief that this is a Jewish
war."[29] A widespread anti-Semitic slur was draft dodging, and Jewish defense agencies worked energetically to stress the presence of
Jews in combat. (The American press had had some assistance from
the ADL in discovering that Colin Kelly's cockpit mate was Meyer
Levin.)

There is no direct evidence to sustain this explanation cum accusation — which doesn't mean that it's wrong, but reminds us that
it's not necessarily right. It is sometimes said that the fact that the
Jewish-owned *New York Times* did not give greater prominence to
Nazi actions against Jews illustrates this syndrome. While it is true
that the *Times* was coy about printing Jewish-sounding bylines on its
front page, its reticence on atrocities against Jews has been greatly
exaggerated — witness its massive coverage of Kristallnacht. Certainly
one of the reasons why mainstream Jewish organizations opposed the
Bergson group was its provocative style: it drafted a newspaper advertisement saying that "there's going to be a very happy Christmas this
year because by December there just wouldn't be any Jews left for the
Christian world to spit at."[30] (The more important reasons for hostility to the Bergson group were defense of organizational turf against an
upstart outsider and the perception, shared by the leaders of world
Zionism and of the Yishuv, that Bergson's group represented terrorist thugs.)[31] As measured by polls, anti-Semitism remained high in
the United States during the war. In retrospect, it is clear that American anti-Semitism, though broad, was relatively shallow; otherwise, it
could not have declined as precipitously as it did after 1945. But this, of
course, was unknown to Jews during the war. It probably *is* true that
fear of "making rishis" played a role in inhibiting Jewish wartime efforts for rescue.[32]

Another argument is that American Jews in general, and Rabbi

Stephen Wise in particular, were so much in thrall to FDR that they were unwilling to confront his administration on the rescue issue. That American Jews in those years were deeply devoted to the president is clear. They believed, it was said, in three worlds: *die velt* (this world), *yene velt* (the world to come), and *Roosevelt*. And though Wise's naïveté has sometimes been overstated, it is true that he was extravagantly deferential, not to say fawning, in his relations with FDR and inordinately proud of their alleged close relationship. A former student of Wise's recalled years later:

> One day Rabbi Wise called some of his students into his office having returned from Washington. He told of a conference he had with President Roosevelt, and he dramatized it, as was his way. At one point he said, "... and then I said, Franklin, I think...." At that point I had the terrifying feeling that for the privilege of calling Roosevelt "Franklin" the Jewish people would pay heavily. He had obviously taken so much pride in that accomplishment.[33]

In the circumstances, there was no possibility of threatening the loss of Jewish political support as a lever with Roosevelt. James Baker, Ronald Reagan's secretary of state, is alleged to have said in 1992, when warned of Jewish political reprisals if he withheld loan guarantees from Israel, "Fuck 'em, they didn't vote for us anyway." Roosevelt could have said, if the question had arisen (it didn't), "Fuck 'em, they'll vote for me anyway." Even if a switch had been possible, the Republican alternative would surely have been worse. During the war, Republican campaigners, referring to Roosevelt's prominent Jewish associate Sidney Hillman, put up billboards across the nation: "It's Your Country — Why Let Sidney Hillman Run It."[34] And without necessarily willing it, Republicans were well aware that it was they who benefited from all the talk of "Jew Deal" and "President Rosenfeld." In any case, it was against mostly Republican opposition that Roosevelt had led the United States into the war against Hitler. It probably *is* true that Wise was inhibited by the peculiarities of his relationship with FDR from pressing as hard as he might have wished on the issue of rescue. But would it have made any difference?

As far as overall Zionist priorities were concerned, in the United States as in Palestine, it is clear that working for the creation of a Jewish state took precedence over working to save Europe's Jews. Even David Ben-Gurion's sympathetic biographer acknowledges that Ben-

Gurion did nothing practical for rescue, devoting his energies to post-war prospects.[35] He delegated rescue work to Yitzhak Gruenbaum, who insisted that "Zionism is above everything." When it was proposed that money for rescue be taken from the Jewish National Fund, devoted to the purchase of Arab land, Gruenbaum replied: "They will say that I am anti-Semitic, that I don't want to save the Exile, that I don't have *a varm Yiddish hartz*. . . . Let them say what they want. I will not demand that the Jewish Agency allocate a sum of 300,000 or 100,000 pounds sterling to help European Jewry. And I think that whoever demands such things is performing an anti-Zionist act."[36]

Zionists in America — apparently spontaneously and without urging from the leadership in Palestine — took the same position. At a May 1943 meeting of the American Emergency Committee for Zionist Affairs, Nahum Goldmann argued, "If a drive is opened against the White Paper [the British policy of restricting Jewish immigration to Palestine] the mass meetings of protest against the murder of European Jewry will have to be dropped. We do not have sufficient manpower for both campaigns."[37] A few months later, at the broad-based American Jewish Conference, the Zionists precipitated a split by insisting on a resolution calling for a Jewish state, thus driving out the non-Zionists. Subsequently the Zionist leadership of the conference disbanded a joint committee on which Zionists and non-Zionists had worked together on rescue-oriented activity, insisting that such matters could be handled by the conference itself. Whatever tenuous unity had existed on the rescue issue dissolved. In May 1944, at a meeting of the (renamed) American Zionist Emergency Council, Abba Hillel Silver worried that

> our overemphasizing the refugee issue has enabled our opponents to state that, if it is rescue you are concerned about, why don't you concentrate on that and put the politics aside. . . . It is possible for the Diaspora to undermine the Jewish state, because the urgency of the rescue issue could lead the world to accept a temporary solution. . . . We should place increased emphasis on fundamental Zionist ideology.

Emmanuel Neumann agreed:

> It is not a question of a conflict between stressing the refugee issue and stressing Zionist ideology. It is a matter of emphasis. The main issue is

whether we place our stress on the present Jewish refugee problem or the eternal Jewish refugee problem. . . . The typical non-Jew thinks that the Jewish problem is the refugee problem perpetrated by Hitler. In reality, it is the recurrence of such tragedies that is peculiar to Jewish life and that has to be addressed.[38]

The decision to give priority to postwar state-building over immediate rescue can easily be made to look appalling: ideological zealotry blind to desperate human need. But was it? One can criticize this or that choice, but overall the decision to "write off" European Jewry and concentrate on building for the future was based on a thoughtful, if chilling, appraisal of what was and was not possible. It was based on the belief, shared by most Jewish leaders, Zionist and non-Zionist alike, that little could be done for the Jews caught in Hitler's net. Speaking to the convention of the Zionist Organization of America, shortly after hearing of Gerhard Riegner's telegram from Switzerland, Nahum Goldmann lamented his generation's tragic position: "One-half of the generation is being slaughtered before our eyes, and the other half has to sit down and cannot prevent this catastrophe." He urged his audience not to despair, but instead to work for a Jewish state that would make future tragedies impossible.[39] At a private gathering at about the same time, Goldmann said:

> Nothing can be done to check them; we can only work for victory. . . . The only thing that would really impress Hitler would be the shooting of 100,000 Nazis in America; Americans, however, could never do that. . . . Even if we had done everything that was suggested here — and within twenty-four hours — it still would not have saved any Jewish lives. We are helpless; all we can hope to do is to establish a record, which will help us after the war.

The same concern that actions be taken "to establish a record" recurred when, some months later, Goldmann remarked that while prospects for rescuing Jews through negotiation with Germany were quite hopeless, "Germany should have been approached for the record, so that we may not go down in history as not having done the necessary."[40]

The belief that there was nothing to be done to rescue European Jews was common. When a delegation of Jewish leaders, after receiving the terrible news from Switzerland in 1942, planned for a meeting with

FDR, all they could think of to ask for was "a statement, just as he made a statement after Lidice," warning that those responsible for the murder of Jews would be held accountable after the war.[41] The statement was issued promptly. In the spring of 1943 Max Weinreich of YIVO (the Yiddish Scientific Organization) prepared a petition to Roosevelt that was signed by hundreds of academics, again asking for a warning to the Nazis, and for the president to "apply hitherto unused methods to save the millions of European Jews doomed to death by the enemy of civilization." Lucy Dawidowicz, an associate of Weinreich's, reflected many years later that "for all of his intellectual brilliance, Weinreich was just as helpless as the rest of us when it came to practical suggestions. He could only propose 'hitherto unused methods.' "[42] For the most part, Jewish leaders accepted the official Allied position that the only effective rescue strategy was rapid military victory. The *National Jewish Monthly* (B'nai B'rith) favored protest "for the record," but warned lest such activities "divert our energies one whit from the immediate task at hand. . . . There is only one way to stop the Nazi massacres, and that is by crushing the Nazis in battle, wholly, completely and irrevocably. . . . Everything for victory!" *New Palestine* (Zionist Organization of America) echoed this view: "spiritual catharsis" was all very well, but the main task was "doggedly, grimly, resolutely, defiantly [turning] our full attention to the task of crushing the enemy."[43]

Zionists, like non-Zionists, were not "writing off" European Jewry, as critics claim. The Jews of Europe were, in their view, already written off by circumstances beyond their control — Nazi domination of *Festung Europa*. Meanwhile, Zionists could take advantage of wartime sympathy for the plight of Europe's Jews, and the expected postwar political changes, to create what they believed to be a very different kind of "final solution" to the Jewish question.

In pursuit of their strategy, important gains were made. Before the end of the war three quarters of the members of Congress had gone on record in favor of a Jewish commonwealth in Palestine. Zionism had made even greater strides among American Jews. No doubt much of this — particularly among Jews, but to some extent among gentiles as well — was a kind of displaced action. One couldn't do what one most wanted to do — save the Jews of Europe. The energy thus frustrated was channeled into working for the postwar and the long term.

The defense of the Zionism-first strategy depends, of course, on the correctness of the calculation on which it was based. Granting, as I think one must, that the calculation was made in good faith, was it the case that in reality little could have been done by the American government to save European Jews?

[3]

"The Abandonment of the Jews"

S INCE THE 1970s it has come to be widely accepted that numerous promising rescue opportunities were willfully disregarded by the Roosevelt administration. Again, book titles tell the tale: it was *The Abandonment of the Jews, The Failure to Rescue; Roosevelt fiddled While Six Million Died,* offered *No Haven for the Oppressed; The Jews Were Expendable.*[1] Their authors differ about exactly how many European Jews could have been saved by an energetic rescue policy; some say many hundreds of thousands, others millions. There is said to be a sense in which *all* of the victims of the Holocaust are the responsibility of the Allies, since the Nazis took Allied indifference as a signal to proceed with the killing.[2]

"Complicity" and "accomplice" are the words typically applied to the American (and British) governments. Deborah Lipstadt is more moderate than others when she describes Allied policy as merely "border[ing] on complicity" in the Final Solution. What prevented Auschwitz from being bombed, says Lipstadt, was the "deep antipathy" toward "contemptible" Jews held by key figures in Washington and London.[3] David Wyman, perhaps the most-cited member of the prosecution team, is at one with Lipstadt in seeing anti-Semitism at the core of the "abandonment."[4] Just as the later claim that American Jews had been delinquent during the war had a practical moral for the future, so did the U.S. government's wartime "failure to rescue": in both cases, a compelling obligation to expiate past sins through unswerving support of Israel in later years.[5]

In recent decades the charge of culpable American inaction has been, with varying degrees of explicitness, accepted by American leaders (when addressing Jewish audiences). Seeking to mend fences in the immediate aftermath of President Reagan's controversial trip to the German military cemetery at Bitburg, Secretary of State George Shultz said that after the Holocaust the American people had pledged "never again would we let the Jewish people stand alone"; Vice President George Bush promised that "never again will the cries of abandoned Jews go unheard by the United States government." At the dedication of the United States Holocaust Memorial Museum in Washington in 1993, President Bill Clinton said that "far too little was done": "Before the war even started, doors to liberty were shut, and even after the United States and the Allies attacked Germany, rail lines to the camps within miles of militarily-significant targets were left undisturbed."[6] American complicity in the Holocaust has been offered as one of the principal justifications for there being an *American* Holocaust museum. The chairman of the museum's education committee told the press that those who did nothing were "just as guilty" as those who performed the killing.[7] Both prewar American immigration policy and the failure to bomb Auschwitz are featured prominently in the museum's permanent exhibition.

The popular consensus around what one historian has called "the comfortable morality tale that has passed for history" is not matched by a scholarly consensus.[8] There is, in fact, no scholarly consensus on the subject, but most professional historians agree that the "comfortable morality tale" — notably as advanced by David Wyman in *The Abandonment of the Jews*, which has achieved a certain canonical status — is simply bad history: estimates of the number of those who might have been saved have been greatly inflated, and the moralistic version ignores real constraints at the time. Lucy Dawidowicz, who can hardly be accused of insufficient empathy with the agony of European Jewry, has been the sharpest critic of Wyman's interpretation. Martin Gilbert, author of *Auschwitz and the Allies*, thinks it unlikely that American or British action could have saved *any* lives in the death camps. Henry Feingold, author of *The Politics of Rescue*, doubts that even if the Roosevelt administration had been more open to rescue options it would have had much effect on the fate of European Jewry.[9]

There are three counts in the indictment of the United States for complicity in the Holocaust: a restrictive prewar immigration policy, which prevented European Jews from escaping before the trap closed; the failure to pursue various prospects for threats, reprisals, or negotiations to alleviate the situation of Jews within Hitler's grasp; and, more cited than any other, the unwillingness of the U.S. Air Force to bomb either the rail lines leading to Auschwitz or the killing facilities themselves. What can be said about each of these?

As is well known, relatively free immigration to the United States came to an end with the passage of the Immigration Act of 1924, which set strict quotas by country of origin. The racist intention of the law was manifest: the quotas were based on the national origins of the American population as measured not in the census of 1920 but of 1890, before the era of mass immigration from Eastern and Southern Europe. In 1930, as the Depression deepened, President Herbert Hoover directed the State Department to interpret more strictly the provision in the law having to do with the immigrant's becoming a "public charge." Whereas previously a visa could be (but seldom was) refused on the basis of the "likelihood" that a person might become a public charge, the new directive excluded those who might "possibly" become such. When this went into effect, there was an overall decline of immigration from 242,000 in 1931 to 36,000 in 1932, of whom fewer than 3,000 were Jews. All this, of course, was before Hitler came to power.[10] In 1935 Roosevelt had the State Department order American consulates to give refugees "the most considerate attention and the most generous and favorable treatment possible under the laws," and reinstated the more lenient "likelihood" standard.[11] But the new policy was not consistently implemented down the line, sometimes the result of anti-Semitism among American officials in Europe. It didn't help matters that many of the consular and visa officers had attended the Georgetown University School of Foreign Service, where the dean, the Reverend Edmund A. Walsh, emphasized in seminars that "the Jew was . . . the entrepreneur [of the Bolshevik Revolution], who recognized his main chance and seized it shrewdly and successfully."[12] From 1938 to Pearl Harbor, the German (now merged with the Austrian) quota was filled almost entirely by Jews. Paradoxically, Jews fleeing Germany and Austria were the beneficiaries of the large German quota under the racist 1924 law: honorary Aryans. But of course there were many more applicants than spaces, and quotas for other countries were not affected. (The Hungarian quota had a twenty-five-year waiting list.)

The natural question is why the immigration law wasn't changed to meet the desperate circumstances of European Jewry. One reason — not adequate, to be sure, but a partial explanation — is that no one knew how desperate the circumstances were. Before 1941, and surely before the outbreak of the European war in September 1939, it appeared to be a matter of Jews escaping from likely persecution, not certain death. The Holocaust, now long in the established past, was then in the unimagined future. Anti-Zionist polemicists, ignoring this elementary fact, have made much of David Ben-Gurion's response when, after Kristallnacht, the British suggested transferring thousands of Jewish children from Germany to England: "If I were to know that it was possible to save all of the [Jewish] children of Germany by sending them to England and only half by transferring them to Palestine, I would still choose the latter. Because before us is not only a responsibility to those children, but a historic responsibility to the Jewish people."[13] Different readers, depending on their moral and ideological dispositions, will have different reactions to this expression of single-mindedness, even in the absence of foreknowledge of the Holocaust to come. But the remark forces us to remember that it was not considered, by Ben-Gurion or anyone else, to be a matter of saving the children from the gas chambers.

In early 1939 the American government was unwilling to admit the Jewish refugees on the German liner *St. Louis*, stranded in the Caribbean when their Cuban visas were canceled — a dismal episode in American history.[14] With no foreknowledge of the Holocaust that was to follow, it seemed no more than the equivalent of the United States, a half century later, turning back Haitians, which is bad enough. And the *St. Louis* story appeared to have a happy ending, as the passengers avoided return to Germany and were given refuge in Belgium, Holland, France, and England; only the last, in the event — but again, who knew? — proved a real haven. (The *St. Louis* passengers fared no better with the Jewish Agency in Palestine than with the American authorities. The agency refused the request of the American Joint Distribution Committee, which was trying to find them a home, for several hundred immigration certificates from the quota allotted under the British mandate.)[15]

Even if not considered a life-or-death matter, and "merely" a matter of humanitarian succor, why didn't the Roosevelt administration, or for that matter organized American Jewry, press for changes in the immigration law, especially after Kristallnacht? This question, at least, is easily answered. In the first place, there were priorities to consider. FDR was, from 1938 onward, dedicated to moving the United States closer to the anti-Axis coalition, and after 1939 to securing American entry into the war. Roosevelt had to convince the public at large, and in particular nativists and isolationists, that the greater involvement he sought in the European conflict was in the American national interest — a matter of self-defense, not some globalist do-gooding; he was not letting Jewish interests determine American policy. In the face of those who were all too ready to see Roosevelt as a tool of the Jews, for the president to take any special measures on behalf of Jewish refugees would be to give hostages to isolationists, to jeopardize the larger foreign-policy goal to which American Jews, more than any other group, gave highest priority.

In addition, with the United States still not out of the Depression, with unemployment still high, public opinion and congressional opinion were strongly in favor of reducing, not increasing, existing quotas — or even closing down immigration altogether. At the beginning of the 1930s, a bill cutting all quotas by 90 percent had passed the House of Representatives and probably would have passed the Senate if the legislative year hadn't come to an end. Such legislation was introduced repeatedly thereafter. As if matters weren't bad enough, the stepping up of Nazi pressure against the Jews of Germany coincided with the worst phase of the "Roosevelt Recession" in 1937–38. Unemployment had been falling since 1933; the situation then worsened, and throughout 1938 and the early months of 1939 it hovered between eight and ten million, with the economy not reaching 1937 levels again until after the war began. It was nearly impossible to counter restrictionist arguments that every entering refugee who found a job would put an American out of work.[16]

Anti-immigration sentiment was so strong in Congress and among the general public that to open the question for debate seemed likely to worsen rather than to ease conditions; better to leave bad enough alone. Immediately following Germany's absorption of Austria in early 1938, two New York Jewish congressmen introduced bills to open America's doors to refugees. The bills were withdrawn, however, after their sponsors became convinced that hearings on the legislation could only benefit restrictionists. This was also the fate of a bill introduced by Senator Robert Wagner later that year to admit twenty thousand Jewish children over the quota. After the bill had been amended beyond recognition, its sponsors decided to let it die rather than pursue it. The Non-Sectarian Committee for German Refugee Children, which had been backing the legislation, concluded that "pressure for this Bill would constitute a hazard to the general immigration situation" because "such a move would rouse to life antialien bills of all kind." All Jewish organizations, with the exception of the Communist-front Jewish People's Committee, agreed. This was the view of several leading members of the administration as well, and was probably Roosevelt's own view, which may have accounted for his failure to press the measure. The same general climate prevailed after the beginning of the war in Europe. In 1940 FDR's commissioner of immigration told him that after carefully monitoring all the sessions of the immigration committees of both houses of Congress, he had concluded that restrictionist sentiment was so strong that "the chances of any liberalizing legislation seemed negligible."[17]

In the aftermath of Kristallnacht Roosevelt, by administrative action, extended indefinitely permission to stay in this country to fifteen thousand refugees with expiring visitor's visas. This seemed the outer limit of the possible in a period when presidential prerogatives were much more circumscribed by congressional oversight than was to be true in subsequent decades. To go further risked successful backlash. (If there had been any thought of pressing forward, which seems unlikely, Democratic losses in the 1938 elections would have put an end to it.)[18] As a practical political matter, any wider opening of America's gates was not feasible.[19]

It might be remarked that it is a curious aspect of our psychology that we think of technical or military obstacles as intractable, but attitudinal or political obstacles as capable of being overcome. Thus the suggestion that great fleets of American transport planes should have swooped down on Treblinka and, like the Israelis at Entebbe, overcome the guards and spirited the prisoners away would be instantly dismissed as an absurd and impossible fantasy. Yet we readily imagine dramatic reversals in mass attitudes toward immigration, which were every bit as impossible and absurd. In fact, comparing our relative successes in surmounting technical and attitudinal obstacles, we should perhaps reverse our expectations.

There were various proposals for negotiated ransom of Jews, but except at the very end of the war, when the Third Reich was collapsing, nothing came of them. For the most part they were not pressed energetically — sometimes, to the shame of those involved, even obstructed by bureaucratic inertia and turf wars. It is possible that such opportunities were underestimated. At a Chicago rally in 1943 the governor of Illinois urged "some bargain or agreement" to rescue Jews, but acknowledged that "it is much like bargaining with a maddened, hungry lion which has been caged with a lamb."[20] The conviction that Nazism was a charging wild beast whom one could kill, from whom one could flee, but with whom one could certainly not negotiate, probably inhibited enthusiasm for rescue through negotiations. Working in the same direction was an underestimation of the conflicts and jealousies within the reputedly unified Nazi regime, and of tensions between Germany and its allies.[21]

But it seems unlikely that the proposals would have come to fruition in any case. There was an offer from Romania to ransom seventy thousand Jews which reached the West in February 1943, and was the occasion of much publicity by the Bergsonites. The possibility vanished almost as soon as it appeared — vetoed by the Germans.[22] There was Adolf Eichmann's famous proposal to release a million Jews in return for ten thousand trucks, which, he guaranteed, would be used only on the eastern front. The proposal was outlandish on the face of it: supplying the enemy with the means to conduct war against one's ally. It was rightly seen by the Western powers (many Jewish leaders agreed) as an attempt to sow dissension between themselves and the Soviet Union. Indeed, the proposal seems to have been in large part an insincere cover for a serious plan to make a separate peace with the Western powers.[23] Fear of arousing Stalin's suspicions was a specter that surrounded all negotiation schemes with Germany or its allies. (The offer to pay a ransom to Romania came at a time when Romanian troops were fighting side by side with the Germans at Stalingrad.) Even proposals for the exchange of sick and wounded Allied prisoners were often delayed by the United States and Great Britain for months, or canceled altogether, when it became clear that the arrangements being proposed by the Germans were designed to disrupt Allied military operations — obviously one of the German aims in dangling possibilities of ransom.[24] A further consideration militating against ransom deals was that until the invasion of France in 1944, the economic blockade of Nazi Germany was a central component of Allied strategy, aiming at undermining the regime from within before the invading armies delivered the death blow. Though the strategy was not, in the end, very effective, it was pursued with the utmost seriousness, and policy-makers took a dim view of accepting the precedent of breaching it.

There was the desperate suggestion from Jews inside Hitler's death trap that the Allies threaten to kill German civilians and POWs under their control in order to halt the killing of Jews. This was hardly acceptable on moral grounds, apart from the fact that the Germans held almost 200,000 British Commonwealth and American POWs as "counter-hostages." Not much more appealing was the suggestion that the West threaten reprisals from the air against German civilian populations. German civilians were already being targeted, but the fiction that unlike the Axis, the Allies aimed only at military targets was not to be discarded lightly.

Particularly in the closing stages of the war, negotiations, diplomatic pressure, and threats did seem to have some effect, though it was often modest. Warnings to Romania, Bulgaria, and Hungary appear to have had some impact. Raids on Budapest in 1944 may in fact have persuaded the Hungarian government, before the German takeover, to halt the deportation of Jews. Latin American countries were pressured to honor questionable passports. Countries where Jews found refuge were assured that the United States would help cover their costs and guarantee their resettlement elsewhere. The War Refugee Board, established at the beginning of 1944, did important work, though its accomplishments have often been exaggerated. It is surely unfortunate that it was not founded earlier, but it is unlikely that before the last year of the war the few rescue opportunities that arose would have been available.

The "rescue" proposal that has been discussed more than any other, which has become the symbol of American culpable inaction, was the suggestion — rejected by the American military — that the rail lines to Auschwitz, or the camp itself, be bombed. The failure to bomb Auschwitz is in some ways the climax of the U.S. Holocaust Museum's narrative. After walking through graphic representations of the death camps, the visitor encounters a floor-to-ceiling display condemning the refusal to bomb Auschwitz — as if to say, "The American government could have, but chose not to, put an end to this." Unlike complex and problematic negotiations, the plan seems so clear cut: doable and effectual. Its rejection seems sheer perversity. But was it?

The question of bombing the rail lines can be dismissed immediately. Massive experience had taught the Allies that bombing rail lines was hardly ever effective: the few hits scored could be quickly repaired. Railways might be bombed in support of tactical operations — to prevent the enemy from moving troops and materiel for several hours, perhaps a day or two. Beyond that, the method was nearly useless.

The problems with bombing the killing facilities themselves were of a different order. The greatest military myth of the Second World War was pinpoint-precision bombing, "dropping a bomb through a pickle barrel from twenty thousand feet." While the myth was assiduously promoted for civilian consumption, strategic bombing was known by military leaders to be exceedingly inaccurate. One of the reasons for the (unavowed) adoption of terror bombing of civilian populations was that it was often hard for Allied pilots to reliably hit anything smaller than a city. Consider two massive raids on a synthetic-fuel plant in the vicinity of Auschwitz during the very time that bombing the concentration camp was under discussion. In one, aerial photography revealed that there was no damage to five of the six primary targets, some damage to the sixth. In another raid, by ninety-six heavy bombers dropping more than a thousand 500-pound bombs from relatively low altitude, photographs showed "only slight damage," most to "small stores buildings and labour barracks."[25]

There were more than 100,000 Jewish prisoners at Auschwitz. How would they have fared in the event of an aerial assault on the killing facilities? No one can know for sure, but the most careful study to date suggests that one third of the bombs that would have been required for the operation would have fallen on the prisoner barracks area, and additional bombs in other areas where prisoners worked.[26] The U.S. Air Force had faced a similar question when considering the bombing of factories at Dachau and Nordhausen. In both cases the missions were rejected on grounds that the factories could not be destroyed without killing the slave laborers who worked in them.[27] (With breathtaking insouciance, David Wyman has suggested that if precision bombing was insufficiently precise, the air force could have used saturation bombing from high altitudes.)[28]

It is often said that the Jewish prisoners at Auschwitz fervently hoped for bombing; they did not care if they were themselves killed so long as the facilities were destroyed. The evidence is mixed. No doubt some did feel this way, though probably fewer than the number who reported this feeling after the Allied failure to bomb Auschwitz had become a standard trope of Holocaust discourse. Others have vigorously dissented. In the fall of 1944 prisoners knew that liberation was near at hand; how ironic to die by Allied action in the waning days of their imprisonment.[29]

Apart from the problem of massive prisoner casualties, how effective would such an operation have been? It is often said that the destruction of the gas chambers and crematoria would have so disrupted the killing operations that they would have been delayed for months or suspended altogether. This seems extremely unlikely — unfounded speculation fueled by the conviction that there *must* have been a promising solution. Though Allied intelligence knew about some of the gas chambers at Auschwitz, they had no knowledge of two cottages converted to killing facilities in the woods west of Birkenau, one no longer used and the other used on a standby basis.[30] Even had the gas chambers and crematoria been hit hard, they might well have been quickly repaired or replaced. Newly arrived Hungarian Jews were frequently killed in makeshift gas chambers in wooden barracks, or shot and then burned in pits in the nearby woods. By late 1944 the Germans had partially reverted to earlier methods and were no longer relying on elaborate, difficult-to-replace installations. Of course there was no shortage of slave labor to do the job. As the commandant of Auschwitz, Rudolf Höss, said in his memoirs, "In Auschwitz everything was possible."[31] All of this aside, if the gas chambers could not have been replaced, would Himmler have hesitated to revert to the mass shootings that earlier had killed more Jews in less time than at Auschwitz? It is said that a shortage of military personnel at this stage of the war would have prevented this, but the terrible lesson of the *Einsatzgruppen* was how few troops it took to kill so many. And could not — would not — a few hundred "Ivan the Terribles" have been easily recruited to do the job?

At the U.S. Holocaust Museum the exhibit on the failure to bomb Auschwitz begins by asserting that American Jewish organizations repeatedly asked the War Department to bomb the camp, which accords with the common impression of a broad consensus within American Jewry in favor of the operation. But the assertion, and the impression, are wrong. There is no record of any American Jewish organization ever asking the War Department to undertake such an operation. The requests came from Jewish individuals and groups in occupied Europe and Switzerland, from some exile governments, and from the Orthodox Agudath Israel World Organization; there were mixed and inconsistent messages on the subject from the World Jewish Congress and the Jewish Agency in Palestine. Some Jewish groups abroad did urge such action, others opposed it, many vacillated.

The exhibit contains a framed August 1944 letter from A. Leon

Kubowitzki, head of the Rescue Department of the World Jewish Congress, to Assistant Secretary of War John J. McCloy, passing on, without endorsement, a request from a member of the Czechoslovak State Council that Auschwitz be bombed. Not on display is Kubowitzki's letter written a month earlier, in which he categorically opposed bombing the camps: "the first victims would be the Jews."[32] Nor is there a display of the minutes of the Jewish Agency Executive, chaired by Ben-Gurion, which had considered the idea in June and concluded that "it ought not be proposed to the Allies to bomb places where there are Jews."[33]

Like a number of others, Kubowitzki wavered on the question. At one point, in desperation, he sought to avoid the issue of Jewish casualties by a proposal — straight out of the films of Errol Flynn — that the killing installations be attacked in force either by the underground or by Allied paratroopers.[34] The Jewish Agency also vacillated: while its London office was pushing the idea, the leadership in Palestine opposed it. The British representatives of the agency acknowledged that the bombing was not likely to be effective; they urged it for its symbolic value.[35]

John Pehle of the American War Rescue Board — one of the most ardent advocates of all plans for saving Europe's Jews — distanced himself from the suggestion throughout the debate: in October he passed along the proposal "for such consideration as it may be worth";[36] he gave it his qualified endorsement only in November 1944, after the mass killings at Auschwitz had ceased. Though the proposal to bomb Auschwitz had circulated among American Jewish groups during the summer of 1944, it seems never to have attracted any support among them.

The reasons McCloy offered for rejecting the bombing idea have been dismissed as transparent lies meant to cover up willed indifference to the fate of those at Auschwitz. But at least some of the reasons seem sound. When he wrote that the bombing "could be executed only by the diversion of considerable air forces now engaged in decisive operations elsewhere," it was in the immediate aftermath of the Normandy invasion, when they were indeed so engaged. Surely there is a case in support of his assertion that "such an operation would be of . . . doubtful efficacy." His third reason, that bombing "might provoke even more vindictive action by the Germans," is bizarre. He might have meant that the Germans would revert to mass shootings rather than the "more humane" gassings; probably he meant nothing at all. He may indeed have been engaged in a coverup, but of something other than callousness. It was impossible for him to acknowledge that pinpoint precision bombing — not only a leading wartime myth, but the public relations groundwork for the air force's grandiose plans for postwar expansion — was a fraud. A not unlikely worst-case scenario, in which thousands of Jewish inmates of Auschwitz were killed without appreciable damage to the killing apparatus, would not only jeopardize the mystique, but could have serious consequences for the career of whoever was responsible. McCloy may even have been concerned about the prisoners.[37]

Much surrounding the abortive initiative to bomb Auschwitz remains obscure, and is likely to remain so. But the current received version — a fruitful opportunity, fervently pressed and frivolously dismissed — must contend with the strong possibility that this ambivalently presented suggestion was a well-intentioned but misbegotten idea that we can perhaps be grateful was turned down.

The (in my view) dim practical possibilities for substantial rescue are relevant to the consequences of American inaction, not to its morality. A much more energetic program of rescue on all fronts might have reduced the overall toll by perhaps 1 percent, conceivably 2 percent. Given the absolute numbers involved, this would have been a worthwhile achievement indeed. Unhappily, the perception that the overall impact of American efforts would be marginal probably served to inhibit action by government officials — and by American Jews. It shouldn't be so, but it seems to be the case that we become energized only when we feel we can make a big difference.

It may be that if the practical possibilities had been greater, the same inaction would have prevailed. We can't know. And however much it mattered in the end, there was plenty of torpor, indifference, mindless routine, and callousness to be found in matters relating to rescue. In short, all the unlovely characteristics of the modern bureaucratic state. We would of course like it if governments were different; to *expect* them to be different is more than a little utopian. Utopianism has its uses — holding out an ideal standard — but with at least part of our minds we should try to distinguish that sort of standard from those we ordinarily employ.

But we've gotten ahead of ourselves, because the practice of rendering harsh moral judgments on the American government (or American gentiles, or American Jews) with respect to the Holocaust had yet to emerge in a serious way. As a widespread practice, it would be twenty years and more after the war's end before it emerged, and we will consider that emergence in due course. In the early 1940s hardly anyone inside government — and hardly anyone outside it, Jew or gentile — would have understood the phrase "abandonment of the Jews." The verb "to abandon" has a perfectly straightforward meaning: to withdraw support or help in spite of an existing commitment or obligation. The notion that the rescue of threatened foreign civilian populations was an obligation of a country involved in total war didn't occur to Americans during World War II or in its immediate aftermath.

At the end of the war almost all Americans, certainly the overwhelming majority of American Jews, were proud of the role of the U.S. armed forces in defeating Hitler; justifiably or not, proud of whatever their own contribution to victory had been. What we now call "the Holocaust" — what seemed to most people at the time simply the Jewish portion of the worldwide holocaust that had consumed between fifty and sixty million victims — had come to an end, thanks to the efforts and sacrifices of the United States and its allies. Dealing with the Holocaust's legacy, along with other legacies of the war, was now on the agenda.

Part Two

THE POSTWAR YEARS

[4]

"The DP Camps Have Served Their Historic Purpose"

A CENTRAL THEME of the commemoration of the fiftieth anniversary of the end of World War II was Americans' belated "confrontation with the Holocaust," as U.S. troops liberated Dachau, Buchenwald, and other sites of horror. Americans in 1995 heard how previous ignorance, doubts, and evasions had been replaced by shocked awareness as Americans encountered — could no longer avoid acknowledging — the reality of the Holocaust. In the spring of 1945, recalled one major news magazine, in a special supplement, "at breakfast tables across America, the Holocaust sprang from the newspaper page. It crackled over the radio. Delegations of congressmen and editors came back from the camps to affirm that the reports were no exaggeration. The newsreels delivered a like message."[1] In the anniversary year, recordings of Edward R. Murrow's awestruck radio commentary from Buchenwald were played and replayed. Veterans, at ceremonies across the country, recounted their personal, horrifying exposure to the Holocaust at the liberated camps. The U.S. Postal Service issued a commemorative stamp, based on a famous photograph by Margaret Bourke-White, showing gaunt figures behind barbed wire, captioned "Allies Liberate Holocaust Survivors, Early 1945."

The liberation of the camps had for some time been made emblematic of Americans' face-to-face encounter with the Holocaust. The Washington Holocaust Museum's narrative is crafted so that the visitor's initial confrontation with the Holocaust replicates that of American soldiers as they encountered heaps of emaciated bodies and hardly less emaciated survivors. Pictures of the horrors seen by those who liberated the camps — pictures that, as the Chinese proverb has it, are worth ten thousand words — are the first thing the visitor sees. Carved in stone on the exterior wall of the museum are the words of General Dwight Eisenhower:

> The things I saw beggar description. . . . The visual evidence and the verbal testimony of starvation, cruelty and bestiality were . . . overpowering. . . . I made the visit deliberately in order to be in position to give firsthand evidence of these things if ever, in the future, there develops a tendency to charge these allegations merely to "propaganda."[2]

But all of this talk of an American "encounter with the Holocaust" is quite misleading. That was not what Americans encountered, directly or indirectly, in 1945.

The shock and horror were clearly real. Equally real was the breadth and depth of the initial reactions to the camps in the United States. A traveling exhibition of Signal Corps photographs of the camps was viewed by stunned audiences across the country. Susan Sontag recalls her negative epiphany on seeing photographs of the camps as a twelve-year-old in California: "Nothing I have seen . . . ever cut me as sharply, deeply, instantaneously. . . . When I looked at those photographs, something broke. . . . I felt irrevocably grieved, wounded, but a part of my feelings started to tighten; something went dead; something is still crying."[3]

Yet none of this was an encounter with "the Holocaust" as we understand the term today. Indeed, everything about the contemporary presentation of the reports, testimonies, photographs, and newsreels was congruent with the wartime framing of Nazi atrocities as having been directed, in the main, at political opponents of the Third Reich.

The words "Jew" and "Jewish" do not appear in Murrow's broadcast about Buchenwald, nor do they appear in Margaret Bourke-White's account of photographing the camp.[4] General Eisenhower described the sites he wanted legislators and editors to visit as "German camps in which they have placed political prisoners." That was how they were described in the the report of congressional visitors to the camps; the newspaper editors' report spoke of "political prisoners, slave laborers and civilians of many nationalities."[5] Virtually all newspaper reports, picture captions, and newsreel commentary described the victims in this way. A *Life* reporter, describing those whom he had encountered at Dachau, wrote of "the men of all nations that Hitler's agents had picked out as prime opponents of Nazism." The *Saturday Evening Post* wrote of the program of "extermination for people who had dared to oppose the Nazi regime . . . had let slip some remark . . . had been members of the resistance [or] had the misfortune to be born Jews."[6]

Thus Jews did not go unmentioned. Particularly in the more detailed reports, they were included along with other groups of victims, and often it was pointed out that Jews fared worse than most others in the camps. But there was nothing about the reporting on the liberation of the camps that treated Jews as more than *among* the victims of the Nazis; nothing that suggested the camps were emblematic of anything other than Nazi barbarism in general; nothing, that is, that associated them with what is now designated "the Holocaust."

Deborah Lipstadt, in her book on the American press and the Holocaust, treats this as willful blindness, the consequence of inexcusable ignorance — or malice:

> Even now that correspondents were witnessing the grim results of the Final Solution, they could not grasp what they were seeing. . . . They found it difficult to admit to themselves — and to their readers — what they were witnessing. . . . They did not associate what they were now seeing in these camps, where most of the survivors were Jews, with the Final Solution.[7]

Was this a failure of perception? In fact, most of those victims Americans encountered in the camps were not Jews. The best estimates are that Jews accounted for about one fifth of those liberated from concentration camps in Germany by American troops. *The Encyclopedia of the Holocaust* estimates that something under one fifth of those at Buchenwald, something over one fifth of those at Dachau, were Jews; proportions varied at other camps.[8] The murder camps in the East, where all or almost all of the victims were Jews, had been either closed before Allied forces arrived or liberated by the Soviets, with few American reporters and photographers in attendance. If Jews did not figure prominently in contemporary accounts of Dachau, Buchenwald, and the other camps liberated in the spring of 1945, it was not because of malice or insensitivity, but because they did not figure that prominently among those liberated.[9]

A picture may be worth ten thousand words *if you know what you're looking at*. Otherwise, as *Newsweek* photographer Shlomo Arad has observed, "you need ten thousand words to understand a picture."[10]

The emaciated survivors of Buchenwald captured in Margaret Bourke-White's pictures now proclaim, and symbolize, "the Holocaust"; we "see" Jews. These pictures were seen — not inaccurately —quite differently in 1945.

No doubt there were many American Jews who in 1945 had a more "particularist" interpretation of the liberated camps, one more in line with that which later became canonical. But even here we would do well to bear in mind that American Jews were usually influenced at least as much by American as by Jewish ways of thinking. After being present at the liberation of Mauthausen, the journalist Fred Friendly wrote a letter home that he asked to have put away and read to the family every Yom Kippur. The letter included several mentions of the special victimhood of Jews. Expressing a common wartime feeling, he noted that "if there had been no America, we, all of us, might well have carried granite at Mauthausen." But he concluded by observing that he had been "allowed to see the ordeal which our fellow brothers and sisters of the human race have endured . . . Czechs, the Jews, the Russians . . . the people of 15 different lands."[11]

One final observation should be made about the impact of the glimpse into hell that came with the liberation of the camps. The immediate impact was doubtless great, but how enduring was it? How clearly did it stand out from all the other dramatic news of that spring? Buchenwald was liberated on April 11; on April 12 President Roosevelt's sudden death plunged the nation into mourning. Dachau was liberated on April 29; the previous day Mussolini had been executed; the following day Hitler committed suicide. Mauthausen was liberated on May 6; the next day Germany surrendered unconditionally. And no sooner was the war in Europe over than the war in the Pacific — always of greater interest to Americans — heated up, producing the bloodiest battles in which Americans would be engaged, on Iwo Jima and Okinawa. Then came Hiroshima, Nagasaki, and V-J Day. The impact of the ghastly photographs from Dachau and Buchenwald was real and substantial, albeit not, for most, highlighting special Jewish victimization. But by singling out that encounter, ignoring all the other headlines that often overshadowed it, its enduring impact is easily exaggerated.

Forty years after the liberation, Werner Weinberg wrote of the changes in the language with which he and others who had been in the camps were described:

Immediately after the war, we were "liberated prisoners"; in subsequent years we were included in the term "DPs" or "displaced persons.". . . In the US we were sometimes generously called "new Americans." Then for a long time . . . there was a good chance that we, as a group, might go nameless. But one day I noticed that I had been reclassified as a "survivor."[12]

The term "Holocaust survivor," in recent American usage, has a very explicit meaning: it always, or almost always, refers to a Jewish survivor of the Nazi murder program. And it is a lifelong attribute, something to which Weinberg and others have objected.

> One survives an earthquake, a shipwreck, but after a while one returns to one's former identity, despite possible scars left by the calamity. However, Holocaust-survivorship is terminal. . . . I have been categorized for the remainder of my natural life. I have been set apart for having been in the Holocaust, while in my own sight I am a person who lived before and who is living after. True, I am essentially changed; but I do not feel that I have joined a club. The ones to be set apart are the nonsurvivors. To be categorized for having survived adds to the damage I have suffered; it is like wearing a tiny new Yellow Star. . . . It is a constricting designation that can easily make its bearer appear — to others and himself — as a museum piece, a fossil, a freak, a ghost.[13]

The most common postwar term, "displaced person" or "DP," was both nonspecific and referred to a temporary condition of displacement, however occasioned. In the immediate aftermath of V-E Day there were more than ten million displaced persons in Germany and Austria, of whom only a tiny fraction were Jewish camp survivors. Before the end of 1945 the great majority had been repatriated, but there remained nearly two million DPs. They included former POWs and forced laborers who preferred not to return to their homes in the East, *Volksdeutsch* who had been expelled from Eastern Europe, Baltic and Ukrainian German auxiliaries and their families, and various others who, for whatever reason, preferred a precarious life in the DP camps of Germany to whatever awaited them at home.

While the number of gentile DPs in Germany decreased rapidly after the end of the war, the number of Jewish DPs increased over the next year and a half, though they remained a fraction of the overall total. In the first few months after their liberation, almost all Jewish camp survivors from Western Europe, as well as many from the East, returned to their countries of origin. There were perhaps no more than 50,000 Jewish DPs in Germany in late 1945. But over the next year their ranks swelled as Jews returning to Poland confronted not just the total devastation of their communities but murderous Polish pogroms. The largest single addition to the ranks of Jewish DPs were those Polish Jews who had found refuge in the Soviet Union during the war, and who, after a brief stopover in the Jewish graveyard that was postwar Poland, usually continued their journey westward. They were joined by smaller numbers of Jews who had survived the war in Eastern Europe but who preferred to pick up their lives in the West. By the end of 1946 the number of Jewish DPs (mostly in Germany, smaller numbers in Austria and Italy) was estimated at about 250,000.[14] Perhaps a fifth of these were survivors of the camps, but all were in one or another sense survivors of the Holocaust.[15]

In recent years "Holocaust survivor" has become an honorific term, evoking not just sympathy but admiration, and even awe. Survivors are thought of and customarily described as exemplars of courage, fortitude, and wisdom derived from their suffering. The views in 1945 were more complex, particularly among Jews, who were, on the whole, the only ones who gave much thought to the matter.

Sympathy there was aplenty in the postwar years, expressed not just in words but in substantial exertions on behalf of survivors. To assist them, American Jews mobilized politically and contributed monetarily as never before. There were, to be sure, tributes to the victims' courage and fortitude. But along with these, and the omnipresent sympathy, there were characterizations that are shocking to read fifty years later. They were "walking corpses," "the living dead," "human wreckage." (When someone who had worked with Jewish DPs, and was impressed by their vitality, challenged these descriptions, he was criticized by Jewish communal leaders for "undermining the Appeal.")[16]

Another theme was that a twisted evolutionary process had taken place. Samuel Lubell wrote in the *Saturday Evening Post*: "For the Jews of Eastern Europe the Nazi gas chambers constituted a kind of grim, perverted Darwinism, psychologically and physically. Six years of systematic extermination — through a process that might be called 'unnatural selection' — bred a strange pattern of tenacious survival." Nazi persecution, Lubell said, "toughened the bodies, hardened the hearts and sharpened the wits of the few who survived. . . . It was a survival not of the fittest, not of the most high-minded or reasonable and certainly not of the meekest, but of the toughest."[17] "Often," wrote one local Jewish official, "it was the 'ex-ghetto' elements rather than the upper class or white collar groups who survived . . . , the petty thief or leader of petty thieves who offered leadership to others, or developed techniques of survival."[18] From Europe, a top leader of the American Jewish Committee wrote to a colleague in New York: "Those who have survived are not the fittest . . . but are largely the lowest Jewish elements, who by cunning and animal instincts have been able to escape the terrible fate of the more refined and better elements who succumbed."[19]

The negative views of the survivors held by many American Jews were even more prevalent in the Yishuv, where years of Zionist ideology had disposed the population to contempt for the Diaspora Jew. One prominent youth leader in Palestine said that for him, "rejection of the Diaspora . . . now turned into personal hatred of the Diaspora. I hate it as a man hates a deformity he is ashamed of."[20] And there was, repeatedly, the theme of "survival of the worst." The future Israeli general David Sh'altiel, who accompanied a boatload of survivors to Palestine, reported his belief that "those who survived lived because they were egotistical and looked out, first and foremost, for themselves."[21] And in David Ben-Gurion's view, the survivors included "people who would not have survived if they had not been what they were — hard, evil and selfish people, and what they underwent there served to destroy what good qualities they had left."[22]

Such perceptions, in America and Israel, faded with time, as did the widespread false and slanderous belief that those who survived probably had done so through shameful acts of collaboration. Gradually it came to be realized that it was mostly sheer contingency and not personal qualities that determined whether one survived the Holocaust: not being in the wrong place at the wrong time, not having distinctively Jewish features. And, to repeat, the early perceptions, however hateful, did not interfere with great exertions, among Jews in both countries, on their behalf.

The Holocaust and the birth of Israel were separated by only three years. So it's hardly surprising that many find a direct causal or even an organic connection between what is (for everyone) the worst event in post-exilic Jewish history and what is (for a great many) the best. But what exactly is the connection?

The claimed connection is often supernatural. For many traditional Jews, both the Holocaust and the birth of Israel were (as with everything else) part of God's divine plan, and perhaps, in different ways, auguries of the day of redemption. Most less traditional Jews nowadays reject this, along with the notion that Israel was — or that anything could be — divine compensation for the Holocaust. But the belief in some sort of connection, or causal nexus, remains widespread.

One frequently alleged connection is the claim that the Holocaust "tragically vindicated" Zionism. Publicly, Zionists made this claim from 1933 on; it was repeated often during the war; it figures in the 1948 Israeli Declaration of Independence; it has been repeated endlessly ever since. Privately, when the devastating news of the scope of the Holocaust began to emerge in 1942, leading Zionists continually voiced the fear that Zionism had been undercut, rendered superfluous. In September 1942 Richard Lichtheim, the Jewish Agency's representative in Geneva, wrote Nahum Goldmann:

> The basis of Zionism as it was understood and preached during the last 50 years has gone. . . . The main argument was: 4 or 5 or 6 million in Eastern Europe need and want a home in Palestine. . . . Now, whatever the number of European Jews will be after this war . . . there will be no need for such mass emigration. After the victory of the Allied Nations there can be no problem in resettling this small number of surviving Jews [in Europe]. Zionism as it was presented to the world during the last 20 years is finished. . . . It might have been the solution for the Jews of Europe, but now it is too late. . . . How can we ask for that State if we cannot show that several million Jews need it or, what is more, want it?[23]

Chaim Weizmann, too, privately feared that with the destruction of most of Eastern European Jewry, Zionism had lost its raison d'être, that demands for a state "based on the imperative necessity of transferring large numbers of Jews speedily to Palestine will . . . fall to the ground."[24] David Ben-Gurion confessed privately that he did not want to think about this "terrifying vision" that kept him awake nights: "The extermination of European Jewry [meant] the end of Zionism, for there will be no one to build Palestine." Ben-Gurion's official biographer speculates that such a fear of seeing his life's work rendered irrelevant may have led him, "consciously or not . . . to play down the magnitude of the tragedy."[25] In the words of one Israeli historian, "The impact of the Holocaust on the creation of the Jewish State was exactly the reverse of what is commonly assumed. It almost rendered the birth of Israel impossible."[26]

Of all the connections asserted between the Holocaust and the establishment of Israel, none has been more enduring, more constantly reiterated, than that the nations of the world were moved to support the birth of Israel because of guilt over their complicity in the Holocaust. Typically the assertion is not argued or documented but simply advanced as self-evident truth. "As we now know," writes Tad Szulc, Allied guilt over inaction during the Holocaust "played an overwhelming role in persuading all the big powers to create the state of Israel."[27] The Western world, says another writer, "voted in late 1947 to give the Jews their own state as partial remittance for its complicity in the Nazi Holocaust."[28] The Holocaust, writes David Horowitz, "created a guilt complex among non-Jews."[29] "The leadership of the Western world, especially in America," write Dan Raviv and Yossi Melman, "could not escape the guilt. A shamefaced, remorseful postwar West now supported the Jewish demand for an independent state in Palestine."[30]

For all the confidence and frequency with which the notion of Western guilt as the godfather of Israel is asserted, it is quite false. Of the countries that supported the establishment of Israel — for practical purposes, those which voted for the United Nations partition resolution of November 1947 — there is no evidence that any of them were moved by "guilt" for the Holocaust. Not the crucial Soviet bloc, which hoped to weaken British power and get a foothold in the Middle East; not the countries of Latin America, which contributed the lion's share of the votes; not those other countries that supplied the needed two-thirds UN majority. The Allied nation against which charges of guilty complicity have most often been brought, Great Britain, which had closed down immigration to Palestine before the war, did not support partition. The Israeli historian Evyatar Friesel, who has examined all the UN proceedings, found

> little indication in the opinions expressed by the different nations to show that the Holocaust had influenced their positions. . . . The Zionist representatives who appeared before [the UN Special Committee on Palestine] barely alluded to the subject. . . . It is reasonable to assume that a great majority of UN members considered the Palestine question in terms of concrete interests and political realities rather than any feeling of remorse. . . . It was natural and understandable to go along with the Soviet-American proposition, given the great weight which agreement between the superpowers carried.[31]

In fact, rather than the decision's requiring some special and supervening explanation like "guilt," it was a perfectly rational decision:

there was every reason to vote for it and little reason to oppose it, except in the case of those nations with a special link to the Arab states.

What of the United States? There is no evidence that guilt for inaction during the Holocaust played any role in the American government's (halting and ambivalent) support of Israeli statehood. Insofar as there was any group in the American polity against which charges of complicity could be laid, it was the State Department and the Pentagon, which consistently opposed partition. President Harry Truman was the key decision-maker, overruling his foreign policy advisers, and there is no evidence whatsoever that thoughts of guilt ever crossed his mind. American Protestants might be expected to be in the forefront of any discourse of guilt over the Holocaust at this time, but if organized Protestantism did talk about American guilt after the war, it was to declare itself "deeply penitent for the irresponsible use . . . made of the atomic bomb."[32] In any case, Protestant churches were divided over the creation of a Jewish state.[33] The Catholic Church — at least the Catholic press — was, on the whole, cool toward the idea.[34]

During and after the war, Zionists occasionally argued that the United States, or "the West," had been culpably negligent concerning the Holocaust, and that reparations in the form of a state were called for. But such remarks were typically part of internal Jewish discussions and played hardly any role in public advocacy, suggesting that the argument was not expected to convince a gentile audience.[35] A handful of Christian Americans made general references to a Jewish state as recompense for the guilt of Christendom for anti-Semitism (though without any reference to U.S. inaction during the Holocaust), but there is no reason to believe that these scattered remarks had any broad resonance. And gentiles who referred to Western guilt did not necessarily draw Zionist conclusions. The clearest expression of the theme of guilt and recompense by a prominent American gentile came from the celebrated newspaper columnist Dorothy Thompson: "The salvation of the Jews must . . . come in part as an act of repentance from the Christian world." Thompson, who during the war had spoken on behalf of unrestricted Jewish immigration to Palestine, became one of the most prominent anti-Zionists in postwar America, serving for five years as president of the pro-Arab American Friends of the Middle East.[36]

What, then, did move Americans to support a Jewish state? In the first place, one should avoid exaggerating that support: most Americans didn't much care. The "groundswell" of letters, petitions, and resolutions in favor of a Jewish state from non-Jewish citizens, which filled the mailbags of the White House and Congress, were a tribute to the energy of Zionist organizations and the "why not?" of those whose signatures they solicited.[37] Various arguments were advanced in congressional debates (though they were hardly that, since there was no opposition). There were numerous references to a 1922 congressional resolution endorsing the Balfour Declaration, which had favored the idea of a Jewish homeland in Palestine. Christendom, it was said, owed a long-standing debt to the Jewish people:

> It was a Jew who preached the Sermon on the Mount . . . who, by his agonizing death upon the cross, provided redemption for the whole wicked world. . . . Our age-old obligations to the Jews . . . have been greatly augmented by recent events. [Without] the famous Jewish doctors . . . we would still be without the atomic bomb; and without the atomic bomb Japan would still be unconquered.[38]

The theme of Jews as deserving cobelligerents was common. Jews should have a state "not only because of our gratefulness for their ten year fight against our ruthless enemy, but also to pay homage to the five million honored casualties they have suffered."[39] While "the Jew was the ostensible target . . . all of us were the victims." Hitler's *real* target was "the Judaeo-Christian tradition. . . . In their homelessness and defenselessness he recognized . . . the weakest point in the armor of organized society and there he struck."[40] Many members of Congress underlined British guilt. The survivors were "alive today only because Eisenhower, Bradley and Patton got to Germany before they too were removed from concentration camps to the crematories. . . . Perhaps more than a million could have been saved but for the rigid, tragic application of the British white paper."[41] For many, there was something very American about the Zionist project. The United States, after all, had been born in a revolt against British colonialism. And the Zionist venture seemed, to the editor of the *Boston Herald*, and no doubt others, not unlike the "conquest of the Indians and the inevitable giving way of a backward people before a more modern and practical one."[42]

But more than anything else — sometimes combined with those and other reasons for supporting Jewish statehood, sometimes standing alone — was sympathy for the plight of the survivors. Whether on grounds of secular humanitarian traditions or of Christian charity, or simply as a reflexive response to the wretched, desolated, and homeless survivors, it seemed urgent, in America as elsewhere, to do something for them. While Truman's motives for supporting the birth of Israel were mixed — with domestic electoral calculations and the importuning of Jewish friends and associates high on the list — his sincere concern for the survivors was manifest from the day of liberation. The members of the Anglo-American Committee of Inquiry and the UN Special Committee on Palestine visited Jewish DP camps and were visibly moved by the experience.[43] Insofar as moral rather than strictly political and geopolitical considerations motivated Americans and others to support a Jewish state, it was not a response to the Holocaust as such, let alone a guilty response, but concern for the plight of the survivors.

It's not clear how the myth of Israel as the world's atonement for complicity in the Holocaust developed. In recent years we have been so saturated in guilt talk surrounding the Holocaust that we have come to assume it was in evidence in 1945. Even an ordinarily scrupulous scholar like Yehuda Bauer can write that upon encountering the concentration camps, American troops, after ten months of fighting across France and Germany, were seized with guilt "when they realized how little the free world had done to avert the Holocaust."[44] Memories of political leaders are retrospectively refigured to give the Holocaust an impact on political decisions that it didn't have at the time.[45] There has been an apparent slide from the belief that the United States and its allies *were* guilty, to the belief that they *should* have felt guilty, to the belief that they *must* have felt guilty, to the belief that they *did* feel guilty — a tenuous progression. Some seem to confuse sympathy for the survivors, which there was in abundance, and guilt for the Holocaust, of which there is no contemporary evidence — a strange equation. American sympathy for the victims of the Rwandan genocide of 1994, or the Armenian earthquake of 1988, and the offering of aid to their victims implied no feelings of guilt for the events that produced the suffering. Even the modest aid appropriations after those disasters cost Americans more than did supporting Israel's birth, which cost nothing. Indeed, one minor argument for statehood was that it would save American taxpayers' money by lessening the burden of caring for those DPs who would depart the American Zone of Occupation.[46] It's likely that the notion of Israeli statehood as the act of atonement of a repentant West simply appeals to some people's moral and aesthetic sensibilities. And to some unknowable extent, the myth is probably sustained, like many myths, because of its utility: if initial American support for Israel's birth was partial atonement for complicity in the

Holocaust, the never-fully-cancellable obligation demanded continued support of Israel.[47]

There is a parallel myth, widespread in Jewish circles, that American Jews converted to Zionism after the war because of guilt for *their* inaction. Edward Shapiro attributes the great rise in Jews' contributions to the United Jewish Appeal to "the guilt they felt for not having done more to rescue Europe's Jews."[48] Another historian writes that the appearance of the non-Zionist president of the American Jewish Committee before the Anglo-American Committee of Inquiry, and his call for the admission of survivors to Palestine, "testify that he was conscience-stricken because not enough had been done to save European Jewry from destruction."[49]

American Jews did indeed, during and after the war, work with unprecedented zeal first for unrestricted immigration to Palestine and later for statehood. Was this a conversion to Zionism? For some it may have been. But for most, this "refugee Zionism" or "emergency Zionism" bore little resemblance to the Zionist worldview of the movement's traditional supporters. It was a chance to do what could be done for the survivors of the Holocaust, work undertaken not because of guilt for having done nothing for rescue, but, during the war, because rescue then seemed impossible, and, after the war, because rescue had hitherto seemed impossible. It was an outlet for a frustrated desire to do something for European Jewry.

When the word "guilt" surfaced after the war, it usually referred to not having been been *able*, rather than not having been *willing*, to effect rescue. One community leader spoke of his pro-statehood activity as having "relieved me spiritually of a great sense of guilt for not being able to save those six million."[50] Fund-raising appeals featured the slogan "Now after all these years . . . we can reach them, we can help them," and went on: "Where before we stood by helplessly beyond the borders of Nazi territory and waited for a handful to come to us, now we can go to them and give them material help, limited now not by our enemy's power, but only by the extent of our own generosity."[51]

Another kind of guilt — though, again, not guilt for cowardly inaction — was that of unmerited safety and privilege, a deeply felt, albeit unmerited, "survivor guilt." American Jews were acutely aware that only the accident of geography saved them from the fate of their European brethren. At the time of the Kishinev massacre, early in the century, a Yiddish writer in New York wrote a poem described by Arthur

Hertzberg as "full of pain and guilt because he was safe in the United States while his brothers were in danger."[52] At the end of World War II similar feelings were widespread among American Jews.

One should not, in any case, exaggerate the speed or the extent of American Jews' conversion even to "refugee Zionism." The Jewish Labor Committee, the B'nai B'rith, and the Central Conference of American Rabbis (Reform) withheld support for Jewish statehood for more than two years after the end of the war, until it was endorsed by the U.S. government.[53]

Other calculations moved other groups. Agudath Israel (Orthodox), after testifying against the creation of a state before the UN Special Committee on Palestine, offered to accept the idea in return for concessions to religious observance, with another key consideration being fear that "the name of God would be profaned" if the Orthodox were blamed for thwarting it.[54] The previously non-Zionist, or even anti-Zionist, American Jewish Committee balanced many factors before ultimately supporting statehood. One staff member, Milton Himmelfarb, described the two reasons that led the AJC, in 1946–47, to abandon its traditional opposition to a Jewish state:

[The first reason for the reversal was] the desperate situation of the Jewish DP's [and the lack of] migration opportunities to countries other than Palestine [which] made "ideological" objections to partition seem less important than they had been, if not actually inhumane. [This was] closely associated with a real fear that any political evils resulting from the creation of a Jewish state would be greatly exceeded by disastrous consequences [i.e., a clash with U.S. troops] of an anticipated uprising of Jewish DP's in their camps. . . .

The second reason is that it became clear that failure to establish a Jewish state could bring about perhaps a worse state of affairs than the actual establishment of the state. The terrorists' activities in Palestine and the posturings and mouthings of their supporters here . . . led a number of AJC people to wonder whether a Jewish state was the chief enemy. They began to feel that after the state was created, the daily papers in New York at least would no longer carry headlines screaming of King David Hotel explosions and hangings of British sergeants; in short, "better an evil end than an endless evil."[55]

Thus many different considerations moved different segments of American Jewry to mobilize on behalf of a Jewish state in Palestine. Were there those who acted out of guilt for what they believed to have been their inadequate efforts for rescue? Perhaps — but there is no evidence that such a feeling was widespread or influential. Like the notion of general American guilt, it is for the most part a retrospective construction, based on playing fast and loose with the idea of guilt. It is probably also based, like the wider myth, on awareness of its utility for continued mobilization.

Though all sorts of other considerations were involved, in the end, for the American Jewish Committee and other Jewish organizations, as for the Jews of the United States at large, the need of the Jewish DPs and sympathy for the survivors were decisive. In any case, it was not that American Jews "became Zionists." Rather, the need of the survivors for a new home overcame all other considerations, and this drew key segments of American Jewry away from anti-Zionism, which thereafter disappeared as a significant current in American Jewish life.

In countless ways, it was the survivors who were the indispensable middle term in the equation linking the Holocaust and the birth of Israel. For the most part — with the peoples and governments of the United Nations, with Jews around the world — this was a matter of spontaneous sympathy and an attempt to make it possible for them to rebuild their lives. But not everything about the role the survivors played was spontaneous — most notably the use made of them by Zionist leaders, in Palestine and elsewhere, to bring about the fulfillment of the Zionist dream. Like others, these leaders were moved by sincere concern for the survivors, but that concern coexisted, in varying proportions, with an acute awareness of how they could be employed as an instrument of the Zionist project.

From the beginning of Hitler's regime Ben-Gurion, guided by what his biographer terms "his philosophy of . . . the beneficial disaster," had insisted that "it is in our interest to use Hitler . . . for the building of our country"; "the harsher the affliction, the greater the strength of Zionism."[56] In October 1942 he told the Zionist Executive: "Disaster is strength if channeled to a productive course; the whole trick of Zionism is that it knows how to channel our disaster not into despondency or degradation, as is the case in the Diaspora, but into a source of creativity and exploitation."[57] The American Zionist leader Abba Hillel Silver told a wartime audience that two arks accompanied the children of Israel through the desert to the promised land. The "ark of faith" carried the tablets of the Law; the "ark of death" carried the body of the Patriarch Joseph. Now, said Silver, another ark of death, carrying millions of Jews killed by Hitler, was "leading us . . . through the wilderness to Palestine."[58]

Such minimal rescue efforts as the Yishuv was able to carry out during the war undoubtedly represented sincere attempts to do what one could. But they were also motivated by anxiety that those who survived would turn their backs on Zionism if Zionism turned its back on them. When a member of a parachute mission into occupied Europe, whose most famous member was Hannah Senesh, asked Ben-Gurion about their central task, he answered "that Jews should know that Eretz Israel is their land and their stronghold"; their mission was to ensure that the survivors "will knock *en masse* on the locked gates of Palestine."[59]

Addressing Jewish survivors at the Landsberg displaced persons' camp after the liberation, Ben-Gurion told them:

> In the coming struggle you will play a decisive role. I know what you have gone through and it is not easy to make this demand of you. You must do it, for you are an enormous factor. You are not only needy persons, you are also a political force. . . . You must not regard yourselves subjectively but rather from the standpoint of the Jewish nation.[60]

Emissaries from the Yishuv deliberately concentrated Jewish survivors in the American Occupation Zone of Germany so that the United States would be led to demand that the British allow them into Palestine. Recruitment for illegal immigration was shifted to relatively intact Jewish communities so that the Yishuv could be reinforced while the DP camps would keep up the pressure. Overall, illegal immigration was only secondarily meant to help survivors. In the words of the Israeli historian Anita Shapira, it was "first and foremost a theater in the battle for the Jewish state."[61] And it was to a great extent a public relations battle. The voyage of the *Exodus*, loaded with survivors who eventually were returned to Germany, was the greatest triumph of this battle. The captain of the ship believed it would be possible to land the passengers on the shores of Palestine, but he was overruled by the senior Mossad representative on board: the goal was to "show how poor and weak and helpless we were, and how cruel the British were."[62]

Inside the DP camps, emissaries from the Yishuv organized survivor activity — crucially, the testimony the DPs gave to the Anglo-American Committee of Inquiry and the UN Special Committee on Palestine about where they wished to go. The results were gratifying to the proponents of a Jewish state. In response to a UN survey, more than 97 percent said that Palestine was their goal. Many wrote down "First choice, Palestine. Second choice, crematorium."[63] Palestine *was* the first choice of many, and survivors with other preferences were often willing to dissimulate for the visitors.[64] But they had some assistance. The Jewish Agency envoys reported home that they had been successful in preventing the appearance of "undesirable" witnesses at the hearings. One wrote to his girlfriend in Palestine that "we have to change our style and handwriting constantly so that they will think that the questionnaires were filled in by the refugees."[65]

In the event, about two thirds of the survivors who left Europe went to Palestine/Israel, one third to the United States. The extent to which this represented spontaneous choice is in dispute. Lucy Dawidowicz, who worked with DPs in the camps, reports having seen "how pressure was exerted against immigration to places other than Palestine." She remarks, rather harshly, that "the Zionists believed that the end justified the means, political goals prevailing over humanitarian need."[66] That there was such pressure, sometimes even coercion, seems clear; it's far from clear how much there was, and how much it influenced the outcome.[67] Much more important was the timing of available options. Yehuda Bauer surmises that if American immigration had been opened up earlier, or Israeli statehood postponed, the proportions might have been reversed, with only a third choosing Israel.[68]

By the time of the birth of Israel there was a certain weariness with the DP problem in Germany among some Jewish elites. Chaplain Abraham Klausner, a militant Zionist who had worked with Jewish survivors and, earlier, closely identified with them, sounded the alarm:

The great majority of the people are idle. . . . The number of people involved in the black-market is estimated at a minimum of 30%. This excludes those who traffic in what may be termed the "gray market" or the basic food market. . . . The demoralization of the people increases rapidly. There is hardly a moral standard to which the people adhere. Nothing seems to be wrong and everything can be excused, no matter how serious, with a shrug of the shoulder or the oft-heard comment, "he is still a Jew." . . . It was suggested . . . that the liberated concentration camp victims having suffered for a number of years . . . were in need of rehabilitation. This is not the case. . . . The great percentage of the people are not concentration camp victims. . . . Judging from recent experience . . . we may predict that perhaps 30% of the people [i.e., those then remaining] will go to Palestine. . . .

The people must be forced to go to Palestine. They are not prepared to understand their own position or the promises of the future. To them, an American dollar looms as the greatest of objectives. . . . The Jewish community at large [must] reverse its policy and instead of creating comforts for the displaced persons make them as uncomfortable as possible. . . . It must be borne in mind that we are dealing with a sick people. They are not to be asked, but to be told what to do. They will be thankful in years to come.[69]

At a meeting of Jewish organizations to discuss Klausner's report, there was disagreement about whether his picture was overdrawn, and little support for his suggestion of the use of force. There was widespread agreement, however, that demoralization and black market activity was rampant, and that something had to be done about that portion of the Jewish DP population that did not want to go to Palestine and which, as of that date, was unlikely to surmount the American immigration restrictions then in force. Nahum Goldmann gave voice to a theme echoed by others:

The DPs, in general, do not represent the human material Eretz Yisroel needs today. . . . In the interest of the State, we have to choose the better material, young, willing people, not those who have to be forced. Besides, the DPs represent no political argument for Palestine any more either. This angle does not make any impression on General Marshall any more, it is therefore a politically irrelevent thing from the point of view of the Jewish State. We have reached the brutal phase where the interests of the State count alone.

Except for those unable to work, DPs not wishing to go to Palestine should be moved into the German economy. "The subterfuge of DP resistance to 'strengthening Germany' cannot be accepted in this scandalous situation any longer."[70]

William Haber, then the official Jewish adviser to the American Military Government, writing shortly after the establishment of Israel, reiterated the theme of the DPs' role having been fulfilled: "The DP camps, containing the most conspicuous concentration of Jews, pressing for a new home, have served their historic purpose in emphasizing the need for a Jewish homeland." Henceforth, "for their own good" they must be given a realistic view of their prospects.[71] A similar view was voiced by Haber's deputy, Major Abraham S. Hyman:

DP camps served their historic role by dramatizing the homelessness of the Jew and his need for a homeland. . . . It is seriously doubted whether the Jewish DPs serve as a pressure group any longer. . . . The issues in Palestine will be decided without any reference to the existence or non-existence of the DP problem in Europe. . . . Not only can Israel and the Jewish DPs expect no benefit from the perpetuation of the DPs as a pressure group but, on the contrary, the whole DP complex is such as to poison the minds of the non-Jew and encourage the growth of antisemitism.[72]

Though many more survivors would go to Palestine, increasing numbers made it to the United States, where well over a hundred thousand ultimately found refuge. But neither their arrival nor, for many years, their presence did much to increase American interest in the Holocaust.

With restrictive immigration laws still in force and public opinion overwhelmingly hostile to overturning them, special efforts were required to bring Holocaust survivors to the United States. The details of those efforts have been recounted elsewhere and will not be repeated here.[73] For our purposes, a few aspects of the process are particularly relevant, all of which worked against focusing American attention on the Holocaust.

The first is that working for the immigration of survivors was a project undertaken by non-Zionists, often of German Jewish background — the group within American Jewry least inclined to stress Jewish distinctiveness. In the immediate aftermath of the war, with proposals on the table for the admission of 100,000 Jewish survivors to Palestine, even non-Zionists held off working for immigration to the United States, lest such efforts interfere with settlement in Palestine. In 1945, moved primarily by sympathy for the survivors, President Truman both pressed the British to allow 100,000 Jewish DPs into Palestine and issued a directive for the emergency immigration of DPs into the United States. (Ultimately, more than 40,000 DPs came in under the Truman Directive, of whom between two thirds and three quarters were Jewish.) American Zionists could hardly mount a campaign against the humanitarian directive, but they were cool toward anything that shifted the focus from Palestine.[74]

In 1946, when there appeared to be no imminent prospect of Britain's allowing 100,000 Jews into Palestine, leaders of the anti-Zionist American Council for Judaism and the non-Zionist American Jewish Committee decided to work for special immigration legislation on behalf of DPs. Two thirds of the million-dollar budget of the lobbying operation was underwritten by the family of Lessing Rosenwald, the most prominent American anti-Zionist. The goal of the campaign's initiators was to bring in 100,000 Jewish survivors. But since it was impolitic and contrary to American tradition for legislation to specify the religion of immigrants, and since Jews were estimated to comprise 25 percent of all DPs, they pressed for a law that would bring in a total of 400,000 DPs over four years. To this end, the Citizens' Committee on Displaced Persons was established — ostensibly nondenominational, but in fact largely funded and staffed by Jews.

Because of the nature of the legislation sought, the ecumenical alliance created, and the desire to short-circuit anti-Semitic opposition to the bill in Congress and elsewhere, the CCDP, whatever its inclinations, systematically downplayed the presence of Jews among the DPs. In the process it further reinforced the tendency to think of the victims of Nazism in general rather than particular terms. Publications of the CCDP often described the DP population as a whole as survivors of concentration camps, which they were not. It was constantly reiterated that at least three quarters of the DPs were Christians. An official of the American Jewish Committee described the desired kind of publicity: "where the case story is of a non-Jew, or one who plans to settle elsewhere than in New York or Chicago."[75] A Jewish CCDP staff member responded with frustration to a photograph in the *New York Daily News* that showed a Jewish-looking couple disembarking: "Something has got to be done to ease up or completely eliminate [this] type of publicity. . . . We have been spending thousands of dollars to try to get across the idea that displaced persons are not all Jews, and if we continue to see such photographs . . . our campaign — public-relations-wise — is a dead duck."[76]

In the prevailing anti-immigrant climate, the passage of any sort of DP bill was a triumph. To some extent the "ecumenical" nature of the campaign had paid off. One Republican senator complained that "he could not walk down the streets of his home town without someone like his banker, butcher, or former Sunday School teacher stopping him and saying, 'Senator, why aren't you a good Christian? Why are you against the DPs?' "[77] But the legislation that finally emerged in 1948 contained several provisions that placed Jewish DPs at a disadvantage compared to other groups, so much so that Truman signed the bill with some reluctance. In the event, however, the law was administered in ways that overcame the provisions that discriminated against Jewish DPs, and these provisions were removed in the amended law of 1950. By the early fifties, approximately 100,000 survivors had come to the United States, a number later augmented by many who had first gone to Israel, then came here.

After their arrival, Holocaust survivors were not a very visible presence, even within American Jewry. They were, on the whole, quite young, only beginning to learn English, and in any case preoccupied with rebuilding their lives. While some spread out around the country, most settled in urban Jewish neighborhoods, especially in New York City, where they usually kept to themselves and rarely, at least in the early years, had much to do with existing Jewish communal organizations, except as the recipients of assistance.

It is said that survivors' memories were so painful that they repressed them, that only after the passage of many years could they bear to speak of what they had undergone. No doubt this was often true, but there is considerable evidence that many were willing, indeed anxious, to talk of their experiences but made a deliberate choice not to do so, except among themselves. Both in Israel and the United States survivors found listeners reluctant to hear of their ordeal. Jews in Palestine, according to Israel Gutman, listened to survivors' stories with a "forced patience" that was soon exhausted.[78] One survivor in the United States recalled being told by his aunt: "If you want to have friends here in America, don't keep talking about your experiences. Nobody's interested and if you tell them, they're going to hear it once and then the next time they'll be afraid to come see you. Don't ever speak about it."[79] To an unknowable extent, survivors' silence was a response to "market" considerations: few were interested. (Thirty and forty years later, with increased demand there was increased supply.)

But more was involved than tacit calculations. Survivors were constantly told — again, this was true both in Palestine and in the United States — that they should turn their faces forward, not backward; that it was in their interest, insofar as possible, to forget the past and proceed to build new lives. A 1947 advertisement by the Federation of Jewish Philanthropies told the story of a "typical" DP family haunted by memories, and concluded, "They need to go to Palestine, or America, or England, or some other place — where they can forget the past."[80] American Jews, or Jews in the Yishuv, would have been incredulous at the idea, later a commonplace, that survivors' memories were a "precious legacy" to be preserved. There is, in fact, an eerie symmetry between the messages survivors received in the forties and fifties and those of the eighties and nineties. Earlier, they were told that even if they wanted to speak of the Holocaust, they shouldn't — it was bad for them. Later they were told that even if they didn't want to speak of it, they must — it was good for them. In both cases, others knew what was best.

The title of the agency that resettled survivors in the United States was pregnant with meaning: the United Service for New Americans. And of course this emphasis on repudiating the past was even greater in Palestine. Of the two survivors quoted earlier in this chapter, Werner Weinberg, in the United States, remained Werner Weinberg; the new Israeli Shlomo Arad had been born Manfred Goldberg.

In the United States as in Israel, the integration of survivors was a matter of relegating the Holocaust to history. The DPs had to be cared for, said one leading American Jewish official, because they represented "unfinished business of the war against Hitler's racial ideas."[81] Caring for the survivors, along with the establishment of Israel, meant liquidating the legacy of the conflict recently concluded — all the more urgent because of the new conflict now beginning.

"That Is Past, and We Must Deal with the Facts Today"

B Y THE LATE 1940s and throughout the 1950s, talk of the Holocaust was something of an embarrassment in American public life. This was not, as many have claimed, because of any shame or guilt on the part of Americans concerning their response to the Holocaust. Rather, it was a consequence of revolutionary changes in world alignments. These changes required far-reaching ideological retooling in the United States, after which talk of the Holocaust was not just unhelpful but actively obstructive.

During World War II Nazi Germany was widely regarded as the apotheosis of human evil and depravity. (The Japanese, as "subhumans," were in a different category.) Reports, and especially photographs, from the liberated concentration camps underlined this perception. Indeed, they provided, retroactively, the symbol that defined the meaning of the war. Ordering that all available troops tour a liberated camp, General Eisenhower observed: "We are told that the American soldier does not know what he is fighting for. Now, at least, he will know what he is fighting *against*."[1]

World War II was "the good war": the forces of human decency pitted against the most criminal regime the world had ever known. The aura of Allied virtue extended to our Soviet allies, who had played the greatest role, and suffered the greatest losses, in defeating the Germans. In the wartime press, the USSR was portrayed in glowing terms: though clearly unlike America in many respects, it was still one of "us" — contrasted morally, as well as militarily, with "them."

All of this changed with breathtaking speed after 1945. The Russians were transformed from indispensable allies to implacable foes, the Germans from implacable foes to indispensable allies. In 1945, Americans had cheered as Soviet forces pounded Berlin into rubble; in 1948, Americans organized the Airlift to defend "gallant Berliners" from Soviet threat. The apotheosis of evil — the epitome of limitless depravity — had been relocated, and public opinion had to be mobilized to accept the new worldview. Symbols that reinforced the old view were no longer functional. Indeed, they were now seriously dysfunctional, reminding Americans of how recently our new allies had been regarded as monsters.

On both a theoretical and rhetorical level, the transition from one set of alignments to another was smoothed by invoking the category of totalitarianism. Coined in the interwar years, but coming into wide usage only after 1945, the term pointed to features of Nazi and Communist regimes that were said to make them "essentially alike" and that distinguished them from traditional autocracies. These common traits included a comprehensive ideology, a centrally controlled economy, one-party dictatorship, the ruthless elimination of all opposition, and a populace terrorized by means of a ubiquitous secret police. Such regimes were understood to be limitlessly expansionist and incapable of reform from within; they could only be overthrown by external force.[2]

Whatever the theory's analytic merits, in the 1940s and 1950s it performed admirable ideological service in denying what to the untutored eye was a dramatic reversal of alliances. It only *seemed* this way, the theory asserted; in fact the cold war was, from the standpoint of the West, a continuation of World War II: a struggle against the transcendent enemy, totalitarianism, first in its Nazi, then its Soviet version.

In the early years of the cold war, the designation "totalitarian" was a powerful rhetorical weapon in deflecting the abhorrence felt toward Nazism onto the new Soviet enemy. Anticipating what some time later became a common theme, *Time* magazine, within a month of the liberation of the concentration camps, was warning against viewing their horrors as a German crime. Rather, they were the product of totalitarianism, and its victims' deaths would be meaningful only if we drew the appropriate anti-Soviet moral.[3] In principle, the theory proclaimed equal opposition to "totalitarianisms of the right and of the left." In practice, after 1945, with the Axis defeated, it was deployed exclusively against leftist regimes.

Not only did the cold war make invocation of the Holocaust the "wrong atrocity" for purposes of mobilizing the new consciousness, but the theorizing about totalitarianism itself served to marginalize the Holocaust. The ruthless persecution of political opponents in concentration camps and slave labor camps was an important link connecting Nazi Germany and Soviet Russia under the rubric of totalitarianism. The constant reiteration of this theme reinforced the already-existing tendency to define the victims of Nazism in political rather than ethnic terms. Conversely, any suggestion that the Nazi murder of European Jewry was a central, let alone defining, feature of that regime would undermine the argument for the essential identity of the two systems. As a result, one will search in vain through the vast literature on totalitarianism for any but the most glancing and casual mention of the Holocaust.

The theory of totalitarianism also had important implications for the question of German guilt. During the war, official American statements had emphasized that, in the words of Assistant Secretary of State Adolph A. Berle, guilt for the murder of European Jewry was "generalized throughout the German people [and this fact] must constitute one of the basic considerations in dealing with the German people in the hour of their final and conclusive defeat." One piece of evidence that would weigh heavily in the treatment meted out to defeated Germans, said Berle, was whether the German people were willing to take action to halt the murders or would "take refuge in whining excuses of fear."[4]

The theory of totalitarianism suggested a more understanding attitude; indeed pointed toward a plenary indulgence. According to the theory, opposition within the totalitarian state was impossible, since "terror embraces the entire society." Even active support of the Nazi program could not be considered criminal, because "totalitarian regimes insist [on] enthusiastic unanimity (and not merely passive acquiescence)."[5] The theory was hardly the reason that the United States abandoned plans for treating the German population harshly, but it surely helped in rationalizing and justifying a forgiving attitude.[6]

There was another corollary of the theory of totalitarianism — more precisely, of the proposition that from the beginning of World War II through the cold war the United States had been engaged

in one continuous battle against totalitarianism in its different em-
bodiments. If the exigencies of fighting the Nazi variety of totalitarianism had required that the United States ally itself with Soviet
totalitarians — and few Americans, certainly few Jews, had objected to
that wartime alliance — then how could one now object to fighting Soviet
totalitarianism in alliance with what were at most *former* totalitarians?

The evolution of American policy toward displaced persons offers a
clear example of how the cold war led to marginalizing the Holocaust.
Those who initiated the campaign to admit DPs were, in their concern
for the surviving Jewish victims of the Holocaust, looking backward to
World War II. But by the time the campaign got under way, in 1947,
most eyes were turned to the emerging cold war.

The Christian organizations recruited to the campaign were more
interested in helping those fleeing Communism than with the "ancient
history" of Nazism, as their publications made clear. The Jewish leadership of the Citizens' Committee on Displaced Persons resisted this
theme for a time, but by early 1948 the CCDP was also stressing that
the DPs were fleeing Communism.[7]

More troublesome to Jewish leaders than the arguments necessary
to win support for DP legislation was the effect of the changed climate
on the substance of the legislation. From the beginning of the campaign, Jewish leaders had recognized that if they succeeded in getting a
bill passed, "there is a chance that more anti-Semites than Jews would
benefit by it."[8] But in 1946 they were thinking of Eastern European
Christians who were at most presumptive anti-Semites. As the legislation took shape in the Displaced Persons Acts of 1948 and 1950 — and
even more, as it became evident how the legislation was going to be
administered — it was increasingly a matter of Eastern European veterans of the Waffen-SS, pro-Nazi *Volksdeutsche* who had been expelled
from their homes in the East, and "nominal" Nazi Party members. As
one official of the International Refugee Organization put it, not victims of Nazism but "victims of the Allied victory."[9]

Christian groups in the CCDP had worked with Jewish organizations to remove provisions in DP legislation that discriminated against
Jews. They were much less sympathetic to Jewish protests against the
admission of *Volksdeutsche* or former SS men — or even to subjecting
them to rigorous screening.[10] Just as Jewish groups' principled decla-
rations against totalitarians did not prevent them from seeking entry

for Jews who had been Communists, so the Christian groups' equally sincere hostility to totalitarianism did not prevent them from seeking admission for their coreligionists who were former Nazis. In late 1948 a Jewish journalist charged in the *New York Post* that a high proportion of non-Jewish DPs were Nazi collaborators. The allegation was denounced in the Jesuit magazine *America* as " 'anti-Christianism' quite comparable to . . . anti-semitism."[11] An open breach between Jewish and Christian groups was only narrowly averted.

The Displaced Persons Commission, with the support of the State Department, and after active lobbying by American Lutherans, ruled that members of Latvian and Estonian SS divisions were eligible for entry to the United States as DPs.[12] When the DP Commission met with officials of Protestant, Catholic, and Jewish private agencies in 1950, the representative of the National Catholic Welfare Conference argued that the provision in the DP law that barred totalitarians from entry as DPs was intended to apply only to Communists, not Nazis or Fascists. To the dismay of the Jewish representatives present, only they and the one Jewish member of the DP Commission disagreed.[13]

In their private meetings, leaders of the various Jewish agencies dispiritedly discussed whether anything could be done to stem the tide. The answer was, clearly, not much. Motives were mixed and hard to disentangle. Representatives of the American Jewish Congress who were for denouncing and abandoning the entire DP program because of the direction it was taking were Zionists who had been suspicious of the program all along because it diverted survivors from Israel. Groups like the American Jewish Committee and the Anti-Defamation League, concerned with preserving their relations with Christian organizations, were more inclined to swallow their reservations. It might be distasteful to admit Eastern European SS veterans, but most were "peasants . . . frequently illiterate . . . not politically active . . . who drift along with the prevailing political winds" — a judgment borne out by their subsequent record in this country.[14] Eugene Hevesi of the American Jewish Committee argued to his colleagues that while it was true that the *Volksdeutsche* were a dangerous and disreputable lot, they'd do less harm here than in Germany.[15] The issue was academic, however. The DP program had been started to aid survivors of the Holocaust; but by the early 1950s it was the displaced victims of Stalin, not of Hitler, who were fashionable, and the Holocaust figured hardly at all in discussions of DPs. The Jewish initiators of the DP campaign had lost all influence over its direction. Their only choice was with what ill or good grace they adapted to the new cold war climate.

Much more consequential was the great turnaround the cold war produced in American policy toward Germany. At the end of the war it was not just American Jews who favored harsh treatment of defeated Germany. Under the impact of the atrocities vividly revealed in the liberated camps, many Christians also believed that the mark of Cain should and would long be borne by the German people. At the beginning of the Allied occupation of Germany, the ban on fraternization with the German population and sweeping plans for de-Nazification and for the judicial prosecution of those implicated in the crimes of the regime were all emblematic of Germany's pariah status.

But that status was not to last long. The nonfraternization policy could not withstand the allure of the frauleins. The notion of a wholesale purge of German society fell victim, in the first instance, to the need of the occupiers to find experienced administrative cadres, of whom a great number had been Nazis. So far as judicial prosecutions were concerned, the involvement of countless Germans in Nazi criminality of one kind or another meant that who was prosecuted and who was not was often a matter of chance. (One businessman, sentenced to prison because his firm had contracted to build gas chambers, had his conviction overturned because it turned out his firm hadn't gotten the contract after all: his bad luck in the early forties; his good luck in the late forties.)[16] There were other practical problems. But it was primarily the rapidly developing struggle with the USSR that led to the turnaround in American policy toward Germany, to the extraordinary spectacle of the conquerors wooing the recently conquered, to what amounted in practice to "all is forgiven." De-Nazification was dismantled, and amnesties multiplied; German "reeducation for democracy" came to focus less on the crimes of Hitler and more on the threat of Stalin. Above all, it became clear that the American government was laying the groundwork for the rearmament of Germany, and that sweeping the Nazi past into the dustbin of history was the price German elites were extracting for their cooperation in the anti-Soviet crusade.

American Jews were dismayed by the speed of the turnaround. While Jewish organizations expressed their opposition to Germany's rapid rehabilitation and moves toward German rearmament, there was something ritualistic and "for the record" about their protests.

As early as 1947 the American Jewish Committee's representative in Washington reported that policy-makers were totally indifferent to Germany's Nazi past and concerned with Germany only as a bulwark against Bolshevism. Their commitment to this position was "now so complete as to preclude any idea of changing it."[17] By 1949 the Committee's foreign policy expert, Eugene Hevesi, concluded that "as far as Germany is concerned, America has almost completely lost the hard-won victory in World War II."[18]

In the late forties and early fifties, American Jewish leaders were pulled in two directions. On the one hand, there were the strong anti-German sentiments of most American Jews, sentiments the leaders themselves shared. On the other hand, there was their special obligation to safeguard the reputation and position of Jews in American society. Overall, in the climate of growing cold war mobilization, this meant seeing to it that Jews were not perceived as out of step with other Americans. In addition, there were particular constraints on publicly grounding their opposition to Germany's rehabilitation on the Holocaust.

One constraint was fear of confirming a long-standing and widely held negative perception of Jews. No lesson in comparative theology was as assiduously taught in Sunday schools across the United States as the contrast between the Old Testament God of Vengeance and the New Testament God of Love and Forgiveness. Recent experience had shown its continued currency. Toward the end of the war, President Roosevelt had casually endorsed, then quickly repudiated, a plan advanced by Secretary of the Treasury Henry Morgenthau for the permanent deindustrialization ("pastoralization") of Germany. Secretary of War Henry Stimson privately called the Morgenthau Plan "semitism gone wild for vengeance." Not only was this view frequently voiced in government circles, but it entered the public arena when the Republicans made an attack on the Morgenthau Plan a central theme in the 1944 election.[19] After the war, an influential anti-Communist journalist charged that the continuation of "politically inexpedient" war crimes trials was due in part to the influence of Jewish refugees "animated by an altogether understandable desire for revenge."[20] (In 1948 the American Military Government in Germany barred the further use of Jewish refugees as civilian investigators on the grounds that they were unlikely to be sufficiently "impartial and objective.")[21] An editorial in the *Saturday Evening Post*, entitled "Nuremberg Verdicts Cool Ardor of Germany for Defending West," thought the ongoing trials a vestige of "Morgenthauism . . . an unrealistic mixture of morality and vengeance."[22] Repeatedly, in their internal discussions, representatives of Jewish groups spoke of the need to convince the public that their attitude toward Germany did not stem from any "vindictiveness" or desire for "revenge."[23] Accordingly, Jewish statements on Germany directed to a general audience (unlike Jewish "insider" discourse) rarely mentioned Germany's crimes against the Jews. Rather, they invoked the broad American interest and cold war considerations: abandoning de-Nazification would provide fodder for Soviet propaganda; Germany would make an unreliable ally; its rearmament and the employment of former Nazis would alienate other countries in Europe.

There was a much more serious constraint on public Jewish discourse about the Holocaust and Nazism in the early cold war years: fear of seeming to confirm a less ancient but potentially more threatening stereotype.

The popular association of Jews with Communism dated from the Bolshevik Revolution. Most of the "alien agitators" deported from the United States during the Red Scare after World War I had been Jews. In the interwar years the Communist Jew was a staple of anti-Semitic propaganda in both the United States and Europe. The Russian-American alliance during World War II temporarily muted charges of Jewish pro-Sovietism. At the same time, the fact that American Jews, for obvious reasons, were the Red Army's greatest cheerleaders during the war, and often retained positive feelings about the Soviet Union long after other Americans had abandoned them, helped lay the groundwork for the renewal of the charges after 1945.[24]

Lucy Dawidowicz — later well known as an historian of the Holocaust, but in these years the American Jewish Committee's expert on Communism — kept running tabulations for the Committee on the percentage of Jews among "hostile witnesses" before various investigative bodies. Jews, she found, often made up 75 percent or more of the totals.[25] Worst of all, producing something near panic among mainstream Jewish organizations, was the number of Jews figuring in espionage prosecutions: the *Amerasia* case, the Canadian Spy Ring, the Judith Coplon case — culminating in that ultimate disaster for Jewish public relations, the case of Julius and Ethel Rosenberg, Morton Sobell, Harry Gold, and David Greenglass.

Jewish organizations worked frantically to combat the Jew-Communist equation, but it was a difficult brief. They could insist, correctly, that only a small proportion of Jews were Communists, or even well disposed toward the Soviet Union. But it was also correct, and becoming manifest, that a great many — perhaps most —American Communists in these years were Jews. (An American' Jewish Committee memorandum in the late 1940s cited a private FBI estimate that 50 to 60 percent of Communist Party members were Jews; a few years later the chairman of its Committee on Communism thought the proportion of Jews in the party was even greater, "because the members of other groups have fled the party in droves.")[26]

One of the most striking features of Communist and pro-Communist rhetoric in the late forties and fifties — and particularly of the Jewish Communists and pro-Communists from whom the mainstream Jewish organizations were desperately trying to dissociate themselves — was the frequency with which that rhetoric invoked the Holocaust. Such invocations became the dominant argument, at least in Jewish circles, for opposition to cold war mobilization.

Holocaust themes appeared in Henry Wallace's 1948 presidential campaign — especially in material addressed to New York audiences. Only a strong Wallace showing, it was argued, could prevent "a repetition of the Hitlerite holocaust."[27] One Wallace campaign leaflet asked "Pres. Truman! Did You Forget This?" over a photograph of stacked corpses at Buchenwald. "You free Nazi torturers like Ilse Koch," the leaflet proclaimed. "This is the kind of Western Germany to which you give Marshall Plan billions. . . . A vote for Truman is a vote to rebuild Nazi Germany. . . . A vote for Wallace is a vote to destroy Nazism in Germany."[28] On the occasion of the fifth anniversary of the Warsaw Ghetto Uprising, the Communist periodical *Jewish Life* insisted that the clear lesson of the uprising was the imperative of resistance to American fascism — as exemplified by Harry Truman.[29] Louis Harap, the editor of *Jewish Life*, told the House Un-American Activities Committee that he wouldn't answer its questions because the committee was producing in America "the same condition under which six million Jews were murdered."[30] An open letter to Senator Joseph McCarthy's aide Roy Cohn called him

a representative of the American *Judenrat*, which like the German *Judenrat* and the Warsaw Ghetto *Judenrat*, hopes to buy security for itself. . . .

You will be remembered like the German and Warsaw Ghetto *Judenrat* members, if at all, along with the traitors, renegades, opportunists, sycophants . . . who are a disgrace in the history of every people.[31]

No doubt some of the invocations were spontaneous, but featuring the Holocaust was also Communist Party policy. Party members were advised that in arguing against German rearmament, "it is essential to recall the tragic experiences of the last war, the concentration camps and gas chambers, and to repeat as slogans 'Remember Buchenwald and Dachau,' 'Remember the six million murdered,' 'Remember Warsaw,' and to reprint in leaflets and other material pictures of Nazi atrocities."[32]

Nowhere was there more talk of the Holocaust than among the partisans of Julius and Ethel Rosenberg. The Rosenbergs themselves invoked it often. At his trial Julius testified that the USSR "contributed a major share in destroying the Hitler beast who killed 6,000,000 of my co-religionists, and I feel emotional about that thing."[33] "We are not the first victims of tyranny," he wrote to his attorney. "Six million of our co-religionists and millions of other innocent victims of fascism went to the death chambers."[34] The Rosenberg case was frequently described as the overture to an American holocaust. William L. Patterson of the Communist-dominated Civil Rights Congress warned that "the lynching of these two innocent American Jews, unless stopped by the American people, will serve as a signal for a wave of Hitler-like genocidal attacks against the Jewish people throughout the United States."[35] After the conviction of the Rosenbergs, appeals for clemency often contrasted their fate with that of the authors of the Holocaust. Ethel Rosenberg wrote to President Eisenhower: "Today, while these ghastly mass butchers, these obscene racists, are graciously receiving the benefits of mercy and in many instances being reinstated in public office, the great democratic United States is proposing the savage destruction of a small unoffending Jewish family."[36] It appears to have been a rare public event on behalf of the Rosenbergs that was not filled with references to the Holocaust. Often — and at their funeral — the "Song of the Warsaw Ghetto" was sung.

Jewish organizations, throughout the fifties and well into the sixties, worked on a variety of fronts to prevent, or at least limit, the association of Jews with Communism in the public mind. Their principal cooperative venture was the "Hollywood Project," in which they jointly employed a West Coast representative who lobbied movie producers to avoid any unsympathetic representations of Jews. A good deal of this lobbying dealt with the Jew-Communist issue. The producer of *I Married a Communist* promised to see that no Communist character had a "name that can even remotely be construed as Jewish."[37] An executive of another studio making an anti-Communist film gave assurances that "he was a 'rabid' Jew and I should trust him to treat the Jew right in the story."[38] In *The Red Menace*, "the Jew in the picture was the only really sympathetic character."[39] The Hollywood representative was enthusiastic about the egregiously McCarthyite *My Son John*, since the central religious symbol was "the Tablets that Moses got from God."[40] There was some uneasiness about the treatment of Jews in Warner Brothers' *I Was a Communist for the FBI*, but in the end no protest was made, since "Mr. Warner would undoubtedly be annoyed with criticism from the Jewish community which would jeopardize his very large contribution to the Jewish Welfare Fund."[41]

Separately, the Jewish organizations pursued parallel agendas, though with individual differences. David Petegorsky of the American Jewish Congress said that offsetting the danger of the equation of Jews and Communists was the principal contribution Jewish agencies could make in the worldwide struggle with the Soviet Union. The Congress conducted a sweeping purge of its staff and expelled its leftist chapters, which included some of the largest ones.[42] The Anti-Defamation League, along with the American Jewish Committee, offered to share its files with the House Un-American Activities Committee, so that only bona fide Jewish Communists would be called to testify.[43] It was the American Jewish Committee — in these years the wealthiest and best connected of the major Jewish organizations — that was most active in this area. The hard-line anti-Soviet articles in its monthly magazine, *Commentary*, were, according to Norman Podhoretz, "part of a secret program to demonstrate that not all Jews were Communists."[44] One of the Committee's staff members secured agreements from *Time* and *Life* and several New York newspapers not to publish letters from readers commenting on the Jewishness of accused Communists. He also claimed to have prevented the summoning of "at least three prominent American Jews . . . who shall be nameless" by the Un-American Activities Committee.[45] After considerable staff debate, the American Jewish Committee participated in and financially supported the McCarthyite All-American Conference to Combat Communism and, like other mainstream Jewish organizations, stayed aloof from the campaign for clemency for the Rosenbergs.[46] Committee staffer Edwin J. Lukas, with gallows humor, observed in an internal memorandum, "While one shrinks from entertaining such diabolical notions, it would appear likely that any current aggressiveness toward Jews might indeed be discharged vicariously — but only temporarily — when the sentences are executed."[47] Lucy Dawidowicz (writing on her own and not as a Committee employee) argued in *The New Leader* that, except for pro-Communists, one could in good conscience oppose the death penalty for the Rosenbergs only if one also opposed it for Hermann Göring.[48]

The same concern to dissociate Jews from Communism in the public mind which preoccupied Jewish organizations in the domestic realm governed "Jewish foreign policy." In matters having to do with Germany there was a virtual taboo on mention of the Holocaust, except for private and in-house Jewish discourse. Its constant invocation by the Jewish left had made it suspect; there was still nervousness about the charge of "vengefulness," and overall, a disinclination to use arguments that might suggest American Jews were viewing the question from other than an "all-American" standpoint. In the first years after the war, Jews had non-Communist gentile allies in opposing Germany's rapid rehabilitation. But by the late 1940s all non-Jews, except for the Communist Party and its periphery, had become reconciled to accepting Germans as cold war allies. The prospect of being allied *only* with Communists on this issue made Jewish leaders acutely uncomfortable.

A good example of the dilemma in which Jewish organizations found themselves was the controversy over a German Industrial Fair, sponsored by the American Military Government and scheduled to open in New York in 1949. All the Jewish organizations thought the fair a bad idea and believed that it was serving to rehabilitate German industrialists who had been ardent Nazis. There were calls for picketing the fair from some Jewish circles: the Yiddish-language newspaper *The Day* urged its readers to picket, as "our most holy duty to the 6,000,000 martyrs." And certainly Communist groups were going to join in. Since the idea of a picket line composed exclusively of Jews and Communists was terrifying, the national Jewish organizations opposed picketing by their members and those whom they could influence.[49] But, as the executive director of the umbrella National Community Relations Advisory Council asked, could the Jewish groups simultaneously "whip up public opinion against the [fair] and at the same time control our constituencies not to picket"?[50] On the other hand, as one Brooklyn Jewish leader insisted, "for the NCRAC to abdicate leadership at this point would be to play into the hands of the Communists." Jewish groups in Brooklyn had been dissuaded from independent action only by assurances that the national organizations would do something.[51]

In joint deliberations on what that "something" would be, the fear of appearing vengeful was voiced by George Hexter of the American Jewish Committee. He reminded the group that

> in the public mind the Morgenthau plan for Germany was generally thought of as a Jewish plan; and that if this view was abetted by the Jewish community, through actions which appeared to substantiate the belief that the Jews of the U.S. desired to take vengeance upon the German people, the impression might be created that the Jews of the U.S. constitute a political enclave. Should this come about, the Jewish community in the U.S. would be isolated, with resultant grave danger to all Jews.... We cannot afford to be pushed by any feeling which exists in the Jewish community; but we must rather accept the responsibility for leadership and try to educate the Jewish community in all the complexities of the issue.[52]

And hovering over all the deliberations was the Communist issue. As the executive director of NCRAC reminded its members, "Opposition [to the industrial fair] would be construed as opposition to the rehabilitation of Germany, and thus as opposition to the official United States government attitude toward Russia — and, by simple reasoning, as an expression of pro-Soviet sentiment."[53] In the end, in part as a result of NCRAC's efforts, picketing was limited to groups identified as pro-Communist. The joint statement of the major Jewish organizations avoided any criticism of the fair, restricted itself to a general expression of concern about the politics of German industry, and endorsed German economic restoration so that it could become a bulwark against the totalitarian threat.[54]

Concern about controlling emotional Jewish responses to questions having to do with Germany and the Holocaust was reiterated frequently in the deliberations of Jewish groups. A representative of the Philadelphia Jewish Community Relations Council spoke of the need to educate Jews to something beyond "the understandable but irrational emotional point of view."[55] His colleague from the Cleveland

JCRC endorsed the necessity of national organizations moving their constituencies away from "emotional reactions."[56] An American Jewish Committee staff memorandum deplored the fact that "for most Jews reasoning about Germany and Germans is still beclouded by strong emotion."[57] Albert Vorspan of NCRAC thought it would be a terrible blunder if Jewish organizations "pander[ed] to the deep emotions within the . . . Jewish community."[58] Elliot Cohen, the editor of *Commentary*, spoke of the need to educate Jews to a "realistic attitude rather than a punitive and recriminatory one," for upon Germany "rested the future of western democratic civilization."[59]

All of this points to ways in which cold war exigencies contributed to a continuing gap between private and public discourse of Jews on issues relating to Germany and the Holocaust, a gap between the spontaneous-personal and the considered-official. From the standpoint of many (not all) Jewish communal leaders in these years, popular Jewish attitudes had regrettably not kept up with the demands of changed times. One Jewish official complained to a colleague that American Jews were "not taking anywhere near the measures or using the efforts in combating Communism as they do against Nazism. I know, they'll bring up the question of two world wars, and 6,000,000 Jews exterminated. But that is past, and we must deal with the facts today."[60]

One should never confuse the calculated public posture of Jewish officialdom with the "around the kitchen table" feelings of American Jewry, and especially not with respect to cold war inhibitions about discussing the Holocaust. But these inhibitions (along with others, to be discussed in the next chapter) meant that to a considerable extent the Holocaust was a private, albeit widely shared, Jewish sorrow. Without official sanction, it could not become a public communal emblem; without official reinforcement, it tended, at least for many, to decline in salience.

While the principal impact of the cold war was to limit talk of the Holocaust, there was one realm in which it could be conscripted to the new crusade. At the center of American Jewish foreign policy during the early cold war was protest against anti-Semitism in the Soviet bloc. A particular target was the trial of Rudolph Slansky and other Jewish leaders of the Communist Party in Czechoslovakia in late 1952. There is no doubt that Jewish groups were sincere in their protests, and in their anxiety — which abated somewhat after the death of Stalin in early 1953 — that "anti-Zionist" campaigns threatened wider circles of Eastern European Jews. But neither is there any doubt that they were aware of the domestic "defense functions" their protests served. One memorandum on the objectives of the American Jewish Committee's program to combat Soviet anti-Semitism noted that "even if no Jewish lives were at stake abroad, concern for the security of Jews in the United States would require us to act. Soviet policy opens up opportunities which must not be overlooked . . . to reinforce certain important aspects of AJC's domestic program."[61] "The Prague trial," said another, "is the best opportunity we ever had to 'dissociate Jews from Communism' in the eyes of the general public."[62] The summary of a staff discussion noted general agreement that "tremendous Jewish public outcry on the subject will serve to dissociate Jews from Communism in the public mind."[63] The editor of *Commentary* was also struck by the "great opportunity" that protests against Soviet anti-Semitism offered at a time of anxiety about the public relations consequences of the Rosenberg case.[64]

Holocaust references abounded. With the Prague trial, announced an article in *The New Leader*, "Stalin is ready for his 'final solution of the Jewish question.' "[65] Stalin's goal, said an editorial a week later, "is the liquidation of the remnants left by Hitler."[66] "Stalin will succeed where Hitler failed," said an article in *Commentary*. "He will finally wipe out the Jews of Central and Eastern Europe. . . . The parallel to the policy of Nazi extermination is almost complete."[67] An American Jewish Committee press release offered the grotesque fabrication that the East German government was rounding up "non-aryans," basing the selection on Nazi racial laws."[68] A NCRAC press release announced that repression in Hungary was "only the first station on the way to a Russian Auschwitz." ("I'm going all out on this," wrote a NCRAC staffer to a colleague, "because it's a good indirect [answer to] the 'Jews are Communists' charge.")[69] Even on the relatively rare occasions when Jewish organizations promoted works dealing directly with the Holocaust, there was often a cold war slant. When the American Jewish Committee sent out a hundred complimentary copies of a German-language anthology on the Holocaust (a form of tacit subsidy to the publisher), the accompanying letter by its president noted the importance of realizing "the extent to which Nazism [is] the basically identical totalitarian twin of Communism."[70] When the Anti-

Defamation League published *The Anatomy of Nazism* in 1961, the letter announcing its release noted that the book highlighted the fundamental similarity between Nazism and Communism.[71]

I have so far concentrated on Jewish discourse about the Holocaust under the impact of the cold war — the ways in which this discourse was either muted or turned to anti-Soviet purposes. The reason for this focus is that there was hardly any gentile discourse about the Holocaust during these years. One partial exception to this generalization (as we shall see, a very partial exception) was discussion of the United Nations Convention on Genocide. If nowadays the word "genocide" immediately conjures up the Holocaust, that association was much more problematic during the early cold war years.[72]

The man who coined the term "genocide," and who was the principal lobbyist for the UN convention, was Raphael Lemkin, by origin a Polish Jew. Though the word did not appear before the Holocaust, Lemkin had turned his attention to the phenomenon many years earlier. Apparently it was his childhood reading of *Quo Vadis*, with its account of Christian martyrs under the Roman Empire, reinforced by many later events, culminating in the mass killings of Armenians by Turks during World War I, that drew him to the subject of state-sponsored murder directed at groups.[73] Unquestionably it was the recent example of Nazi crimes that put genocide on the United Nations agenda, but from the beginning Lemkin defined the Nazi program ecumenically: "The Nazi leaders had stated very bluntly their intent to wipe out the Poles, the Russians; to destroy demographically and culturally the French element in Alsace-Lorraine, the Slavonians in Carniola and Carinthia. They almost achieved their goal in exterminating the Jews and gypsies in Europe."[74]

As adopted unanimously by the UN General Assembly in 1948, the Genocide Convention defined the crime broadly, in a way that included the Holocaust but went far beyond it. Genocide was the attempt to destroy "in whole or in part, a national, ethnic, racial or religious group as such." Among the acts that might constitute genocide were causing serious "mental harm" or inflicting "conditions of life" aimed at such destruction. (The United Nations rejected Soviet attempts to insert language tying the concept of genocide more closely to the crimes of Nazism.) Despite the broad scope of the language adopted, over the next fifty years, which saw tens of millions die in actions that were, by the UN definition, clearly genocidal, the United Nations has never invoked the procedure for charging the crime of genocide. From the outset, "genocide" was a rhetorical rather than a juridical device, employed for purely propagandistic purposes. And in cold war America those purposes were anti-Soviet.

In lobbying for American ratification of the Genocide Convention, Lemkin himself, except when addressing Jewish groups, used cold war arguments almost exclusively, seldom mentioning the Holocaust. Among his principal supporters, financial as well as political, were Lithuanian Americans and Ukrainian Americans.[75] This was quite natural, because accusations of Soviet genocide against several national groups in the USSR were the principal theme of Lemkin's campaign. (To German Americans, Lemkin suggested that the postwar expulsion of *Volksdeutsche* from Eastern Europe and the Soviets' continued imprisonment of German POWs were tantamount to genocide.)[76] Discussions of genocide and the Genocide Convention, which petered out in the course of the 1950s, hardly ever referred to the Holocaust; they focused almost exclusively on the crimes — often real, sometimes imagined — of the Soviet bloc.[77]

Genocide was a generic category, and examples could be found to fit the needs of the moment. The Holocaust had an awkward specificity, and it was the "wrong atrocity" for contemporary purposes. The problem of an awkward atrocity was one American leaders had faced during the war. It became increasingly clear that the thousands of captured Polish officers whose bodies were found in the Katyn Forest had been murdered by our Russian allies, not our German enemies. To acknowledge the authorship of the crime would have complicated the pageant of Allied virtue versus Axis vice. President Roosevelt and the Office of War Information did their best to see that the issue was buried.[78] When the Polish government-in-exile called on the International Red Cross to investigate, precipitating a crisis in Polish-Russian relations, the American press was sharply critical of the Poles for raising an issue that might threaten the anti-Hitler alliance. Leading newspapers ran editorials with titles like "Unity Comes First" and "Only Hitler Can Profit."[79] *Time* argued that whoever had killed the Katyn victims, the Nazis had already killed "many, many times 10,000 Poles."[80] The arguments prefigured attitudes toward Jews who dwelled on the Holocaust at a time when Germany had to be rearmed to meet the Soviet threat. Whatever the good intentions of those who raised the issue, harping on Katyn during World War II was objectively inter- fering with the necessary mobilization of public opinion — indeed, objectively serving Nazi purposes. And in a way that prefigured the re- sponse of many Jewish organizations in parallel postwar circum- stances, mainstream Polish American organizations kept quiet about Katyn during the war, "to avoid charges of disrupting Allied unity."[81] After the war, of course, when talk of the Holocaust, or other German crimes, was considered unhelpful, talk about the Katyn Forest mas- sacre, along with other Soviet atrocities, was very helpful indeed.

[6]

"Not in the Best Interests of Jewry"

ETWEEN THE END of the war and the 1960s, as anyone who
has lived through those years can testify, the Holocaust made
scarcely any appearance in American public discourse, and
hardly more in Jewish public discourse — especially discourse directed
to gentiles.

Only a handful of books dealt with it, and those that did, with rare
exceptions like *The Diary of Anne Frank*, had few readers.[1] The two historical accounts of the Holocaust available in the United States during
that time were both imports from abroad, and neither attracted much
attention. Gerald Reitlinger's *The Final Solution* was distributed in this
country by an obscure publisher, and so far as I can tell was never reviewed in the general-circulation press. The same was true of Léon Poliakov's *Bréviaire de la haine*; it was translated into English, as *Harvest of
Hate*, thanks to a subsidy by a Jewish businessman, but sold only a few
hundred copies. Neither Reitlinger's nor Poliakov's book was noted by
the major historical journals. Treatment of the Holocaust in high
school and college history textbooks was extremely skimpy — indeed,
often nonexistent.[2] Mention of the Holocaust in other than Jewish
newspapers and magazines was rare and usually perfunctory.

On the new medium of television there were a handful of dramas
that touched on the Holocaust. In the movies (*Anne Frank* again excepted) there was almost nothing before the 1960s — and not much
then. Alain Resnais's *Nuit et brouillard* (*Night and Fog*, 1955) is often remembered as a Holocaust film, but in fact it dealt primarily with German action against members of the French resistance, and the word
"Jew" does not appear. (Resnais intended the film as a warning against
the atrocities then taking place in the Algerian War.)[3] *Judgment at*

Nuremberg — a 1959 television play that became a 1961 movie — is also often talked about as a Holocaust film, but while the murder of Jews receives peripheral mention in it, the focus throughout is on other crimes of Nazism. *Judgment at Nuremberg,* despite its all-star cast, and *The Diary of Anne Frank,* despite all the attention the book had received and a barrage of publicity surrounding the movie, were not hits at the box office.[4]

There was the same absence in other realms. Contemporary American Jewish religious thinkers had nothing to say about the Holocaust, and with the exception of the occasional insertion of mentions in Seder rituals, no provision was made for religious commemoration of the event.[5] Secular commemoration was mostly restricted to survivors. Throughout the 1950s the World Jewish Congress, with uneven success, encouraged Jewish groups around the globe to hold annual commemorations of the Warsaw Ghetto Uprising. Nowhere did they have less success than in the United States. The WJC's files are filled with accounts of failure and disappointment. The Association of Jewish Musicians was "lukewarm and indifferent" toward participation; most campus Hillel chapters "felt that local circumstances are such as to make such a memorial either unwise or non-practicable"; a meeting with members of the American Jewish Congress showed "how little importance these circles ascribe to the commemoration." Each year the WJC collected information on commemorations in countries with Jewish communities large and small. One year, Isaac Schwarzbart of the WJC wrote at the bottom of the American report, "Very poor — even for Indonesia."[6]

No monuments or memorials were constructed, except for a few commemorative plaques on synagogue walls. By any standard — certainly compared with the omnipresence of the Holocaust in the 1980s and 1990s — nobody in these years seemed to have much to say on the subject, at least in public.

When speaking of public Holocaust discourse, we have the contemporary record to draw on — even if it is largely the record of an absence — and well-grounded generalizations are possible. When it comes to how much the Holocaust was talked about or thought about in private, we're on shakier ground, because the evidence is thinner, fragmentary, often indirect, and sometimes of doubtful reliability. So we'd do well to be tentative about our generalizations here. (With respect to private discourse, I restrict myself to Jews, because there's virtually no evidence concerning non-Jews.]

Contemporary observers who commented on the matter were struck by how little American Jews talked about — or, so far as they could tell, thought about — the Holocaust between the end of the war and the 1960s. In his 1957 *American Judaism*, the only scholarly survey of Jews in the fifties, Nathan Glazer observed that the Holocaust "had had remarkably slight effects on the inner life of American Jewry."[7] In the same year Norman Podhoretz surveyed contemporary Jewish attitudes in the article "The Intellectual and Jewish Fate" — a title that might seem to promise a discussion centering on the Holocaust. It was not even mentioned.[8] There was one unpublished scholarly investigation of the postwar American Jewish response to the Holocaust. Leo Bogart, who went on to become a highly regarded analyst of public opinion, was a graduate student in sociology at the University of Chicago in the late 1940s, and wrote a thesis on just this subject. Bogart began with the hypothesis that an event of this magnitude "would manifest itself through changes in group behavior and belief" — specifically, that "Jews in America would react . . . with an increased sense of group unity and cohesion, and perhaps with some symptoms of psychic disorganization."[9] One of his approaches to testing this hypothesis was soliciting lengthy written statements from a number of young Jews. He found that except for two individuals who were in the armed forces in Europe at the end of the war, it did not appear that "the extermination of Europe's Jews had had any real emotional effect upon the writers of the statements, or that it has influenced their basic outlook." At the center of the project was the administration of an open-ended questionnaire to a hundred Chicago Jews of various backgrounds. The responses of his Chicago sample led him to conclude that "the murder of Europe's Jews has not strongly affected the basic pattern of thought and feeling of Jews in the United States."[10]

Three published symposia offer indirect evidence of how much of a role the Holocaust played in the thought of young American Jews. In 1957 *The New Leader* ran a series of eighteen personal essays to see "what's going on in the minds of the five million Americans who have graduated college since Hiroshima." At least two thirds of the respondents were Jewish. In writing of what had shaped their thinking they mentioned a variety of historic events, from the Great Depression to the cold war. Not a single contributor mentioned the Holocaust.[11] Two other symposia, this time restricted to Jews, were published in 1961, just after the period with which we are concerned. Appearing at a time when there was a great upsurge in discussion of the Holocaust, occasioned by the capture of Adolf Eichmann (to be considered in the next chapter), it's likely that they present an inflated index of how salient the Holocaust was in the fifties. Thirty-one people participated in a symposium in *Commentary*, "Jewishness and the Younger Intellectuals." A few referred to the Holocaust in passing, but in only two cases did contributors speak of it in a way that indicated it loomed large in their sense of their Jewish identity.[12] Later that year the quarterly *Judaism* presented a symposium on "My Jewish Affirmation," with twenty-one participants — most a bit older and less secular in outlook than the *Commentary* contributors. Only one, who had fled Austria after the Anschluss, mentioned the Holocaust.[13]

It's a rule among historians, and a good one, to place greater reliance on contemporary sources than on recollections produced years later, after memory has been reprocessed and refigured. For whatever they're worth, the memoirs and autobiographies of many highly committed Jews bear out the contemporary evidence that suggests the Holocaust wasn't much talked about. Alan Dershowitz, growing up in an intensely Jewish neighborhood in Brooklyn in the forties and fifties, recalls no discussion of the Holocaust either with his schoolmates or at home.[14] Daniel J. Elazar, an observant Jew who later immigrated to Israel, reports that in his Detroit Zionist milieu, in the same period, the Spanish Civil War was a more evocative symbolic event than the Holocaust.[15] As a young man Norman Podhoretz had sufficient Jewish commitment to study at the Jewish Theological Seminary during his four years as a Columbia undergraduate. His 1967 memoir *Making It* details a number of influences during his youth; the Holocaust is not mentioned.[16] But there are other memoirs, particularly in recent years, in which the authors report the Holocaust as being very present during their childhoods in the fifties. The leftist activist Todd Gitlin, writing of his youthful support for nuclear disarmament, recalls that for him and his friends "American bombs . . . were the closest thing to an immoral equivalent of Auschwitz in our lifetimes. When the time came, we jumped at the chance to purge ourselves of the nearest thing to the original trauma."[17] Other writers remember it as (literally) a recurring nightmare, as in the title essay of Daphne

Merkin's *Dreaming of Hitler*, or Meredith Tax's report of every night "look[ing] under the bed for men from Mars, witches, and Nazis."[18]

Recollections concerning how much American Jews talked and thought about the Holocaust in the fifties vary so greatly that any generalization can be met with many counterexamples, and has to be offered very tentatively. In any case, the sources we've so far looked at are not representative of all strata of American Jewry, since they focus on the scribbling classes. Apart from the direct and indirect evidence I've mentioned, we have to ask, given the absence of much public discussion, whether it's likely that there was that much private discussion. The two realms aren't all that autonomous. It seems plausible that if there'd been a great deal of private discussion, this would have been reflected in much more public discussion than there was. And it works the other way too. Even in the way we talk about our direct experiences and feelings, we rely on our culture to provide us with a menu of appropriate responses. Eavesdrop sometime on the conversation of lovers, and note how often what's said is highly stylized, based on pop-culture models. When it comes to dramatic events that are much talked about — the death of JFK or of Princess Di — the things we say in private either reflect or are in reaction to things said in public. Public discourse doesn't just shape private discourse, it is its catalyst; it sends out the message "This is something you should be talking about." When, as in the case of the Holocaust in the 1950s, there isn't much public discourse, the opposite signal is being sent. Such a signal won't, of course, be followed by everyone — in this case, was least likely to be followed by those whose families immigrated relatively recently, or those living in densely Jewish neighborhoods, or those with a strong traditional Jewish identity. But I think it likely that the negative signal was followed by a great many.

The absence of much talk about the Holocaust during these years can be explained in different ways. As I remarked in the Introduction, and for the reasons I outlined there, I don't think the explanation is to be found in "trauma" giving rise to "repression." It seems to me more fruitful to consider choices — albeit tacit and less-than-fully-conscious choices — about whether to talk much about the Holocaust. Some of the grounds for those choices — like the belief that it was better for survivors not to dwell on the past, and the inhibitions the cold war produced — I've already discussed. Before turning to some of the general considerations that influenced decisions to marginalize the Holocaust in this period, let's take a look at a few particular realms where there were special factors.

Concerning the movies, it is sometimes said that the Jewish executives so prominent in that industry were reluctant to call attention to their own Jewishness or open themselves to charges of parochialism by making movies on Jewish subjects. There's probably something to this. At the same time, both the movies and television have always been notoriously dominated by "the bottom line." When, during the war, an employee had suggested to Darryl F. Zanuck that he make a film about concentration camps, he scoffed at the idea: nothing would be "less inviting to an audience"; every venture in this direction had "laid an egg."[19] During the 1950s and for some years thereafter, the Jewish organizations' representative in Hollywood reported that such assessments were a continuing obstacle to the industry's undertaking Holocaust-related projects.[20]

The avoidance of Jewish theological discussion of the Holocaust reflected widespread dissatisfaction with the traditional explanation of Jewish catastrophe as a wake-up call from God occasioned by Jewish sin. I have found only one example from the early postwar years of a Jewish religious explanation of the Holocaust offered to a general audience, and it was the traditional one. Louis Finkelstein, chancellor of the Jewish Theological Seminary, was interviewed by *Time* for a cover story on him in 1951.

> When I was a seminary student 40 years ago it seemed . . . that our faith could not survive. . . . The great First Century Rabbi Eliezer once said: "The Messiah will never come until the Jewish people repent." When they asked him, "What if the Jews do not repent?" he answered: "The Lord will raise up a king worse than Haman to smite them, and then they will repent." This is just what happened. . . . Six million. . . . That dreadful calamity — and the whole spiritual and material crisis of our time — are bringing American Jews back to the faith of their Fathers.[21]

From the late sixties on, various religious voices attempted to offer alternatives to viewing the Holocaust as divine punishment — or as marking the expiration of the special covenant between Jews and God. Even then, these voices were to have no discernible impact on popular Jewish religious consciousness. But as of the fifties, there were no such voices.[22] Rabbi Eugene Borowitz has suggested another inhibition on postwar Jewish theological discussion of the Holocaust. In his view most Jews in this period were in fact agnostics, who had abandoned belief in a God who punishes and rewards. They joined synagogues in order to find a satisfactory niche in a culture that accepted Jews as part of the Protestant-Catholic-Jew triad: "To raise a cry against the God who tolerated such an enormity would expose the full extent of Jewish unbelief to Christian America, thereby undermining Judaism's status as one of America's equivalent faiths."[23]

Later on, survivors were to be important in initiating Holocaust memorialization, especially at the local level. But in the first decades after the end of the war survivors were quite young and were busy finding their feet in a new country. Their command of English was often shaky, and they were usually somewhat isolated from the mainstream of American Jewish life. Most commemorative activity took place within the survivor community, without much effort to involve others. Rabbi Irving Greenberg recalls attending a Holocaust remembrance service in those years, and, like other outsiders, being made acutely aware that he didn't belong. "It felt," he said, "like we were crashing a funeral."[24]

(There was in fact one important and widely observed de facto ritual of Holocaust remembrance that was not initiated by survivors. This was the spontaneous and never-formally-proclaimed boycott by American Jews of German-made goods, coupled with a tacit ban on travel to Germany. There were paradoxes here. American Jews shunned Volkswagens and Grundig radios at a time when Israel, as a result of reparations payments, was awash in German consumer durables. And unlike the formal ban on setting foot in Spain after 1492, which was primarily observed by the Sephardim who were most directly involved, in the postwar years those American Jews *least* likely to observe the informal ban on travel to Germany were Jews of German origin who had fled Hitler in the 1930s. In a somewhat similar category of symbolic actions — though this time rather more public — were postwar Jewish protests against the appearance or employment in the United States of musicians implicated in one way or another with the Nazi regime.)[25]

Apart from those particular realms, what can we say of the general considerations that inhibited talk of the Holocaust? One of the most powerful inhibitions was straightforward and obvious. The Holocaust was a horrifying spectacle, painful and nauseating to contemplate, the sort of thing to which most of us respond by averting our eyes. This kind of self-protective aversion is often talked about as a moral failing. To be sure, a good case can be made that it is morally and politically irresponsible for us to turn our eyes away from distressing sights when, if we confronted them directly, we might be moved to useful action. This is, of course, the basis of the criticism of bystanders' averting their eyes during the Holocaust. But in the first postwar years, much more than nowadays, the Holocaust was *historicized* — thought about and talked about as a terrible feature of the period that had ended with the defeat of Nazi Germany. The Holocaust had not, in the postwar years, attained transcendent status as the bearer of eternal truths or lessons that could be derived from contemplating it. Since the Holocaust was over and done with, there was no practical advantage to compensate for the pain of staring into that awful abyss. This was surely the prevalent American perception, and it was the perception of a great many Jews as well. A writer in the American Jewish Congress quarterly, *Judaism,* surveying the postwar scene, remarked that for "the vast majority of American Jews . . . what occurred before and in other parts of the world happened just that way: in other times and other places."[26] Dwelling on these atrocious scenes seemed like unhealthy voyeurism to many. Even those with a professional obligation to do so often could not bear the prospect. In accounting for the reluctance of his colleagues to address the Holocaust in the first postwar years, the historian Lloyd P. Gartner recalled "the inhibition of loathing and revulsion."[27]

The year 1945 brought not just the full revelation of the horrors of the death camps but another horror as well. Hiroshima had a much greater impact on Americans than did the Holocaust, and a much more enduring impact, for perfectly sensible reasons having nothing to do with "comparative atrocitology." If the Holocaust was emblematic of the era that had just come to an end, Hiroshima, as the emblem of nuclear devastation, defined the present and future. Unlike the Holocaust, Hiroshima did seem to carry with it urgent lessons for Americans, which made it disreputable to avert one's eyes. For many, including leading clergymen, viewing images of the dead and maimed of Hiroshima yielded the lesson "God forgive us." For almost all Americans it yielded the lesson "God — this could be us."

Not just Christian pacifists, but also anti-pacifist Christian theologians like Reinhold Niebuhr, saw Americans as having committed a "morally indefensible" act by which we had "sinned grievously against the laws of God and the people of Japan."[28] Harry Emerson Fosdick,

one of America's best-known Protestant clergymen, continued to insist that Germany be punished for its "monstrous program of cold-
blooded torture and extermination," but after Hiroshima thought that
Americans were "in no position to wash our hands in innocency and
call others guilty."[29] An editorial in the *New York Herald Tribune* found
"no satisfaction in the thought that an American air crew has produced what must without doubt be the greatest simultaneous slaughter in the whole history of mankind, and even in its numbers matches
the more methodical mass butcheries of the Nazis or of the an-
cients."[30] Lewis Mumford wrote, "Our aims were different, but our
methods were those of mankind's worst enemy."[31]

If it was only a minority of Americans who saw the United States
as the perpetrator of a ghastly atrocity, the overwhelming majority
had little doubt that they might themselves share the fate of the people
of Hiroshima. The press drove home this prospect. Local newspapers
ran graphics of the Hiroshima circle of devastation superimposed on
their communities; *Life* devoted nine pages to descriptions of a future nuclear war, culminating with a technician testing the rubble of
New York City for radioactivity under the blank eyes of the (surviving)
lions in front of the public library on Fifth Avenue.[32]

As we saw in a previous chapter, at the time of the liberation of the
camps there had been those who urged that Americans confront the
horrors so they could grasp the full dimensions of Nazi criminality.
But insofar as such an encounter took place, it was short-lived. Hiroshima, coming only a few months later, engaged Americans with
much greater immediacy. Unlike the Holocaust, Americans were involved both as perpetrators and as potential victims; unlike the Holocaust, there were practical reasons for undergoing the ordeal of facing
the horror. The anthropologist Ruth Benedict wrote that to grasp the
prospect before us, it was necessary to confront "scenes of the burned
and wounded staggering endlessly along the roads, of living burial . . .
of vomit and suppuration and lingering death."[33] The economist Stuart Chase urged that "all of us, children as well as adults," should see
photographs and films of Hiroshima. "We should see the dead, the
wounded, the smashed hospitals, the agony. [The pictures] should be
run in every theatre. . . . We should take these horrors straight, hard,
and unvarnished. [Only] first hand experience can hold us to the task
of saving our civilization."[34] Another well-known writer urged dramatic re-creations of the devastation "until man . . . has seen with his
own eyes [and] felt with immediate emotion, the possibility of his

own destruction."[35] Although the willingness of the American public to confront the grisly specter of Hiroshima had its ups and downs, there was never any shortage of renewed incentives: the Soviet Union's acquisition of first nuclear then thermonuclear weapons, the shelter mania, anxiety about fallout from testing, and the Cuban missile crisis. There were no comparable incentives, in these years, for Americans to contemplate the horrors of Nazism.

Various writers, without making invidious comparisons between them, talked of Auschwitz and Hiroshima as terrible twin symbols of manmade mass death. For some, Auschwitz was seen as the curtain raiser for a new and greater holocaust to come, a truly final solution for all mankind, as projected in movies like *On the Beach, Planet of the Apes,* and *Dr. Strangelove.* The physicist I. I. Rabi wrote of the nuclear arms race as "the nations lined up, like those prisoners of Auschwitz, going into the ovens."[36] Bernard Rosenberg in *Jewish Frontier*, and A. Alvarez in *Commentary*, saw in the Holocaust what they described as a "rehearsal" or "a small-scale trial" for a nuclear war.[37] It is certainly not impossible to immerse oneself in the awful details of the Holocaust *and* nuclear devastation, and there are individuals, like John Hersey and Robert K. Lifton, who have done just that. But for most people psychic equilibrium seemed to demand that at most they deal with one, and they often chose the encounter that pointed toward dealing with the present and the future rather than the past.

Some years after the period we're looking at — in the 1970s, when the Holocaust moved to the center of American culture — it came to seem an appropriate symbol of contemporary consciousness. American social morale was at a low ebb, where it has stayed ever since. The previous decade had seen the assassination of John and Robert Kennedy, along with that of Martin Luther King. The hopes of radicals for "the movement," of liberals for the Great Society, of blacks and others for the civil rights crusade, had all been dashed. It had been the years of Vietnam and Watergate. The Holocaust was to become an aptly bleak emblem for an age of diminished expectations.

The postwar years, by contrast, were extraordinarily upbeat. The Vietnam War was to divide Americans; World War II had united them. Despite (perhaps, for some, because of) the mushroom-shaped cloud just over the horizon, Americans had never been more cheerful and optimistic. The novelist Herbert Gold, taking as his text instructions given to television writers to produce "happy stories about happy people with happy problems," titled his book of essays on the fifties *The Age of Happy Problems*.[38] Triumphant in the war, with a booming economy that had avoided the widely expected postwar slump, now by far the world's richest and most powerful nation, the United States and its people took for granted that they stood on the threshold of what Henry Luce had called "the American Century."

No group in American society shared more wholeheartedly in this ebullient mood than American Jews. The fifteen or twenty years after the war saw the repudiation of anti-Semitic discourse and its virtual disappearance from the public realm. Opinion polls are a crude instrument for measuring private sentiments, but for what they're worth, they show dramatically declining anti-Semitism during the postwar years. In 1946 an unpublicized poll commissioned by the American Jewish Committee asked a national sample of gentiles whether there are "any nationality, religious or racial groups in this country that are a threat to America." Eighteen percent named Jews. By 1954, after which the question was abandoned, this was down to one percent.[39] Of greater consequence was the rapid collapse of anti-Semitic barriers to Jewish ascent in every area of American life.[40] The Holocaust was almost certainly one of the reasons for the dramatic postwar decline of anti-Semitism in the United States, but the evidence is contradictory.[41] Other social and cultural factors may have been of equal or greater importance, not least the fact that Jews were by now much less "foreign" than they had been. By the 1950s three quarters of American Jews were native born — mostly of the third generation in this country. The reasons for the decline in anti-Semitism need not concern us here, as they didn't much concern people then. The fact of the decline, and the ease with which they were able to rise in all spheres, soon became clear to Jews in the postwar years, and led them to become enthusiastic participants in the prevailing optimistic cultural climate. Philip Roth thought that

> much of the exuberance with which I and others of my generation of Jewish children seized our opportunities after the war — that wonderful feeling that one was entitled to no less than anyone else, that one could do anything and could be excluded from nothing — came from our belief in the boundlessness of the democracy in which we lived and to which we belonged. It's hard to imagine that anyone of intelligence growing up in America since the Vietnam War can have had our unambiguous sense, as young adolescents immediately after the victory over Nazi fascism and Japanese militarism, of belonging to the greatest nation on earth.[42]

All of this meant that American society was increasingly disposed to treat Jews no differently from other Americans, and think of them as an integral rather than a foreign part of that society. Edward Shapiro began his history of postwar American Jewry with twin symbols of that integration: Bess Myerson, the 1945 Miss America, and Hank Greenberg, whose ninth-inning grand-slam home run that year won the American League pennant for the Detroit Tigers, and who went on to lead the Tigers to victory in the World Series.[43] And as an increasing number of Americans came to think of Jews as not significantly different from other Americans, an increasing number of American Jews came to think of themselves in the same way. An integrationist rather than a particularist consciousness was the norm in the postwar decades: difference and specificity were at a discount; a "brothers under the skin" and "family of man" ethos was dominant. Blacks weren't yet being brought effectively under this umbrella, but Jews were, and Jewish groups did everything in their power to further this. An official of the American Jewish Committee recalled that her first assignment, in the late forties, was promoting stories in the press that would show "Jews were as nice as anybody else; show them that they're football players, they're not all intellectuals."[44] It's worth noting that the three leading promoters of the postwar "consensus school" of American history — which stressed what united Americans rather than what divided them — were all Jews.[45]

In recent decades many have insisted that a sustained encounter with the Holocaust militates against callow optimism and meretricious universalism. The argument has force. For our immediate purposes, we might turn the observation on its head. Dispensing with the invidious adjectives, those whose outlook is basically optimistic and universalist — as Americans, including American Jews, were in the fifties — are not going to be inclined to center the Holocaust in their consciousness. It was an inappropriate symbol of the contemporary mood, and that is surely one of the principal reasons that it stayed at the margins.

The upbeat and universalist postwar mood not only muted discussion of the Holocaust, it colored what discussion there was. To be sure, one couldn't make the Holocaust an upbeat experience, but what one *could* do was, in the words of a contemporary popular song, "ac-cent-tchu-ate the positive" and "latch on to the affirmative." One way of doing this was making the Warsaw Ghetto Uprising the central symbol of the Holocaust. The New York office of the World Jewish Congress explained that

> the imagination and hearts of peoples cling to deeds of courage, sacrifice, heroism, shining examples of self-defense, strength and pride, rather than to mourning over general calamities, passive defeatism, and destruction.... [The] Warsaw Ghetto Uprising ... has thus captured the imagination of the people and became more ... the symbol of the Catastrophe than other events.[46]

Those who participated in the uprising had demonstrated their faith in "the ultimate triumph of humanity despite the temporary victories of barbarism."[47]

The other way of keeping representation of the Holocaust upbeat was by focusing on the successful postwar lives of survivors. Unlike later years, when the emphasis was on the permanence of their scars, depictions of survivors in the fifties featured their success in overcoming the past. An article on survivors in the *New York Times Magazine* reported that most were "fitting into the American way of life as though born to it." The lesson was "that no matter how great the catastrophe, the human spirit ... is durable."[48] Contestants on the television program *Queen for a Day* were chosen for the honor by audience response to the wish they wanted granted if crowned. Lili Meier, a survivor of Birkenau, was chosen when she said: "Each time I look down at my left arm and see my tattoo I am reminded of my terrible past.... If only my tattoo could be removed!"[49] Hanna Bloch Kohner was a survivor of Westerbork, Theresienstadt, Auschwitz, and Mauthausen; her husband and parents had been murdered. She was one of those surprised by a recounting of her biography on the equally popular program *This Is Your Life*, whose host, Ralph Edwards, said:

> Out of darkness, of terror and despair, a new life has been born in a new world for you, Hanna Kohner. This is your life. Even as your heart goes out to those less fortunate than you, you rejoice humbly in the bounties America has given you.... The never-to-be-forgotten tragic experiences of your life, Hanna, have been tempered by the happiness you've found here in America. ... To you in your darkest hour, America held out a friendly hand. Your gratitude is reflected in your unwavering devotion and loyalty to the land of your adoption.[50]

Even more widespread than the upbeat representation of the Holocaust was its universalist framing, with an emphasis on the diversity of the victims of Nazism rather than on what was singular about Jewish victimhood. As we have seen, both during the war and afterward, "the Holocaust," as a Jewish-specific conceptual entity, hardly existed. As we have also seen, the fact that Jews were a relatively small minority of those liberated from German camps in 1945, the exigencies of the campaign for displaced persons, and the cold war emphasis on an undifferentiated totalitarianism as the author of genocide all furthered this framing. This was not merely a gentile perception; a universalist approach was, in these and other contexts, often taken by Jewish organizations. An official of the American Jewish Committee wrote to a Hollywood executive about a line in the script of the movie *Body and Soul* which read, "In Europe today they're killing people like us just because they are Jewish": "It isn't quite true to say that Jews in Europe were killed just because they were Jews," he said. "It was because the Nazis were using anti-Semitism and anti-Jewish atrocities as a propaganda weapon, first in order to seize power, and then to exploit it."[51] A speech drafted by the American Jewish Congress staff for one of their local leaders, while noting that Jews had been the "first" and "most tragic" victims, insisted that "Hitler felt that only by eradicating the Jews could he succeed in his campaign to destroy Judeo-Christian civilization and supplant it with primeval paganism."[52] Leaders of the Anti-Defamation League, viewing an ADL film strip, "The Anatomy of Nazism," thought it focused too narrowly on Jewish suffering. They wanted frames added to show that millions of non-Jews also perished.[53]

In recent decades, the leading Jewish organizations have invoked the Holocaust to argue that anti-Semitism is a distinctively virulent and murderous form of hatred. But in the first postwar decades their emphasis — powerfully reinforced by contemporary scholarly opinion — was on the common psychological roots of all forms of prejudice. Their research, educational, and political action programs consistently minimized differences between different targets of discrimination. If prejudice and discrimination were all of a piece, they reasoned that they could serve the cause of Jewish self-defense as well by attacking prejudice and discrimination against blacks as by tackling anti-Semitism directly. And this reasoning was reflected in their allocation of energy and resources. (When going through the papers of the American Jewish Congress, I saw, in a list of 1949 research projects, an investigation of "Adjustment of a Newly-Arrived Minority Group."

I assumed that this would refer to Jewish DPs. Wrong. It was "a study of the community relations of a group of Puerto Rican Negroes recently arrived in a Utah mining town.")[54]

By far the best-known representation of the Holocaust in the 1950s was the adaptation of Anne Frank's diary to stage and screen by the husband-wife team of Albert Hackett and Frances Goodrich. The 1955 Broadway play was a box-office smash that won a Pulitzer Prize, the Tony Award for best play, and the New York Drama Critics Circle Award. George Stevens, who as a Signal Corps officer had made the film of the liberation of Dachau, which now unrolls continually at the Washington Holocaust Museum, produced and directed the 1959 movie version, which was seen by millions. Jewish groups hailed and promoted both the stage and screen adaptations. The National Community Relations Advisory Council, the coordinating body of leading Jewish organizations, enthusiastically recommended the film for its "portrayal of Jews finding solace and strength in their Jewishness, for its depiction of the selfless courage of Christians who risked their lives to save Jews from the Nazis, and for its evocation of horror and revulsion against the Nazi program of Jewish extermination."[55]

Forty years after the appearance of these roundly acclaimed adaptations, they became the representations of the Holocaust that nearly everyone who writes on the subject loves to hate. What captured audiences in the 1950s — Anne's "universalism," both in character and in outlook, together with her luminous optimism — was precisely what outraged writers in the 1990s. Among those who inveigh against the universalizing or "de-Judaizing" of the Holocaust — "stealing our Holocaust" — the Hacketts' adaptations are repeatedly invoked as the most egregious examples of this process, exhibit A in the case for the prosecution.[56] Cynthia Ozick, writing in *The New Yorker* in 1997, suggested that the universalizing of Anne's story had gone so far, and its results had been so pernicious, that it might have been better if her diary had been "burned, vanished, lost."[57]

The Broadway and Hollywood versions of the *Diary* assuredly *were* upbeat and universal. As one typical review remarked, "like the diary itself . . . a moving document about the durability of the young in spirit."[58] The curtain line on both stage and screen repeated words from the original *Diary:* "In spite of everything, I still believe that people are really good at heart." The director Garson Kanin had urged the

Hacketts to omit lines from a diary entry in which Anne remarked that Jews had always suffered. This, he thought, was "special pleading." He preferred to have Anne say, as she wound up doing, on stage and screen: "We're not the only people that've had to suffer . . . sometimes one race . . . sometimes another."[59]

Hardly anyone at the time suggested that there was anything inappropriate about the upbeat and universal approach being taken, which, besides being à la mode, also had the endorsement of the person who would seem to have had the greatest interpretive authority, Anne's father, Otto Frank. In later years much would be made of the substitution of "sometimes one race . . . sometimes another" for the *Diary*'s sentences on past Jewish suffering, but in the mid-1950s this was scarcely mentioned. The majority of reviewers stressed how faithfully the play (and later the movie) followed Anne's diary.

There was one dissenting voice, the novelist Meyer Levin, whose stage adaptation had been rejected by Otto Frank and the producers. At first Levin's grievance had nothing to do with the substance of the adaptation chosen and everything to do with its authorship. He wrote Otto Frank that he was "disgusted and enraged at the thought that a non-Jew has been selected to write the play. . . . To have it produced by a Gentile . . . is scandalous beyond measure. I will not stand for this. I will write about it wherever I can."[60] And write about it he did — endlessly, obsessively, desperately — until his death in 1981, in a crusade that carried him to the brink of insanity and beyond. Levin was, in any case, not in a good position to object to universalizing Anne's experience or focusing on her optimism. Reviewing the *Diary* in the *New York Times Book Review* at the time of its publication in 1952, he had assured potential readers that "this is no lugubrious ghetto tale, no compilation of horrors":

> It is so wondrously alive, so near, that one feels overwhelmingly the universalities of human nature. These people might be living next door; their . . . emotions, their tensions and satisfactions are those of human character and growth, anywhere. . . . This wise and wonderful young girl brings back a poignant delight in the infinite human spirit.[61]

In a review in *Congress Weekly*, the organ of the American Jewish Congress, Levin quoted Anne's longing for a time "when we are people again, and not just Jews":

> Her book is, in essence, a song to life, no matter what the conditions, no matter what the threat. . . . The whole world now lives with the same sense

of threat, waiting momentarily for the doom of war. It is for this reason that Anne's book can break the sectarian circle. . . . For all who read her words, the "time when we are people again" has arrived.[62]

After the Hacketts' dramatization of the *Diary* opened, Levin, in arguing for the superiority of his rendition, came to insist that they had presented a "de-Judaized" version, that his was more authentically Jewish. But his was an isolated complaint, garnering hardly any support in the 1950s.[63]

The charge, made repeatedly in recent years, that the Hacketts' version systematically de-Judaized Anne, can be sustained only by a very selective reading of both the original diary and the play. As the literary scholar Robert Alter has observed, Anne's Jewish identity was marginal; for her, "being a Jew is like being freckled or being left-handed . . . [it] has no specific content or deep resonance." Of the invented "sometimes one race . . . sometimes another" in the play, Alter remarks that "it is not exactly a violation of the spirit of the book." He concludes that "it is impossible to 'universalize' a document that is already universal."[64]

From the *Diary*'s first publication in the United States, there were those who noted, in a tone and spirit very different from Alter's, that its author wasn't all that Jewish. An early reviewer in *Jewish Social Studies* complained that

> what one misses in Anne's portrait is the attachment to any specific Jewish values. . . . [She] was deprived of the spiritual power and comfort inherent in the Jewish tradition. There is considerable evidence that the children (as well as adults) stemming from Eastern Europe weathered the Nazi plague more successfully. Who knows — perhaps the strength derived from Judaism might have given her the endurance needed to hang on several weeks until Belsen was liberated.[65]

A similar complaint about Anne's being a poor symbol of the Holocaust victim because of her inadequate Jewish identity was voiced a few years later by Israel Gutman of Yad Vashem:

> Anne Frank is unlike many of the Jewish young people in the communities of Eastern Europe. The Dutch girl is not an organic part of Jewish national life and a Jewish atmosphere. . . . There are other books in which we become acquainted with a different environment, not just one or two Jewish families but a whole segment of deeply rooted Jewish living.[66]

Recently Lawrence Langer, a specialist in Holocaust literature, has cited Anne's failure to practice Jewish rituals, the lack of a mention of Passover in the two years covered by her diary, and, in general, her "limited concern with Jewish issues" as grounds for considering whether the time had come to expel her *Diary* from the canon of important Holocaust texts.[67]

While in some respects additions and deletions in the play made Anne and her family less Jewish, in other respects the play made them more Jewish, something Jewish reviewers noted at the time but later commentators have ignored. The theater reviewers for two Zionist magazines, *Jewish Frontier* and *Midstream*, pointed out that while in the *Diary* Anne had referred to Hanukkah once in passing, immediately adding that "St. Nicholas Day was much more fun," the play dwells at length on the Hanukkah celebration and ignores St. Nicholas Day. "All of this is good public relations for the Jews' traditional observances," remarked the reviewer in *Midstream*, "but it is not what Anne Frank wrote in her diary."[68]

Commentators in recent years have complained that the adaptation removed the *Diary*'s Zionist message. Edward Alexander, in an article entitled "Stealing the Holocaust," charged the adapters with having "expunged from the stage version all of Anne's references to her hopes for survival in a Jewish homeland."[69] In fact, Anne, in the *Diary*, cites her sister Margot's desire to become a midwife in Palestine as an example of the "narrow cramped existence" about which she was "not at all keen." For herself, she longed to spend years in Paris and London, learn the languages and study the history of art, "see beautiful dresses and interesting people." So far as her national consciousness was concerned, "My first wish after the war is that I may become Dutch! I love the Dutch, I love this country. . . . Even if I have to write to the Queen myself, I will not give up until I have reached my goal."[70]

Whatever "universalization" of Anne took place in the 1950s, and there certainly was some, pales in comparison with her "particularization" in recent years. The *Diary* was not twisted into an optimistic and universalist document by the Hacketts, Garson Kanin, George Stevens, or anyone else; it *was* such a document, and it was that fact which commended it to Americans in the 1950s, including most of the organized Jewish community.[71] Every generation frames the Holocaust, represents the Holocaust, in ways that suit its mood.

There was another aspect of postwar American culture that led Jews to marginalize the Holocaust in their own minds — even more in how they represented themselves to others.

Whereas nowadays the status of victim has come to be prized, in the forties and fifties it evoked at best the sort of pity mixed with contempt. It was a label actively shunned. The self-reliant cowboy and the victorious war hero were the approved (masculine) ideals. Few wanted to think of themselves as victims, and even fewer to be thought about that way by others. American Jews — at least young male Jews of the post-immigrant generation — accepted these norms as enthusiastically as did other Americans, were as much in the thrall of Gary Cooper and John Wayne. Hundreds of thousands of them, as members of the American armed forces, were charter members of the postwar victory culture. As Israelis were "negating" the Diaspora victim condition (very much including the Holocaust), American Jews, in a parallel fashion, regarded the victimhood symbolized by the Holocaust as a feature of the Old World that they, likewise, were putting behind them. Many years later, a Jewish journalist recalled what Hank Greenberg and Bess Myerson had meant to him as a ten-year-old in 1945: "Hank and Bess were winners, like DiMaggio and Grable — only smarter. They were as American as apple pie and the Fourth of July — and as Jewish as *knishes* and Yom Kippur. They belonged to a race of victors, not victims."[72]

Postwar Jews' repudiation of the status of victim — and their attendant distancing of themselves from the most recent and ghastly symbol of that status — was largely spontaneous and tacit. But it was also the result of strategic calculation.

Toward the end of World War II the American Jewish Committee sponsored an academic conference on American anti-Semitism, which brought together many of the social-scientific heavy hitters of the day. Shortly thereafter John Slawson, the chief executive of the Committee, reported its findings to a meeting of the National Community Relations Advisory Council (NCRAC). He began by noting that in the experts' view, dedicated anti-Semites, though they claimed Jews were powerful, subconsciously knew they were weak, and this perception stimulated their sadistic impulses. Thus, he said, Jewish organizations

should avoid representing the Jew as weak, victimized, and suffering. . . . There needs to be an elimination or at least a reduction of horror stories of victimized Jewry. . . . We must normalize the image of the Jew. . . . War hero stories are excellent. . . . The Jew should be represented as *like* others, rather than unlike others. The image of Jewish weakness must be eliminated. . . . In an effort to arouse the conscience of the world, as the one possible means of alleviating the tragic plight of our brethren in Europe, we have had to publicize the mass atrocities committed by the Nazis. That was unavoidable. . . .

It is necessary first to identify and analyze the characteristics that seem to distinguish the Jewish from the non-Jewish American, and then to encourage the adaptation of the Jewish mores to the mores prevailing in this country. [What is implied] is neither segregation nor assimilation, but an adjustment to the American scene by means of a cultural integration . . . retention of positive and useful traits and the gradual sloughing off of useless and outworn characteristics in favor of desirable American characteristics.[73]

Here was a perfect fit between the experts' view that the victim image worsened rather than alleviated anti-Semitism and Slawson's preference for Jews' taking on "desirable American characteristics." Among the "useless and outworn characteristics" to be sloughed off was the common negative stereotype of the whining, complaining, or self-pitying Jew — the stigmata of the Jew as victim.

Of the leading Jewish organizations, Slawson's American Jewish Committee was the most assiduous in combating the victim image. The Committee suspended work on a picture album of Nazi barbarities when the émigré scholar Max Horkheimer, then its director of scientific research, advised that "harp[ing] on the atrocity story . . . might have an undesirable effect on the subconscious mind of many people."[74] Elliot Cohen, the editor of *Commentary*, criticized the 1947 movie *Crossfire*, which dealt with the murder of a Jew by an anti-Semitic soldier. The producers, he said, would have done better to find a "more vigorously human character for its Jew than the stereotype of the eternal helpless victim of brute force."

The exhibition of sadism and slaughter does not automatically cause revulsion and rejection. On the contrary, it may make the forbidden and horrible familiar and customary, and link up hidden emotions with open action. . . . More than one careful observer believes that the ghastly pitiful newsreel pictures of Buchenwald stirred very ambiguous emotions; the sight of Jewish corpses stacked like butcher's meat made Jewish life cheap.[75]

A Committee staffer was distressed by the 1958 movie *Me and the Colonel*, which starred Danny Kaye as a Jewish refugee fleeing the Nazis. It reinforced "long-ingrained stereotypes . . . the hunted wanderer, inured to universal hatred and contempt."[76]

There were other grounds for thinking that the featuring of the Holocaust was counterproductive. A film about Nazism was shown to thousands of high school students across the country to test its impact. The percentage of students who thought Jews were treated unequally in the United States fell by more than a third after seeing the film: it set a standard of "unequal treatment" that made discriminatory practices in America not worth noticing. Marie Jahoda — like Horkheimer, one of the authors of the Committee-sponsored *The Authoritarian Personality* — thought "these figures ought to be considered very seriously by everyone making use of Nazi atrocities for propaganda here."[77]

Not all of the views just presented reflected a consensus among Jewish leaders, but on one point there was striking unanimity among the principal Jewish agencies: the danger that promoting widespread consciousness of the Holocaust would inevitably promote the image of the Jew as victim. This was made clear by the fate of a request to the leading Jewish organizations in the late 1940s that they lend their support to a proposed Holocaust memorial in New York City. The proposal had won the endorsement of several prominent Jews and gentiles but could not go forward without Jewish institutional sponsorship. On three separate occasions — in 1946, 1947, and 1948 — the representatives of the NCRAC organizations, including the American Jewish Committee, Anti-Defamation League, American Jewish Congress, Jewish Labor Committee, and Jewish War Veterans, unanimously rejected the idea — and effectively vetoed the initiative. They were concerned that such a monument would result in Americans' thinking of Jews as victims: it would be "a perpetual memorial to the weakness and defenselessness of the Jewish people"; it would "not be in the best interests of Jewry."[78]

Through the 1950s, this remained the judgment of most American Jewish leaders.[79] In the 1960s and 1970s, changed circumstances were to alter that judgment.

Part Three

THE YEARS
OF TRANSITION

[7]

"Self-Hating Jewess
Writes Pro-Eichmann Series"

As we've seen, the Holocaust wasn't talked about very much in the United States through the end of the 1950s. As we all know, it's been talked about a lot since the late 1970s. In this chapter, and the two chapters that follow, we'll be looking at how this changed.

Part of the background to the new readiness to talk about the Holocaust was a certain loosening of the cold war culture that had previously inhibited it. The cold war was by no means over — indeed, John F. Kennedy was a much more fervent cold warrior than Dwight Eisenhower, and the early sixties saw, in the Cuban missile crisis, the cold war's most dangerous moment. There were still those who resisted talk of the Holocaust on the grounds that it weakened the Atlantic Alliance. And the Holocaust was still being recycled for cold war purposes. (Secretary of Labor Arthur Goldberg, laying a wreath at the Anne Frank House in Amsterdam in 1961, carried a message from President Kennedy: Anne's words, "written in the face of a monstrous tyranny, have significant meaning today as millions who read them live in the shadow . . . of another such tyranny.")[1] But the death of Stalin and the fall of McCarthy, limited liberalization in Eastern Europe and the Sino-Soviet split, the rise to a kind of legitimacy of critics of the nuclear-arms race, perhaps above all the impossibility of sustaining the level of ideological mobilization of the late forties and early fifties — all worked to relax previous constraints on talking of the Holocaust. Alternatively — but it comes to the same thing — one could argue that by the early sixties the cold war outlook was so institutionalized that it was no longer threatened by reminders of World War II alignments.

William L. Shirer's record-breaking 1960 bestseller *The Rise and Fall of the Third Reich* resonated throughout American society. After years of inattention to the subjects, the book put Nazism and World War II on the American cultural map in a big way.[2] (Shirer devoted 2 or 3 percent of his 1,200-page book to the murder of European Jewry, a proportion that, to the best of my knowledge, no critic commented on.) In the very last week of the 1950s young thugs who daubed swastikas on West German synagogues found imitators first in other parts of Europe, then in the United States. The outburst was short-lived, but it served, along with other catalysts, to put Nazism back in the headlines. Another headline grabber was George Lincoln Rockwell, whose tiny American Nazi Party succeeded in provoking confrontations that got it a fair amount of press coverage. In the early months of 1960 the East German regime stepped up its campaign of revealing the Nazi pasts of prominent West German officials, which kept alive doubts, particularly among Jews, about whether the Bonn republic was completely discontinuous with the Third Reich. Leaders of the American Jewish Committee were moved to consider whether they had gone too far in accepting the argument that "criticism of Germany plays into Communist hands," and whether the outbreaks of vandalism meant more attention should be directed to teaching about Nazism not just in Germany but in America as well.[3] A top official of the American Jewish Congress thought the swastika daubings in both Europe and the United States would have been inconceivable when "the memory of Nazism and the concentration camps was fresh." Jewish educators and community leaders were told that they needed to do more to keep this memory alive.[4]

Would those things by themselves have been the catalyst of a sustained increase in talk of the Holocaust? We'll never know, for close on their heels came a much greater catalyst: David Ben-Gurion's dramatic announcement to the Knesset that Israeli agents had captured Adolf Eichmann in Argentina and secretly transported him to Israel, where he would stand trial.

The reaction of Americans to the Israeli announcement was mixed. All expressed pleasure that the criminal had been captured and would be called to account. But a great many were distressed about the manner in which Eichmann had been apprehended, and rejected Israel's claim to jurisdiction. In the first weeks after Ben-Gurion's announcement, newspaper editorials, by a margin of more than two to one, were negative in one way or another.[5] *The New Republic* thought Israel "would do well to confess error and hand Eichmann back to the Argentine authorities."[6] Telford Taylor, the chief American prosecutor at the Nuremberg Trials, argued that the Israeli action undermined the principle, established at Nuremberg, that genocide was an offense against the international community, not a private matter for the aggrieved party.[7] Jewish-owned newspapers were often among the critics. The *Washington Post* thought what was planned was a "passion play in the guise of a trial . . . a prostitution of the forms of law."[8] The *New York Post* said the trial should take place in Germany, which "needs the educational value of such a trial far more than Israel. . . . A death sentence from an Israeli court would be interpreted as a simple act of vengeance; a life sentence handed down in Germany would be a far more meaningful verdict."[9] Leading Jewish academic figures, like the historian Oscar Handlin of Harvard and Herbert Wechsler of Columbia Law School, joined in condemning the Israeli decision on procedural grounds.[10]

Two other lines of press commentary — sometimes made separately, sometimes joined — were more troublesome: that the trial would benefit the Soviets and that it illustrated the difference between Christian forgiveness and "Jewish vengefulness." The *Wall Street Journal* wrote that the trial not only risked reviving anti-German feeling, which could only benefit the Communists, but that it was pervaded by "an atmosphere of Old Testament retribution."[11] A Unitarian minister wrote that he could see little ethical difference between "the Jew-pursuing Nazi and the Nazi-pursuing Jew."[12] A strong version of this argument appeared in the Catholic newspaper *The Tablet*:

> All this Eichmann business that has been filling the papers lately sadly reminds us that there are still some influential people around who — like Shylock of old — demand their pound of flesh. . . . They are a powerful group largely responsible for this country's unconditional surrender demands which prolonged the Second World War and for the disgraceful Morgenthau Plan aimed at reducing our conquered foe to abject slavery. This identical thinking was back of the notorious Nuremberg trials. And the same believers in "an eye for an eye" continue today unregenerate and unashamed. Forgiveness is not in their makeup, not even forgiveness of the

completely vanquished. For these warped minds there is no such word as pardon.[13]

The general-circulation magazine that outdid all others in the frequency and vehemence of its attacks on the trial was William F. Buckley's *National Review*. Its first commentary on Eichmann was noteworthy in that, at a time when all the other media were reporting his millions of victims, it spoke of Eichmann's being "generally believed to have had a primary hand in exterminating hundreds of thousands."[14] Two weeks later the magazine returned to the subject, attacking the "pernicious" trial that was "manipulat[ing] a series of *ex post facto* laws . . . to give assassination a juridical rationale." It was "an international apparatus of vengeance."[15] *National Review*'s Eichmann coverage then turned to anti-Semitic "humor." The magazine presented the imagined conversation of a vulgar Jewish couple: "Sylvia" spoke to "Myron" about Eichmann (and gold, and hairdressers) in their Central Park West apartment while "doing her nails . . . on an enormous crescent-shaped, gold-on-gold, French provincial Castro convertible."[16] A bit later, the *National Review* devoted an editorial to how the Communists were profiting from the "Hate Germany movement" being furthered by the Eichmann trial.[17] As the trial opened, the magazine made its fullest statement on the subject:

> We are in for a great deal of Eichmann in the weeks ahead. . . . We predict the country will tire of it all, and for perfectly healthy reasons. The Christian Church focuses hard on the crucifixion of Jesus Christ for only one week out of the year. Three months — that is the minimum estimate made by the Israeli Government for the duration of the trial — is too long. . . . Everyone knows the facts, and has known them for years. There is no more drama or suspense in store for us. . . . Beyond that there are the luridities. . . . The counting of corpses, and gas ovens, and kilos of gold wrenched out of dead men's teeth. . . . There is under way a studied attempt to cast suspicion upon Germany. . . . It is all there: bitterness, distrust, the refusal to forgive, the advancement of Communist aims.[18]

The magazine's final observation on the trial was an expression of satisfaction that despite the efforts of Israeli publicists, who were "titillating the world's appetite for horror stories," Yuri Gagarin's space flight and the Bay of Pigs invasion, which coincided with the opening of the trial, had chased Eichmann from the front pages.[19]

The line taken by Buckley's *National Review* was, to be sure, not typical of press commentary, but it represented just the sort of backlash Jewish organizations feared. Uncertainty about how the trial would be received in America led to a nervous ambivalence in how leading Jewish groups responded to Eichmann's capture and trial.

As we saw in the previous chapter, there was a widespread reluctance to seeing Jews portrayed as victims, a fear that parading atrocities might spark anti-Semitic incidents. Israelis often agreed. Meier Grossman had been a long-time member of the Jewish Agency Executive. On the eve of the trial he objected to "Jews stripping and showing their scars to the world like old beggars years after the sores have healed. The State of Israel has created an image of the courageous and self-reliant Jew standing up for his rights and fighting irrespective of odds which will be replaced by the old image of the sufferer crying his wrongs."[20] Ben-Gurion was sufficiently concerned about a worldwide backlash that he ordered the Mossad to monitor anti-Semitic incidents during the trial.[21]

In the United States, several Jewish leaders privately expressed concern about the trial's promoting the Jewish-victim image; all thought it likely that at least in some circles it would exacerbate anti-Semitism. The American Jewish Congress noted the widespread expectation that the trial might have a "boomerang effect" on Israel and American Jews. A Congress memorandum said it was "not altogether unfortunate" that the Soviet space flight and the Bay of Pigs invasion cut down coverage of the trial's opening; this "helped guard against disproportionate, spectacular and unnatural emphasis in the press."[22] An Anti-Defamation League memorandum to local affiliates urged that Jews not hold public meetings on the trial, believing that "the American people will have their fill of the matter without such events and they should not be encouraged."[23] The ADL also worried that the trial could "damage the image which many people have of Jews as a fair-minded and merciful people." It reassured its members that a death sentence was very unlikely: "this seems to be a universal Jewish attitude," it claimed. The ADL distanced itself from Eichmann's kidnapping and Israel's claim of jurisdiction, insisting that American Jews could not be held responsible for Israel's actions.[24] A representative of the Union of Orthodox Jewish Congregations worried that "visual reminders of the horrors and atrocities committed by the Nazis would have a negative effect upon an American audience by leading the general public to reject the victims of the atrocities."[25] One staff member of the American Jewish Committee echoed this concern, fearing that the presentation of "gruesome details" in the press and television might lead to the public's blaming Jews for inflicting these horrors on them.[26] Another was concerned that gentiles might learn that "for over 2,000 years Jews have cheered joyously in the synagogues when the Megillah readers annually told of the hanging of Haman and his ten sons with him."[27] Within the Committee there was a debate. Some wanted to condemn Israel's "violations of legal norms" and thus "uphold our good name among our natural allies, the liberals of America." Others worried that such a stand would alienate Jewish opinion.[28] In the end, no statement was issued.

Both the Anti-Defamation League and the American Jewish Committee (this was less true of the American Jewish Congress) worked to present the Eichmann case to the public in a universalist fashion. At the opening of the trial, Attorney General Gideon Hausner placed Eichmann in a genealogy that extended from Pharaoh through Haman, Chmielnicki, and Petlura. In Jerusalem, the Zionist moral — the Holocaust as the apotheosis of life in the Diaspora; the vulnerability of Jews outside the Jewish state — was repeatedly driven home. But according to the ADL, the Israeli government's intention was "to alert the conscience of the world to the fearful consequences of totalitarianism." The trial was "not a case of special pleading for Jews. . . . What happened to the Jews of Europe . . . can very well happen to other peoples oppressed by totalitarianism."[29] In a meeting with radio and television executives, whose purpose was to influence the spin put on trial coverage, the American Jewish Committee leader John Slawson told them that the object of the trial was to confront "hatred and totalitarianism . . . and their continued presence in the world today." The themes to be stressed were "this must never happen again anywhere to any people" and "this is the result of letting bigotry grow."[30]

With only a few exceptions, the backlash that the Jewish agencies anticipated never took place. Criticism of the Israelis fell off considerably between Eichmann's capture and the beginning of his trial, and even more after the trial began. Whatever the negative consequences of the trial's portrayal of Jews as victims, it was counterbalanced by the image of Israeli Jews as activists, for capturing and trying Eichmann. Though there were those who continued to mutter about Jewish vengefulness, such voices were heard less and less during the course of the affair. There seems little doubt that in the wake of the trial American Jews lost a good deal of their inhibitions about discussing the Holocaust. Aside from the discovery that the dangers of discussing it had been exaggerated, or had diminished over time, they had more to discuss: both in direct coverage of the trial and in historical feature stories surrounding it, much more information about the Holocaust became widely available.

In the end, for our purposes, the most important thing about the Eichmann trial was that it was the first time that what we now call the Holocaust was presented to the American public as an entity in its own right, distinct from Nazi barbarism in general. In the United States, the word "Holocaust" first became firmly attached to the murder of European Jewry as a result of the trial — which makes this a convenient point to address some controversies about its use.

In recent years it has been said that the word is hatefully inappropriate because its original meaning was a religious sacrifice consumed by fire; it thus represents a pernicious Christianization of Jewish suffering. On these grounds, as well as what might be called cultural-nationalist grounds, the Hebrew word for catastrophe, "*shoah*," is said to be superior — a purely Jewish and purely secular term, free of odious theological implications. In fact, archaic original meanings are relevant only to someone looking to pick a fight. The *Oxford English Dictionary* gives, as the first definition for "victim," "a living creature killed and offered as a sacrifice to some deity." Since long before the Second World War, "holocaust," in everyday usage, was almost always used to describe widespread destruction, particularly by fire, with no more theological freight than "victim." And "*shoah*," in the Hebrew Bible, was repeatedly used to describe punishments visited by God on the Jews — hardly a more palatable connotation.[31]

"Holocaust" began to be widely used in connection with the Nazi murder program in the 1960s, not as the result of a gentile plot, but as an import from Israel. Large numbers of American journalists, covering the Eichmann trial, learned to use the word that Israelis had for many years chosen to translate "*shoah*" into English. This choice dates, literally, from the establishment of the state. A reference in the preamble to the 1948 Israeli Declaration of Independence to "the Nazi *shoah*," appears, in the official Israeli English translation, as "the Nazi holocaust."[32] Starting in the late fifties, English-language publications of Yad Vashem regularly rendered "*shoah*" as "holocaust." The American journalist Paul Jacobs, in a dispatch from Jerusalem where he was covering the Eichmann trial, wrote of "The Holocaust, as the Nazi annihilation of European Jewry is called in Israel."[33] What had formerly been one of a variety of terms came, in the early sixties, to be (still usually uncapitalized) the most common one; by the late sixties (usually capitalized), it had become clearly dominant.

While it is true that the Eichmann trial was the first time that the American public was presented with the Holocaust as a distinct — and distinctively Jewish — entity, it was as yet by no means *as* distinct, or *as* distinctly Jewish, as it was later to become. It's not clear how much, if at all, the efforts of Jewish organizations to stress the trial as an indictment of totalitarianism influenced media coverage. The media were surely, on their own, disposed to frame it in this way, and did. (The media certainly did not stress, indeed rarely picked up on, the pointed Zionist lessons that the trial sought to drive home.) The theme emphasized more than any other in newspaper editorials was that of the Eichmann trial as a warning against the constant threat of totalitarianism — that is, Communism. Insofar as editorials noted the responsibility of the Western powers for the Holocaust, it was most often for the Allies' having failed to resist Hitler earlier; this was "the lesson of appeasement," which was applicable to dealing with the Soviets in the present. While some of the editorials in the Christian press were self-critical, at least as many were self-congratulatory, emphasizing the role of Christian rescuers. (Of seven articles on the Eichmann case that the news service of the National Catholic Welfare Conference distributed to Catholic papers, five dealt with this subject.) More generally, all segments of the press drew "Brotherhood Week" lessons from the trial: the phrase appearing more than any other was "man's inhumanity to man."[34] Midge Decter of the American Jewish Committee staff analyzed press reaction to the Eichmann case in an internal memorandum. She thought the universalism of American press commentary, its encapsulation within a "liberal democratic worldview," meant that the trial, "far from reminding the world of Jewish fate may, in America at least, have closed the books on it forever."[35]

There was an epilogue to the Eichmann trial: the furor occasioned by Hannah Arendt's 1963 series of articles on the trial in *The New Yorker*, which were published the same year in book form as *Eichmann in Jerusalem: A Report on the Banality of Evil*. The German Jewish émigré philosopher became, for a time, American Jewish Public Enemy Number One.[36] "Self-Hating Jewess Writes Pro-Eichmann Series for New Yorker Magazine" was the headline in one Jewish newspaper.[37] The Anti-Defamation League, in its campaign against what it called this "evil book," endorsed and sent to its branches scurrilous reviews of her work.[38] The Jewish Publication Society of America distributed a 400-page attack on Arendt's book.[39] What was all the fuss about?

Eichmann in Jerusalem is a dense work, probably best understood, in retrospect, as part of Arendt's ongoing inquiry into the nature of totalitarianism. For our purposes, what is interesting about the book is in what the controversy surrounding it reveals about Jewish sensibilities in the early sixties and the way in which it directs our attention to themes that continue to resonate in discussions about the Holocaust.

The first set of charges against Arendt had to do with her treatment of Eichmann himself. Rabbi Joachim Prinz, president of the American Jewish Congress, claimed that she sympathetically described him as a "sweet, misguided man."[40] One of the reviews distributed by the ADL, and described as "on target," said that Arendt regretted that Eichmann failed to "beat what the author clearly regards as a 'bum rap.' "[41] The historian Barbara Tuchman said that Arendt wrote out of "a conscious desire to support Eichmann's defense."[42]

All of this was not just false but the reverse of the truth. Arendt's loathing and contempt for Eichmann was manifest on every page of her book. Unlike many at the time, including many Jews, she quarreled neither with Israel's right to try him nor with the death sentence. The subtitle of Arendt's book refers to what Arendt found most striking about Eichmann, his terrifying ordinariness: that far from being the demonic monster portrayed by the Israeli prosecutor, he was a bland and mindless though all-too-efficient bureaucrat, motivated principally by personal ambition; that while he zealously carried out his orders, he had no influence on policy; that he was not even particularly anti-Semitic. By "the banality of evil" Arendt meant

> the phenomenon of evil deeds, committed on a gigantic scale, which could not be traced to any particularity of wickedness, pathology, or ideological conviction in the doer, whose only personal distinction was a perhaps extraordinary shallowness. . . . However monstrous the deeds were, the doer was neither monstrous nor demonic. . . . [Evil] can spread over the whole world like a fungus and lay waste precisely because it is not rooted anywhere. . . . It was the most banal motives, not especially wicked ones (like sadism or the wish to humiliate or the will to power) which made Eichmann such a frightful evil-doer.[43]

This was far from the dominant image, which was that of a monstrous sadist and a driven anti-Semite with sweeping powers. According to the ADL:

It is common knowledge that Eichmann himself deliberately planned the cold-blooded senseless liquidation of an entire people. . . . Eichmann personally conceived the idea of liquidating Jews as a means of "solving" the Jewish problem, and . . . these were the only orders he had from his Nazi bosses. . . . He probably could have successfully proposed mass Jewish emigration to his superiors [but] instead he selected the gas chamber, the crematorium and the soap factory.[44]

Arendt's scaled-down version of Eichmann was no doubt resented because it could be read as trivializing the Israeli accomplishment and undermining the claim that he was an appropriate symbol of eternal anti-Semitism. But more important, Arendt's picture of Eichmann upset long-standing and deeply rooted assumptions — never a recipe for popularity. Norman Podhoretz clearly spoke for many when he wrote that it "violates everything we know about the Nature of Man": "No person could have joined the Nazi party, let alone the S.S., who was not at the very least a *vicious* anti-Semite; to believe otherwise is to learn nothing about the nature of anti-Semitism. . . . No banality of a man could have done so hugely evil a job so well; to believe otherwise is to learn nothing about the nature of evil."[45] Podhoretz was also voicing a widespread feeling when he wrote that the traditional version — pure evil versus pure good — was preferable to her story: "complex, unsentimental, riddled with paradox and ambiguity."[46] Arendt's picture, said one writer in the *New York Times Magazine*, was "a natural outgrowth of the behavioristic, materialistic interpretation of the world, given 'scientistic' sustenance by the works of Darwin, Marx, Freud, Pavlov and others." It would, he said, be rejected by those who "accept the Judeo-Christian principle of free will."[47]

While the Eichmann trial was still going on, and well before Arendt had written on the subject, Stanley Milgram, a psychologist at Yale, was carrying out experiments that would lend considerable support to Arendt's argument, and then some. Arendt had said that under conditions of totalitarianism, ordinary moral scruples were likely to collapse, that obedience to the dictates of authority could lead quite normal and ordinary people to commit, or collaborate in, atrocious crimes. Milgram recruited citizens of the not-particularly-totalitarian city of New Haven to participate in what was described to them as an experiment in the influence of pain on learning. The experiment called on them, as "teachers," to inflict on a "learner" (in fact, an actor) what they believed were increasingly painful electric shocks in response to wrong answers. The upper range of shocks were described on the (fake) generator they operated as "Extreme Intensity Shock," "Danger: Severe Shock," and "XXX." At various points as one moved up the scale, the "learner" shouted "Get me out of here," "I can't stand the pain," and screamed in agony. More than 60 percent of the "teachers" continued (so they believed) to crank up the voltage to the top of the scale. Among those assigned the subsidiary role of reading out the questions, but not directly administering the shock, more than 90 percent continued to the end.[48]

In the mid-sixties Milgram's work began to reach an audience wider than the readership of the *Journal of Abnormal* [?] *Psychology.* By then, Arendt's version of Eichmann had also entered common discourse. In a post-experiment interview one "teacher" told Milgram: "As my wife said: 'You can call yourself Eichmann.' "[49] From the sixties on, a kind of synergy developed between the symbol of Arendt's Eichmann and the symbol of Milgram's subjects, invoked in discussing everything from the Vietnam War to the tobacco industry, and, of course, reflecting back on discussions of the Holocaust. It was in large part as a result of the acceptance of Arendt's portrait of Eichmann (with an assist from Milgram) that "just following orders" changed, in the American lexicon, from a plea in extenuation to a damning indictment.[50]

In the long run, almost all scholars have come to accept Arendt's thesis that the typical Holocaust perpetrator was "terrifyingly normal" and by no means a driven anti-Semite. Yehuda Bauer, an Israeli Holocaust historian, writes: "The Germans did not have to hate the Jews in order to kill them. . . . One suspects that, had they received instructions to murder all the Poles, or all the Frenchmen, they would have performed equally well."[51] For this reason, among others, scholars of the Holocaust have rejected the argument of Daniel Jonah Goldhagen that generations of systematic socialization into murderous hatred of Jews was a necessary condition for the Holocaust.[52] (It is a comforting argument: if such deep and long-standing hatred is a necessary precondition for mass murder, we're a lot safer than many of us think.) But the desire to frame the perpetrators in the traditional way remains powerful — which is why Goldhagen's book was a runaway bestseller.

The second set of charges against Arendt were in part as wrongheaded as the first, in part not without justification. These charges had to do with her treatment of Jewish behavior during the Holocaust. It was widely asserted that she had blamed Jews for going passively to their deaths. Nahum Goldmann, head of the World Zionist Organization, attacked Arendt before a New York audience for accusing the

Jewish victims of "cowardice and lack of will to resist."[53] At a special meeting of the National Community Relations Advisory Council, members wondered how to respond to what was described as her charge that Jews "went docilely to their graves."[54] (One suggestion was to renew efforts to have a Hollywood movie made about the Warsaw Ghetto Uprising.)[55] And the assertion endures: the entry on Arendt in the *Encyclopædia Judaica* says that in her book she blames victims for their "failure to resist."[56]

Again, what was attributed to her was the reverse of what she wrote. To be sure, in *Eichmann in Jerusalem* she had remarked in passing that Jewish resistance had been rare, weak, and ineffectual — but that, she said, was inevitable under ruthless totalitarian rule. "No non-Jewish group or people had behaved differently," she insisted. In her book she called the prosecutor's repeated questions to survivors about why they didn't resist "cruel and silly." She thought them a propagandistic attempt to contrast Israeli heroism and the alleged "submissive meekness" of Diaspora Jews.[57]

Why, then, was it so often claimed that she had blamed Jews for not resisting? One partial explanation is that by her offhand characterization of Jewish resistance as inconsequential, she was breaking with the myth of widespread Jewish resistance which, for various reasons, had been assiduously promoted since the war. This was not a Jewish peculiarity: all peoples who had lived (and died) in Hitler's Europe inflated their resistance credentials, the French being perhaps the best-known example. Passivity under the heel of the oppressor was regarded as discreditable, and history was adjusted accordingly. Jewish spokesmen had more reason than most to claim that their people had zealously resisted, since from the beginning there were many Jews who had scorned those who went "like sheep to the slaughter."[58] The cult of Jewish resistance was particularly strong in Israel, where the full name of Yad Vashem is "Yad Vashem Martyrs and Heroes Remembrance Authority"; the full name of Yom Hashoah is "Day of the Holocaust and of Heroism." (The heroism in question is almost always that of Zionist groups.) But in the United States as well, the breadth and depth of Jewish resistance was a major theme of what Holocaust commemoration there was — the anniversary of the Warsaw Ghetto Uprising being the principal occasion of memorialization. Thus the event most atypical of the Holocaust was made emblematic of it — suggestive evidence of the (quite unjustified) shame that many Jews felt because of the absence of substantial Jewish resistance. At the time of the Eichmann trial a top ADL official wrote that "perhaps a million . . . Jews were killed resisting the Nazi conqueror, fighting back against Hitler's juggernaut, dying *not* on their bedraggled knees but on their blood-soaked feet."[59]

Also, Arendt got caught up in the onslaught against two prominent Jewish authors who shortly before her book came out *had* written scornfully of "Jewish passivity," attributing to the Jews of Europe a craven and submissive attitude acquired over the centuries, even a "death wish." Bruno Bettelheim, in *Harper's Magazine*, chastised the Frank family for huddling defenseless in the secret annex. They should have bought a gun and killed the police who came for them. If Jews had resisted, he said, many fewer would have died.[60] Raul Hilberg's *Destruction of the European Jews* attracted a good deal of attention because it came out in the middle of the Eichmann trial. His book was filled with disparaging remarks about the Jewish failure to resist. Arendt, before her *New Yorker* articles appeared, had taken Bettelheim to task in the pages of a Zionist journal. She rejected his notion that Jews had failed to resist because of "ghetto thinking": "There is such a thing as an inverted chauvinism, and when discussing the wrongs of the Jewish people one must be careful not to fall into that trap. . . . Under these conditions all groups, social and ethnic, behaved alike. . . . Mr. Bettelheim looks for a Jewish problem where it does not exist."[61]

Despite this, Arendt got caught in the field of fire that Jewish writers directed at Hilberg and Bettelheim on the issue of resistance. In part this was because in her own book she had drawn on and praised Hilberg's scholarship. Most importantly, both Hilberg and Bettelheim supported what was by far the most controversial and provocative of the arguments in her book: that the leadership of European Jewry — in Germany, in the occupied countries of Western Europe, in the ghettos of the East — had culpably cooperated with the German murder program.[62]

"To a Jew," she wrote, "this role of the Jewish leaders in the destruction of their own people is undoubtedly the darkest chapter of the whole dark story."

> Wherever Jews lived, there were recognized Jewish leaders, and this leadership, almost without exception, cooperated in one way or another, for one reason or another, with the Nazis. The whole truth was that if the Jewish people had really been unorganized and leaderless, there would have been chaos and plenty of misery but the total number of victims would hardly have been between four and a half and six million people.

She wrote of this, she said, because "it offers the most striking insight into the totality of the moral collapse the Nazis caused in respectable European society . . . not only among the persecutors but also among the victims."[63]

Once again, it could be said that her point was being distorted by critics. Whereas Arendt wrote of leaders — always clearly distinguishing the mass of Jews from those who spoke and acted on their behalf — she was usually charged with having said that "the Jews" had cooperated.[64] The distinction is not unimportant. But unlike the other dimensions of the controversy, where her reasonable statements were turned upside down, in this matter her own statements were so unjustifiably sweeping, hyperbolic, provocatively expressed, and supported by often inaccurate factual statements that it is hard to get indignant about her receiving similar treatment.

A few aspects of the furious response to Arendt's assertion are noteworthy. The first was the frequent claim that on the subject of Jewish collaboration Arendt was saying something totally new. This wasn't true. Many published diaries and memoirs were filled with denunciations of officials of the Jewish Councils (*Judenräten*) and the ghetto police they employed as collaborators, traitors, and murderers. After a well-publicized trial in Israel, a government official was told by the judge that in his wartime dealings with the Nazis he had "sold his soul to the devil."[65] (The judgment was reversed on appeal.) Blanket condemnation of the Jewish Councils was a major theme of Menachem Begin's Herut Party throughout the fifties. Indeed, the very law under which Eichmann was tried had been instituted in Israel to punish Jewish collaborators. The Law for the Punishment of Nazis and Their Collaborators included Nazis as a matter of form, but there was no expectation that any would be bagged. Its real targets, everyone acknowledged, were collaborators among the survivors. Before Eichmann's capture, dozens of Jews in Israel had been prosecuted under the law. (Some were sentenced to death, though the sentences were commuted.)[66]

These questions did not loom as large in the United States, but they were hardly unknown — certainly not to those familiar with the diary and memoir literature, and certainly not within the survivor community. In the early fifties Jewish Communists used the term *"Judenrat"* for Jewish anti-Communists precisely because they knew it was regarded as a vile epithet among Jews.[67] But with only one exception known to me — an article in *Life* in 1950 about a New York rabbinic court proceeding against a surviving Jewish camp official accused of beating another prisoner to death — discussion of the phenomenon was confined to Jews.[68] Much of Arendt's offense was that she had written of these matters before a large gentile audience.

It is true that a great many Jews, and all survivors, were aware of the phenomenon she described. But awareness and willingness to confront are not the same thing. Raul Hilberg tells of presenting to his *Doktorvater* at Columbia, the tough-minded Marxist émigré scholar Franz Neumann, the portion of his dissertation that talked of how "the Jews had cooperated in their own destruction": "Neumann did not say that this finding was contradicted by any facts; he did not say that it was underresearched. He said, 'This is too much to take — cut it out.' I deleted the passage, silently determined to restore it to my larger work."[69]

The Holocaust had not, at this point, become as sacralized as it was subsequently to become. But there was already a great deal of visceral resistance to its being discussed in terms other than the confrontation of pure evil and pure virtue. Arendt's failure to abide by these norms — her insistence on stressing complexity and ambiguity — was clearly, and understandably, one of the things that gave the greatest offense. (There was also, to be sure, her sardonic mode of expression, which rubbed many the wrong way.)

A great deal of the harsh criticism directed at Arendt predicted dire consequences from what she had written. It was "a well of poisonous slander for all enemies of our people to draw from."[70] Arnold Forster of the Anti-Defamation League predicted that "anti-Semites will point to this Arendt document as evidence that Jews were no less guilty than others for what happened to six million of their co-religionists."[71] But it was not just a matter of anti-Semites; it also had to do with depletion of moral capital. A committee of the National Community Relations Advisory Council met to consider the impact of Arendt's work. Its members agreed that her conclusions would "furnish a ready 'out' for those Christians who have never faced up to their full responsibilities in permitting the Nazi holocaust to go unchallenged until it was too late."[72]

There are, I think, both bad and good reasons for refraining from sweeping judgments on individual Jews or Jewish institutions that "cooperated" with the murderers. One bad reason is commitment to a black-and-white distinction between diabolical perpetrators and saintly victims. While insisting that to confuse murderers with their victims is "a moral disease," Primo Levi emphasized the existence of a "gray zone."

> It is naive, absurd, and historically false to believe that an infernal system such as National Socialism sanctifies its victims: on the contrary, it degrades them, it makes them resemble itself. . . . The harsher the oppression, the more widespread among the oppressed is the willingness, with all its infinite nuances and motivations, to collaborate.[73]

Another bad reason is the cowardly injunction "Judge not lest you be judged," which if followed — it can't be — could only lead to a paralyzing relativism. Still another bad reason is that malicious people will cite your judgments for hateful purposes. There's no help for that. ("Even the Jew Yehuda Bauer," say the deniers, "admits that the figures for Auschwitz deaths were inflated.")

One good reason for avoiding sweeping judgments is that important distinctions, exceptions, qualifications, and nuances get swept away. Those intent on making what they think is an important theoretical point are likely to ignore this, as Arendt did, and as others do for other purposes. Another good reason for at least being very cautious about judging moral choices made under totalitarian terror is that in such circumstances choices are terribly constrained — hardly seem to the actors like choices at all. No one knew this better than Hannah Arendt, but Arendt the stern moralist triumphed over Arendt the sophisticated analyst.

The aftermath of the Arendt controversy saw a good deal of scholarly writing about the *Judenräten*. Much of it was originally undertaken to refute Arendt, but the evidence turned out to be ambiguous and contradictory. At an academic conference in Israel in the early 1980s, there seemed to be general acceptance of Saul Friedländer's suggestion that "*objectively* the *Judenrat* was probably an instrument in the destruction of European Jewry, but *subjectively* the actors were not aware of this function, and that even if they were aware, some of them — or even most of them — tried to do their best according to their very limited strategic possibilities in order to stave off the destruction."[74]

The final "Holocaust event" of the early sixties addressed an issue that is still very much alive: the "silence of Pope Pius XII" — his failure to publicly denounce the Holocaust during the war. Whereas nowadays this is something Jewish spokesmen discuss openly, and often angrily, in the early sixties leading Jewish organizations either refrained from comment or actively sought to make the issue go away.

What put the pope's silence on the agenda was the announcement that *The Deputy*, by the young German Protestant playwright Rolf Hochhuth, would be opening on Broadway early in 1964.[75] His play was a savage indictment of Pius's inaction, attributing it to his Germanophilia, his anti-Sovietism, and the preeminent importance he attached to the narrowest of Vatican interests. In Europe, the performance of the play had everywhere produced angry confrontations, sometimes including violence; the antagonists were usually Protestants and Catholics, with Jews on the sidelines. But America, for various reasons, was a different playing field.

Almost all Jewish organizations, particularly the Anti-Defamation League and the American Jewish Committee, were heavily involved in interreligious dialogue, whose agenda was "make nice" and "can't we all just get along?" *The Deputy* was definitely *not nice*, not a contribution to getting along. Catholic spokesmen publicly and privately called on their Jewish dialogue partners to put pressure on the Jewish producer and director to cancel the play, or at least to join them in denouncing it.[76] Implicitly they were saying that if the shoe was on the other foot — if what was at issue was a play sullying the reputation of the world's most venerated Jewish leader — Jews wouldn't hesitate to call on *them*. And Jewish groups' maneuvering room was limited by the fact that at the time of Pius's death in 1958 they had vied with each other in fulsome tributes to his wartime role in rescuing Jews.[77]

There was a more urgent consideration. All of this took place at the worst possible time: the height of tense politicking at Vatican Council II in Rome over a declaration repudiating anti-Semitism and absolving Jews of culpability in the death of Jesus. It was touch-and-go whether the declaration would be shelved or weakened, as clerical conservatives and churchmen from Arab countries wished. American prelates, reflecting their background in American ecumenism, were in the forefront of those pressing for adoption of the declaration. How would they respond to what many of them would be bound to interpret as a slap in the face from American Jews?

So . . . the American Jewish Committee did its best, albeit unsuccessfully, to prevent the play from going on — and made sure that church officials knew that it had tried. The Committee also attempted to get media executives to downplay the controversy.[78] The public statement it finally issued omitted a passage in earlier drafts that was mildly critical of Pius's silence, contenting itself with leaving the matter to "future historians."[79] The Anti-Defamation League went further: its foreign affairs expert, Joseph Lichten, wrote a pamphlet for the National Catholic Welfare Conference (which the ADL also distributed) defending Pius's silence. "A formal statement would have provoked the Nazis to brutal retaliation and would have substantially thwarted further Catholic action on behalf of Jews." The evidence, he said, suggested it was for the best.[80] A few other Jewish leaders also attacked the play: an official of the Jewish War Veterans said it would "serve no useful purpose except to continue 'the lie' about our brethren in the Catholic world."[81] Most refrained from comment, though there were individual Jewish leaders who supported the play, including a few officials of rabbinical organizations.[82] Some Jewish magazines, without engaging the support of their organizational sponsors, printed articles critical of Pius.[83]

Catholic spokesmen, if not completely appeased, seem overall to have been satisfied with the Jewish response. The play was not judged theatrically successful by most critics. Alfred Kazin was voicing a common reaction when he said it reminded him of "an anti-Nazi movie of the John Garfield period."[84] Plans for a national tour were canceled, whether because of pressure on theater owners, as the producer maintained, or on other grounds, it is impossible to say. In 1965 Vatican II finally did produce a declaration on anti-Semitism and deicide: not as strong as many had hoped, not as weak as many had feared. In the same year Pope Paul VI took the first steps toward the elevation of Pius XII to sainthood.

The Eichmann trial, along with the controversies over Arendt's book and Hochhuth's play, effectively broke fifteen years of near silence on the Holocaust in American public discourse. As part of this process, there emerged in American culture a distinct *thing* called "the Holocaust" — an event in its own right, not simply a subdivision of general Nazi barbarism. There was a shift in focus to Jewish victims rather than German perpetrators that made its discussion more palatable in the continuing cold war climate. Despite the fact that American Jews had taken no initiative in placing the Holocaust on the agenda in the early sixties, many experienced the end of silence on the subject as liberating. At the same time, as we've seen, "official" Jewish responses to the trial, to Arendt's book, and to Hochhuth's play were often nervous, embarrassed, and defensive — emblematic of widespread Jewish ambivalence toward public discussion of the Holocaust. This was soon to change dramatically, as the Holocaust came to be regularly invoked — indeed, brandished as a weapon — in American Jewry's struggles on behalf of an embattled Israel.

[8]

"A Bill Submitted 'for Sufferings Rendered'"

I<small>T HAS BECOME</small> a commonplace in recent years that Israel and the Holocaust are the twin pillars of American Jewish "civil religion" — the symbols that bind together Jews in the United States whether they are believers or nonbelievers, on the political right, left, or center. But through the mid-1960s Israel, like the Holocaust, didn't loom that large in American Jewish consciousness — at least not in public expressions of that consciousness. In the late sixties and early seventies, Israel became much more important to American Jews, and, in a set of spiraling interactions, concern with Israel was expressed in ways that evoked the Holocaust, and vice versa.

It had been the American Zionist movement that had energized American Jews on behalf of a Jewish national home in Palestine. But after the establishment of that home, American Zionism was deliberately eviscerated by Israeli Prime Minister David Ben-Gurion. Many American Zionist leaders had backed Ben-Gurion's opponents in Israel; in any case, for both fund-raising and lobbying purposes, he thought it more useful to establish relations with wealthier and more politically connected non-Zionist American Jews.[1] Though all American Jewish leaders, as well as their constituents, were generally supportive of Israel, their degree of attachment to the new state was very uneven. Nathan Perlmutter of the Anti-Defamation League later became a strong Zionist. Before 1967, he wrote in a memoir, he had been glad that Israel existed as a home for displaced Jews, but "I had no feelings of a 'Jewish homeland.' ... On a would-you-rather-visit list, Israel ranked behind Paris, England, Japan."[2] Lucy Dawidowicz, who worked for the American Jewish Committee, was also in later years a fervent supporter of Israel. In the 1950s she was a sharp critic of the new state, contrasting Israel's willingness to accept German reparations with its failure to take responsibility for displaced Palestinians. "Morality," she wrote, "cannot be that flexible."[3] Groups like the American Jewish Congress were more Israel oriented, but in 1961 its president, Joachim Prinz, was willing to declare that "Zionism is — for all practical purposes — dead."[4] At the time of the 1956 Sinai Campaign, American Jewish lobbying on behalf of Israel had been quiet and diffident; in the immediately following election, Eisenhower, who had sharply rebuked the Israelis, received a greater share of the Jewish vote than he had in 1952.[5] Despite their increasing prosperity, American Jews' donations to Israel steadily declined throughout the years before 1967. In a study conducted in the late 1950s, Jews in a midwestern suburb were asked what kinds of behaviors were essential to be considered a good Jew. "Support Israel" was listed by 21 percent, compared with 58 percent who listed "help the underprivileged."[6] While there's no way to measure just how important Israel was to American Jews through the mid-sixties, it was clearly less important than it later became.

However much or little American Jews thought or spoke of Israel in these years, to what extent was their support for Israel tied to the memory of the Holocaust? Here, too, it's hard to give a precise answer, except to say that the link was much looser than it later became.

After the establishment of Israel had provided a home for survivors of the Holocaust, there was a marked decline in the extent to which Israel and the Holocaust were connected in Jewish public discourse. To be sure, the Holocaust sometimes figured in fund-raising appeals for Israel, but this was much less true in the fifties and early sixties than it had been in the late forties, and than it would be from the late sixties on. Some American Zionists pressed the connection, but their overall influence is questionable. And those who attended closely to Israeli discourse — a small minority of American Jews — received mixed messages.

On the one hand, Israeli leaders claimed a certain symbolic ownership of the Holocaust. One assertion of this claim was the plan, at Yad Vashem, to grant posthumous Israeli citizenship to all those killed in Europe.[7] Israeli ownership was reasserted at the time of the Eichmann trial. Israel, Ben-Gurion said, "is the heir of the six million . . . the only heir. . . . If they had lived, the great majority of them would have come to Israel."[8] At the same time, several factors worked to minimize Israel's association with the European catastrophe. The way Israel represented itself before the sixties downplayed the Holocaust; looked to the future rather than the past; emphasized the discontinuity between the debased life of Jews in the Diaspora and the stalwart "new Jews" of Israel. Yom Hashoah — Holocaust Remembrance Day — was largely ignored, and school textbooks paid little attention to the Holocaust. In those years Israelis were as little inclined as American Jews to present Jews as victims.[9] The image of Israel held by most American Jews was not a land of memory-haunted survivors, but one typified by bronzed, blue-eyed young sabras, singing as they marched into the fields with hoes over their shoulders — "making the desert bloom."[10]

As is well known, the spring of 1967 was a dramatic turning point in American Jews' relationship to Israel. Less dramatically, and in a less thoroughgoing way, it marked an important stage in their changing relationship to the Holocaust.

In the escalating Middle East crisis, Arab spokesmen proclaimed their determination to "wipe Israel off the map" and "drive the Jews into the sea." One said that "the surviving Jews will be helped to return to their native countries," but, he added, "there will be very few survivors."[11] The great majority of American Jews, including many who had not previously shown the slightest interest in Israel, were in a state of high anxiety, and plunged into a flurry of rallies and fund-raising. In fact, Israel was hardly in serious peril. Shortly before the outbreak of war in June, President Lyndon Johnson's intelligence experts debated whether it would take a week or ten days for Israel to demolish its enemies.[12] But this was not the understanding of American Jews, for whom Israel was poised on the brink of destruction — and it is our perceptions of reality, not the reality itself, that shape our responses. Though there were surprisingly few explicit references to the Holocaust in American Jewish mobilization on behalf of Israel before the war, thoughts of a new Holocaust were surely present.[13] The Holocaust, for many, was suddenly transformed from "mere," albeit tragic, history to imminent and terrifying prospect.

Within a few days, despair turned to exhilaration as Israeli forces, humiliating their combined Arab adversaries, captured Jerusalem and the West Bank from Jordan, the Golan Heights from Syria, Gaza and the Sinai from Egypt. The Six Day War — and even more, its anxious prelude and triumphal aftermath — effected a permanent reorientation in the agenda of organized American Jewry. Israel moved to the top of that agenda — in fund-raising, in lobbying, and in electoral politics. Oscar Cohen, a long-time official of the Anti-Defamation League, wrote to a friend that by the 1970s organized American Jewry had become "an agency of the Israeli government . . . follow[ing] its directions from day to day."[14] Popular Jewish attitudes underwent a profound "Israelization." The hallmark of the good Jew became the depth of his or her commitment to Israel. Failure to fulfill religious obligations, near-total Jewish illiteracy, even intermarriage, were all permissible; lack of enthusiasm for the Israeli cause (not to speak of public criticism of Israel) became unforgivable. The change extended to language, as *kippa* replaced *yarmulke* and as Israeli (Sephardic) pronunciation of Hebrew — *Shabbat* instead of *Shabbos*, *bat* rather than *bas* mitzvah — became dominant. The presence of Israeli artifacts in the living room became as mandatory as a mezuzah on the doorpost. (In none of this was any knowledge of Israel required. A survey in the 1980s revealed that fewer than a third of American Jews knew that the archenemies Menachem Begin and Shimon Peres were members of different parties.)[15]

In American Jews' relationship to Israel, the Six Day War was the immediate and most important cause of a new closeness. As concerns the Holocaust, and the connections American Jews made between the Holocaust and Israel, it's harder to locate a single decisive moment. We have to look not just at the Six Day War but at the Yom Kippur War of 1973, as well as domestic developments (to be considered in the next chapter) that reinforced the impact of those events. But the Six Day War was certainly important. The fears of a renewed Holocaust on the eve of that war left their mark on American Jewish consciousness. Also important was the way the image of Jews as military heroes worked to efface the stereotype of weak and passive victims, which, as we've seen, had previously inhibited Jewish discussion of the Holocaust. (There were many jokes and cartoons about turning the faltering American military effort in Vietnam over to General Moshe Dayan.)

The "miraculous" victory of Israel also made it easier to integrate the Holocaust into Jewish religious consciousness. For Jews with any shred of traditional religious belief, the Holocaust had posed the most serious problem. This was not simply the age-old problem of theodicy, shared by all religious traditions: how one reconciles a God who is omniscient, omnipotent, and benevolent with the presence of enormous suffering. For religious Jews, the problem went beyond theodicy:

it was how to reconcile the Holocaust with the Covenant — God's special protective relationship with the Jewish people. There was the answer of traditionalists: that like previous catastrophes, the Holocaust had been another wake-up call from God to Jews who weren't abiding by their side of the covenant — "tough love." This explanation appealed to few Jews outside ultra-Orthodox circles; most found it hateful. A common response was evasion: the principal of one Jewish religious school is reported to have vetoed the teaching of the Holocaust because it "made God look bad."[16]

But in a way that seems to have appealed to many Jews, the Six Day War offered a folk theology of "Holocaust and Redemption." In Jacob Neusner's words, it was a salvation myth: "of the darkness followed by the light; of passage through the netherworld . . . then, purified by suffering and by blood, into the new age."

> The extermination of European Jewry could become *the Holocaust* only on 9 June when, in the aftermath of a remarkable victory, the State of Israel celebrated the return of the people of Israel to the ancient wall of the Temple of Jerusalem. On that day the extermination of European Jewry attained the — if not happy, at least viable — ending that served to transform events into a myth, and to endow a symbol with a single, ineluctable meaning.[17]

Rabbi Irving Greenberg was later to become director of the President's Commission on the Holocaust, which recommended the building of a museum in Washington. In the aftermath of the Six Day War, he wrote that it had given God a second chance:

> In Europe, He failed to do His task. . . . The failure to come through in June would have been an even more decisive destruction of the covenant. (When we heard the news of the outbreak of the war, a layman asked me: what will we do if we lose? My answer was: you will find a sign outside our synagogue that we are closed.)[18]

Among the most common ways of dealing with the Holocaust theologically has been the concept of *hester panim*, God's temporary "hiding of His face." To those so inclined, the outcome of the 1967 war served as proof that the hiding was over; He was back on the job.[19]

But the legacy of the Six Day War — in particular, the triumphal mood in the period after the war — did not point unambiguously toward the centering of the Holocaust in American Jewish consciousness. The war's outcome suggested that the fears of a renewed Holocaust, though understandable, had been misplaced. It appeared to teach the radical discontinuity between the bad old days of Jewish vulnerability and the new era of Jewish invincibility. To be sure, as Jacob Neusner suggested, the Holocaust, combined with the Six Day War, could now be integrated into a salvation myth. But such myths, in his words, tell of "the old being and the new, a vanquishing of death and mourning . . . the passing away of former things."[20] Had the victory of 1967 brought an end to Israel's travails, the Holocaust might have entered American Jewish consciousness in this fashion — as a subordinate, historicized and transcended element in a salvation myth. But that is not the way in which the Holocaust gained a central place in American Jewish consciousness. Rather, like many other national myths, it came to define an enduring, perhaps permanent, Jewish condition.

It was the Yom Kippur War of October 1973 that was decisive in converting many to this worldview. Though Israel was ultimately victorious, the victory came only after serious and terrifying early reverses and after substantial Israeli casualties. The escape from catastrophe was due in large measure to the airlifting of American supplies during the fighting. The implications of the war, for both Israelis and American Jews, were far-reaching. Illusions of Israeli invincibility and self-sufficiency were among the casualties of this war. A related casualty was the contrast, traditionally drawn by Zionists, between the vulnerability of Jews in the Diaspora, culminating in the Holocaust, and the security that Jews could find in a Jewish homeland. Clearly there was no place in the world *less* secure for Jews than in Israel.

And there was great concern over Israel's increasing isolation in the world. At the time of the Six Day War, most people in the West had hailed the Israeli victory. But for a variety of reasons, by 1973 Israel was becoming estranged even from erstwhile friends. The American government was still supporting Israel, but how sure could one be of the continuation of that support, particularly if it proved costly? From the standpoint of American foreign policy, strong backing of Israel could threaten the sought-after détente with the USSR. At home, with Arab states using oil prices as a political weapon, support of Israel could entail another kind of cost. Above all, how would the American people, just emerging from the Vietnam nightmare, respond to calls to make sacrifices to defend a small state, on the other side of the world, threatened by larger neighbors? A likely response was "Been there, done that."

Among American Jews (Israelis as well) the situation of a vulnerable and isolated Israel came to be seen as terrifyingly similar to that of European Jewry thirty years earlier. What in May 1967 had been a brief and soon-dissipated fear of a renewed Holocaust became an enduring specter. It was in the aftermath of the 1973 war that the song at the top of the charts in Israel was "The Whole World Is Against Us"; that, in the United States, Cynthia Ozick wrote "All the World Wants the Jews Dead." And though, as we'll see in the next chapter, there were other factors at work, it was at the same time that talk of the Holocaust not only "took off" in America but became increasing institutionalized.[21]

Sometimes, particularly in internal and informal Jewish discourse, connecting Israel's plight with the Holocaust was reflexive and unstudied: the association was made without any strategic calculation or consideration of its rhetorical effectiveness. We're not just looking at the sum total of private conversations, however, but at massive investments by Jewish communal organizations in promoting "Holocaust consciousness." Making strategic calculations, thinking about what means are likely to achieve desired ends, and developing effective programs on the basis of their conclusions is what communal leaders are chosen to do. Their concerns, and the choices they make about how to proceed, are influenced and constrained by the views of their constituents. But if they're successful in their work, they'll also be reshaping those views. After the process has been in operation for a while, it's impossible to disentangle the spontaneous and the contrived.

In the wake of the Yom Kippur War, American Jewish leaders were confronted with an agonizing problem, which was summed up by Leonard Fein, editor of the Jewish magazine *Moment*:

> A complex fear has taken hold of us since October of 1973. Its roots lie in our renewed awareness of Jewish vulnerability, now widely perceived as permanent, perhaps even ultimate. . . . The terrible isolation of Israel, the dramatic ascendance of the Arabs . . . Israel's near-total dependence on the United States — all these are aspects of our present gloom.
>
> We cast about uncertainly for a way of making the case for Israel, a way that will be sufficiently compelling to overcome the threat of an oil embargo, of Arab economic reprisal . . . a way sufficiently compelling to persuade a post-Vietnam America to assume the burdens and the risks of Israel's defense. . . . With the stakes so large, and the perils so manifest, we

search for the most powerful arguments. . . . We speak tentatively, testing the strength of one approach against another.[22]

As American Jewish leaders sought to understand the reasons for Israel's isolation and vulnerability — reasons that might suggest a remedy — the explanation commanding the widest support was that the fading of the memories of Nazism's crimes against the Jews, and the arrival on the scene of a generation ignorant of the Holocaust, had resulted in Israel's losing the support it had once enjoyed. Among those pressing this argument were the two top officials of the Anti-Defamation League, Arnold Forster and Benjamin Epstein, who laid it out in a widely discussed book written just after the Yom Kippur War.

> For a long while after World War II, sympathy for the six million Jewish victims of Nazi genocide . . . helped to open doors long closed to Jews here and abroad. Certainly the State of Israel was one direct beneficiary of world empathy with the Jewish victims of nazism. . . .
>
> In the postwar world . . . the time during which the non-Jewish world continued to view Jews as oppressed was incredibly short. Within twenty-five years after the photographs of the bestiality in the concentration camps shocked the world . . . Jews had ceased being victims.

It was the fact that the Holocaust had been forgotten, they argued, that had produced the "palpable erosion in worldwide sympathy and friendship for Jews." Jews, they concluded, were acceptable to the non-Jewish world only insofar as they were perceived to be victims. When they were no longer perceived as victims, the world found this "hard to take" and mounted an effort "to render them victims anew."[23]

We are all attracted to explanations that make clear that our troubles are someone else's fault, that we are blameless. In fact, the most important reason for Israel's declining standing wasn't anyone's fault. It was the result of a massive shift in global currents of thought between the initiation and the coming to fruition of the Zionist venture. When political Zionism was born, in the 1890s, it was at the high tide of European expansion, when nothing seemed more right and proper than European settlement in non-European areas, the establishment of outposts of European sovereignty around the world, and bringing Western enlightenment to the benighted East. Zionism was not simply or merely an example of this phenomenon — far from it — but it was surely *also* that. Indeed, Theodore Herzl argued that a Jewish state in Palestine would be an outpost of Western civilization against Eastern barbarism, and many Christian supporters of Zionism continued to see it in that way. By the time Israel was established in 1948, the tide was turning, and over the next generation this became a tidal wave, as colonial empires were swept away, as the revolt of non-European peoples against Europeans in their midst became à la mode. In the 1950s, Israel's Suez venture, undertaken in partnership with the former imperial powers of Britain and France, was almost universally condemned as an anachronistic exercise in neo-colonialism. "Settler regime" became a term of abuse. And the turnaround was politically institutionalized, as the UN General Assembly came to be dominated by representatives of scores of non-European countries recently liberated from European dominion.

Before 1967, all of this had had some effect on Israel's global standing, but the problem wasn't that serious. Israel had cordial relations with a number of newly independent African states. Then came its smashing victory — and territorial expansion — in the Six Day War. For Jews, the victory of tiny Israel over its larger neighbors recalled David and Goliath. For many around the world it summoned up bitter memories of previous cases (Cortés in Mexico, Clive in India) in which a small force of Europeans had conquered "the natives." Extending the colonial analogy, as many were inclined to do, Israel had now established itself as the ruler of more than a million Palestinians in the West Bank and Gaza. Immediately after the Six Day War, David Ben-Gurion, in retirement, pleaded with his countrymen to return the captured territories on any terms obtainable. Their retention, he said, would distort, or even destroy, the Jewish state.[24] He was ignored. Within a year of the war, Israel began the creation of "facts on the ground" with ever more Jewish settlements in the newly acquired lands. Israeli Prime Minister Golda Meir, in words reminiscent of "a land without people for a people without a land," declared in 1969 that Palestinians didn't exist.[25] There was Israel's rejection of Egyptian President Anwar Sadat's peace overtures in the early seventies. There were incidents like the Israeli attack on a Libyan airliner in early 1973, which resulted in the deaths of a hundred civilian passengers. The point here is not to argue that after 1967 Israel was to blame for all the problems of the Middle East, which was definitely not true — there were crimes and blunders aplenty on the other side. Rather, it is to suggest that explaining Israel's declining world standing didn't require hypotheses about "fading memories of the Holocaust."

Sympathy for Jewish survivors of the Holocaust had certainly been among the factors that in 1947 led the United Nations to promote the establishment of a Jewish state in Palestine. But that decision had given equal weight to the claims of the Palestinians, which is why the UN had voted to *divide* the land. After 1967, and particularly after 1973, much of the world came to see the Middle East conflict as grounded in the Palestinian struggle to, belatedly, accomplish the UN's original intention. There were strong reasons for Jewish organizations to ignore all this, however, and instead to conceive of Israel's difficulties as stemming from the world's having forgotten the Holocaust. The Holocaust framework allowed one to put aside as irrelevant any legitimate grounds for criticizing Israel, to avoid even considering the possibility that the rights and wrongs were complex. In addition, while American Jewish organizations could do nothing to alter the recent past in the Middle East, and precious little to affect its future, they *could* work to revive memories of the Holocaust. So the "fading memories" explanation offered an agenda for action.

Of course, invoking the Holocaust was far from the only rhetorical strategy pursued in mobilizing support for Israel. Depending on the audience and the context, one might argue that Israel was an important American strategic asset or stress the support given to Israel's enemies by the Soviet Union. With some Christian audiences, biblical claims were effective. And the belief that talking about the Holocaust would help Israel was, as we'll see, far from the only reason there came to be so much "Holocaust programming" by Jewish organizations. It's relatively easy to find instances of the purposive introduction of the Holocaust into discussions of the Middle East, harder to say how often the latent function of Holocaust discourse was to firm up support for Israel. There are occasional indications. Only a few months after the top officials of the Anti-Defamation League had proclaimed that it was fading memories of Nazism's crimes against the Jews that accounted for Israel's isolation, the ADL decided to embark on an ambitious venture in Holocaust programming. Its public relations consultant submitted a memorandum on the shape the program should take. The memo concluded by insisting that everything done should be "against the background of a powerful *J'Accuse* that is now submitting its bill 'for Sufferings Rendered.' "[26]

There wasn't one unified discourse connecting the Holocaust to Israel — there were many, with different authors, taking different forms, addressed to different audiences, emphasizing different themes. To the extent that these various approaches succeeded with their targeted audiences, the overall effect was more than the sum of its parts. Insofar as the Middle East imbroglio could be seen in a Holocaust framework, its complex and ambiguous rights and wrongs faded into the background. Current conflicts were endowed with all the black-and-white moral clarity of the Holocaust, which came to be, for the Israeli cause, what Israel was said to be for the United States — a strategic asset. Holocaust deniers, according to David Singer of the American Jewish Committee, seek to "rob the Jewish people and the State of Israel of their moral capital."[27] The wrong interpretation of Nazi atrocities could have the same effect: Edward Alexander complained that those who "universalized" the Holocaust sought to "plunder moral capital" that Jews had accumulated.[28] Others complained of the "kidnapping" or "appropriating" of what it became increasingly common to call the "moral capital" derived from the Holocaust.[29] The leader of one Jewish organization claimed that the presence of Christian symbols at Auschwitz "could ultimately affect Israel," since much of the Jewish state's legitimacy "is based on assumptions about what happened to Jews during the Holocaust."[30]

Accordingly, particular linkages were often less important than a diffuse, symbolic connection. Thus, when the American Israel Public Affairs Committee (AIPAC) was lobbying against the sale of American aircraft to Saudi Arabia, it sent a copy of the novel based on the TV series *Holocaust* to every member of Congress.[31] Oscar Cohen of the ADL advised the president of the National Conference of Christians and Jews regarding Holocaust activities sponsored by that organization:

> Unless there is some relationship between the Holocaust and the position of Jews today, I feel that we . . . gain very little from these Holocaust conferences how wonderful though they may be. . . . Specifically I would refer to Israel and the dangers which confront that nation as well as the support it must receive. This subject in conjunction with discussions of the Holocaust make the conferences and colloquia tremendously more meaningful.[32]

Wolf Blitzer, reporting on a gathering of Holocaust survivors in Washington, noted that while Israeli officials and American Jewish political activists were "always careful . . . to characterize it as a nonpolitical event," and while there was "a deliberate effort not to go too far in

making the connection," they were agreed that "raising public awareness of the Holocaust . . . was bound to generate heightened sympathy
and support for Israel."[33] A similar sentiment was expressed by Hyman
Bookbinder when serving as a member of President Jimmy Carter's
Commission on the Holocaust. He expressed the hope that its recom-
mendations on a memorial would "contribute to sustaining and increasing an American consciousness and conscience which is essential
to maintaining our commitment to Israel." He immediately added that
this wasn't the same thing as "desiring that the Commissioners get involved in a conscious effort in support of Israel."[34] Within two years he
seems to have changed his mind about this restriction. At a time when
West Germany was considering the sale of arms to Saudi Arabia,
Bookbinder wrote to the German ambassador to the United States in
his capacity as a member of the U.S. Holocaust Memorial Council —
though he was not, he made clear, speaking for the council. Plans for
the Washington museum were now being developed, he said. "How
Germany will be treated in that museum might well be affected by the
decision you make pertaining to the sale of arms to Saudi Arabia."[35]

Beyond a diffuse relationship between the Holocaust and Israel's
cause, specific themes were developed. One was connecting Arabs in
general, and Palestinians in particular, with Nazism. In part this was
just a matter of rhetorical flourishes. ("The checkered kaffiya of the
PLO has replaced Hitler's blackshirt.")[36] In part it was a trope of shlock
fiction. In Leon Uris's *Exodus* (both the novel and the film), Palestinian terrorism is masterminded by an escaped Nazi in the background.
In dozens of thrillers (like Frederick Forsyth's *The Odessa File*), unre-
pentant Nazis collaborate with Arabs to destroy Israel. But serious arguments were also advanced about continuity between Nazism and
the Palestinian movement. "The Arabs cannot pretend they played no
role in the Holocaust," said I. L. Kenen, the head of AIPAC.[37] "The
Palestinians, or many of them," wrote Leon Wieseltier, "were Hitler's
little helpers in the Middle East."[38] The claims of Palestinian complicity in the murder of the European Jews were to some extent a defensive
strategy, a preemptive response to the Palestinian complaint that if Israel was recompense for the Holocaust, it was unjust that Palestinian
Muslims should pick up the bill for the crimes of European Christians.
The assertion that Palestinians were complicit in the Holocaust was
mostly based on the case of the Mufti of Jerusalem, a pre–World
War II Palestinian nationalist leader who, to escape imprisonment by

the British, sought refuge during the war in Germany. The Mufti was in many ways a disreputable character, but postwar claims that he played any significant part in the Holocaust have never been sustained.[39] This did not prevent the editors of the four-volume *Encyclopedia of the Holocaust* from giving him a starring role. The article on the Mufti is more than twice as long as the articles on Goebbels and Göring, longer than the articles on Himmler and Heydrich combined, longer than the article on Eichmann — of all the biographical articles, it is exceeded in length, but only slightly, by the entry for Hitler.

The themes in Holocaust discourse used more often than any others in support of Israel were "the world's silence," "the world's indifference," and "the abandonment of the Jews." These had been discussed from time to time since 1945, but almost exclusively in internal Jewish talk; they didn't figure much in remarks directed to a gentile audience.[40] This changed somewhat in 1967. During the period of anxiety before the Six Day War a leaflet distributed at Yale exhorted Christians that "because of their special ties to the people of Israel, they cannot again be silent when their existence is being threatened."[41] After Israel's victory, some Jewish leaders who had been involved in ecumenical dialogues were angered by the "silence and indifference" of Christian church groups during the crisis, and talked of suspending such dialogues. But the anger soon abated, particularly as the Jewish participants came to acknowledge privately that they could hardly blame Christians for not realizing how important Israel was to American Jews, since they had never made that clear — indeed, to some extent had not realized it themselves. The initial outraged reaction was, in any case, confined to fairly narrow circles.[42] Most Jews were gratified at how supportive their gentile neighbors had been.[43] By coincidence, 1967 saw the serialization in *Look* magazine of Arthur Morse's *While Six Million Died*, a searing indictment of America's wartime behavior. When Morse's book was published the following year it was well and widely reviewed in the Jewish and general-circulation press without (so far as I have found) the suggestion that its subject had any contemporary relevance to Israel's situation. For, in the triumphal mood following the Six Day War, it didn't seem to have any.

In the radically transformed situation after 1973, charges of wartime silence, indifference, and abandonment came to seem very relevant indeed. Beginning after the Yom Kippur War, they moved to the center of American Holocaust discourse. Elie Wiesel wrote of being, for the first time in his adult life, "afraid that the nightmare may start all over again." For Jews, he said, "the world has remained unchanged . . . indifferent to our fate."[44] Martin Peretz thought "indifference" the wrong word to describe America's role during the Holocaust; it had been "acquiescence and perhaps even complicity," and he warned that this might be true again if Israel was threatened with destruction.[45] In the midst of concern that President Carter was being too "evenhanded" in the Middle East, David Wyman concluded an article on the wartime failure to bomb Auschwitz by observing that American inaction in the face of the Jews' plight carried lessons for the present.[46] When Pope John Paul II met with Yasir Arafat, an editorial writer for *The New Republic* was reminded of "the indifference of Pius XII to the extermination of the Jews."[47] The popular notion that the world in general, and the United States in particular, had supported the birth of Israel out of guilt was important here. The very existence of Israel was thus *proof* of the world's guilt. And if that guilt had been partially expiated by Israel's creation, full expiation — if such were possible — demanded continuing support for Israel.

Not all invocations of the Holocaust in support of Israel were aimed at gentiles. Often they were directed at Jews, to spur them to greater efforts on Israel's behalf, to see that new generations drew the correct lessons from the catastrophe. The slogan "Never again" was an exhortation Jews directed at themselves. "Never again, we meant, would we let others fool us or would we fool ourselves about the intention of those who intended to destroy the Jews," Milton Himmelfarb said. "Never again would we lean on that broken reed, enlightened opinion. Never again would we do less than all we could do. Never again would we expose ourselves to our own reproaches for having done less."[48]

From the late sixties on, talk about "our timidity," "our cowardice," and "our failure" figured prominently in American Jewish discourse about the Holocaust. The explicit moral was the need to behave differently in the face of dangers to Israel. It's worth remarking that what was, on the surface, self-reproach was in fact self-aggrandizement: we today, unlike they then, are *not* timid, *not* cowardly, will *not* fail. And this was largely an internal discourse, because, if pressed too far, the argument that American Jews had not demanded action during the Holocaust tended to undermine the indictment of the American government for not having acted.[49]

"Can You Appreciate Israel If You Haven't Seen Auschwitz?" This was the headline of a Jewish newspaper's report on the March of the Living, in which thousands of Jewish adolescents tour death camps in Poland, where they commemorate Yom Hashoah, then are flown to Israel, where they celebrate Independence Day.[50] American teenagers join Jewish youths from around the world in a meticulously orchestrated "Holocaust to Redemption" pageant in which the Zionist message is driven home. At Auschwitz, an American rabbi, Shlomo Riskin, tells them: "The world is divided into two parts: those who actively participated with the Nazis and those who passively collaborated with them."[51] At Maidanek, another rabbi informs the kids that the camp could become operational again within a few hours.[52] Armed Israeli security guards who accompany the tour do everything possible to convince the youngsters that they're in constant danger in Poland. "Run straight to the buses. Don't stop for anything."[53] The kids get the message. A participant from Cleveland: "Six million were killed by a country — Germany — where Jews were living the good life. I hate to draw the parallel, but Jews are living the good life in America."[54] "I don't see any place for Jews in the Diaspora," said another student.[55] A California student: "We are leaving this awful place tonight and tomorrow we will be in Israel. All I want to do is go home and I realize now that tomorrow I will be home, my real home, Israel."[56] "I'm so scared, I can't go on, I want to be in Israel already," said a girl from Connecticut."[57] The Israeli journalist Yossi Klein Halevi reported "feeling sick" as a Yad Vashem official delightedly described the tearful attachment to Israel of a girl who had just returned from a tour of the camps. "Do we think we can scare kids into Zionism?" he asked.[58] The tentative answer, based on surveys of March of the Living participants, appears to be yes.[59] One Jewish educator, commenting on the march, concluded that the participants "achieved a Zionist perspective which many hours in suburban Jewish classrooms could not transmit."[60]

In retrospect — though it was quite a while before this became clear — the peak of using the Holocaust to mobilize support for Israel came in the late 1970s. What made this difficult to see was that sheer momentum kept the practice going for some time thereafter. In the years immediately following the Yom Kippur War, the sense of Israel's vulnerability, of its isolated and beleaguered situation, was nearly universal within American Jewry, which made the use of Holocaust imagery almost a reflex.

But from the late 1970s on, the parallels between the circumstances of Jews in Hitler's Europe and in the contemporary Middle East came to seem less and less appropriate. The 1979 Camp David accords, signed by Israeli Prime Minister Menachem Begin and Egyptian President Anwar Sadat, split off the largest and most powerful Arab state from the anti-Israel alliance. Sadat was among those Arab leaders who had been described by American Jews as a Nazi because, as an anti-British Egyptian nationalist leader during World War II, he had seen Germany as a de facto ally. But could the man clasped by Menachem Begin in a warm embrace really be "the Hitler of the Nile"?

None of this, of course, led Begin to lessen his invocations of the Holocaust: throughout his premiership (1977–1983) it appeared constantly in his speeches. If West German Chancellor Helmut Schmidt spoke of the rights of Palestinians, Begin snapped back that Schmidt, a Wehrmacht officer in World War II, had "remained faithful to Hitler until the last moment."[61] The Palestine Liberation Organization was a "neo-Nazi organization."[62] All of this reached a peak during the 1982 Lebanon War. Inflicting massive devastation on the civilian population of Beirut was, in Begin's view, justified, because 1982 was just like 1945: Arafat in Beirut was Hitler in his bunker under the Reichschancellery.[63] There were those American Jews who, taking their cue from Begin, became even more prone to describe the conflict in the Middle East in the language of the Holocaust. But, overall, Begin's promiscuous use of such imagery probably tended to discredit it. Israel's previous wars had had the wholehearted backing of the Israeli population. In 1982 the country was deeply divided, and many Israelis thought Begin's Holocaust obsession had led to the ill-fated venture. An article in the *Jerusalem Post* concluded by observing that the war's epitaph would be "Here lies the international stature and moral integrity of a wonderful people. Died of a false analogy."[64] This was an argument often advanced by American writers as well. "How Much Past Is Enough?" asked Roger Rosenblatt in *Time*. "At what point does a devotion to history cease to be a weapon against present and future error, and begin to cripple those who seek its protection?"[65]

Questions of the Holocaust came into discussions of the Middle East in an unanticipated and embarrassing way with the massacre of Palestinians — including many old men, women, and children — by Christian Phalangists at the Sabra and Shatila refugee camps. The surrounding Israeli forces dispatched the Phalangists into the camps, illuminated the scene with flares, and later claimed not to have known what was going on. David Shipler wrote in the *New York Times* that "to a country that rose out of Hitler's death camps, the answers 'We did not do it' and 'We did not know' are not enough. To a people who remember that six million Jews were slaughtered as others turned their backs, the standards of behavior are more exacting, the questions more troubling."[66] Similar remarks appeared elsewhere in the American press.[67]

Throughout the 1980s, and particularly after the beginning of the Palestinian uprising (*intifada*) in 1987, the Holocaust framework for thinking about Israel's situation grew ever more implausible. Israel was by now clearly the dominant military power in the region. It was manifest that Israel's security problems derived less and less from hostile foreign forces, more and more from its prolonged military rule over a million and a half Palestinians. Americans were repeatedly bombarded with television images of Israeli troops shooting and beating young rock-throwing Palestinian protesters. There was widespread reporting of Israeli Defense Minister Yitzhak Rabin's recipe for dealing with protesters: "force, might, beatings"; of Prime Minister Yitzhak Shamir's strategy: "to recreate the barrier of fear between Palestinians and the Israeli military . . . put the fear of death into the Arabs of the area."[68]

Calling Israelis "the new Nazis," as some Communist bloc and Third World spokesmen did, understandably and justifiably outraged Jews. Nazi Germany was neither the first nor the last foreign occupying regime to behave brutally toward those whom it dominated. Even democratic regimes — the British in India, the French in Algeria — wound up committing atrocities when repressing popular nationalist insurgency. But for a number of American Jews and Israelis, Nazi imagery came to mind — though it was always introduced apologetically and in highly qualified fashion. An American rabbi: "We condemn the silence of good people during the Nazi era. There is certainly no genocide in Israel. Such comparisons are obscene. [But] the storm troopers did not begin with the ovens, but with beatings in the streets."[69] An Israeli, reporting on his annual reserve service in Gaza at an internment camp for Palestinians:

> The unjust analogy with those other camps of fifty years ago won't go away. It is not suggested by anti-Israel propaganda. It is in the language the soldiers use as a matter of course. . . . And I, too, who have always abhorred

this analogy, who have always argued bitterly with anyone who so much as hints at it, I can no longer stop myself. . . . I go over and over again . . . the list of differences. There are no crematoria here, I remind myself. . . . But then I realized that the problem is not in the similarity — for no one can seriously think that there is a real similarity — but that there isn't enough lack of similarity.[70]

It was a small minority who ventured to say such things (smaller in the United States than in Israel), and, as in these examples, the parallels were typically advanced tentatively and somewhat guiltily. That they could be put forward at all was emblematic of the loss of legitimacy of the older framework, which saw Israelis as potential victims of an Arab-sponsored holocaust.

As that older framework declined in mainstream Jewish discourse, it came increasingly to be the hallmark of Jewish hawks in opposing Jewish doves. This development began well before the *intifada*. In the spring of 1978, at a large demonstration in Tel Aviv, the Israeli organization Peace Now urged flexibility in negotiating with the Palestinians. In the United States, Americans for a Safe Israel responded by running an advertisement showing the piled-up bodies of Holocaust victims, described as "Six Million Jews Who Were Not Intransigent."[71] In the aftermath of the Lebanon War, Norman Podhoretz accused those Jews who had criticized it of granting Hitler a "posthumous victory."[72] Rabbi Richard Rubenstein wrote that the *intifada* made the Holocaust more relevant than ever as a "reminder of the fate that awaits Israel should its defenses ever falter."[73] In 1992, when Prime Minister Yitzhak Rabin urged Jews to talk more about friends than enemies, the *New York Times* columnist A. M. Rosenthal wrote that this was "condescending to anybody, but to Israeli Holocaust survivors, insulting." (Henry Siegman, head of the American Jewish Congress, replied: "I am a Holocaust survivor, and I do not find Mr. Rabin's advice insulting. I find it absolutely liberating.")[74]

Ideas have consequences — not necessarily the consequences intended by those who promote the ideas. If Arabs are really latter-day Nazis, surely it's a good idea to kill them before they kill you. One who took this to heart was the Holocaust-obsessed Baruch Goldstein. Shortly before his murderous rampage in Hebron, the Brooklyn born and bred physician told Israeli interviewers that "again, the Arab Nazis attack the Jew."[75] And if the Arabs are Nazis, there is a well-established category for Jews who urge accommodation with them. Abraham

Foxman of the Anti-Defamation League was a member of an Orthodox congregation whose rabbi, in 1995, urged Jews not to listen to "the
blatherings of the Rabin Judenrat."[76] Messages of this kind — even
more common in Israel than in the United States — were, as we know,
heeded by Rabin's assassin, Yigal Amir.[77]

In Israel, even before the *intifada*, there had been those who worried about the consequences of obsession with the Holocaust for public debate and public policy. The novelist Amos Oz, invoking an ancient enemy of the Hebrews, asked whether, along with an obligation
to remember, there wasn't also a right to forget.

> Are we . . . to sit forever mourning for our dead? to sit behind barred doors
> and shuttered windows, telephone disconnected, our backs to the wicked
> world and our faces to the awful past, our backs to the living and our faces
> to the dead, to sit thus, day and night, and to remember what was done
> unto us by Amalek, until the coming of the Messiah — or until the second
> coming of Amalek?[78]

In the first year of the *intifada*, the distinguished Israeli philosopher
Yehuda Elkana, who had been in Auschwitz as a child, published "A
Plea for Forgetting." The Holocaust's "lesson" that "the whole world is
against us," that "we are the eternal victim," was, for Elkana, "the tragic
and paradoxical victory of Hitler." This lesson, he thought, had contributed to Israeli brutalities in the West Bank and to the unwillingness
to make peace with the Palestinians.

> It may be that it is important for the world at large to remember. I am not
> even sure about that, but in any case it is not our problem. Every nation,
> including the Germans, will decide their own way and on the basis of their
> own criteria, whether they want to remember or not.
>
> For our part, we must *forget*! Today I see no more important political
> and educational task for the leaders of this nation than to take their stand
> on the side of life, to dedicate themselves to creating our future, and not to
> be preoccupied from morning to night, with symbols, ceremonies, and
> lessons of the Holocaust. They must uproot the domination of that his-
> torical "remember!" over our lives.[79]

The very moderate (and very religious) Israeli political scientist
Charles Liebman wrote that the way the Holocaust was interpreted in
Israel "reinforces and legitimates closed-mindedness, unrealistic foreign policies and barbaric behavior toward Arabs."[80] After the Hebron
massacre, Ze'ev Chafets, who had been head of the government press

office under Menachem Begin, wrote that "dwelling on genocide may be a good fund-raising strategy, but it also encourages an us-against-the-world mentality that deranged zealots like Benjy Goldstein translate into a religious obligation to murder."[81] After Rabin's assassination in 1995, three prominent Holocaust survivors in the United States — Abraham Foxman, Benjamin Meed, and Miles Lerman — issued a statement deploring "the use of Holocaust imagery in argument about the Arab-Israeli peace process. . . . Applying the vocabulary of the Holocaust — which is intended to evoke deeply felt emotions and forceful responses — inflamed the atmosphere and helped to stir passions beyond control. Language matters."[82]

Invocations of the Holocaust in discussing Israel's situation, once common, have for various reasons now become rare, except at the hawkish end of the spectrum. Sometimes, as we've seen, for American Jews thinking about the Middle East in a Holocaust framework was spontaneous and unstudied. But it was also a deliberate strategy for mobilizing support for Israel among American Jews, among the general American public, and in the American government. How effective has it been?

The first thing to say is that any judgment is bound to be speculative — this isn't a realm in which anything can be proven. At least through the late 1980s it seems likely that it *was* effective with American Jews. Probably the most powerful argument was that American Jews during World War II had been cravenly silent and that — like God — they were now given a second chance. The peaks of monetary contributions to Israel were in 1967 and 1973 when the Jews of Israel were thought to be on the eve of another Holocaust. If American Jews were, once again, and through no merit of their own, to be spared the fate of Jews in danger, at least they could give — and demonstrate. I've said earlier that one of the consequences of placing Israel's situation in a Holocaust framework was to invest the tangled Middle East conflict with the moral clarity of the Nazi period. But before the 1982 Lebanon War there is little reason to believe that even without the Holocaust framework, American Jews would have seen Israel's situation in other than black-and-white terms. And since then, while remaining on the whole supportive of Israel, increasing numbers of American Jews no longer see things as quite so black-and-white. This is both cause and effect of the diminishing inclination to see the Middle East through

Holocaust lenses. But at least for many years, the Holocaust connection almost certainly did energize Jews on Israel's behalf; in a vestigial way, it probably still does.

As concerns the American gentile population, there doesn't seem much reason to believe that the Holocaust has substantially influenced public opinion toward Middle Eastern conflicts. The very idea of "public opinion" on such questions is something of an illusion. Israel's cause has never much concerned the American public, whose interest in international affairs is usually limited to those situations which directly engage American interests — and troops. If there has been, over the years, a generally pro-Israel tilt among Americans, this had mostly to do with the fact that Israel was aligned with the West in the cold war; to an unknowable but probably significant extent, it has reflected pervasive, often racist anti-Arab attitudes. The memory of the Holocaust has probably tended to inhibit public criticism of Israel. (The Holocaust made most Americans bend over backward to avoid anything that could be represented, or misrepresented, as anti-Semitism.) But earlier there wasn't that much criticism of Israel to inhibit; in recent years, criticism hasn't been that inhibited.

There remains the most important question of all: the extent to which invoking the Holocaust has affected U.S. government policy. Here again, nothing can be proven. The question is how *plausible* it is to believe that American policy toward Israel has been shaped by the memory of the Holocaust. Not very. It was when the Holocaust was freshest in the minds of American leaders — the first twenty-five years after the end of the war — that the United States was *least* supportive of Israel and more interested in overtures to Arab states. It was not when Israel was perceived as weak and vulnerable, but after it demonstrated its strength, in the Six Day War, that American aid to Israel changed from a trickle to a flood. And the president who forged the close American alliance with Israel, and inaugurated the massive annual grants to Israel, was Richard Nixon, of all postwar American political leaders surely the one least likely to be moved by moral or sentimental considerations. For Nixon — and this was true of his successors as well — Israel was supported primarily because it was a force to be deployed against the USSR and its clients in the Middle East. After the end of the cold war, Israel continued to be supported, although somewhat less fervently, in an effort to preserve peace in the region through maintenance of balance, and for other services Israel could perform.[83]

In addition to the geopolitical considerations that governed decisions in the executive branch, there has been the much-vaunted "Jewish lobby," centering around the American Israel Public Affairs Committee. AIPAC, operating through hundreds of political action committees, has lavishly rewarded members of Congress who have supported Israel and ruthlessly punished those who have been critical of Israeli policies. Its most dramatic triumph (though far from the only one) was the 1984 defeat of Senator Charles Percy, chairman of the Foreign Relations Committee, who had spoken out in favor of Palestinians once too often. "All the Jews in America, from coast to coast, gathered to oust Percy," boasted AIPAC's director Tom Dine. "And American politicians . . . got the message."[34] Yet the significance of AIPAC's work, and that of other formal and informal Jewish lobbying efforts, can easily be exaggerated. Pro-Israel lobbyists have sometimes been able to push aid levels higher than administration requests, but when they have gone head to head with the executive branch on important policy issues, they've usually lost. One of the things that eased the task of pro-Israel lobbyists is that unlike just about every other issue on which interest groups work to win congressional support — things like abortion, gun control, and affirmative action — there have been no significant forces in the legislative arena opposing them. The political rewards for supporting Israel have been manifest and substantial; on the other side, nothing but aggravation. In soliciting Jewish contributions to PACs that rewarded friends and punished adversaries, there were certainly appeals to emotions deriving from the Holocaust. But in interactions between PACs and legislators, the primary appeal was to greed and fear.

In the end, there seems little reason to believe that memories of the Holocaust have had any real influence on American policy toward the Middle East. To be sure, plenty of political figures will speak — particularly to Jewish audiences — of an American obligation to assist the country that provided a refuge for the survivors, or of expiation of American guilt for inaction during the Holocaust. There are those who believe that politicians' explanations of their actions reflect their actual motives, those of us who believe politicians say what they think their audiences want to hear.

Ironies surround the reciprocal relationship between American memories of the Holocaust and American support of Israel. For many years it was official Israeli policy to insist that diplomatic visitors to the country stop first at Yad Vashem — a somewhat heavy-handed use of the Nazi slaughter to garner support for Israel.[85] Israelis who backed that policy were not always delighted about American Jewish emphasis on the Holocaust. For one thing, more modern and better funded American Holocaust museums threatened to eclipse cash-strapped Yad Vashem, which had now, Israelis worried, "slipped from being the world's center of the Holocaust to being the poor relative from Israel."[86] Even apart from the challenge to Israel's hegemony over the Holocaust, there was concern, as American Jews poured more and more effort into commemorating it, that the Holocaust was displacing Israel at the center of American Jewish consciousness. When, at a Yom Hashoah commemoration in New York in 1984, Mayor Ed Koch announced a proposal for a Holocaust memorial at the southern tip of Manhattan, Israeli Ambassador Meier Rosenne responded, "The Jewish people do not want any more monuments to the memory of the dead. We have only one monument . . . the state of Israel."[87] A writer in the *Jerusalem Post* saw Jewish donors to Holocaust memorials in the United States as motivated by "subconscious denial of the centrality of Israel in Jewish life and an affirmation that America is indeed the promised land."

> The Jews behind the projects . . . have evidently failed entirely to absorb the lesson of the Holocaust . . . that the Diaspora rests on shifting sands; that today's carnival may be tomorrow's St. Bartholomew's night. . . . Those who sincerely wish to commemorate the Holocaust . . . should understand that the only means of memorializing the suffering of the Six Million is to participate in the upbuilding of the Jewish State.[88]

The other side of the coin — the way in which concern about Israel influenced the Holocaust awareness of American Jews — was even more ironic. In the 1970s, American Jews' anxiety about Israel's security, and their viewing Israel's situation within a Holocaust framework, was the single greatest catalyst of the new centering of the Holocaust in American Jewish consciousness. In the course of the 1980s and 1990s, concern with Israel's security declined, and that framework no longer seemed applicable to Israel's situation. But the consequence of this was an even *greater* centering of the Holocaust for American Jews. Of course, there were already in place, or under construction, countless Holocaust institutions of one sort of another, and a growing cadre of "Holocaust professionals." Even more important, as larger numbers of American Jews no longer saw the Israeli-Palestinian conflict in black-and-white terms, the Holocaust offered a substitute symbol of infinitely greater moral clarity. At a discussion of the central role of the Holocaust in American Jewish life, held a few years ago at the University of Chicago, a local rabbi suggested that there was nothing at all surprising about this fact: "God and Israel are too controversial."[89]

[9]

"Would They Hide My Children?"

THE MOST SIGNIFICANT collective memories — memories that suffuse group consciousness — derive their power from their claim to express some permanent, enduring truth. Such memories are as much about the present as about the past, and are believed to tell us (and others) something fundamental about *who we are now*; they express, or even define, our identity. For a memory to take hold in this way, it has to resonate with how we understand ourselves: how we see our present circumstances, how we think about our future. And the relationship is circular. We embrace a memory because it speaks to our condition; to the extent that we embrace it, we establish a framework for interpreting that condition.

A corollary of all this is that when a memory doesn't reflect our self-understanding (and how we want others to see us), we marginalize it. This, as we've seen, is what American Jews had done with the Holocaust, up to some point in the mid-1960s. The shift of the Holocaust from the margins to the center of American Jewish consciousness from the late 1960s on reflected (and, in turn, promoted) far-reaching changes in the way American Jews came to understand themselves and their circumstances. Previously, Jews had seen America as different. They had emphasized the contrast between the precariousness of Jewish existence elsewhere with the security and acceptance they had achieved in the United States. Jews had viewed with satisfaction the rapid decline of anti-Semitism in American society — the fact that they were no longer outsiders looking in, but now were insiders to whom no doors to advancement were closed.

Beginning in the late sixties, and increasingly in the course of the seventies, influential Jewish leaders began to insist that a "new anti-

Semitism" had arisen; that in contrast with the previous period, American Jews were now threatened, isolated, and vulnerable. Formerly, Jewish organizations had had an outward orientation, had emphasized building bridges between Jews and gentiles, had stressed what Jews had in common with other Americans. Now there was an inward turn, an insistence on the defense of separate Jewish interests, a stress on what made Jews unlike other Americans. Previously, the history of Jews in America was seen as a success story. Now, increasingly, American Jews came to see themselves as an endangered species, and searched for themes and programs that could promote Jewish solidarity and stem the hemorrhage of assimilation and intermarriage. Overall, there was a shift away from the posture of the earlier period when American Jews rejected the status of "victim community," and in consequence marginalized the Holocaust. Now the posture adopted by an increasing number of Jewish leaders — and embraced by a substantial segment of American Jewry — was one in which Jews defined themselves by their history of victimization and in which the Holocaust became the central symbol of Jewish identity.

Jewish leaders began to warn that the good days for Jews in America had ended in the 1960s; hard times were on the horizon. Benjamin Epstein of the Anti-Defamation League said that he and his colleagues had developed "sensitive antennae that alert us to hostile winds of change that threaten Jewish security."

> The antennae of many of us who monitor the climate for Jewish security in America have been vibrating vigorously. [By 1970] we in ADL were convinced that the golden age of progress for Jewish security that marked the 20 years between 1945 and 1965 had indeed ended and that the pendulum was swinging in the opposite direction. . . . The 20-year honeymoon with Jews [is over]. Leaders must verbalize and clarify the unarticulated gut feelings of the rank-and-file in the community. It is our job to . . . document their instinctively accurate gut feelings — to sound the alert.

The belief that American Jews enjoyed greater acceptance and security than at any time in the past was "an obsolete viewpoint. . . . We have been forced into a far more defensive position."[1] Norman Podhoretz also warned that the "golden age" was over: no longer were Jews fully accepted as equals — indeed, even their physical safety could no longer be assumed. Comparing the early sixties with the early seventies, he claimed that hostile references to Jews in the media had increased "by a factor of ten or even fifty, or even a hundred."[2] Earl Raab, a leading figure in Jewish communal life, also spoke of the end of the golden age. America was becoming "inhospitable" and "hostile" to Jews. It was necessary to undertake a "general reconsideration of the relation between the Jewish community and American society as a whole."[3] Even those who rejected this view acknowledged the extent to which it had taken hold. Henry Siegman, in the seventies the executive vice president of the Synagogue Council of America, spoke of the Jewish community's being — quite unjustifiably in his view — in the grip of a "siege mentality . . . an 'everyone has turned against us' attitude."[4]

At the time these alarms were being sounded, anti-Semitism in the United States was, by every measure, continuing its long-term decline, diminishing to the point that it presented no significant barriers or disadvantages to American Jews. What was going on?

The proximate occasions for these "vibrating antennae," and the far-reaching conclusions drawn from the vibrations, were almost laughably trivial: a series of anti-Semitic remarks made by a few militant blacks in the late sixties, as the civil rights movement was collapsing into impotence and disarray. As the Student Non-Violent Coordinating Committee (SNCC) dissolved into warring factions, some of its leaders, seeking to bolster their "revolutionary" credentials, started spouting ill-digested slogans about "Zionist imperialism," which quickly slid over the line to raw anti-Semitism. Some sections of the Black Panthers followed the same trajectory. A number of the most-publicized incidents took place in New York City, the capital of American Jewry. The black talk-show host of a local radio station invited a guest to read an anti-Semitic poem by a Harlem teenager; the Metropolitan Museum of Art's catalogue for an exhibition on Harlem included anti-Semitic remarks by another black adolescent. Above all, there was the New York City school strike of 1968, when black advocates of local community control of schools were pitted against the largely Jewish United Federation of Teachers. When anonymous anti-Semitic leaflets were distributed at some schools, the UFT promptly printed a half-million copies of the leaflets to win support for its cause. Suddenly, black anti-Semitism was all over the front pages. The Anti-Defamation League issued a report announcing that anti-Semitism in the New York school system was at a "crisis level."[5]

It was these trivial incidents — irritating, to be sure, but nevertheless trivial — that were the basis for claims that the golden age for

American Jews was over, that a new anti-Semitism had appeared, that one must abandon as obsolete the belief that Jews were accepted and secure in America. All of this, of course, helped prepare the ground for making the Holocaust emblematic of an eternal Jewish condition, as relevant to the situation of American Jews as to Jews at other times, in other places. So it's worth asking what generated these perceptions and these claims.

The assertion that American Jewry was in danger was first advanced in the aftermath of the Six Day War, and it continued to be advanced in the years after the Yom Kippur War. These were days when American Jews were mobilized by a combination of high anxiety and activist resolve. Rabbi Irving Greenberg, speaking in 1968 of the legacy of the Six Day War, noted that in Diaspora history "no home for the Jews has proven to be more than a temporary *succah.*" While one might hope that America would be different, he said, it was likely that it would not. Heightened Holocaust awareness, Greenberg said, would prepare American Jews for the day when they might have to flee the United States.[6] Norman Podhoretz spoke of a new determination, born of the 1967 victory, "to resist any who would in any way and to any degree and for any reason whatsoever attempt to do us harm. . . . We would from now on stand our ground."[7] When a handful of black demagogues linked "Zionist imperialism" with New York Jewish schoolteachers, Jews could imagine themselves — in Ocean Hill–Brownsville or at the Metropolitan Museum — standing shoulder to shoulder with Moshe Dayan: "We are one!"

Also relevant is the position of Jews in the racial crisis of the sixties. Despite retroactive myth-making, there was never much of a black-Jewish alliance on the communal or organizational level. There were a great many individual Jews who over the years had worked on behalf of blacks, but, with some exceptions, they were leftist and liberal activists who had little connection to the Jewish community. This was certainly true of the Jewish lawyers and student volunteers who worked with the black movement in the South in the 1960s. (Neither Andrew Goodman nor Michael Schwerner, the civil rights activists murdered in Mississippi with a black coworker, had a Jewish funeral.) There is a larger point. During the McCarthy era, Jewish organizations repeatedly pointed out that it was a fallacy to infer from the fact that a great many (perhaps even a majority of) Communists were Jews that a great many, let alone a majority of, Jews were Communists. The logic was impeccable with respect to alleged Jewish pro-Communism, and equally impeccable with respect to alleged Jewish civil rights activism.[8]

As the focus of the civil rights movement shifted to campaigns against de facto segregation in housing and education in northern cities and suburbs, Jewish organizations found their constituencies increasingly resistant to the black agenda. All of this was during the Martin Luther King era, some years before the turn to Black Power and before the "crisis" of 1968–69.[9]

By 1968, leaders of national Jewish organizations had a new worry: the appearance of a dynamic Jewish group that denounced the traditional leadership for timidity in the face of the threat militant blacks posed to Jews. Meir Kahane's Jewish Defense League, which popularized the slogan "Never again," invoked it, in the first instance, in anti-black posturing. The JDL picketed the radio station on which the Harlem teenager's anti-Semitic poem had been read, with signs reading "No Auschwitz Here" and "They Will Not Make Lampshades Out of Us."[10] Nathan Perlmutter of the Anti-Defamation League, responding to charges that his organization had exaggerated the threat of black anti-Semitism in 1968, said that, to the contrary, the growing support for the JDL showed that mainstream Jewish organizations, including his own, had been too slow to sound the alarm, had allowed Kahane to become the spokesman for Jewish concerns about black militancy.[11] A confidential survey by the American Jewish Congress, the most liberal of the leading Jewish organizations, revealed that more than a third of its members said they approved of the tactics of the JDL.[12] The responsive chord struck by Kahane's repeated invocation of the Holocaust gave rise to a fear among established Jewish organizations that he was establishing a kind of rhetorical ownership of it. In order to block this takeover bid by the usurper, they themselves began to talk more about the Holocaust.[13]

It's hard to say how many American Jews were caught up in the anxiety that Jewish spokesmen claimed to be reflecting, and were certainly promoting. It is harder still to say how much the specter of the Holocaust fed into the anxiety, and how much the anxiety fed into increased talk about the Holocaust. In any case, many were struck by the extent of the anxiety and the ways in which it was expressed. In 1969 a Catholic journalist in New York wrote that "Jewish friends, whom I have never heard raise the subject, now assure me that American Jews are about in the same position as German Jews when Hitler came to power. One, apparently echoing a widespread fear, gave me a long explanation of how the Gentile was determined to raise the black man at the Jew's expense."[14] The Weimar analogy was frequently made — German Jews, too, one was reminded, had thought themselves accepted and secure. The assertion that gentiles, particularly elite gentiles, would buy social peace with blacks at the expense of Jews was also common. "If the crunch ever comes between the 'haves' and the 'have-nots,' " said Rabbi Arthur Hertzberg, "the 'haves' are perfectly willing to sell out the Jews to the blacks to save what they have."[15]

No major Jewish leader (unless one counts Meir Kahane) predicted an American holocaust, but privately many Jews gave voice to heightened nervousness. In the early 1970s Stephen Isaacs, a reporter for the *Washington Post*, wrote a book on Jews in American politics for which he interviewed a number of prominent Jewish public figures:

> One question was repeated to most of those who gave longer interviews. . . . "Do you think it could happen here?" (Never was it necessary to define the "it.") In almost every case, the reply was approximately the same: "If you know history at all, you have to presume not that it could happen, but that it probably will," or "It's not a matter of if; it's a matter of when."[16]

The perception of the "end of the golden age" for Jews in America, and of mounting anti-Semitism, persisted throughout the seventies and eighties and into the nineties. Jonathan Sarna, a leading historian of American Jewry, surveyed recent books on American anti-Semitism in 1981. He observed with dismay that, "influenced by the current obsession with the Holocaust, they ask only one question: could it happen here? And to this question they have only one answer: yes."[17] Throughout the 1980s the chimera of resurgent anti-Semitism continued to haunt American Jews. Indeed, in the course of the decade the percentage of American Jews who said that anti-Semitism was a "serious problem" in the United States rose dramatically, to more than 80 percent by 1990.[18]

The reality in those years was that the "golden age" for American Jews, rather than receding, became even more golden. The last pockets of anti-Jewish discrimination disappeared; surveys showed anti-Semitic attitudes continuing to decline; Jewish senators came to be regularly elected in states with virtually no Jewish voters; any hint of anti-Semitism from a figure in public life was immediately and roundly reprobated. There were predictions that the oil crisis, the Jonathan Pollard espionage case, or the Wall Street insider-trading scandal would produce an anti-Semitic reaction; it never happened.

But the relationship between reality and perceptions is tenuous at best. Where did the perceptions of high and rising levels of anti-Semitism come from? And what was the (reciprocal) relationship between these perceptions and increasing talk of the Holocaust?

These questions can't be answered precisely or definitively. I suggested earlier, and it's worth repeating, that to some unknowable extent Jews' perceptions of increasing anti-Semitism were probably a reflexive gesture of solidarity with a beleaguered Israel and with Jews in the Soviet Union and elsewhere who were thought to be in danger. It also seems likely that at a time when American Jewry was publicly defining itself as militantly Zionist (not, of course, enough to immigrate to Israel), many were, albeit ambivalently, coming to accept classic Zionist ideological propositions: that murderous anti-Semitism was always latent in the "unnatural" condition of Jews living in the Diaspora, that only in Israel were Jews safe. (Where once American Jews had contrasted Jewish insecurity in Europe with safety in the United States, now the dichotomy was between insecurity in the Diaspora, including the United States, and safety — at least in principle — in Israel.)

American Jews, like everybody else, get their views of what's going on in the world not from independent reflection but from what they're told by those whom they're inclined to believe. Many Jewish agencies and much of the Jewish media told them that the level of American anti-Semitism was high and rising. Why should they doubt it? From the 1970s on, the growth sector in the Jewish organizational world consisted of old and new *"schrei gevalt"* agencies, while those with other agendas, like the American Jewish Committee and the American Jewish Congress, declined. The Anti-Defamation League, together with the enormously successful Simon Wiesenthal Center, bombarded Jews with mailings announcing new anti-Semitic threats. (The ADL was especially assiduous in giving wide circulation to anti-Semitic remarks by obscure black hustlers and demagogues, thus vastly increasing their audiences.)[19] Of the dozens of local Jewish newspapers in the United States, all but a handful were organs of local Jewish Federations, whose success in fund-raising was directly proportional to the level of anxiety among potential contributors.

The reciprocal relationship between perceptions of increased anti-Semitism in the United States and increased attention to the Holocaust is at once manifest and difficult to pin down. From the late sixties on, those who claimed that there was a new anti-Semitism often attributed its appearance to fading memories of the Holocaust. It was the immediate impact of the Holocaust, they said, that had produced the "golden age."[20] By the late sixties, said Norman Podhoretz, "the moral statute of limitations ran out on the Holocaust."[21] Michael Berenbaum, in 1982, bemoaned the end of "the period of sanitization. . . . The shield of the Holocaust is gone."[22] Ten years later, claiming that "antisemitism has gained a new respectability not seen in the U.S. since World War II," Abraham Foxman attributed this alleged respectability to the fact that the Holocaust was now "ancient history."[23] Given the overwhelming evidence that in recent decades anti-Semitism in the United States has become less and less respectable, and given that in recent decades Americans have been much more aware of the Holocaust than they were in the postwar years, it's hard to know what to say about those assertions. But they were probably believed by those who made them, and thus gave Jewish leaders a pragmatic incentive to spread Holocaust consciousness.

Perceptions of growing American anti-Semitism clearly played a role — it's hard to say how large a role — in stimulating thinking and talking about the Holocaust among American Jews. Once the Holocaust became centered in Jewish consciousness, and to the extent that it became centered, it provided a language and framework that deepened anxiety about American anti-Semitism, and a spiraling interaction came into play. Once one starts using imagery from that most extreme of events, it becomes impossible to say anything moderate, balanced, or nuanced; the very language carries you along to hyperbole. A journalist who supported black community control of schools was told by Norman Podhoretz in 1969 that he was one of those who wanted to "shove the Jewish people back into the gas ovens."[24] "The ovens" recurred again and again. In Brooklyn a militant protester against busing for school integration insisted that "we wouldn't be led to the ovens this time."[25] At a public forum on relations between blacks and Jews, the black psychologist Kenneth Clark wondered why the issue was so charged, observing that he never got invitations to discuss relations between Catholics and blacks. A woman in the audience said that the reason was because "the Catholics aren't worried that the blacks are going to shove them into the oven." Clark, according to an observer, "winced, as though he had been physically struck. 'My goodness,' he said very softly. . . . 'Did you say something about blacks shoving people into ovens?' "[26]

As I remarked in an earlier chapter, in the first postwar years the

Holocaust was viewed, by Jews as well as Americans in general, as part of history. It was an event that had taken place there and not here; it was an aspect of a period — the era of fascism — that was now ended; it had been the result of a particular constellation of forces. As the Holocaust moved from history to myth, it became the bearer of "eternal truths" not bound by historical circumstances. Among other things, the Holocaust came to symbolize the natural and inevitable terminus of anti-Semitism: first stop, an anti-Semitic joke; last stop, Treblinka. Every loudmouthed Farrakhan acolyte was the opening act in the Julius Streicher Show. The insistence on the incomprehensibility and inexplicability of the Holocaust furthered this inclination. If the Holocaust defied rational explanation, who could know what trivial event might be the precursor to "the ovens"? With this mindset, there could be no such thing as overreaction to an anti-Semitic incident, no such thing as exaggerating the omnipresent danger. Anyone who scoffed at the idea that there were dangerous portents in American society hadn't learned "the lesson of the Holocaust." Defending what some had called Jewish overreaction to anti-Semitic remarks by a handful of blacks in 1968, an official of the American Jewish Committee insisted that "not enough people, including Jews, believed that Hitler was serious."[27] In succeeding decades, this became a recurring theme in official Jewish responses to every incident. A quarter century later, in a remark that took the fashionable form of the-apology-that-really-isn't, Abraham Foxman of the ADL said that he was "sorry if I have offended some in the black or white community by being too quick to yell. The last time Jews didn't, they paid a very heavy price."[28]

In the late sixties and early seventies, at the same time that the arrival of the "new anti-Semitism" was announced, American Jewish organizations were changing their priorities and their posture, a change that has so far proved permanent. It is probably best described as an inward turn — a shift away from the previously dominant "integrationist" perspective and toward an emphasis on the defense of distinctive Jewish interests, a kind of circling of the wagons. Those who promoted the idea of a new anti-Semitism argued that the new version, unlike the old, did not necessarily reflect any animus toward Jews. Often it was a matter of policies that might harm Jewish interests, even if the policies weren't intended to harm Jews. Support by white elites of black community control of schools — which threatened the position of Jewish teachers — was one example. Another was affirmative action programs, which the major Jewish organizations campaigned against on the grounds that Jews would be disadvantaged by their operation.[29] Such initiatives were seen as examples of what was at the core of the new anti-Semitism: "callous indifference to Jewish concerns"; a failure to appreciate "the most profound apprehensions of the Jewish people."[30]

Gentile indifference to Israel's plight and gentile indifference to the well-being of American Jews were seen as instances of a general phenomenon, of which the most dramatic example — often invoked — was gentile indifference to Jews' fate during the Holocaust. No aspect of the Holocaust received greater attention than the role of bystanders in Hitler's Europe. The discussion of bystanders — the minority who helped rescue Jews and the majority who did not — became one of the principal ways in which talk about the Holocaust promoted the notion of Jews as vulnerable and alone in a hostile or indifferent world.

The unsurprising reality of bystanders' behavior during the Holocaust is that the overwhelming majority of gentiles acted just as one would expect under circumstances of ruthless foreign occupation: they kept their heads down and looked out for number one. Insofar as one can generalize about differences in the amount of help extended in different countries — and it's very hard to measure — those differences were also predictable. Where the conditions of German occupation were relatively mild, and where Jews were well integrated into local society — as in Denmark — more help, and more effective help, was forthcoming. In places where the Germans behaved with particular brutality and where Jews were less well integrated — as in Poland — there was less help, and it was less often successful. But the discourse about bystanders was not part of a search for historical comprehension; it was intended to point a moral.

In other contexts it was common to speak of "innocent bystanders." These were held to be *guilty* bystanders who were contrasted with "Righteous Gentiles" — the term officially adopted at Yad Vashem to designate Christian Europeans who had helped to save Jews.[31] The qualifications for certification as a Righteous Gentile had little connection with the everyday meaning of "righteousness": following accepted moral norms and doing what people could reasonably be expected to do. The criteria were to have risked one's life, and often the lives of the members of one's family as well, to save another; to have displayed self-sacrificing heroism of the highest and rarest order.[32] At Yad Vashem nominees for Righteous Gentile status are carefully screened. Often the process takes many years, and the most rigorous standards are applied. (Thus fishermen who transported Danish Jews to Sweden in 1943 are not eligible because they were paid.)[33]

The intention of most commemoration of the "righteous minority" has been to damn the vast "unrighteous majority." The article "Righteous among the Nations," in *The Encyclopedia of the Holocaust,* stresses that "the acts of those few show that aid and rescue were possible . . . had there been more high-minded people."[34] The director of Yad Vashem's Department of the Righteous explained that "spicing" the history of the Holocaust with stories of rescuers was indispensable in showing the delinquency of European Christians "against the background of the righteous."[35] In the United States, the head of the Anti-Defamation League discussed a book by the director of the ADL's Foundation for Christian Rescuers. He insisted that "what is important about the book is that the reader comes away understanding that rescue of Jews was a rare phenomenon. [The fact is] that 700 million people lived in Nazi-occupied Europe; to date 11,000 have been honored by Yad Vashem for rescuing Jews."[36] The ratio of unrighteous to righteous gentiles — thousands to one — is repeatedly underlined by commentators. "For every righteous person," said Benjamin Meed, "there were thousands upon thousands who collaborated . . . or who, at best, stood idly by and did nothing."[37]

Those who have written or spoken about gentile rescuers, for purposes other than underlining their rarity, report that they often receive a hostile reception from Jewish audiences. One recounts that the critics of his lectures "accused me of everything from lulling American Jews into a false sense of security . . . to endangering Israel by fostering the illusion that it can rely on American support."[38] One of the most common Jewish complaints about Steven Spielberg's *Schindler's List* was that it distorted the meaning and lesson of the Holocaust by focusing on a Christian rescuer.[39] Some *individuals* who pressed for recognition of Christian rescuers wanted to combat blanket condemnation of gentiles; in the words of one such individual, to break down the "fortress-like mentality" of American Jews.[40] But the *institutional* use of the commemoration of Righteous Gentiles as "the exceptions that prove the rule" has usually been in the service of shoring up that mentality — promoting a wary suspicion of gentiles. Whatever the intention, this seems to have been the consequence, judging by reports that come with remarkable frequency from otherwise apparently sensible American Jews. "When I move to a new town," writes a university teacher, "I give great thought to whom, among my gentile friends, I might entrust my children, should that ever become necessary."[41] A prominent Jewish feminist: "Every conscious Jew longs to ask her or his non-Jewish friends, 'Would you hide me?' — and suppresses the question for fear of hearing the sounds of silence."[42] A professor of psychology:

> Many Jews report that the unspoken question they ask themselves when interacting with a non-Jew is, "Would she or he have saved me from the Nazis?" I have asked myself this question innumerable times: sometimes I surprise myself by answering, "I don't know," when asking this question of a non-Jewish friend I had otherwise assumed was close to me. The answer is the ultimate standard by which to measure trust in a non-Jewish person.[43]

Hovering over all of this is the absurd maxim *In extremis veritas* — that it is in imagining the most desperate circumstances that one gains insight into what gentiles really think of Jews. To be preoccupied with the question of whether one could be sure that one would be saved by gentile friends if a holocaust came to America is to actively solicit anxiety and doubt, because who could ever be sure of such a thing? The asking of this pointless question seems to have become culturally approved, a sign that one has learned "the lesson of the Holocaust."

Other dimensions of the inward turn of organized American Jewry, not all of them directly connected to growing Holocaust consciousness, often contributed to the fortress mentality that was both source and consequence of that consciousness. One indication of the extent of this new inwardness is that in a 1988 survey, more than a third of Reform rabbis — traditionally the most "integrated" and "outreaching" of the major Jewish denominations — endorsed the proposition that "ideally, one ought not to have any contact with non-Jews."[44] To the extent that one became convinced that only Jews could be depended upon to care about Jews, it made less and less sense for Jews to care about those who didn't care about them. At a minimum, it was foolish to squander Jewish resources on their behalf. There was growing impatience with those Jews who were still behaving in the manner of the "golden age" and hadn't adapted to the new situation. Nathan Perlmutter, who headed the Anti-Defamation League during the early

1980s, said that local Jewish groups might foolishly promote "doomed to failure" projects to increase opportunities for minorities, but he was not about to "waste the manpower of this agency. . . . We have made clear our opposition to programs that are not related to the interests of Jews."[45]

Not all Jewish leaders went as far as the leader of the ADL, but the turn to an inward orientation could be seen across the board. There was a shift in policy within Jewish charitable institutions. During the first postwar decades, as a result of demographic changes, many Jewish hospitals, orphanages, and the like had increasingly come to serve a non-Jewish (often black) clientele. This development had not been unwelcome to many of those involved who had a nonsectarian, "need-based" philosophy. From the late sixties on, this policy changed, and Jewish resources were increasingly reserved for exclusively Jewish purposes.[46] Even among those organizations which retained some commitment to the old liberal agenda, like the Union of American Hebrew Congregations (Reform), there was a marked decrease in the attention paid to broader issues and a concomitant rise in parochial concerns.[47] A Reform rabbi, an erstwhile liberal activist, justified the turn by quoting Elie Wiesel:

> By working for his own people a Jew . . . makes his most valuable contribution. . . . By struggling on behalf of Russian, Arab or Polish Jews, I fight for human rights everywhere. . . . By striving to keep alive the memory of the holocaust, I denounce the massacres in Biafra and the nuclear menace. . . . A Jew fulfills his role as a man only from inside his Jewishness.[48]

There was, around this time, a gradual but marked change in the personnel of the leading Jewish agencies. Whereas formerly almost all had been secularists, or at most were minimally observant, there came to be a significant and growing Orthodox presence in their ranks.[49] The fact that Christianity, in principle, is universalist has not prevented individual Christians from being the narrowest of chauvinists. And the particularism of traditional Judaism has not prevented individual Jews — even some observant Jews — from endorsing universalist values. But it remains true that, overall, observant Jews have been much more particularist in their concerns. As the organizations' agendas moved in this direction, it was natural for more observant Jews to come on staff, and their presence furthered the shift away from universalist concerns. The Talmudic epigraph of Steven Spielberg's *Schind-*

ler's List, "Whoever saves one life saves the world entire," surely reflected the universalist values of liberal Judaism as it had evolved in recent centuries. The observant knew that the traditional version, the one taught in all Orthodox yeshivot, speaks of "whoever saves one life of Israel."[50]

The inward turn on the part of much of American Jewish leadership — their insistence that "Is it good for the Jews?" be the first, if not the only, question that Jews ask themselves — inevitably mandated a rightward turn as well. By the 1970s Jews were preeminent among the "haves" in American society, and the gap between Jews and non-Jews, in income as well as in representation in all elite positions, widened over subsequent decades Jews had everything to lose and nothing to gain from the more equal distribution of rewards which had been the aim of liberal social policies. The rightward turn also manifested itself in questions of foreign policy. Those who would cut American defense spending, wrote Irving Kristol in the magazine of the American Jewish Congress, would "drive a knife into the heart of Israel."[51] Lucy Dawidowicz denounced Jews who voted for Walter Mondale over Ronald Reagan in 1984: they had not only "voted with groups who are not our allies but our enemies," but "voted for the party with a direct line to the PLO."[52] A country that fails to back the right against the left in Nicaragua and El Salvador, said the head of the ADL, "is a country that will be indifferent to catastrophe in the Middle East."[53] The political movement called neo-conservatism was almost exclusively a Jewish affair; *Commentary,* published by the American Jewish Committee, became America's best-known conservative magazine.[54]

Despite the jeremiads from Jewish conservatives, most American Jews resisted appeals to shift their allegiance to the Republicans.[55] But it ceased to be true that Jews were markedly more liberal than other Americans of similar age, education, and income when it came to bread-and-butter issues like welfare, income distribution, and aid to blacks. (Their greater liberalism was mostly restricted to questions of sexual morality, like abortion and gay rights.)[56] Though Jewish voting patterns lagged behind other changes, the former symbolic identification of Jews with liberalism became anachronistic: increasingly, Jews were as likely to be found on the conservative as on the liberal side in the political arena, in the press, and in the academic and literary culture.

It's difficult to say how much growing attention to the Holocaust contributed to the Jewish rightward turn, and vice versa. It was often claimed that the Holocaust taught deeply conservative lessons about the nature of man, that it undercut the Enlightenment optimism that had been the foundation of liberalism. ("It is a dangerous illusion to think one can do much for more than a very few," says Saul Bellow's Artur Sammler, freed by the Holocaust from liberal fantasies.)[57] But Jewish leftists, though less and less influential from the early seventies on, were equally assiduous in drawing their own kinds of lessons from the Holocaust. FDR's alleged abandonment of the Jews did double duty: for conservative Jews, it showed the error of relying on liberals and Democrats; for leftist Jews, it illustrated the foolishness of trying to ally with the "ruling class" rather than the masses, of turning to any "power structure" for protection.[58] While right-wingers found invoking the Holocaust philosophically useful, providing an historical justification for a conservative worldview, left-wingers and counterculturists found it psychologically congenial: it offered a vehicle for the outraged confrontational style, and "letting it all hang out," left over from the sixties. Rabbi Avi Weiss, scaling the wall of the Carmelite convent at Auschwitz to provoke a confrontation with the nuns, was a direct descendant of the Free Speech Movement activists at Berkeley's Sproul Plaza in 1964 provoking the police.[59] Particularly in *Tikkun*, the best-known Jewish magazine on the left, there was a good deal of psychobabble about "therapeutic rage" concerning the Holocaust. An insert with suggestions for modifying the Passover Haggadah argued that "to get beyond the pain, we must first be allowed to express our anger." It included a stage direction: "Stop here and let seder participants speak about their righteous indignation."[60] On both the Jewish right and the Jewish left it's often difficult to sort out chickens and eggs: the extent to which thinking about the Holocaust led to a particular posture or, alternatively, provided a convenient mode of expressing a posture arrived at independently. But there was something for everybody in the Holocaust.

What I have up to now described as American Jewry's inward turn can also be called, and often is called, a shift in strategic priorities from "integration" to "survival." Integration — winning acceptance on every level and in every area of American society — could hardly any longer be a priority, since it was an accomplished fact. But that acceptance came at a price. The survival to which Jewish leaders increasingly turned their attention did not mean the physical survival of Jews in a hostile environment. Rather, it was the *absence* of hostility to Jews that was threatening. Individually American Jews were prospering; collectively they were being killed with kindness. In the words of one Jewish leader, "the melting pot has succeeded beyond our wildest fears."[61] A decline in Jewish commitment and sense of Jewish identity, particularly among the young — dramatically reflected in soaring rates of intermarriage — threatened demographic catastrophe for American Jewry. The word used to describe the most ghastly consequence of murderous hostility toward Jews was also used to describe the predicted consequence of benevolence toward Jews. The threat of assimilation was frequently described as a "quiet," "silent," "bloodless," or "spiritual" Holocaust.[62] Norman Lamm, president of (Modern Orthodox) Yeshiva University: "With a diminishing birth rate, an intermarriage rate exceeding 40%, Jewish illiteracy gaining ascendance daily — who says that the Holocaust is over? . . . The monster has assumed a different and more benign form . . . but its evil goal remains unchanged: a *Judenrein* world."[63]

From the mid-1960s on, Jewish communal leaders became more and more worried about what *Look* magazine, in a 1964 cover story, called "The Vanishing American Jew."[64] By the late sixties more than 40 percent of young Jewish men (but only a quarter as many young Jewish women) were marrying gentiles.[65] Over the next decades, newly liberated young Jewish women were becoming "equal opportunity intermarriers," and by the time of the 1990 National Jewish Population Survey, the overall rate of intermarriage was above 50 percent, with only about a quarter of the children of these unions being even nominally Jewish.[66] Even if the rate remained constant — and why shouldn't it continue to rise? — the ranks of American Jews, a few generations down the road, would be drastically reduced. Small wonder that, from the 1970s on, "survival" became the American Jewish watchword.

Two factors had been the guarantors of a substantial Jewish presence in the United States over the centuries. The first was renewal through immigration. The first Jews in America, Sephardim, had begun to assimilate and intermarry at an increasing rate when American Jewry was renewed by German Jewish immigration. As this cohort's commitment to a distinctive Jewish identity waned, there was the massive influx of Eastern European Jews at the turn of the century. As the children and grandchildren of the Eastern European immigrants began to assimilate, there was a (smaller) source of renewal — refugees from, and survivors of, the Holocaust. Apart from a certain number of

Soviet Jews (not very Jewish) and Israelis (an embarrassment), there was no further external source of unassimilated Jews, to make up for those whose Jewishness was dissolving. There has been much talk of a third-generation renaissance of ethnic consciousness — "what the son wishes to forget, the grandson wishes to remember"; many claims of the "unmeltability" of ethnicity.[67] But the evidence is clear that for all European immigrant groups, very much including Jews, ethnic identity continues to thin and attenuate (though often not quite to the vanishing point) from generation to generation.[68] By the third and fourth generations it usually amounts to little more than symbolic ethnicity — the performance of undemanding rituals that only minimally interfere with the melting process.[69] Perhaps most important, ethnic identity — again, including Jewish identity — has increasingly come to be something chosen rather than taken for granted.

The second factor that had, for many years, held Jews together was anti-Semitism. Before World War II and into the first postwar years, both a general disdain for Jews and discriminatory practices had resulted in a good deal of separateness — residential, occupational, social. As anti-Semitism declined so did separateness, with all of its daily reminders of having a distinctive identity. The decline of anti-Semitism also meant that it was less dishonorable than formerly to let one's Jewish identity atrophy: it was no longer "cowardice in the face of the enemy."

What could Jewish organizations do to shore up Jewish identity, particularly among the assimilating and intermarrying younger generation? Various initiatives had varying degrees of success. Mobilization on behalf of Israel may have provided some with a sense of purpose, but hardly an identity. There was a minor religious revival, with some young Jews becoming involved in small, informal religious communities (*havurot*), but such activities attracted only a handful. A few began to study Jewish culture and history. These things were not insignificant, and were certainly gratifying to those who worried about diminishing Jewish commitment. But only rarely did they engage the marginal Jews who were the principal source of anxiety among communal leaders. In any case, those who were becoming more Jewish continued to be greatly outnumbered by those who were becoming less Jewish.

From the beginning of the concern for survival, in the late sixties and early seventies, it was suggested that the noninvolvement of the young in Jewish affairs — their thinning Jewish identity — was a consequence of their insufficient awareness of the Holocaust. Rabbi Joachim Prinz told the convention of the American Jewish Congress that young Jews' unwillingness to consider "Jewish identification and solidarity," their "indifference in matters Jewish," was largely attributable to their ignorance of the European catastrophe. Unless something was done, "within one or two generations the beautiful edifices which have been built in Jewish communities all over the land may be empty."[70] Bertram Gold, head of the American Jewish Committee, likewise attributed young American Jews' "lack of a sense of 'being Jewish' " to the fact that the Holocaust was not "seared into the memory of a generation born after World War II."[71] This view was echoed at the 1971 convention of the Union of American Hebrew Congregations, where leaders bemoaned their failure to "instill in youth a deep-rooted awareness of what the holocaust means to contemporary Jewry"; to overcome the gap between those who lived through the Nazi period and those born after 1945.[72] A 1972 article in the journal of the American Jewish Congress, entitled "How to Make the Children Understand," again repeated this explanation of why young Jews "depreciate ethnic or group loyalties": "They didn't live through the period of the Holocaust; they have learned about it at second hand, from their parents and their history books. But they are accustomed to discredit much of what they hear from their parents . . . and they don't pay much attention to history."[73] A conference sponsored by the North American Jewish Students' Network began with participants' being asked to write an essay, "How Would You Present the Holocaust to an Uninvolved Sixteen Year Old Jewish Student?"[74] A number of speakers at a meeting of the National Jewish Community Relations Advisory Council observed that programming on the Holocaust could attract young people who were "indifferent to and 'turned off' by most approaches."[75]

No central decision-making body of American Jewry concluded that it was the absence of Holocaust consciousness that explained the declining Jewish commitment of the young, that the way to keep straying sheep in the fold was through Holocaust programming. There has never been any such body; that's not the way things work. Rather, it was a matter of market forces. Young Jews did indeed seem to be "indifferent to and 'turned off' by" synagogue attendance, learning Hebrew or Yiddish, immersing themselves in Jewish culture, or participating in mainstream Jewish organizations. The Holocaust looked like the one item in stock with consumer appeal. Jewish college students who had shown no interest in other academic courses with Jewish subject matter oversubscribed offerings on the Holocaust. Supply responded to demand, and the number of such courses rapidly multiplied throughout the seventies. According to one (possibly inflated) estimate, they were being offered at more than seven hundred colleges by 1978.[76]

Public events related to the Holocaust drew audiences far exceeding those on other subjects, and were scheduled with increasing frequency. Whereas other Jewish activities tended to attract those who already had a fairly high degree of Jewish commitment, programs related to the Holocaust showed a capacity to pull in Jews with an otherwise marginal Jewish identity. These, of course, were precisely the people who were the object of "survival anxiety." Though this was most easily measurable on campuses, it seemed to be true among older Jews as well, judging by the relative appeal of Holocaust-related events and institutions and those devoted to other aspects of Jewishness. The millionaire who provided most of the original funding for the Simon Wiesenthal Center told a reporter that it was "a sad fact that Israel and Jewish education and all the other familiar buzzwords no longer seem to rally Jews behind the community. The Holocaust, though, works every time."[77] Certainly none of those who have promoted Holocaust programming to meet the problem of "the vanishing American Jew" intended that Jewish identity should end there. The hope has been, in the words of Rabbi Irving Greenberg, one of the leading promoters of Holocaust consciousness, that it would "become a channel to the recovery of the rest of Judaism."[78] No doubt sometimes it has been, but no one knows how often, or how permanently.

If one of the contexts in which a Holocaust-centered Jewish identity developed was survival anxiety, another was the growth in American society of "the new ethnicity" and "identity politics." The roots of these many-sided phenomena were various and tangled — too complex to be detailed here. The background against which they developed was a diffuse disillusionment with an idealized image of America in the years that spanned JFK's assassination and Watergate, and included the Vietnam War and the collapse of the civil rights movement. In an influential book, Benedict Anderson suggested that we think of nations as "imagined communities" in which we project onto the nation the feelings found in small, face-to-face communities — "family" sorts of feelings.[79] Increasingly, from the 1960s on, many Americans ceased imagining the United States as a community — or an extended family — in the old sense. The United States came to be seen as an inappropriate (or unworthy) object of "we" feelings. That highly charged pronoun came to be used to refer to smaller entities, or entities that crossed national boundaries: "we blacks," "we women," "we gays," "we Jews." Such usages were by no means new, but the balance shifted sharply in the direction of particular identities, as opposed to "all-American" identity. In the Jewish version of this (every group had its own version), a survey of American Jewish volunteer fund-raisers in the late seventies found three quarters agreeing that "I feel more emotional when I hear Hatikvah [Israel's national anthem] than when I hear the Star-Spangled Banner."[80] In historical writing — to pick the area I know best — there was less and less discussion of the contributions that members of particular groups had made to the larger society and culture, more and more insistence on what was distinctive to each group.[81]

The reach of the new ethnicity has sometimes been exaggerated. In the case of most European immigrant groups — Irish, Italians, Poles, Greeks, and so on — there was never a successful mobilization of collective consciousness. Intermarriage over the generations had drastically reduced the number of "pure" ethnics; those who remained, apart from a handful of activists, were usually satisfied with the kind of occasional symbolic assertion found in the St. Patrick's Day parade or the San Gennaro festival. "Asian American" as an ethnicity was a purely academic (and purely specious) category, about as meaningful as "Euro-American." (The distance between Seoul and New Delhi, culturally as well as geographically, is twice the distance from Moscow to Dublin.) Apart from Jews, the groups among whom "identities" really took hold — became the basis of successful mobilization and collective consciousness — were blacks, women, gays, and, to a lesser extent, Hispanics.

Their group mobilization and "raised consciousness" was based on their shared experience of collective disadvantage or their individual experience of discrimination, usually both. They organized on the basis of shared grievances against the dominant society, which continued to deny them full and equal participation and gave them less than what they saw as their fair share of rewards. Their shared identity was thus, above all, a victim identity. The hallmark of the fully participating and fully conscious member of the group was belief — however well one was doing personally — in shared victimhood.

Other features of American culture from the sixties on furthered sympathetic attention to the condition of victimhood. Vietnam was the first war in American history in which images of the victims, like the naked napalmed girl running down a road, displaced traditional images of heroism. After the inspiring scenes of struggle in the South in the mid-sixties, the predominant image of blacks, when it was not of burning and looting rioters, was of people trapped in despair and hopelessness in urban ghettos. A new focus on spousal abuse and child abuse extended the range of perceived victims, as did the visible presence on city streets of the homeless. Also new was a strong emphasis in historical and literary works on the experience of losers rather than winners.[82]

It was against this background, and in this cultural climate that virtually celebrated victimhood, that efforts to firm up faltering Jewish identity were mounted. It is not that Jewish leaders deliberately and opportunistically latched on to a fashionable victimhood as the basis for an identity that could mobilize Jews and ensure Jewish continuity. (In any case, as I have said, there is no united Jewish leadership capable of making such choices.) Rather, the heightened status of the victim removed inhibitions that had in previous decades led them to shun that label. The "culture of victimization" didn't *cause* Jews to embrace a victim identity based on the Holocaust; it *allowed* this sort of identity to become dominant, because it was, after all, virtually the only one that could encompass those Jews whose faltering Jewish identity produced so much anxiety about Jewish survival.

It was very hard to find any other basis on which to ground a distinctive identity shared by all Jews. It couldn't be grounded in distinctive religious beliefs, since most Jews didn't have much in the way of such beliefs. It couldn't be grounded in distinctive cultural traits, since most didn't have much of these either. Support of Israel exerted a certain centripetal force, but in recent years questions having to do with Israel have divided more than they have united Jews. The only thing that all American Jews shared was the knowledge that but for the immigration of near or distant ancestors, they would have shared the fate of European Jewry. Insofar as the Holocaust became the defining Jewish experience, all Jews had their "honorary" survivorship in common. Insofar as it attained mythic status, expressing truths about an enduring Jewish condition, all were united in an essential victim identity.

Many Jewish leaders were distressed at this outcome. But there were reasons — aside from the fact that the Holocaust seemed the only symbol to which all Jews could feel a strong sense of connection — that a victim identity took hold. That sort of self-understanding had strong roots in the European Jewish tradition. "Jewish history," the novelist Aharon Appelfeld said, "is a series of holocausts, with only some improvement in technique."[83] Simon Wiesenthal compiled a chronicle of Jewish martyrdom in almanac form, so that one could look up where, and by whom, Jews were murdered over the centuries on every day of the year.[84] This kind of traditional identity had instinctive appeal to many more observant and more conservative Jews. But a victim identity had equal appeal for many Jewish secularists on the left, like *Village Voice* columnist Ellen Willis, for whom "the status of Jews as . . . persecuted outsiders is at the core of what Judaism and Jewishness is all about."[85] A victim identity was reassuringly comfortable to all sorts of Jews who found it disturbing that Jews were no longer seen as victims or underdogs; that, as one Jewish leader complained, through "some sort of sociological sleight-of-hand . . . Jews have become part of the 'white majority.' "[86] Especially in campus settings, Jewish students were restive under policies that, one Hillel rabbi complained, "recognize[d] the special status of historically oppressed racial minorities and women, while casting Jews in the unfamiliar role of the white oppressor."[87] An editorial in *Tikkun* insisted that Jews weren't really white:

> In current discourse, who gets labeled "white" and who gets labeled "person of color" derives not from the color of one's skin . . . but from the degree to which one has been a victim of Western colonialist oppression. By that measure, Jews have been the greatest victims of Western societies throughout the past two thousand years and must certainly be understood to be one of the "peoples of color."[88]

Whatever other functions they serve, the yellow stars Jewish students proudly wear on Yom Hashoah are their passport to the ranks of the oppressed.

Jews were by no means alone in pressing for acknowledgment of past injustices. Japanese Americans spoke of their wartime internment;

Chinese Americans memorialized the Rape of Nanking; Armenian Americans directed attention to the 1915 genocide; Irish Americans sought commemoration of the Potato Famine of the 1840s. As a rule, these claims for recognition did not involve the groups in competition, except in the relatively benign sense that public attention was limited, and each had to elbow its way onto the stage. But the success of Jews in gaining permanent possession of center stage for their tragedy, and their equal success in making it the benchmark against which other atrocities were judged, produced a fair amount of resentment — "Holocaust envy."

Discussing the refusal of the Smithsonian Institution to return the skeletons of thousands of Indians to the tribes that wished to rebury them, Clara Spotted Elk asked: "What would happen if the Smithsonian had 18,500 Holocaust victims in the attic?"[89] A leading Holocaust scholar concluded his argument that the massacring of the Pequot Indians wasn't really genocidal by noting that many Pequot survived: "As recently as the 1960s, Pequots were still listed as a separate group residing in Connecticut," he said. "While the British could certainly have been less thorough, less severe, less deadly in prosecuting their campaign against the Pequots, the campaign they actually did carry out, for all its vehemence, was not, either in intent or execution, genocidal."[90] Commenting on this, an historian of American Indians wondered what the response would be to the argument that the Holocaust wasn't genocidal because while the Nazis "could certainly have been less thorough, less severe, less deadly" in their policy toward Jews, after all, some Jews survived, "a number of whom even live in Connecticut."[91]

Armenian Americans were offended by what they saw as Jewish insistence on making the Holocaust "unique," while portraying the Armenian genocide as "ordinary." A Jewish magazine published a symposium in which Jewish writers responded to an Armenian who, in moderate language, questioned the uniqueness of the Holocaust and suggested numerous ways in which it paralleled the events of 1915. Lucy Dawidowicz (quite falsely) accused the Armenian of "turn[ing] the subject into a vulgar contest about who suffered more." She added that while the Turks had "a rational reason" for killing Armenians, the Germans had no rational reason for killing Jews. Other contributors offered various reasons why the Holocaust, unlike the Armenian genocide, was "special": that it took place in the heart of Christian Europe; that anti-Semitism was "sui generis"; that what happened to the Jews, unlike what happened to the Armenians, "represents a new divide in human history."[92]

Armenians had other grievances. The designers of the Washington Holocaust Museum went back on earlier commitments to give significant space to the Armenian genocide as part of the background of the Holocaust. They yielded to those in the museum's governing councils who objected to any dilution of the Holocaust's "unprecedented" character. They yielded as well to the urgent lobbying of the Israeli government, which was anxious not to offend Turkey — at the time, the only Muslim country with which Israel had diplomatic relations.[93] (Turkey has consistently denied that there ever was an Armenian genocide.) Israeli lobbying also led a number of prominent American Jews, including Elie Wiesel, Alan Dershowitz, and Arthur Hertzberg, to withdraw from an international conference on genocide in Tel Aviv when the Israeli organizers, despite heavy pressure from their government, refused to remove sessions on the Armenian case.[94]

Perhaps most infuriating of all to Armenians — given how forthcoming the American Congress had been with proclamations and funding for commemorating the Holocaust — Israeli diplomats and important American Jewish activists joined in a coalition that helped defeat a congressional resolution memorializing the Armenian genocide. Major Jewish organizations that had originally planned to support the resolution backed off and stayed silent in response to urgings from Israel.[95] One veteran Jewish leader explained what motivated his lobbying against the resolution: "Many contend the Holocaust was simply a terrible event, neither unique nor particular. To compare . . . Armenians [in 1915] to the situation of Europe's Jews in 1933 or 1939 is a dangerous invitation to revisionism about the Holocaust. . . . If Jews say every terrible event . . . is genocide, why should the world believe the Holocaust is distinctive?"[96] There were those in the American Jewish world who supported the congressional resolution commemorating the Armenian genocide. But it would be hard to quarrel with Armenian or other observers who concluded that, as far as "official" Jewry was concerned, some memories were more equal than others.[97]

As so often in these years, the most-publicized conflicts in this realm were between Jews and blacks. Those that attracted the greatest attention featured Louis Farrakhan and his merry band. "Don't push your six million down our throats," Farrakhan said, "when we lost 100 million."[98] "The black holocaust," said his aide Khalid Abdul

Muhammad, "was a hundred times worse than the so-called Jew Holocaust."[99] Though one would be hard-pressed to find blacks outside the Nation of Islam who would endorse this sort of trash talk, a sense of being perpetually one-upped by Jews, and of Jews' having stolen from blacks their rightful place as America's number-one victim community, was widespread. Farrakhan's kind of numerical competition was rare outside his circle, but it could turn up in unexpected places. Toni Morrison's 1987 novel *Beloved* is dedicated to "Sixty Million and More." This, Morrison says, is the number of enslaved blacks who died before they made it to the United States. The figure bears no relation to any scholarly estimate, but it is, of course, ten times six million.[100]

Apart from the numbers game — indeed, apart from any explicit invidious comparison between slavery and the Holocaust — it seems clear that as the Holocaust loomed ever larger in American culture as the central symbol of oppression and atrocity, and as American Jews increasingly defined themselves as the quintessential victim community, many blacks were resentful — though they usually expressed this in private.[101] One public statement came early in the process, in the late sixties. James Baldwin wrote:

> One does not wish . . . to be told by an American Jew that his suffering is as great as the American Negro's suffering. It isn't, and one knows that it isn't from the very tone in which he assures you that it is. . . .
>
> It is not here, and not now, that the Jew is being slaughtered, and he is never despised, here, as the Negro is, *because* he is an American. The Jewish travail occurred across the sea and America rescued him from the house of bondage. But America *is* the house of bondage for the Negro, and no country can rescue him.[102]

Blacks, as Baldwin's words suggest, were not much interested in global comparisons. Their grievance was that in America, the group that was by a wide margin the most advantaged was using European crimes to trump American crimes against what was, by an equally wide margin, the least advantaged group. As succeeding decades saw ever-diminishing concern with the misery of blacks and ever-greater concern with past Jewish suffering, resentment grew. The greatest symbolic affront was that while Jews had a federally funded museum memorializing their victimhood, proposals for a museum of the black experience never made it through Congress.[103] Blacks were well aware of the irony, which some Jewish commentators have also noted. It was American Jews' wealth and political influence that made it possible for them to bring to the Mall in Washington a monument to their weakness and vulnerability. Those who remained weak and vulnerable — who were oppressed here rather than there — lacked the wherewithal to carry off such a venture.[104]

The most common Jewish response to the charge that Jews were intent on permanent possession of the gold medal in the Victimization Olympics has been to protest that it was others, not they, who were engaged in competition. Jews were the aggrieved party — "they are stealing the Holocaust from us," said Elie Wiesel; others were illegitimately appropriating language and imagery to which they were not entitled.[105] (As we saw in the previous chapter, this was often described as the theft of Jewish moral capital.) The use of the word "ghetto" for black slums was frequently cited as an example of "stealing the Holocaust": "there is no barbed wire across 125th Street and there are no guard towers"; "no place in New York or Los Angeles or Chicago was even remotely like Buchenwald in 1938 or Warsaw in 1942 or Auschwitz in 1944."[106] The most commonly expressed Jewish grievance was the use of the words "Holocaust" and "genocide" to describe other catastrophes. This sense of grievance was rooted in the conviction, axiomatic in at least "official" Jewish discourse, that the Holocaust was unique. Since Jews recognized the Holocaust's uniqueness — that it was "incomparable," beyond any analogy — they had no occasion to compete with others; there could be no contest over the incontestable. It was only those who, out of ignorance or malice, denied the uniqueness of the Holocaust who could be so foolish as to engage in competition. (Some scholars in fact characterized denial of the Holocaust's uniqueness as a form of "Holocaust denial.")[107]

The word "unique" is often used loosely and casually as an attention-getting intensifier: "try our unique dishwashing liquid"; "I met this guy last night and he's, like, unique." Claims that one's own suffering is unique, incommunicable to others, are also common: "Nobody knows the trouble I've seen / Nobody knows my sorrow." But in the case of the alleged uniqueness of the Holocaust, we're in the presence not of loose usage and hyperbole but of serious philosophical and historical arguments — indeed, a substantial scholarly literature — which aim at logical and empirical demonstration that the Holocaust is unlike any other atrocity, a demonstration that will compel non-Jews to acknowledge this "fact."

Over the years, various grounds for the Holocaust's uniqueness have been offered, but many, for one or another reason, were found wanting: Stalin killed more innocents than Hitler; over the centuries many other targeted populations suffered greater proportional losses than did European Jews during World War II. Other criteria presented other difficulties.[108] The most comprehensive argument for the uniqueness of the Holocaust was also the most radical. Whereas many other writers were willing to acknowledge that there had been other genocides but only one Holocaust, Steven Katz, in a book of more than seven hundred pages (the first of three projected volumes), argued that even the word "genocide," if correctly understood, could be applied only to the travail of European Jewry in World War II. It was on the basis of this book that Katz was named head of the Washington Holocaust Museum — which suggests the appeal of its argument.[109]

I remarked in the Introduction that the very idea of uniqueness is fatuous, since any event — a war, a revolution, a genocide — will have significant features that it shares with events to which it might be compared as well as features that differentiate it from others. The claim that an event — as opposed to some features of an event — is unique can be sustained only by gerrymandering: deliberately singling out one or more distinctive features of the event and trivializing or sweeping under the rug those features that it shares with other events to which it might be compared. For Katz, what makes the Holocaust unique, makes it the only real genocide, is that "never before has a state set out . . . to annihilate physically every man, woman, and child belonging to a specific people."[110] If Katz is historically correct on this point — and historians who have examined his arguments have their doubts — this would indeed be a distinctive feature of the Holocaust.[111] How did Katz decide that this is the criterion by which one should decide whether the Holocaust is unique, the only genocide? He himself supplies the answer when he writes that while the Final Solution had many other features, "only the element of intentionality can serve as the individuating criterion by which to distinguish the Sho'ah from other instances of mass death."[112] Translation: I was determined to find that feature of the Holocaust which set it apart — made it unique — and this is the one I settled on.[113]

Putting aside for the moment the question of why this "individuating criterion" was chosen, and accepting for the moment that it is *the* crucial criterion for determining uniqueness, a question immediately arises, which was stated nicely by the philosopher Berel Lang: "*So what if the Holocaust is unique?*"

> What follows if the Shoah *was* the first of its kind in the respects Katz indicates? What significance does *that* have? . . . It is as though the effort to establish the "fact" becomes an end in itself, with any further justification self-evident. But such justification is *not* self-evident, indeed not evident at all. [Or] suppose an example that (by hypothesis) did meet all Katz's criteria of "uniqueness." . . . Nothing in the enormity of the Nazi genocide would change if that series of acts turned out to be the second — or fifth — instance of its kind.[114]

The question transcends Katz's book, which is of interest to us only insofar as it is the most systematic exposition of the doctrine of uniqueness, which sits astride all of contemporary Jewish discourse on the Holocaust. Katz, like virtually everyone else who makes this argument, asserts again and again that "unique" doesn't mean "worse," that the claim is not for *greater* but only for *different* Jewish victimization, that no one is saying the Holocaust is *more evil* than other atrocities, just that it's . . . unique. Such disavowals are either naïve or, more often, disingenuous. They are naïve or disingenuous because all the talk of uniqueness takes place in a context in which, for various purposes, atrocities are constantly compared. And the talk of uniqueness coexists with, overlaps with, and is inextricably intertwined with repeated insistence that the Holocaust is the archetype and yardstick of evil. This insistence comes from secularists like Raul Hilberg, for whom the Holocaust is "the benchmark, the defining moment in the drama of good and evil"; from rabbis like Michael Berenbaum, for whom it is "the paradigmatic manifestation of evil."[115] The claim that the assertion of the Holocaust's uniqueness is *not* a form of invidious comparison produces systematic doubletalk. A rabbi, in an op-ed piece for the *New York Times*, writes that "it is degrading, even ghoulish, to seek to prove preeminence in suffering." But, he continues, "the holocaust was unique," and proceeds to offer a statistical demonstration.[116] Does anyone (except, just conceivably, those making the argument) believe that the claim of uniqueness is anything *other* than a claim for preeminence?

"Holocaust envy" contends with "Holocaust possessiveness." Claims by others that they have experienced genocide or a holocaust — claims that are indeed sometimes hyperbolic — are treated as felonious assault.[117] At the same time, within the Jewish world there have been many critics of the fetishism of the Holocaust's uniqueness — some of them, like Ismar Schorsch, the chancellor of the Jewish Theological Seminary and a refugee from Nazi Germany, quite eminent. For Schorsch the obsession with uniqueness is a "distasteful secular version of chosenness," which introduces pointless enmity between Jews and other victims.[118] For Jacob Neusner the elaborate arguments for uniqueness are "intellectually vulgar":

> It comes down to why the Shoah was "worse" than what the Armenians went through. [It's] grotesque for us to be arguing with other ethnic groups that our Holocaust was worse than their Holocaust. Is our blood redder than theirs? . . . It's not a discussion that pays tribute to . . . our sense of self-worth. If you know who you are, you don't have to make statements like that.[119]

But these and other protests against the cult of uniqueness — and against the larger drive for acknowledgment of Jewish preeminence in suffering of which it is a part — have been unavailing. Why?

In part it may be because many Jews *don't* know who they are, except insofar as they have a "unique" victim identity, and because the uniqueness of the Holocaust is the sole guarantor of *their* uniqueness. As we've seen, it was frequently asserted, beginning in the seventies, that a rise in anti-Semitism in the United States made the Holocaust particularly relevant to American Jews. One could turn this around and argue, as does Rabbi Arthur Hertzberg, that it was not coincidental that interest in the Holocaust began "at the point when anti-semitism in America had become negligible."

> Every major area of American life . . . was now open to Jews. The children who had been born after the end of the Second World War . . . were free to choose their politics, . . . their sexual mores, and their connection, or lack of it, to Jewish faith and memory.
>
> Middle-aged parents saw what freedom had wrought and became frightened at the evaporation of the Jewishness of their children. The parents evoked the one Jewish emotion that had tied their own generation together, the fear of antisemitism. The stark memory of Auschwitz needed to be evoked to make the point that Jews were different. . . .

Historians . . . will no doubt see the unparalleled effort and passion which created the greatest of the Holocaust memorials in the United States on the Mall in Washington as the contemporary version of the building of a "national Jewish cathedral." It enshrines the Holocaust as the via dolorosa and crucifixion of the Jewish people. Those who come to remember are transformed in this shrine into participants in the great sacrifice. They are confirmed in their Jewishness, leaving with "never again" on their lips. It is their prayer, even as they remember that "Hear O Israel, the Lord, Thy God, the Lord is one" was the holiest of all verses for their ancestors.[120]

Hertzberg's remarks are a reminder that it's often hard to tell where "civil religion" leaves off and "the real thing" begins. Insistence on the uniqueness of the Holocaust — more broadly, the centering of the Holocaust in Jewish consciousness — proceeded apace with the Holocaust's increasing sacralization. (Important religious symbols, like the Covenant, or the Crucifixion, are always regarded as unique; to the extent that the Holocaust has become a central symbol not just of Jewishness but of Judaism, it too must be unique.)[121] For some religious Jews there was another criterion of uniqueness. Abraham Foxman, head of the Anti-Defamation League, said that the Holocaust was "not simply one example of genocide but a near successful attempt on the life of God's chosen children and, thus, on God himself."[122]

The Holocaust's sacralization has been ambiguous — "uneven" or "contested" might be better words. Some have insisted that the Holocaust should occupy a prominent place in Jewish religious thought and ritual. Emil Fackenheim formulated a "614th Commandment," to be appended to the 613 that, according to tradition, were received from God at Mount Sinai: "the commanding voice of Auschwitz."

> The authentic Jew of today is forbidden to hand Hitler yet another, posthumous victory. [We are] commanded to survive as Jews, lest the Jewish people perish. We are commanded [to remember] the martyrs of the Holocaust, lest their memory perish. We are forbidden . . . to deny or despair of God . . . lest Judaism perish. . . . To abandon any of these imperatives, in response to Hitler's victory at Auschwitz, would be to hand him yet other, posthumous victories.[123]

Rabbi Irving Greenberg was one of the most effective individuals in working to place the Holocaust at the core of American Jewish thought. He was the founder of ZACHOR: The Holocaust Resource Center, which promoted and coordinated various forms of commemoration; he went on to become the first director of the U.S. Holocaust Memorial Commission. For Greenberg, the Holocaust was a "revelational event" on a par with Sinai and the Exodus, and he urged that, accordingly, it be given a central place in a renegotiated Covenant and in Jewish liturgy.[124] The sacramental eating of matzo to commemorate the Exodus should, he suggested, be matched by the sacramental eating of "the rotten bread of Auschwitz, or the potato peelings of Bergen-Belsen" to commemorate the other "revelational" event.[125] (Greenberg called the comparison of the Holocaust with any other genocide "blasphemous.")[126]

Despite these efforts, the Holocaust has not assumed a central place in formal Jewish religious belief or practice as they are defined by rabbinical associations and by the tacit consensus of leading religious thinkers. In part this is simply the bias against major innovation within any religious establishment. But it also reflects widespread uneasiness about "what to do with" the Holocaust — seen as an embarrassment for traditional notions of the Covenant. Most Jewish religious leaders see nothing revelational about the Holocaust; they would prefer to relegate it to the margins of religious consciousness. "Should the Holocaust cease to be peripheral to the faith of Israel," wrote one Jewish scholar,

> should it enter the Holy of Holies and become the dominant voice that Israel hears, it could not but be a demonic voice that it would be hearing. There is no salvation to be extracted from the Holocaust, no faltering Judaism can be revived by it, no new reason for the continuation of the Jewish people can be found in it. If there is hope after the Holocaust, it is because to those who believe, the voice of the Prophets speaks more loudly than did Hitler, and because the divine promise sweeps over the crematoria and silences the voice of Auschwitz.[127]

As far as "official" Judaism is concerned, this position seems to be the dominant one.

Yet in what might be called American "folk Judaism" — less bound by tradition and less scrupulous about theological consistency — a de facto sacralization of the Holocaust has taken place. This assumes various forms. Even many observant Jews are often willing to discuss the founding myths of Judaism naturalistically — subject them to rational, scholarly analysis. But they're unwilling to adopt this mode of thought when it comes to the "inexplicable mystery" of the Holocaust, where rational analysis is seen as inappropriate or sacrilegious. Con-

sider "awe," which my dictionary defines as "a mixed emotion of rever-
ence, respect, dread, and wonder." For how many Jews does the word
describe their emotions when contemplating God (as tradition mandates)? For how many their emotions when contemplating the Holocaust? It has become standard practice to use the term "sacred" to describe the Holocaust and everything connected with it. "Sacred Image,
Sacred Text" was the title of an exhibition of art dealing with the Holocaust at the B'nai B'rith's Klutznick Museum in Washington.[128] Survivors' accounts are routinely described as sacred, as are the survivors
themselves: "the American Jewish equivalent of saints and relics,"
says Leon Wieseltier, himself the son of a survivor.[129] An important
influence in all of this, of course, has been Elie Wiesel, the most influential American interpreter of the Holocaust. Like Greenberg,
Wiesel sees the Holocaust as "equal to the revelation at Sinai" in its
religious significance; attempts to "desanctify" or "demystify" the
Holocaust are, he says, a subtle form of anti-Semitism.[130] And Wiesel,
with his insistence that "any survivor has more to say than all the historians combined about what happened," appears to have persuaded
many Jews to treat the Holocaust as something of a "mystery religion,"
with survivors having privileged (priestly) authority to interpret the
mystery.[131] "The survivor has become a priest," the education director
of Yad Vashem said, with some irritation; "because of his story, he is
holy."[132]

Certainly not all Jews view the Holocaust as a sacred mystery
or think of it as an event with profound, albeit often unspecified,
religious significance. But a great many seem to — enough that it is
probably a mistake to treat the Holocaust as a primary tenet only in
American Jewish *civil* religion.

However described, and for all the reasons discussed in this and the
previous chapter, the Holocaust has, in recent decades, moved from
the margins to the center of how American Jews understand themselves and how they represent themselves to others. So far as self-
understanding is concerned, there's no way of knowing just how many
American Jews, and which American Jews, ground their Jewish identity in the Holocaust, but the number appears to be large. (It's clear
that the Holocaust has less relative importance for those Jews with an
identity firmly rooted in Jewish religious belief or who are otherwise
grounded in Jewish culture, but that's a rather small percentage of
American Jewry.)[133] Though no one can specify with any precision the

breadth and depth of Holocaust-based Jewish identity, we can note the hundreds of millions of dollars American Jews have contributed to Holocaust-related projects, the way they turn out for Holocaust-related events as for no others, the continuing high demand for scholarly (and not-so-scholarly) books on the Holocaust — greater than for books on any other Jewish subject. For those who prefer "harder" data, and for what it's worth, there are the results of the American Jewish Committee's "1998 Annual Survey of American Jewish Opinion." Those responding were asked to rate the importance of various listed activities to their Jewish identity. The year 1998 was the first in which "remembrance of the Holocaust" was included in the list. It won hands down — chosen as "extremely important" or "very important" by many more than those who chose synagogue attendance, Jewish study, working with Jewish organizations, traveling to Israel, or observing Jewish holidays.[134]

When it comes to how American Jews represent themselves to others, there is no question but that the Holocaust is at the center of that representation. The U.S. Holocaust Memorial Museum is the principal symbol and "address" of American Jewry, our "epistle to the gentiles" about what it means to be Jewish. The museum on the Mall is matched by dozens of smaller Holocaust museums in cities across the country. In the late 1980s — before the opening of the major museums in Washington, Los Angeles, and New York — the Detroit Holocaust Museum boasted that it was "this Nation's most toured Jewish institution."[135] The smaller museums serve the same function of communal definition locally as the Washington museum does nationally: these monuments to suffering and death are described by their builders as "the natural site for interfaith services"; they function to "explain our Jewish heritage and our Jewish needs to the Gentile as well as to the Jew."[136]

As we have seen, while the Holocaust has proved "popular" with American Jews, its rise to the top of the Jewish agenda was by no means a spontaneous development. More than anything else, it was the consequence of decisions made by communal leaders in response to their appraisals of current communal needs — of what worked in dealing with immediate problems. That the end result of these decisions would be to put the Holocaust at the center of how Jews understood themselves and wanted others to understand them was neither foreseen nor intended by most of those who set the process in motion. Some of those who, from the sixties on, urged that Jews "confront" the Holocaust did so because they had been dismayed by the relative silence in the postwar years, when many Jews seemed ashamed of it. Years later, they were often equally dismayed when many Jews seemed proud of it.

Part Four

RECENT YEARS

[10]

"To Bigotry No Sanction"

SINCE THE 1970s, the Holocaust has come to be presented — come to be thought of — as not just a Jewish memory but an American memory. In a growing number of states the teaching of the Holocaust in public schools is legislatively mandated. Instructions for conducting "Days of Remembrance" are distributed throughout the American military establishment, and commemorative ceremonies are held annually in the Capitol Rotunda. Over the past twenty years every president has urged Americans to preserve the memory of the Holocaust. The operating expenses of the Washington Holocaust Museum — originally to have been raised by private contributions — have been largely taken over by the federal government. In Boston, the New England Holocaust Memorial is located on the Freedom Trail, along with Paul Revere's house and the Bunker Hill Monument. Public officials across the country told Americans that seeing *Schindler's List* was their civic duty. How did this European event come to loom so large in American consciousness?

A good part of the answer is the fact — not less of a fact because anti-Semites turn it into a grievance — that Jews play an important and influential role in Hollywood, the television industry, and the newspaper, magazine, and book publishing worlds.[1] Anyone who would explain the massive attention the Holocaust has received in these media in recent years without reference to that fact is being naïve or disingenuous. This is not, of course, a matter of any "Jewish conspiracy" — Jews in the media do not dance to the tune of "the elders of Zion." It's not even a matter of Jews in the media per se, which is an old story, but of what sort of Jews. Beginning in the 1970s, a cohort of Jews who either didn't have much in the way of Jewish concerns or were diffident about voicing the concerns they did have came to be replaced by a cohort that included many for whom those concerns were more deeply felt and who were more up-front about them. In large part the movement of the Holocaust from the Jewish to the general American arena resulted from private and spontaneous decisions of Jews who happened to occupy strategic positions in the mass media.

But that movement was not completely private and spontaneous. If, as many in Jewish organizations believed, Americans could be made more sympathetic to Israel, or to American Jews, through awareness of the Holocaust, efforts had to be made to spread that awareness throughout American society. Blu Greenberg, the wife of Rabbi Irving Greenberg, wrote that she had originally favored exclusively Jewish commemoration of the Holocaust; such occasions were "a moment to withdraw into the embrace of one's own group." After attending an interfaith Yom Hashoah ceremony, however, she found it "moving and comforting to see Christians share tears with us, acknowledge Christian guilt, and commit themselves to the security of Israel."[2] Indeed, even the aim of promoting awareness of the Holocaust among Jews — for "survivalist" or other purposes — could be accomplished only by making that awareness general. "For Jews to solidify the place of the Holocaust within Jewish consciousness," wrote Michael Berenbaum of the Washington Holocaust Museum, "they must establish its importance for the American people as a whole."[3]

Not all of the initiatives in spreading awareness of the Holocaust have been Jewish — and the exceptions will later be noted — but they almost always have been, frequently with considerable investment of communal resources. Sometimes these initiatives took the form of outreach to targeted audiences, like the Catholic and Protestant churches, or the schools. Sometimes the independent initiatives of others were promoted, as in the case of NBC's 1978 miniseries *Holocaust*. What were, de jure, government initiatives were often, de facto, those of Jewish aides, simultaneously promoting projects in which they believed and helping their employers score points with Jewish constituents. There is certainly nothing improper in any of this; every group does it; American pluralism in action. But the phenomenon is worth bearing in mind, lest we overinterpret the depth and spontaneity of statements by gentile public figures on the Holocaust. What might be termed "ventriloquism between consenting adults" is, in any case, a time-hallowed practice.

On the wall of the Washington Holocaust Museum are engraved the words George Washington used in a letter to the Hebrew Congregation of Newport in 1790: "The Government of the United States . . . gives to bigotry no sanction, to persecution no assistance." A worthwhile sentiment, which should be preserved, and one which the American government has for the most part lived up to, at least as concerns Jews. But while Washington endorsed the sentiment, no doubt sincerely, he was simply playing back to the congregation the words *it* had used in a letter to which he was replying: "we now, with a deep sense of gratitude . . . behold a government . . . which to bigotry gives no sanction, to persecution no assistance."[4]

Whatever the source of the initiatives, and whatever motivated them, the entry of the Holocaust into general American discourse raised new questions. If the Holocaust was to be presented to a mass audience, what were appropriate and what were inappropriate modes of representation? Which compromises were permissible, and which impermissible, in making the subject accessible to the masses? The Holocaust's entry into American discourse has, in many instances, led to a redefinition of the very word "Holocaust." As the Holocaust came to figure ever larger in the American scene, to be invoked in various contexts, the problem repeatedly arose of distinguishing between the (legitimate) "use" and the (illegitimate) "abuse" of the Holocaust and its imagery. Finally, what did non-Jews make of all this talk of the Holocaust?

Without doubt the most important moment in the entry of the Holocaust into general American consciousness was NBC's presentation, in April 1978, of the miniseries *Holocaust*. Close to 100 million Americans watched all or most of the four-part, 9½-hour program.[5] As was often observed at the time, more information about the Holocaust was imparted to more Americans over those four nights than over all the preceding thirty years. The drama followed ten years in the lives of two fictional families — one of assimilated German Jews, the other of a highly placed official of the SS. Through this somewhat labored device, the series was able to cover all of the principal landmarks: the Nuremberg Laws, Kristallnacht, the Wannsee Conference, Babi Yar, the Warsaw Ghetto Uprising; Buchenwald, Theresienstadt, and Auschwitz. The miniseries was a mini–survey course.

NBC went all out to promote the series — its answer to ABC's enormously successful *Roots* in the previous year. But its efforts paled in comparison with those of organized Jewry. Coming at a time when, as we've seen, Jewish organizations were getting into Holocaust programming, it was an opportunity not to be missed. The Anti-Defamation League distributed ten million copies of its sixteen-page tabloid *The Record* to promote the drama. Jewish organizations successfully lobbied major newspapers to serialize Gerald Green's novelization of his television play, or to publish special inserts on the Holocaust. (*The Chicago Sun-Times* distributed hundreds of thousands of copies of its insert to local schools.) The American Jewish Committee, in cooperation with NBC, distributed millions of copies of a study guide for viewers; teachers' magazines carried other curricular material tied to the program. Jewish organizations worked with the National Council of Churches to prepare other promotional and educational materials, and organized advance viewings for religious leaders. The day the series began was designated "Holocaust Sunday"; various activities were scheduled in cities across the country; the National Conference of Christians and Jews distributed yellow stars to be worn on that day.[6]

Those activities were directed at gentiles. But, following Berenbaum's dictum that making the Holocaust important to all Americans would also make it more important to Jews, the NBC miniseries offered an unmatched opportunity to further that task as well. Thus, much of the promotional work conducted by the Jewish agencies, and the activities that accompanied the miniseries, were directed at American Jews, virtually all of whom seem to have watched. ("For Jews," said one Jewish magazine, watching the program "has about it the quality of a religious obligation.")[7] The director of a Jewish school in Pittsburgh called *Holocaust* a "shock treatment for developing Jewish identity."[8] There were differences between the materials Jewish agencies prepared for gentile and for Jewish viewers. The miniseries contained several references to Christian anti-Semitism and the churches' silence during the Holocaust, as well as to Eastern Europeans who participated in the Nazi killings. The ADL's *Record* contained no reference to any of this, but did have four items on churchmen who opposed Nazism or rescued Jews — presumably the result of community-relations considerations. The study guides for Jewish young people, prepared by a consortium of Jewish organizations, were rather different. Christian anti-Semitism and Eastern European collaborators were frequently mentioned. There were disparaging references to how assimilated the family of Jewish protagonists were, and that they weren't bothered by the son's marriage to a gentile. Intermarriage was one suggested theme for group meetings to be held after viewing the program. Among the questions for discussion recommended in the study guides were "What can we learn from the TV program about those who wanted to forget . . . that they were Jews?" "Should Jews always keep their passports up-to-date, just in case?" "Do you own a gun?" "Do you think you ought to?"[9]

With a handful of exceptions, television critics and journalistic commentators were highly enthusiastic, not to say rhapsodic, about *Holocaust*. (Several commentators were bothered by the intrusion of commercials, which produced some grotesque juxtapositions, but most wearily accepted this as the price of having the program on network TV.)[10] Having spent so much effort promoting it, the leading Jewish organizations were, predictably, effusive in their praise. "I've seen the complete film three times," said Rabbi Marc Tannenbaum of the American Jewish Committee. "And each time I came away bawling like a baby. It really has a transforming power. It really could make a difference."[11]

But this first representation of the Holocaust before a mass audience was also the catalyst for a denunciation of the very idea of such a representation. On the day the NBC series began to air, the *New York Times* featured an article by Elie Wiesel entitled "Trivializing the Holocaust."

> Untrue, offensive, cheap . . . an insult to those who perished and to those who survived. . . . It transforms an ontological event into soap-opera. . . . We see long, endless processions of Jews marching toward Babi Yar. . . . We see the naked bodies covered with "blood" — and it is all make-believe. . . . People will tell me that . . . similar techniques are being used for war movies and historical re-creations. But the Holocaust is unique; not just another event. This series treats the Holocaust as if it were just another event. . . . Auschwitz cannot be explained nor can it be visualized. . . . The Holocaust transcends history. . . . The dead are in possession of a secret that we, the living, are neither worthy of nor capable of recovering. . . . The Holocaust [is] the ultimate event, the ultimate mystery, never to be comprehended or transmitted. Only those who were there know what it was; the others will never know.[12]

Not everyone was willing to endorse Wiesel's claim that the Holocaust was a sacred mystery, whose secrets were confined to a priesthood of survivors. In a diffuse way, however, the assertion that the Holocaust was a holy event that resisted profane representation, that it was uniquely inaccessible to explanation or understanding, that survivors had privileged interpretive authority — all these themes continued to resonate, though their overall influence is hard to calculate. That the Holocaust was, in some undefined way, sacred, and mandated some sort of special rules for its representation, was a proposition to which a great many people at least paid lip service. Many also came to believe that the Holocaust was uniquely inexplicable — a belief based in part, I suspect, on the mistaken conviction that historians ordinarily reach consensus on explaining other complex events. The assertion that only those who were there can know what it was like — with its corollary of privileged authority for the survivor — is in one sense profoundly true. At the same time, it again makes a sharper-than-justified distinction between the Holocaust experience and others. In this connection Raul Hilberg wrote: " 'If you were not there, you cannot imagine what it was like.' These words were said to me in Düsseldorf some years ago by a one-legged veteran of the German army who had been trapped in the Demyansk pocket on the Russian front at the end of 1941. The man had been wounded six times. One cannot deny that he had a valid point."[13]

How consequential has all of this been for how the Holocaust has been presented to a mass audience? My guess is that it hasn't mattered that much. A substantial literature has developed on special problems that are alleged to exist in portraying the Holocaust in film, in fiction, and in scholarship. But it is a very academic literature — written by and for academics, almost always published in academic journals, often jargon-ridden, or written with the assumption that the reader is conversant with current academic theories. None of this is a judgment on the intellectual quality of this work, which of course varies. Rather, it's the question of whether all of this writing has influenced either the producers or consumers of mass media representations of the Holocaust. Probably not much.

There were some writers in the popular press in 1978 who, like Wiesel, or following his lead, attacked *Holocaust* as sacrilegious. Thus the critic Molly Haskell in *New York*: "How can actors, how *dare* actors, presume to imagine and tell us what it felt like! The attempt becomes a desecration against, among others, the Hebraic injunction banning graven images."[14] More common were those, like Peter Sourian in *The Nation*, who argued that it was the very "falsity" of Gerald Green's teleplay that enabled it to fulfill its mission — to move and inform those without any desire to be moved and informed, "at least not during prime time."[15]

Sourian's argument received powerful, indeed decisive, support early the following year, when *Holocaust* was broadcast in Germany. During the debate over whether the program should be shown, those opposed to "wallowing" in the Nazi past deployed the full array of aesthetic objections. Franz Josef Strauss, the Christian Democratic Party's candidate for chancellor, called it "a fast-buck operation." German television executives who opposed the showing termed it "a cultural commodity . . . not in keeping with the memory of the victims." *Der Spiegel* denounced the "destruction of the Jews as soap opera . . . a commercial horror show . . . an imported cheap commodity. . . . Genocide shrunken to the level of *Bonanza* with music appropriate to *Love Story.*"[16]

The airing of the series, in January 1979, became the turning point in Germany's long-delayed confrontation with the Holocaust, which, albeit not without bumps in the road, has continued ever since. It enabled Germans to connect with the Jewish victims, and with the crime, as never before. It was widely credited with a decisive role in the Bundestag's decision, later that year, to abolish the statute of limitations on war crimes.[17] One German journalist wrote:

> It is absolutely fantastic. . . . "Holocaust" has shaken up post-Hitler Germany in a way that German intellectuals have been unable to do. No other film has ever made the Jews' road of suffering leading to the gas chambers so vivid. . . . Only since and as a result of "Holocaust" does a majority of the nation know what lay behind the horrible and vacuous formula "Final Solution of the Jewish Question." They know it because a U.S. film maker had the courage to break with the paralyzing dogma . . . that mass murder must not be represented in art.[18]

A double irony. It was an American "soap opera" that shattered thirty years of German silence on their wartime crimes. It was the German reception of that American "soap opera" which, as a practical if not a theoretical matter, ended debate in America on the ability of the popular media to present the Holocaust effectively.

And — though not for many years on so grand a scale — the American popular media, particularly television, continued to do so: *Playing for Time, Escape from Sobibor, Triumph of the Spirit, War and Remembrance;* there were many, many others.[19] None of these ever achieved the audience, or occasioned as much discussion, as did *Holocaust* in 1978. But in the aggregate (supplemented by a steady stream of imported foreign films on the subject), they served to firmly affix the Holocaust on the American cultural map. The culmination (so far) of this process was Steven Spielberg's 1993 *Schindler's List*, which benefited not just from the director's mega-reputation but from the fact that it appeared in the same year that the Washington Holocaust Museum opened. As *Holocaust* had swept television's Emmy Awards for 1978, *Schindler's List* did with the Oscars for 1993. And whereas in 1978 Jewish organizations felt obliged to promote the television program, in 1993 public officials from the president on down were so actively promoting Spielberg's film that it was hard to find room on the bandwagon. Free showings for high school students were arranged (during class time) across the country, as a contribution to their moral education, following the example of Oprah Winfrey, who announced on her talk show that "I'm a better person as a result of seeing *Schindler's List*."[20]

As with *Holocaust* there were naysayers, but theirs was distinctly a minority view: two negative commentaries were each entitled "A Dissent on *Schindler's List*."[21] Those critical of the movie made excellent points: it was grotesque that what was frequently touted as the definitive Holocaust movie featured that most atypical of Holocaust heroes, a Nazi rescuer; that Spielberg had made "a feel-good entertainment about the ultimate feel-bad experience of the 20th century."[22] Even the movie's critics, however, acknowledged that *Schindler's List* left all of those who saw it — however much or little they'd previously known of the Holocaust — overwhelmed by the horror of the events and deeply moved, often to tears. This was my own experience, and I think it likely that for the majority of viewers, responses of horror and grief overwhelmed whatever redemptive message is carried by the movie. These are, in any case, not inappropriate responses. But this leaves unresolved the question of why the eliciting of these responses from Americans is seen as so urgently important a task.

Six million is an instantly recognizable number, the generally accepted estimate of the Jews killed by Nazi Germany in its murderous crusade.[23] The phrase "the six million" is a rhetorical stand-in for "the Holocaust." But nowadays, for a great many people, the real number of Holocaust victims is eleven million: six million Jews and five million non-Jews. What's at stake, of course, is not numbers as such, but what we mean, what we're referring to, when we talk of "the Holocaust." As we'll see, the question came to be hotly and angrily disputed in official American commemorations. More broadly, the various ways in which "six" and "eleven" have been used shed light on the uses of the Holocaust in American life.

The eleven million figure — or, rather, the notion of five million "other victims" of Nazism, added to six million Jews — makes no historical sense. Five million is either much too low (for all non-Jewish civilians killed by the Third Reich) or much too high (for non-Jewish groups targeted, like Jews, for murder). Where did the number come from? Although there is no detailed paper trail, it's generally agreed that the figure of eleven million originated with Simon Wiesenthal, the renowned pursuer of Nazi criminals. How did he arrive at this figure? The Israeli historian Yehuda Bauer reports that Wiesenthal acknowledged to him in a private conversation that he simply invented it.[24] He was, he once told a reporter, against "dividing the victims": "Since 1948," Wiesenthal said, "I have sought with Jewish leaders not to talk about six million Jewish dead, but rather about eleven million civilians dead, including six million Jews. . . . We reduced the problem to one between Nazis and Jews. Because of this we lost many friends who suffered with us, whose families share common graves."[25]

The date in Wiesenthal's remark is worth noting. In postwar Europe, as in postwar America, while everyone realized that the fate of the Jews was "special," there was an inclination, even among many Jews, to include that fate under the larger heading of "crimes of Nazism." Wiesenthal — all the more so because of his lifetime mission of ferreting out Nazi criminals, and enlisting the help of European governments in that task — was sympathetic to the inclusion. Biography was also important. Many survivors of the Holocaust were strictly observant Jews who were swept as children from the *shtetl* to camps where all their fellow prisoners were Jews. Nothing could have been more natural than for them to frame their experience as a solely Jewish one. Wiesenthal — in this he resembled survivors like Primo Levi — was not religious and had a relatively cosmopolitan background. For four years he survived camps like Mauthausen, where many of his fellow prisoners were not Jewish. Wiesenthal's invention of "eleven million" was bizarre, but given his experiences and the context in which he worked, there was nothing unusual or unnatural in his interpreting Nazi crimes in an "ecumenical" way.[26] In any event, it was with reference to those crimes in general, not "the Holocaust," that he spoke of eleven million.

Before the late seventies, few in the United States had ever heard the figure "eleven million." Wiesenthal's fame in this country had to do with his exploits as a Nazi hunter, not as an interpreter of the Holocaust. This changed in 1977 when, in return for a subsidy for his program of tracking down war criminals, a California rabbi obtained the use of his name for what became a highly visible Holocaust institution, the Simon Wiesenthal Center.[27] "Eleven million" was part of the baggage that came with the name."[28] Inscribed at the entrance to the center's museum was a tribute to "six million Jews and to five million of other faiths"; center publications came to speak of "The Holocaust — six million Jews and five million non-Jews."[29] Though not originally advanced as such, "eleven million" had become a new description of the parameters of the Holocaust.

By itself, the use of "eleven million" by the Wiesenthal Center might not have given wide currency to the figure. What put it on the agenda — what made "eleven million" a slogan for some and fighting words for others — was the setting in motion, in the spring of 1978, of the process that ultimately led to the creation of the United States Holocaust Memorial Museum in Washington.

That process began with the conventional understanding of the Holocaust. At a ceremony on the White House lawn in honor of Israel's thirtieth birthday, President Jimmy Carter announced that he was setting up a commission to explore creating a national memorial to "the six million who were killed in the Holocaust."[30] On this occasion no other definition would have been appropriate, for, as is well known, Carter's initiative was an attempt to placate American Jews, who were increasingly alienated by what they saw as the president's "excessive evenhandedness" in dealing with Israelis and Palestinians.[31] If the estrangement continued, it could be devastating for Carter's prospects for reelection, in part because of Jewish votes in key states, and even more because Jews traditionally contributed a substantial portion of national Democratic campaign funds.[32] Jewish White House staffers who developed the proposal for the memorial weren't moved solely by political calculations; several seem to have had a genuine commitment to Holocaust commemoration.[33] But the potential political payoff was paramount. The final staff discussions of the proposed memorial were conducted amid all the hoopla over NBC's *Holocaust*. This led one of the aides of domestic policy chief Stuart Eizenstadt to worry that it might look like "a tacky effort to ride the coattails of the show." So it might, replied another, but "our relations with Jewish community need every little boost possible."[34]

On the day after Carter's announcement of a proposal to commemorate "the six million," one of Eizenstadt's aides suggested to her boss that the new commission might "consider expanding this to eleven million," following the example of the Simon Wiesenthal Center.[35] There were various reasons to move in this direction. Carter's initiative had preempted a bill recently introduced in the Senate (with twenty cosponsors) to establish a memorial to the Holocaust's "eleven million innocent victims, of all faiths."[36] In congressional discussions after Carter's announcement, senators and representatives who lauded the proposal — Jews and gentiles alike — referred as often to "eleven" or "six plus five" or "six plus millions of others" as they did to "six."[37] When the President's Commission on the Holocaust was formally established some months later, with Elie Wiesel as its chairman, it solicited suggestions from numerous sources, including representatives of ethnic groups. The director of the Ukrainian National Information Service wrote that Ukrainians also "met Hitler's criteria for extermination" and were "numerically the second largest group to be destroyed in . . . Auschwitz, Treblinka, and Dachau." He asked that whatever was done "reflect the various nationalities and the numerical proportions of the victims of the Nazi Holocaust."[38] Aloysius Mazewski, the president of the Polish-American Congress, insisted that it was Poles, not Ukrainians, who deserved second place to Jews: his total of ten million Holocaust victims was made up of six million Jews, three million Catholic Poles, and one million "other nationalities."[39] On the other hand, the president of the Alliance of Poles of America claimed that "more than six million Christians [mostly Poles] . . . lost their lives"; he spoke of "the need to memorialize the sufferings and death of our Polish Catholic brothers and sisters — and not only those of Jewish tradition. To do otherwise would make their suffering and death meaningless."[40]

In April 1979, while the commission was deliberating, the first "Days of Remembrance" of the Holocaust were held in the Capitol Rotunda.[41] By this time, for whatever reasons, the White House had changed its definition of "the Holocaust." President Carter spoke of "eleven million innocent victims exterminated — six million of them Jews." Vice President Walter Mondale spoke of bearing witness "to the unanswered cries of the eleven million."[42] This redefinition was, of course, deeply offensive to Wiesel. His commission's report, delivered to the president in September 1979, was, above all, a rejoinder to Carter's new characterization. It insisted on the Jewish specificity — the Jewish essence — of the Holocaust: "any attempt to dilute or deny this reality would be to falsify it in the name of misguided universalism." The report contained phrases that Wiesel was to repeat frequently over subsequent years — acknowledging that Nazism had other targets, but insisting on the temporal as well as the conceptual priority of Jewish victimhood: "as night descended, millions of other peoples were swept into this net of death"; "Jews might not have remained the final victims of Nazi genocide but they were certainly its first"; "as always, they began with Jews[;] as always they did not stop with Jews alone." There were indeed "other victims," whose existence should be recognized in the museum being recommended, but, the report strongly implied — without quite saying so — they were not victims of "the Holocaust."[43]

The following months saw an intense struggle between Wiesel and Jewish staffers in the White House over how the Holocaust should be described — who would be included. It was "morally repugnant," said one presidential aide, "to create a category of second-class victims of the Holocaust as Mr. Wiesel would have us do."[44] Stuart Eizenstadt urged Carter that in the executive order creating the Holocaust Memorial Council (successor to the presidential commission) he should "make clear the memorial is to honor the memory of all victims of the Holocaust — six million Jews and some five million other peoples."[45] This definition, one staff member pointed out, was that of Simon Wiesenthal, "whose Holocaust credentials are as good as anyone else I know."[46] At the eleventh hour there was an ingenious proposal from Wiesel and the commission's new director, Monroe Freedman, to resolve the question through punctuation. The White House draft spoke of commemorating "The Holocaust, the systematic, state-sponsored extermination of six million Jews and millions of other victims of Nazism during World War II." The proposed alternative would make a conceptual separation through the use of dashes: "The Holocaust — the systematic state-sponsored extermination of six million Jews — and the millions of other Nazi victims."[47] Eizenstadt, in the end, was willing to give in. "For better or worse," he said, Wiesel had become the symbol of the Holocaust, and if he resigned over the issue, "we simply would not be able to get another prominent Jewish leader to serve as Chairman." While Eastern European ethnic groups would prefer the original wording, the definitional issue was not, for them, "a live or die matter as it is with Wiesel."[48] But an exasperated Carter refused to accept the dashes, and the executive order creating the Holocaust Memorial Council referred to eleven million victims. Wiesel did not resign, and the museum he was charged with creating was officially committed to memorializing "eleven million."

This was clearly unacceptable to Wiesel and others for whom the "big truth" about the Holocaust was its Jewish specificity. They responded to the expansion of the victims of the Holocaust to eleven million the way devout Christians would respond to the expansion of the victims of the Crucifixion to three — the Son of God and two thieves. Weisel's forces mobilized, both inside and outside the Holocaust Council, to ensure that, despite the executive order, their definition would prevail. Though Jewish survivors of the Holocaust had no role in the initiative that created the museum, they came, under the leadership of Wiesel, to dominate the council — morally, if not numerically. When one survivor, Sigmund Strochlitz, was sworn in as a council member, he announced that it was "unreasonable and inappropriate to ask survivors to share the term Holocaust . . . to equate our suffering . . . with others."[49] At one council meeting, another survivor, Kalman Sultanik, was asked whether Daniel Trocmé, murdered at Maidanek for rescuing Jews and honored at Yad Vashem as a Righteous Gentile, could be remembered in the museum's Hall of Remembrance. "No," said Sultanik, because "he didn't die as a Jew. . . . The six million Jews . . . died differently."[50]

There were also attempts to mobilize Jewish opinion at large against blurring the distinction between the victimhood of Jews and that of others. Survivor Henry Grynberg even objected to the ancillary role accorded to gentiles in Wiesel's phrase about others being, "as night descended . . . swept into this net of death." This was, Grynberg said, "absolutely false": "Those millions of others would have perished in the war even if the Holocaust had never taken place."[51] Children of survivors were often among those who insisted on the distinction between the deaths of gentiles and of Jews. Gentiles, said one, "died a death invented for the Jews . . . victims of a 'solution' designed for others."[52] For another child of survivors, dismayed by what he saw as the museum's blurring of the issue, the deaths of gentile victims "were of a different, non-theological order, untouched by the mysteries that reign at the heart of . . . the 'Tremendum.' "[53] Yehuda Bauer enlisted in the battle against what he called the "Wiesenthal-Carter definition." It reflected, he wrote, gentile "envy" of the Jews' experience in the Holocaust, which "would seem to be an unconscious reflection of anti-Semitic attitudes."

> The Holocaust created a pro-Jewish reaction among large numbers of non-Jews. . . . A reversion back to "normalcy" regarding Jews requires the destruction of the Holocaust-caused attitude of sympathy. . . . This is achieved by claiming that the Holocaust was . . . something that happened to many millions of others. . . . The Holocaust then becomes lost, flattened out . . . and a "normal" attitude of anti-Jewishness becomes possible again.[54]

Wiesel and his allies no doubt feared that the logic of the museum's "eleven million" mandate foreshadowed "other victims" receiving five elevenths of the space. In the end, largely as a result of the influence of survivors on the council, "other victims" wound up receiving little more than perfunctory mention in the museum's permanent exhibition.[55] Thus, though he had lost in the preliminary skirmish with Carter over the museum's mandate, Wiesel won the war over its content. Carter's "eleven million" never became operational doctrine at the museum, yet there remained a vague commitment to a principle of inclusion, producing endless wrangling over the definition of the Holocaust at meetings of the council. Council member Hyman Bookbinder — the long-time Washington representative of the American Jewish Committee — was frustrated, and after reviewing the various elusive aphoristic formulas that were trotted out, tried to get Wiesel to answer a straightforward question: "Are the 'other millions' victims of *the Holocaust*, or *in addition* to the Holocaust?"[56] Wiesel never gave a direct answer, and neither has the museum.[57] Clarity was undesirable and imprudent; much better to leave the matter ambiguous.

The same ambiguity, the same confusion and uncertainty, characterize general American discourse about the Holocaust. Americans are exhorted that they must "confront" or "remember" the Holocaust, but what is it that they are to confront or remember? This isn't a matter of different interpretations or different theories but of what event we're talking about. It's a truism — Philosophy 101 — that we never directly encounter events, only *representations* of events, which offer different *versions* of events. The more highly charged the event, the more evocative it is, the greater the incentive to become invested in different versions of it. An illustration. No text from the Holocaust is more often quoted than Martin Niemöller's confession of his moral failure during the 1930s:

> First they came for the Communists, but I was not a Communist — so I said nothing. Then they came for the Social Democrats, but I was not a Social Democrat — so I did nothing. Then came the trade unionists, but I was not a trade unionist. And then they came for the Jews, but I was not a Jew — so I did little. Then when they came for me, there was no one left who could stand up for me.[58]

Time magazine, Vice President Al Gore, and a speaker at the 1992 Republican Convention follow the example of *The Encyclopedia of the Holocaust* in moving Jews from last to first place: "First they came for the Jews."[59] *Time*, Gore, and the Republican speaker omitted Communists and Social Democrats; Gore omitted trade unionists as well. All three added Catholics (not on Niemöller's original list). Catholics are also added to the version of the quotation inscribed on the Holocaust memorial in Boston, a heavily Catholic city.[60] The U.S. Holocaust Museum preserves the list and order intact except for prudently omitting Communists.[61] Other versions include homosexuals on Niemöller's list.[62] (The quotation has been invoked for causes ranging from Jewish settlement in the West Bank to freedom of the insurance industry from government regulation.)[63]

This brief survey of the various creative editings of the Niemöller quotation has the merit of underlining the centrality of questions of inclusion and exclusion, but it is in some ways a bad example of what we're looking at. It involves, at least in some cases, deliberate misrepresentation, and it doesn't address the core issue of what it is we're talking about when we talk of "the Holocaust." There is no misrepresentation, deliberate or otherwise, on the part of either those who speak of six or those who speak of eleven. They're talking about different things. But except for those like Henryk Grynberg, who would dig a moat around the six million and raise the drawbridge, these different things are never sharply defined. Even Elie Wiesel, as we saw, preferred ambiguous aphorisms to clear delineation of boundaries.[64]

While many insist upon six and only six, many others (though rather less insistently) routinely talk of eleven in all sorts of contexts.

The executive director of the Chicago Board of Rabbis finds it "un-conscionable" to compare abortion with "the eleven million human beings who were deliberate targets of Hitler's death machine."[65] A spokesman for a campus Hillel organization explains Yom Hashoah to a reporter as "a day of remembering . . . the eleven million people — six million of them Jews — who were killed in the Holocaust."[66] (In a way, the young man is right: Yom Hashoah is as Yom Hashoah does; in dozens of cities the annual ceremonies do indeed commemorate "eleven million.") The executive director of the Baltimore Jewish Council hopes that the renovated Holocaust memorial in that city will be more welcoming to visitors "interested in remembering the eleven million victims of the Third Reich."[67] In the Detroit Holocaust Museum, which opened many years ago and prides itself on being the first such institution in the United States, the memorial flame "burns for the six million Jews and five million non-Jews murdered in the Holocaust."[68] The Tampa Bay Holocaust Memorial Museum in Florida is, as of this writing, the most recent to open. Elie Wiesel spoke at its inauguration. According to the account in the local newspaper, he delivered his remarks "against a background of eleven eternal flames, representing eleven million victims of the Holocaust." He also performed the ceremonial ribbon-cutting. The ribbon was multicolored: "yellow for Jews, red for political prisoners, black for social outcasts, pink for homosexuals, brown for Gypsies, purple for Jehovah's Witnesses and green for professional criminals."[69] Wiesel's private thoughts concerning the iconography were not reported.

The examples in the previous paragraph could be multiplied. The reader will have noted that they come not from gentiles — with a conscious or an unconscious anti-Semitic agenda, as Yehuda Bauer would have it — but from Jews. And they are by no means only highly assimilated Jews; many survivors (and children of survivors) also speak of "eleven."[70]

Has it been a question of bowing to the pressure of other victimized groups who want in? It is true that among the considerations weighed by the Carter White House, as they moved to "eleven," were requests for inclusion by representatives of Polish American and Ukrainian American organizations. But these were solicited, not spontaneous, expressions of opinion. From World War II to the collapse of the Communist bloc, these groups saw themselves not as victims of Nazism but as members of the family of captive nations, groaning under Soviet tyranny. On the whole, they didn't want to get into talk of the Holocaust, they wanted to get out from under it.

Most popular depictions of the Holocaust had portrayed Poles as guilty bystanders, or worse. Thus there was the frequent assertion, by Wiesel among others, that it was "not an accident" that the Germans had located the murder camps in Poland: they had sought a congenial anti-Semitic environment.[71] (Strip mines aren't located in West Virginia because of the local residents' failure to appreciate the beauty of unspoiled landscapes; that's where the coal is, as Poland was where most of the Jews were.) Ukrainians were regularly portrayed as Nazi auxiliaries — which, of course, a certain number (a small minority) had been. Insofar as Poles, Ukrainians, and other Eastern European groups participated in Holocaust commemoration, as they very occasionally did, that participation was primarily defensive. Their claim (true enough) that many Poles and Ukrainians had been victims of the Nazi regime was made to offset assertions (sometimes true, sometimes false, and often much too sweeping) that they had been allies of that regime. In any case, except, in a few instances, on the local level, they never had the political, cultural, or financial resources to press their case. This was even more true of Gypsies, whose proportional losses to the Nazi murder program approximated that of Jews. And there were no lobbyists for former Soviet prisoners of the Germans, whose losses through deliberate starvation, disease, and execution ran into the millions.

Paradoxically, the one group that has actively, and successfully, lobbied for inclusion in the ranks of the "eleven million" is the group whose losses contributed the least to that total. Claims by gay activists and their supporters for the number of homosexuals killed by the Third Reich reach as high as one million, and assertions that it was a quarter of a million or half a million are common.[72] The actual number of gays who died or were killed in the camps appears to be around five thousand, conceivably as high as ten thousand.[73] But unlike other groups that wanted to be recognized as victims of the Holocaust, gays do have political and cultural resources, and they don't face the same hostility to inclusion, based on prewar and wartime experience, encountered by Poles and Ukrainians. Their inclusion, moreover, could be seen as a contribution to the cause of combating homophobia. And many of their spokesmen, who press for inclusion, are Jewish.

If it's not the result of a conscious or an unconscious anti-Semitic agenda, and it's not, with the exception just noted, the result of lobbying by otherwise excluded groups, what *does* account for the fact that so many have chosen to speak of — to engrave in marble — "eleven million"? We ought, in the first place, to note that it's not a matter of either-or. Often "six" and "eleven" coexist. Thus the New England Holocaust Memorial consists of six striking glass columns on a site in downtown Boston, while the descriptive text on a granite panel at its entrance tells of the murder of "as many as eleven million men, women and children. Six million of them were Jews."[74] When one does make a choice to use "eleven" instead of "six," or vice versa, what kind of choice is it? A midwestern schoolteacher, trying, in a class on the Holocaust, to get his students to grasp the enormity of the number "six million," set them to collecting six million pop tops (the tabs you pull off cans of soda). The kids collected enthusiastically and surpassed the original goal, which was therefore recalculated. They would now grasp, or try to grasp, "eleven million."[75] When looking at discussions of the Holocaust in the media, the use of six or eleven often seems haphazard. Is the line of type too long to fit? Change eleven to six. Is it too short? Change six to eleven.

Still, "six" long predated "eleven," and we should at least try to account for the increasing frequency with which we encounter eleven, even if all we can do is speculate. In 1980 Senator William Proxmire told his colleagues of the groundbreaking for the Baltimore Holocaust Memorial, and of how it had been held up by a disagreement between the partisans of "six" and of "eleven," with the latter ultimately being chosen. The decision, said Proxmire, "was a wise and thoughtful one. Genocide is not, as many persons erroneously believe, simply a Jewish issue."[76] The following year Representative Henry Waxman told his fellow members of the House about the decision of the Jewish community of Denver to share its Holocaust memorial — which focused on Babi Yar — with local Ukrainian Americans: "While it is true that the majority of victims were Jews damned by the Germans for the 'Final Solution,' many people of other backgrounds also died there. I salute the Babi Yar Foundation for recognizing the suffering and martyrdom of Ukrainians and other Slavs both at the time of the Babi Yar massacre and throughout the period of World War II."[77]

The values invoked by Proxmire and Waxman are opposition to "parochialism" together with that even more primal value, which both gentile and Jewish children learn in kindergarten — "sharing." They suggest — though neither would have used these words — that it was

wrong for Jews to be possessive or exclusive about the Holocaust, that
it was desirable for them to transcend particularism. Those who resisted these appeals, who insisted on the irreducible Jewish specificity
of the Holocaust, had powerful arguments on their side. But the appeal of sharing was also powerful. The pervasive discourse of multiculturalism generated not just "neo-particularism" but also sentiment
for overcoming particularism. It's been argued that as a condition of
getting along in a pluralist American society, all of the three major re-
ligions have had to, if not abandon, at least fudge key particularist elements in their traditions. For the Protestants, "[only] Jesus saves"; for
the Catholics, "no salvation outside the [one true] Church"; for the
Jews, "the chosen people."[78] The argument can be pushed too far, but
it underlines a real and strong drive in American society toward accommodation. Before World War II, it was common to hear America
described as a Christian country — statistically, a most defensible designation. After the war, the leaders of a no-less-overwhelmingly Christian society had accommodated Jews by coming to speak of our
"Judeo-Christian traditions"; they elevated the 3 percent of American
society that was Jewish to symbolic parity with vastly larger groups by
speaking of "Protestant-Catholic-Jew." For Jews to make room for others in an "expanded" Holocaust may well have seemed to many — I'm
just guessing — simply returning the favor.

And, in the end, how much did this whole six-versus-eleven business matter? To some, of course, a great deal. Particularly for those
Jews for whom the Holocaust was a holy event — the deaths of the
Nazis' Jewish victims sacred, those of their gentile victims profane —
the issue was not negotiable. The same was true of those for whom the
"big truth" about the Holocaust was its Zionist lesson — that Jewish
life in the Diaspora was untenable. For those, including myself, who
value precision of expression, "six" describes something specific and
determinate; "eleven," even apart from being invented and arbitrary, is
unacceptably mushy. (Wiesenthal's invented number may not have
been completely arbitrary, since it combines maximum inclusiveness
with the preservation of a Jewish majority.) But if we're concerned, as
we are in this chapter, with the images and perceptions of the American public at large, these distinctions may not be all that consequential. Even in talk of "eleven," Jews are always taken to be at the center,
others at the periphery. Is it then *that* different from speaking of
six million Jewish victims of "the Holocaust, properly speaking,"
surrounded by a penumbra of other victims of Nazism? In practice,

even Holocaust museums formally committed to the memory of "eleven million victims" devote practically all of their exhibit space to the agony of European Jewry; others figure very marginally, sometimes not at all. How many books, movies, or television programs have there been that focused on "other victims"? During the period when Wiesel was wrangling with the Carter White House over the definition of the Holocaust, he gave voice to his anxiety. Survivors, he said, spoke of six million Jewish victims. "Then some friends . . . began reminding us, 'true, but after all, there were others as well.' It's true; there were others as well. So they said eleven million, six of whom are Jews . . . and in a couple of years, they won't even speak of the six. They will speak only of eleven million."[79] It hasn't (with unimportant exceptions) happened yet, and there are no signs that it's about to happen. But it could.

From the 1970s on, a series of events — sometimes trivial in themselves, but often rich in symbolism — kept the Holocaust on the front pages and on the nightly news. Of course, there's a circularity in trying to disentangle cause and effect: to what extent did all this reportage contribute to placing the Holocaust on the American agenda; to what extent were the events so fully reported because the Holocaust was already taking its place on that agenda? That these events were in the news, rather than in history books, surely contributed to a sense of the Holocaust as contemporary. How closely did Americans attend to these events? How deep, and how lasting, was their impact? How much, and in what ways, did they affect how Americans thought about the Holocaust? We can only speculate, based on fragments of evidence, often ambiguous poll results, and seat-of-the-pants impressions.

In 1977 and 1978 there was the constitutional-cum-emotional controversy over the right of American Nazis to conduct a march in Skokie, Illinois, a town that was home to many Holocaust survivors. (The contemplated march was hardly the Macy's Thanksgiving Day Parade — about a dozen kooks and misfits were slated to participate.) This was widely reported at the time — and later became the subject of a television docudrama starring Danny Kaye — but it soon became yesterday's news, and it's unlikely that it left much of a permanent impression.[80]

In 1985 there was the also short-lived but much more intense (and more intensively covered) controversy over President Reagan's visit to the Bitburg cemetery in West Germany. Would he or wouldn't he visit the resting place of young SS men killed in the war; would he or wouldn't he also visit a concentration camp? American opinion was sharply divided — according to one poll, split right down the middle, with half approving, half disapproving the visit.[81] (Often this was a partisan response, with Republicans approving, and Democrats disapproving, by margins of about two to one.)[82] At the time of the affair, a slim majority of Americans agreed with Reagan's much-criticized remark that "German soldiers buried in the Bitburg cemetery were victims of the Nazis just as surely as the victims in the concentration camps."[83] Three months after Bitburg, the American Jewish Committee commissioned a national survey to probe more deeply into its impact.[84] Although it's always hard to know exactly what such surveys are measuring, the findings were interesting. The educated were much more likely than the uneducated to approve of Reagan's visit — probably, a Committee staffer wrote, because they saw it as a contribution to international goodwill and "the healing of old wounds," while the less-educated were more nationalist. The Committee poll asked whether "the Holocaust is something we need to be reminded of annually, or do you think that after forty years Jews should stop focusing on the Holocaust?" Forty-six percent were for annual reminders; 40 percent thought Jews should let up on the issue.[35]

A year after Bitburg there was the Kurt Waldheim affair. Was the former UN secretary-general, and soon-to-be president of Austria, a Nazi war criminal; should he or shouldn't he be placed on the watch list that barred individuals in that category from the United States? While the discussion of Waldheim's past dragged on for years, and contributed to the cumulative process by which Americans were reminded of the Holocaust, the affair by itself didn't seem to have that much impact. Waldheim was more often seen as a sleazy opportunist (which he was) than as an active participant in the Holocaust (which he probably wasn't).

The Waldheim affair led to the controversy over Pope John Paul II's reception of the Austrian president at a time when he was a pariah throughout Europe. And this was far from the only dispute involving the Holocaust and the Catholic Church which attracted extensive media attention. There was the interminable dispute over the presence of a Carmelite convent at Auschwitz, which Jewish groups insisted be removed. Foot-dragging by Polish Church leaders in effecting its promised removal kept the story alive for several years. American

Catholics' responses to these conflicts varied. Many Catholics joined Jews in criticizing the pope's reception of Waldheim. As far as the convent was concerned, most of the American hierarchy, along with many lay Catholics, were embarrassed by the stalling tactics of the Church in Poland, even apart from their discomfiture at the anti-Semitic remarks of the Polish primate, Cardinal Josef Glemp, during the controversy.[86] Overall, it was more of an occasion for the expression of solidarity between American Catholics and American Jews than of conflict — though some Polish American Catholics were loyal to the gospel as preached by Glemp. It was otherwise concerning American Jews' repeated expressions of hope that the Vatican would apologize for the "silence" of the Church in general, and of Pius XII in particular, during the Holocaust (in the face of the repeated dashing of these hopes with each successive statement from Rome). On this issue, American Catholics — or at least those voicing "official" Catholic opinion — dug in their heels. They continued to defend the role of the Church as a whole and of Pius, a stance that is likely to prove permanent.[87] Many Jewish leaders recognized this, and sought to avoid occasions for continued wrangling. (Among the dozens of sins of commission and omission recorded in the permanent exhibition at the Washington Holocaust Museum, there is no mention of the silence of Pius XII.) In any event, except at the margins, these conflicts don't seem to have had much influence on American Catholic opinion — if one wants to speak of such a questionable entity.

Overlapping the events just discussed has been the Justice Department's program — begun in the late seventies and still continuing — of tracking down, denaturalizing, and deporting immigrants (sometimes of German, more often of Eastern European, origin) who were accused of involvement in the Holocaust. The head of the Justice Department's Office of Special Investigations claimed that so far as the American public was concerned, the pursuit of Nazi war criminals was "up there with mom, baseball, and apple pie."[88] So far as the principle was concerned, and in the early days of the program, he was probably right, with this sentiment reinforced by popular films that romanticized the quest. But most early cases didn't get much publicity, except in the communities where the target resided and within the ethnic group from which he came.[89] (Among some, though not all, Eastern European ethnic organizations there was angry talk of persecution, often with an anti-Semitic subtext, but their complaints didn't attract the attention of the wider public.)

By far the most-publicized case was that of John Demjanjuk, a retired Cleveland automobile worker. He was identified by numerous survivors as "Ivan the Terrible" of Treblinka — a guard who even in that sewer of depravity was outstanding for the glee with which he casually murdered and mutilated Jewish prisoners. The survivors' shocking testimony was reported during the American hearings that led to his extradition to Israel, and more vividly presented on American television during his 1987 trial in Jerusalem, where he was found guilty and sentenced to death. Demjanjuk's trial was seen as a salutary reminder of the human reality behind the bureaucratic phrase "Final Solution" — which it assuredly was. Demjanjuk himself became the emblematic Holocaust murderer — which turned out to be more problematic. After their client's conviction, Demjanjuk's lawyers uncovered documentary evidence that while it was all but certain that Demjanjuk (contrary to his own repeated denials) was a concentration camp guard *somewhere*, there was strong reason to believe that the survivor-witnesses, though testifying in good faith, had been mistaken in their identification of Demjanjuk as "Ivan the Terrible" of Treblinka. In 1993 the Israeli Supreme Court agreed that there was reasonable doubt, reversed the conviction, and freed Demjanjuk, who returned to the United States. After much legal argument, a U.S. court ultimately restored Demjanjuk's American citizenship, on grounds that the Justice Department had suppressed exculpatory evidence during his denaturalization.

The reversal of Demjanjuk's conviction, along with the suggestion of improprieties in Justice Department conduct, led many to become disenchanted with the ongoing pursuit of Holocaust perpetrators and their accomplices. This sentiment was not new. In the American Jewish Committee poll after Bitburg, 41 percent of Americans had been for continuing the search for war criminals; 49 percent chose "the time has come to put it behind us."[90] The Demjanjuk fiasco deepened skepticism. (Jewish opinion had long been divided on the question of pursuing aging Nazis. Israeli Foreign Minister Abba Eban had said, some years earlier, that he really didn't care whether "some wretched man in Paraguay or Brazil" was captured. But even — or especially — after the overturning of Demjanjuk's conviction, some remained implacable: the Holocaust writer Deborah Lipstadt said that she would "prosecute them if they had to be wheeled into the courtroom on a stretcher.")[91]

As of this writing, the most recent item in this by-no-means-exhaustive survey of Holocaust-related events that have made the front pages is the long-running saga of the Swiss banks: their initial reluctance to disgorge "dormant accounts" of Holocaust victims; later charges that the Nazi gold they laundered during the war included gold from Jewish teeth; interminable disputes over the sums they would contribute to make amends. How closely most readers and viewers have followed the reportage of all of this is unclear. But the response of elected officials to the affair illuminates another avenue through which the Holocaust has been placed before the American public: its exploitation by politicians. Political figures who had spent their entire careers stuffing their pockets with contributions of dubious provenance were shocked — shocked! — to discover that there was something illicit about Swiss wartime dealings in gold. Senator Alphonse D'Amato of New York, who faced an uphill reelection campaign in a state with a large Jewish population, took the lead in loudly and repeatedly demanding quicker and more generous action from the Swiss. "I thank you for your sensitivity to Jewish pain, to Jewish memory," Elie Wiesel said publicly to D'Amato.[92] The New York senator was quickly followed by local and state officials — mostly in areas with many Jewish voters — who were quick to seize the moral high ground, threatening the withdrawal of public funds from Swiss banks unless they were more forthcoming.

Opportunistically climbing on the Swiss-bashing bandwagon is only the latest example of politicians' finding invocation of the Holocaust advantageous. And it's an equal-opportunity venture, with participants of all backgrounds and affiliations. Illinois Democratic Senator Carol Moseley-Braun, like D'Amato facing a difficult reelection campaign, joined him in cosponsoring legislation to establish a special commission to investigate the disposition of art works and other assets of Holocaust victims.[93] Politicians at all levels have found it useful to score points by one or another kind of association with the Holocaust. In advance of a trip to Europe to court overseas businesses, New York Mayor David Dinkins was criticized for including on his agenda attendance at a tennis tournament. Bowing to the critics, he announced he would stick strictly to business: his trade mission and visiting Holocaust memorials.[94] Photo opportunities at local Holocaust memorials became a regular feature of the campaign trail; when Vice President George Bush went to Israel, he took along a personal film crew to record his presence at Yad Vashem.[95] The most imaginative and subtle Holocaust photo op came in 1996 when Hillary Clinton, then under heavy fire for various alleged misdeeds, appeared in the gallery of the

House during her husband's (much televised) State of the Union Address, flanked by their daughter, Chelsea, and Elie Wiesel. Another imaginative device was employed by Republican Senator Arlen Specter of Pennsylvania. As chairman of the Judiciary Committee's Juvenile Justice Subcommittee, he held hearings to investigate the fate of Dr. Josef Mengele of Auschwitz. The rationale for his subcommittee's jurisdiction was Mengele's experiments on children.[96] Anti-Semitic remarks by some leaders of the Christian Coalition had harmed the reputation of the organization; to remove the taint, its executive head, Ralph Reed, announced that he'd purchased lifetime memberships in both Yad Vashem and the U.S. Holocaust Museum.[97]

The promoters of many causes sought enhanced legitimacy and visibility by association with the Holocaust. Senator (later Vice President) Al Gore wrote of "An Ecological Kristallnacht," with an "environmental Holocaust" to follow.[98] Anti-Castro activists in Miami erected a "Monument to the Cuban Holocaust."[99] It was also in Miami that the pink triangle, the badge of homosexuals in concentration camps, seems to have taken off as a symbol of gay liberation. It was there that anti-gay crusader Anita Bryant was campaigning to repeal a gay rights ordinance. A columnist in a gay newspaper wrote that "the Jewish vote is essential to our victory in Miami and the pink triangle can make the difference."[100]

Both inside and outside the political arena, it became common to invoke the Holocaust to dramatize one's victimhood — and survival. As "persecuted evangelical Christians," said Ronald Reagan's interior secretary, James G. Watt, he and his wife could see "the seeds of the Holocaust-type mentality here in America," and for that reason they were strong supporters of the Washington Holocaust Museum.[101] Returning to television after a sex and money scandal led to his and his wife's departure from their PTL Ministry, Jim Bakker told viewers that "if Jim and Tammy can survive their holocaust of the last two years, then you can make it."[102] Woody Allen told an interviewer that what enabled him to cope following scandals about his domestic life was "all the reading I'd done through my life on the Holocaust. . . . Those who focused on what was actually happening to them — the daily horror . . . the reality of it — they survived."[103]

In various ways, for various purposes, the Holocaust had entered the American cultural mainstream; it had become part of the language; it had become, except for hermits, inescapable. What did Americans make of all this? How much impact has the Holocaust had on their consciousness?

In trying to answer these questions — without much success, I might as well admit at the outset — we don't have much to go on apart from that blunt and flawed instrument the opinion poll. Awareness of the Holocaust, according to surveys, is higher than it's ever been. In a survey of the public's knowledge of World War II, 97 percent of those polled knew what the Holocaust was. This was substantially higher than the percentage who could identify Pearl Harbor or knew that the United States had dropped an atomic bomb on Japan, and much higher than the 49 percent who knew that the Soviet Union fought on the American side in the war.[104] But what does "knowing what the Holocaust was" mean for that portion of the population — more than a third, according to a recent survey — who either didn't know that the Holocaust took place during World War II or "knew" that it didn't?[105] This last finding did not dismay the acting director of the Washington Holocaust Museum, who said to a reporter: "You're surprised by that in a country that doesn't know where Mexico is?" (She was citing a Gallup poll that found almost half of Americans couldn't locate Mexico on a map.)[106] In a way, it's a fair enough riposte: even a majority of college-educated Americans probably couldn't say much that was coherent about the American Revolution or the Civil War. But it raises the (unanswerable) question of how many Americans have knowledge of the Holocaust that amounts to more than scattered sound bites. All one can say is: some.

Whatever their knowledge of the Holocaust, those who respond to surveys are sure that it's important. A clear majority in a 1990 survey, when presented with a list of catastrophic events, said that the Holocaust "was *the* worst tragedy in history."[107] And there's a high degree of consensus on the Holocaust's lessons: between 80 and 90 percent of those surveyed agreed that the need to protect the rights of minorities, and not "going along with everybody else," were lessons to be drawn from the Holocaust; they agreed in similar proportions that "it is important that people keep hearing about the Holocaust so that it will not happen again."[108]

My colleagues who do survey research are fond of a cartoon showing an exasperated pollster saying to an interviewee: "Those are the worst opinions I ever heard in my life!" No doubt this resonates with their own (unvoiced) exasperation in similar circumstances, but it points to something else that's relevant to our interpretation of these results. Most people have a pretty good intuitive sense of what are "better" and "worse" opinions in response to pollsters' questions, particularly when they're asked whether they agree with benign-sounding propositions. Are these, in any worthwhile sense, opinions? The best reason for skepticism on this score is provided by the responses to a question in one survey: "How important is it for all Americans to know about and understand the Holocaust — is it essential, very important, only somewhat important or not important?" There were separate tabulations for those who said they knew "a great deal," "a fair amount," or "little or nothing" about the Holocaust. Not surprisingly, the more one knew (or said one knew) about the Holocaust, the greater the tilt toward the "importance" end of the scale. But almost two thirds of those who said they knew little or nothing about the Holocaust thought it was either "essential" or "very important" that all Americans know about and understand it.[109] They may not have known much, but they knew what the "better" answer was.

The Washington Holocaust Museum has been overwhelmed by millions of non-Jewish visitors, "voting with their feet" for the encounter the museum provides. Some unknown portion of that stream of visitors have been led to its doors by deeply felt interest and concern. For some equally unknown portion of visitors, the museum has become something that one has to "do" when one tours Washington, just as one has to "do" the Louvre in Paris.

My skepticism about some of the standard measures of American gentiles' involvement with the Holocaust is balanced by my certainty that many have a commitment to its importance, and the clear evidence that, in a diffuse sense, Americans have been receptive to Holocaust commemoration. We don't know for sure what's moved them in this direction, but some suggestions have been offered.

One of the most interesting was put forward by Robert Wuthnow, a sociologist at Princeton. He saw the mass viewing of NBC's *Holocaust* in 1978 as a "public ritual" dramatizing the moral chaos and breakdown that Americans feared, offering reassurance that good and evil remained clearly distinguishable.[110] The program aired in the wake of Vietnam and Watergate, amid continuing racial violence and concerns about the erosion of traditional morality, at a time when there was a sharp rise in the number of Americans who believed that the country had "pretty seriously gotten on the wrong track."[111] Wuthnow wasn't just speculating about the relationship between fear of chaos and the search for moral order, on the one hand, and interest in the Holocaust on the other. On the basis of a very large response to a detailed questionnaire, he found a strong correlation between the two:

> Whether someone was politically liberal, moderate, or conservative, that person was more likely to be interested in the Holocaust if he or she perceived serious problems in the moral order. . . . It was the Holocaust as symbol of everpresent evil rather than the Holocaust as historical event that was of interest to persons troubled about the moral fabric.[112]

Different viewers, he found, understood what they saw differently, and came away with different lessons. Religious conservatives, for example, saw the Holocaust as stemming from the breakdown of traditional Christian values, which dictated their remedies for preventing a recurrence; liberals saw social causes and social remedies. So, in one sense, viewing *Holocaust* was a ritual of solidarity expressing abhorrence of "evil incarnate" — an affirmation of shared values, albeit expressed negatively. In another sense — something we'll look at further in the next chapter — the Holocaust became a screen on which people projected a variety of values and anxieties.

Though Wuthnow's discussion of public ritual was restricted to one television series and its fallout, it's suggestive for understanding the continuing functions of Holocaust commemoration in American society. Anxiety about moral chaos and social disarray, and a yearning for firmer moorings, are more widespread than ever; the Holocaust remains a symbol of both. The leaders of the Washington Holocaust Museum have described it as exemplifying — by showing their negation — traditional American values and have expressed the hope that it would be "a moral compass" for the nation.[113] A newspaper columnist explained the success of the museum this way:

> In an era of moral relativity, the Holocaust museum serves as a lodestone. Here there is no rationalization. . . . Here is an absolute. And in that absolute of Evil, maybe, the prospect of an absolute Good. . . . We live amid the ruins of "the modern" — the era in which Western man discarded age-old standards and creeds and placed his faith in science. [Americans] flocking to the Holocaust museum are searching for answers — in the form of moral certainties. . . . The Holocaust museum offers a basic moral foundation on which to build: a negative surety from which to begin.[114]

I suggested in the previous chapter that a change in attitudes toward victims in American culture influenced how Jews related to the

Holocaust. That change in attitudes neither began nor ended with Jews. As both cause and consequence of this development, Americans of all sorts came to see themselves as victims — oppressed by various aspects of modern life. It's been suggested that this has led many gentiles to identify with Jewish victims of the Holocaust, because those Jews' victimization, unlike their own, was concrete and endowed with meaning.[115] There's probably something to this. It would help to explain why giving victim identity cards to visitors at the Washington Holocaust Museum was a smash hit with the focus groups that exhibition planners convened in advance of its opening.[116]

If it's true — and it seems to be — that American gentiles are more likely to identify with victims of the Holocaust than with the victims of countless other disasters, why is this so? In part because they are more often invited to — explicitly by the victim identification cards at the Washington museum and at the Simon Wiesenthal Center, implicitly in diverse ways. But there are probably other reasons. "Hitler's crimes," wrote Jason Epstein, "are particularly poignant to us because they occurred so to speak in the house next door. . . . The victims were ourselves at barely one remove. . . . The Soviet victims in their faraway country with their unpronounceable names and odd clothing were seen as nothing like us."[117] Phillip Lopate has made much the same argument in trying to explain why "those piles of other victims are not as significant as Jewish corpses."

> Is it simply because they are Third World people — black, brown, yellow-skinned? . . . How much is social class itself a factor? In so many books and movies about the Holocaust, I sense that I am being asked to feel a particular pathos in the rounding up of gentle, scholarly, middle-class, *civilized* people who are then packed into cattle cars, as though the liquidation of illiterate peasants would not be as poignant. The now-familiar newsreel shot of Asian populations fleeing a slaughter with their meager possessions in handcarts still reads to us as a catastrophe involving "masses," while the images of Jews lined up in their fedoras and overcoats tug at our hearts precisely because we see them as individuals.[118]

To repeat an earlier point, we respond not to events but to representations of events. Only a minority of the European Jews murdered by Hitler resembled middle-class Americans, but that's how they've been most often represented to American audiences. Recall that Meyer Levin thought that *The Diary of Anne Frank* could bring home the Holocaust to Americans as nothing else had because "these people might be living next door."[119] Explaining the choice of the very "American" Weiss family as the protagonists of *Holocaust,* Gerald Green said that "we didn't want to do *Fiddler on the Roof* Jews"; that "would vitiate what we were trying to do — appeal to a broad audience."[120] We can't *know* that one of the reasons Americans have been so moved by the fate of the Jews of Europe is because they were perceived to be "like us." But it seems probable.

When we talk of "non-Jews" in America, we're almost always talking of at least nominal Christians. It's impossible to specify what is distinctively Christian in the overall American response to the Holocaust, but something can be said about those responses which are explicitly Christian. The first major public event in which Christians *as* Christians were involved in Holocaust commemoration was a 1974 conference at the Cathedral of St. John the Divine in New York City. The welcoming address, given by the Episcopal bishop of New York, contained two themes that recurred in subsequent Christian discourse on the Holocaust. One was thinking of oneself as a possible perpetrator — something foreign to mainstream Jewish discourse.

> If we look into our own souls, we know that we too were there at Auschwitz; that any one of us could, under certain circumstances, have committed those atrocities. . . . I entered the Marine Corps as a rather decent, Christian American boy; I was trained to kill; and I did kill. . . . I found my soul somehow so warped and immunized by the propaganda to which I was exposed that I could do these things without feeling. . . . I have had my Mylai in my own life, so that our Mylai did not surprise me when it came; and I think that perhaps any one of us could also have had his or her own Mylai, his or her own Auschwitz.

At the same time, he expressed Christians' desire to share, "as fellow human beings,"

> the strange glory of innocent suffering, the strange glory of heroism which came out of the stories from Auschwitz. . . . This innocent suffering is a strange thing in our creation, and Auschwitz may well be its greatest symbol. Perhaps there is some mystery of atonement here. Perhaps this cosmic power of the Holy Innocents can be a means by which we become one. [This symposium] must release within us the power generated by that sacrifice and innocence . . . make it part of our lives: so that we will dare to share in that passion, that vicarious suffering.[121]

Roman soldier with spear *and* Jesus on the cross.

As we've seen, Jewish religious thinkers have sometimes been sharply critical of endowing agony and death with religious significance — it seems to them un-Jewish. But there are no such inhibitions in a religious tradition that has made an implement of agony and death its primary symbol. Apart from this, suffering and redemption is a theme that resonates powerfully for many Christians, and so is guilt and contrition. Martin Jaffee, a professor of Jewish studies at the University of Washington, has described many Christian-Jewish encounters around the Holocaust as rituals with profound religious significance for Christians.

> The Christian partner in Holocaust discourse, standing before the Jew as heir and representative of the Christian culture in which . . . the Holocaust was nurtured, must obediently hear, acknowledge, and memorialize the truth of Jewish anguish and the legitimacy of Jewish outrage. The proper response of the Christian to the Jew is, by a kind of tacit mutual agreement, a spiritual self-annihilation, a confessing openness to one's own guilt that mirrors in subtle ways themes of classical Christian theology.[122]

Many individual Christians have been strongly attracted to such rituals and other forms of symbolic repentance. A relatively small group of Christians — both Protestant and Catholic, some within and some outside the clergy — have devoted themselves to addressing the Holocaust as a specifically Christian problem. In many cases they were energized by what they saw as the inadequate Christian response to the 1967 and 1973 wars. They've worked tirelessly, and with some success, at the admirable task of exploring, exposing, and expunging anti-Semitic elements in Christian doctrine, which they see as having laid the groundwork for the Holocaust. Several became members of the Council of the Washington Holocaust Museum, where they pressed, without much success, to have the Christian background of Nazi anti-Semitism featured. (The leadership of the museum decided that this would be too provocative and off-putting to Christian visitors.)[123] In cooperation with Jewish groups they've promoted the teaching of the Holocaust at denominational colleges and sponsored interfaith commemoration ceremonies. But in their larger aim, inserting the Holocaust at the core of Christian doctrine and liturgy, they haven't met with much success outside limited circles.[124] This group — and those other Christians for whom the Holocaust is an occasion for self-critical religious reflection — are, of all non-Jewish Americans, probably those who have taken the Holocaust most to heart.

What, in the end, can we say about the grassroots, as opposed to the official, American response to the Holocaust? With certainty, let alone precision, not much. When I began this inquiry several years ago, I was impressed by the frequency with which gentiles were talking about the Holocaust. After spending more time with the available material and thinking about it more, my present best guess is that a good deal of such talk is pretty formulaic. Like the ritual greeting in which we express solicitude about each other's health ("How are you?"), the ritualistic acknowledgment of the victimization of other groups is well meant, a worthwhile gesture. But one ought to be cautious about thinking this acknowledgment represents deep and spontaneous feeling, just as one ought to be cautious in evaluating the significance of George Washington's equally well meant words to the Hebrew Congregation of Newport.

Whatever the sources of Americans' concern with the Holocaust, and whatever its depth, there is broad agreement on the rationale for that concern. The Holocaust, everyone agrees, is the bearer of urgently important lessons — not just for Jews but for all of us. It is to those lessons that we now turn.

[11]

"Never Again the Slaughter of the Albigensians"

REMEMBERING THE HOLOCAUST, especially for Jews, needs no pragmatic justification. It is an act of piety analogous to reciting the Mourner's Kaddish on the anniversary of a relative's death, to the remembrance of war dead on Memorial Day. To say that it hasn't needed justification isn't to say that it hasn't received it, and Jewish-specific lessons — Zionist and otherwise — soon became a regular part of Jewish commemoration. As remembering the Holocaust, along with teaching the Holocaust, moved into the wider American community, pragmatic justification did seem required. Why, since there was no real or metaphorical family connection, should non-Jewish Americans mourn Hitler's Jewish victims more than Pol Pot's Cambodian victims? Why make special provisions for teaching about the Holocaust rather than about any of the other atrocious crimes in the record of mankind?

The answer, everybody seems to agree, is that the Holocaust carries messages not just to Jews but to all people. The Holocaust, Elie Wiesel has said, was "a unique Jewish tragedy with universal implications."[1] These implications have been translated into lessons, and it is the rare Holocaust commemoration, or Holocaust institution, or Holocaust curriculum, that is not dedicated to promulgating "the lessons of the Holocaust."

Often the lessons are very general. Thus the Holocaust is said to be a salutary reminder of the presence of evil in the world — something of which many Americans are said to be unaware — an "antidote for innocence."[2] Others draw more far-reaching lessons. According to President George Bush, the Holocaust serves to disabuse us of Enlightenment illusions about the "perfectibility of man."[3] In the same vein, the philosopher Ronald Aronson observes that the Holocaust "explodes . . . the popular belief in steady, irreversible progress."[4] The columnist George Will says that it refutes "the grand Renaissance illusion that man becomes better as he becomes more clever."[5] For others, the Holocaust brings the revelation that science and technology are not necessarily benevolent, or even neutral; they made the Holocaust possible.[6] More sweepingly, the Holocaust is often presented as not just an outcome of but the symbol of "modernity," with its bureaucratic rationality and its division of labor, which fragments responsibility.[7]

The problem with most of these lessons is not that they're wrong but that they're empty, and not very useful. It's hard to believe that there are many American adults today — bombarded as they are daily with images of murder in the streets, terrorist bombings, and mass atrocities — who, without the Holocaust to remind them, would remain oblivious to the presence of evil in the world.[8] I hesitate to say there are *no* Americans who believe in that caricature of Enlightenment thought, the perfectibility of man; who believe that human progress is steady and irreversible; that cleverness equals virtue; or (since Hiroshima at the latest) that technology is an unmixed blessing. But how many? Most Americans don't think deep thoughts about modernity, but if they did, I doubt that they'd deny it has a dark side. While some features of the Holocaust were typically modern, others represented a rejection of much that's characteristic of modernity. Besides, what — short of moving to the woods — does one do with the "lesson" that the Holocaust is emblematic of modernity?[9]

Equally, there's nothing wrong with the affirmative lessons the Washington Holocaust Museum attempts to teach, but they seem, if not useless, hardly necessary. "When America is at its best," a leading official of the museum told an interviewer, "the Holocaust is impossible in the United States." He said that the museum teaches fundamental American values of "pluralism, democracy, restraint on government, the inalienable rights of individuals, the inability of government to enter into freedom of the press, freedom of assembly, freedom of religion, and so forth."[10] If Americans need a demonstration of the way these values were violated in the Holocaust to remain committed to them, we're in worse shape than I'd thought.

At the other end of the scale from the most general (and most un-controversial) lessons of the Holocaust are those which are very pointed, and often very controversial indeed. Elie Wiesel would seem to have been right in speaking of the "universal implications" of the Holocaust, to judge by the number of people who have found that it has implications for their beliefs.

No lesson has a broader and more enthusiastic constituency than the dictum that legalized abortion is "the American Holocaust."[11] To those for whom the fetus was as entitled to protection as any other human life, to legalize abortion was tacitly to endorse the Nazi slogan "life unworthy of life." No less a figure than the surgeon general of the United States, C. Everett Koop, saw a progression "from liberalized abortion . . . to active euthanasia . . . to the very beginnings of the political climate that led to Auschwitz, Dachau, and Belsen."[12] (All of this outraged those on the other side, who often also buttressed their cause by citing the Holocaust. "Genocide begins," said one "pro-choice" activist, "the moment where people's right and ability to control their own bodies is taken away from them.")[13]

Feminists have suggested that the dominance of "patriarchal values" made the Holocaust possible, pointing out that it was "mostly men" who designed and ran the death camps.[14] An Oklahoma congressman, after viewing NBC's *Holocaust*, explained to his colleagues that it taught the dangers of "big government."[15] Animal rights activists call fur farms "Buchenwalds for animals." "In their behavior toward creatures," wrote Isaac Bashevis Singer, a strict vegetarian, "all men are Nazis."[16] In a lawsuit brought by the American Civil Liberties Union, charging that execution by cyanide gas was cruel and unusual punishment, its general counsel noted that the gas's chemical composition was the same as the Zyklon B used in the death camps.[17] Critics of the Harvard sociobiologist Edward O. Wilson accused him of reviving the ideas that "led to the establishment of gas chambers in Nazi Germany."[18] Campaigning against gun control, *The American Rifleman* ran an article entitled "The Warsaw Ghetto: Ten Handguns Against Tyranny."[19] "Had Germany had the right to bear arms," said House Speaker Newt Gingrich, "there might have been no Holocaust."[20] Gay activists' slogan "Silence equals death" argues that in the AIDS Holocaust, as in the Holocaust of the forties, indifference among bystanders permits devastation to proceed unimpeded.[21] An evangelical writer, commenting on the literature on rescuers of Jews, says that the evidence "reinforces fundamental Christian convictions about the centrality of the family and the awesome responsibilities and opportunities of Christian parents."[22]

Before turning to other lessons of the Holocaust, what can we say about the general and particular lessons we've so far surveyed? Most readers will have noticed that while these are presented as lessons *of* the Holocaust, they seem to be not so much lessons drawn *from* the Holocaust as brought *to* it. These lessons reflect values and concerns that originated elsewhere but that seemed to be confirmed by contemplating the Holocaust — in any case, could be dramatically illustrated by grounding them in the Holocaust. This is as true of the most sweeping as of the most specific lessons. It wasn't the Holocaust that made George Bush and George Will into conservatives with a dim view of human nature and human prospects. (More generally, the pessimistic worldview now so fashionable didn't derive from the Holocaust. The first post-Holocaust decades in America were notably cheerful and forward-looking. It was later, when Americans, for various reasons, took a bleaker view of life, that it became common to cite the Holocaust as justification for such a view.)[23] And it's surely the case that feminists, gays, and animal rights activists; opponents of abortion, big government, capital punishment, and gun control; along with promoters of Christian family values, did not arrive at these positions — did not first learn these lessons — from reflecting on the Holocaust.

Does the fact that these lessons didn't originate with the Holocaust mean that they aren't really lessons of the Holocaust, or at least not authentic ones? I don't think we should be in a hurry to say that. That would mean, among other things, that a prewar Zionist who had always believed in the need for an independent Jewish state couldn't later claim that that need was a "lesson of the Holocaust." Are only those who were blank slates before encountering the Holocaust permitted to extract lessons from it?

What makes something a "real" lesson of the Holocaust? Let's look at some lessons drawn by those whose Holocaust experience was direct rather than vicarious, who insist that it was precisely that experience which led them to draw certain lessons. The ACLU lawsuit challenging execution by gas as unconstitutionally cruel was supported by an affidavit from a death-camp survivor: "As a person who saw the daily horrors of mass extermination by gas, I know that execution by gas is torture and it can never be anything less."[24] Was she advancing an inauthentic lesson from her Holocaust experience? Alex Hershaft is a leading animal rights activist and a survivor of the Warsaw Ghetto. His years in hiding, he says, left him with "a passion for justice and a concern for planetary survival. In terms of justice, I just looked for the beings most persecuted on earth."[25] Was Hershaft drawing an improper or illegitimate lesson from his years in hiding? Were the implications he found in the Holocaust *too* universal?

Is it less legitimate for nonsurvivors to endorse and promote these lessons than to embrace more mainstream lessons drawn by other survivors? If it is less legitimate, *why* is it less legitimate? None of this is to suggest that all lessons drawn from the Holocaust are equally appropriate. No one could possibly believe anything so absurd. It would entail, among other things, embracing the lessons that Baruch Goldstein, with evident sincerity, drew. Rather, it's a matter of trying to sort out the grounds on which we accept some lessons as proper or legitimate and reject others as improper or illegitimate.

Most of the time, when we say that an event carries lessons that can be applied in another situation, we're doing what's called making an analogy — pointing out, my dictionary says, a "similarity in some respects between things that are otherwise dissimilar." It won't get us very far to say that there are good analogies and bad analogies, as if we were referring to some impersonal standard, however vague. Analogies — like that between "the unborn" in American and "life unworthy of life" in Nazi Germany — are clear and compelling to those who make them; are dismissed out of hand by others. If an analogy "clicks" with someone, and especially if that person becomes attached to it, you're unlikely to persuade him or her to abandon it. If it doesn't click, if someone is committed to rejecting it, then "that's not the same thing *at all.*" I don't know of any criterion for the aptness of an analogy except the pragmatic one: does it or doesn't it click?

The problem of dividing proper from improper lessons of the Holocaust is made even more difficult by the fact that those, like Elie Wiesel, who insist on the universal implications of the Holocaust are equally insistent that nothing else is comparable to it; they therefore resist "tight" analogies. Rigorous criteria of similarity are irrelevant: it's a matter of being *reminded* of the Holocaust when encountering some later atrocity or injustice, of that later instance evoking some of the emotions one feels about the Holocaust. Even if there were logicians who could codify rules for what's a good and bad analogy, who would have the temerity to tell us in what circumstances it's proper to be reminded of the Holocaust? Our varying judgments about what are proper and improper lessons of the Holocaust, and what are and aren't appropriate occasions to be reminded of it, depend, in practice, on how we feel about the direction in which those lessons and reminders point. I don't see how it could be otherwise.

The very characteristics of the Holocaust that make it such an appealing *illustration* of this or that lesson make it a dubious *source* of lessons. The Holocaust is invoked in support of various lessons because it is so dramatic, so horrific, so extreme. If the Holocaust shows us where technology or modernity or patriarchy lead, or if abortion is really like the Holocaust, surely we have to think more seriously about these questions than we have up to now. But the very extremity of the Holocaust, and the extremity of the circumstances in which it unfolded, seriously limit its capacity to provide lessons applicable in our everyday world.

First, the victims. What lessons for survival have those who lived through it carried out of the inferno? There are those who recount — and we have no reason to doubt them — that mutual aid, communal solidarity, and religious faith allowed them to survive. There are others who say — equally believably — that it was a capacity for ruthlessness, an eye for the main chance, trusting only oneself and not God or man, that saw them through. Some survived because they were married to gentiles or were otherwise able to blend into the surrounding community. Others report that it was only their wary suspicion of any but "one's own" that enabled them to survive. Which of these opposite-pointing lessons of survival should we embrace as the authentic lesson of the victim experience? And what lesson emerges if we embrace that most widespread (and most plausible) of all possible explanations — luck? Above all, what is the relevance of these lessons on surviving in the hell of Hitler's Europe for living our lives, safely and peacefully, in the here and now?

Then there are the lessons we seek in the behavior of the perpetrators. We all want to understand how apparently normal Germans could have willingly complied with orders to inflict torture and death on millions of innocent European Jews. In one sense, this is a strictly historical question, to which many historians have devoted themselves. But it's more than that: we're concerned with the universal implications of the issue. We want, if we can, to emerge with useful lessons, to understand, better than we have hitherto, the human potential. Certainly studying the Holocaust can help us in this, but is it really the most useful avenue to understanding the broader issue with which we're concerned? In an earlier chapter I described Stanley Milgram's landmark experiment that showed how willingly the most ordinary people, in the most ordinary circumstances, would comply with barbaric instructions.[26] There is of course no comparison between the scale of the events: on the one hand, the murder of millions; on the other, a few hundred people briefly deceived, but none injured, in a psychology lab. But while the enormity of the Holocaust boggles the mind, the fact that, particularly in time of war, in response to orders from their superiors, men will murder those whom they have been systematically taught to despise and regard as totally unlike themselves — this is all-too-familiar knowledge. With none of these special circumstances present, citizens of New Haven (women, incidentally, as much as men) were willing — so far as they knew — to inflict excruciating pain on someone just like themselves, against whom they had no animus at all.[27] If it is relevant, usable understanding we're after, there seems to me a sense in which Milgram's work is the more enlightening — and the more terrifying. And as a matter of practical morality — finding useful lessons — should our greatest worry be about people blindly following explicitly genocidal orders? It might be more to the point to consider how readily we delegate our moral decision-making to respectable authorities — as respectable as a Yale professor in a white laboratory coat — who assure us that however questionable the things we're told to do may seem, they're all in a good cause.

And then there are the bystanders and what their behavior is said to teach. No lesson of the Holocaust is pressed more often and more forcefully than "the crime of indifference." The Washington Holocaust Museum, according to its founding director, "facilitates the internalization of the moral lessons embedded in the story." None of these, he said, is more important than the insight that "bystanders, by omission, became accomplices of the perpetrators."[28] We are repeatedly urged to confront, as a negative object lesson, the fact that tens of millions of European civilians "stood by" and "remained silent" while Jews were deported and murdered.

If one were drawing up an indictment against modernity, high on the list of counts would be the atrophy of a sense of mutual obligation — the flip side of the individualism modernity promotes. Whether or not we designate indifference to our fellow man a crime, it is certainly something we ought to be concerned about. But is the failure of Europeans under German occupation to protest the fate of the Jews, and to come to their assistance, the best example of the phenomenon we rightly deplore? I mentioned in the Introduction that when Maurice Halbwachs protested the arrest of his Jewish father-in-law, Halbwachs himself was sent to his death in Buchenwald. Wholly admirable, but is this the model we want to hold up as the alternative to indifference? There *were* moral choices to be made under the German occupation, as at other times and places. But the extremity of those circumstances put powerful constraints on choices. Looking after the welfare of one's own family is a basic obligation — ranking higher, most would say, than one's obligations to strangers. When Poles were caught hiding Jews, not only they but their entire families were shot. Are we certain that in such circumstances the only moral course was to be a Righteous Gentile, whatever the cost and whoever paid it? To ask this terrible question — as terrible as the situation that put it on the agenda — is not to deny the existence of genuinely culpable indifference during the Holocaust. Rather, it's to suggest that we face squarely the extremity of those circumstances and then think about whether behavior in those circumstances is all that relevant to the problems we face.

Those who lived in New York City in the mid-1960s will recall the case of Kitty Genovese. Coming home from work late at night, she was stabbed by a crazed assailant and cried out for help. Thirty-eight neighbors, in apartments overlooking the scene, saw the attack and heard her cries. None called the police. The assailant returned to where Genovese lay bleeding and stabbed her again. He returned a second time, and again stabbed her. Finally, after she was dead, one of the thirty-eight went to the apartment of an elderly neighbor and got *her* to call the police. "I didn't want to get involved," he explained.[29] We don't know what went through the minds of indifferent bystanders, in Hitler's Europe or in New York City. We do know the likely price of speaking out in the former instance, and how totally cost-free telephoning the police was in the latter.

But even the case of Kitty Genovese, and the several analogous cases reported in subsequent years, aren't completely to the point, because, like the Holocaust, albeit on an infinitely smaller scale, they are so extreme. Few of us have been or will be eyewitnesses to murder, which allows us to assure ourselves and others that *we* would never behave like the residents of New York City in the sixties or of Poland in the

forties. On the other hand, all of us are witnesses to injustices, large
and small, about which we don't make a fuss. "It wouldn't make any
difference anyway." "Who wants to be known as a troublemaker?"

Let me relate a personal anecdote that makes my point so well that I
wouldn't blame any reader who thought I was inventing it. In a class
called "The Holocaust and the Uses of History" a few years ago, I was
discussing what I suggested were, for the reasons just stated, rather
simplistic moral judgments on bystanders. Samantha strongly dissented: "It was outrageous and unforgivable that they didn't speak up."
After a brief exchange we moved on to other subjects. Samantha came
to see me the next day about an unrelated matter, and remarked that
after class a couple of students had told her that they were 100 percent
on her side, but, "you know, we didn't want to say anything." On her
way up to my office, she said, she'd encountered still another student
from the class who shared her view that Polish bystanders' failure to
speak out was unforgivable; this student also had wanted to enter the
discussion on Samantha's side, but, "you know . . ." At the next class
meeting I reported what Samantha had told me — and that, of course,
she hadn't identified the other students. "If you spoke out against the
Nazi murders in occupied Poland," I said, "they killed you, killed your
family, and burned down your house. What did you think I was going
to do if you spoke out in disagreement with me in class?" I really
didn't make this up.[30]

Whatever the power of this or that particular lesson, there is the larger
claim that the Holocaust "sensitizes" us, makes us more alert and responsive to other, lesser atrocities. It's not an implausible idea, and
many have believed that this would be the case, judging by the frequency with which the Holocaust is invoked by those seeking to mobilize American public opinion and stir the government to action. How
effective it's been in practice is another matter.

Probably the first case of a catastrophe abroad that was talked about
in these terms was the Nigerian civil war of the late sixties, in which
the blockaded population of secessionist Biafra was described as the
object of genocide. A representative of one relief organization used the
suggestive figure of six million in estimating how many might die of
starvation.[31] Biafra was the most Catholic region of Nigeria, and Catholic missionaries were energetic advocates for the secessionists. "To our
eternal shame," said one missionary, "we sat by while millions of Jewish people and others were put to death before our very eyes. We did

practically nothing then. Have we learned nothing from those days?"[32] One of Biafra's American supporters wrote of their efforts to conjure up "an image of the Nazi regime and Jewish victims."[33] Substantial sums were collected by private charitable groups, but the American government, along with most other powers, continued to back the central government, and the revolt ultimately collapsed.

In the late seventies, after the Vietnamese invaded Cambodia and toppled the Khmer Rouge regime of Pol Pot from power, the world discovered "the Cambodian Holocaust." There had been scattered reports from refugees, between 1975 and 1978, of mass killings in Cambodia, but in the aftermath of the Vietnam War most Americans had had their fill of Southeast Asia, and few paid much attention. It was only after the killing had been brought to an end by the Vietnamese invasion that the full story reached the world. The revelation of the depth and scale of the horrors visited on the Cambodian population exceeded earlier speculation. That it came to be termed "a Holocaust" was in part a spontaneous reaction, but it was also one actively promoted by the Vietnamese. In creating a museum of "the Asian Auschwitz" at Tuol Sleng, the Vietnamese deliberately designed the exhibit to resemble World War II models. They went so far as to send its curator to visit Buchenwald and Sachsenhausen so he could make Tuol Sleng look more like the Nazi "original."[34] A massive relief effort was mounted in the West to succor refugees — who often were Khmer Rouge cadres fleeing the Vietnamese. Asking Americans to contribute, President Carter said: "Thirty-seven years ago a holocaust began which was to take the lives of more than six million human beings. The world stood by silently in a moral lapse whose enormity still numbs the human mind. . . . If a tragedy of genocidal proportions is to be avoided in Kampuchea [Cambodia] we must all help."[35] At the same time (also, of course, the same time that Carter was arguing with Elie Wiesel that the Holocaust should be framed more expansively), the White House was covertly supporting Pol Pot, the author of the Cambodian Holocaust. It was the Vietnamese who were seen as the real threat to American interests, and Pol Pot had to be kept in play as a counterweight. "I encouraged the Chinese to support Pol Pot," said Carter's national security adviser Zbigniew Brzezinski. "Pol Pot was an abomination. We could never [publicly] support him. But China could." The United States, he said, "winked semipublicly" at China's funneling arms to him via Thailand.[36] If Tuol Sleng (publicly) resembled Auschwitz, American policy toward the Khmer Rouge (privately) resembled the post-1945 American posture toward Germany: faced with a current enemy, past crimes could not be allowed to interfere with strategic requirements.

In the 1980s the Islamic Unity of Afghanistan mujahideen announced that what the Soviets were doing after the invasion of their country was "worse than the holocaust that Nazis did in Germany," and the word "holocaust" was occasionally employed by American government officials as well as journalists.[37] But the American government's response had nothing to do with the "holocaustal" dimensions of the invasion; it was strictly a matter of cold war jockeying. There was, of course, no question of a direct American military confrontation with the Soviets; instead, the Central Intelligence Agency trained, armed, and otherwise sponsored local Islamic insurgents.[38]

Holocaust imagery figured much more prominently in mobilizing support for the 1991 Persian Gulf War. Saddam Hussein, President Bush said, was worse than Hitler.[39] "Worse than" was a bit much for some commentators, but the equation (or near equation) was advanced again and again.[40] Stories of doubtful provenance concerning Nazi-like atrocities — newborn Kuwaiti babies torn from hospital incubators by Iraqi troops and left to die on the cold floor — were widely circulated.[41] A columnist for the *New York Times* wrote of Saddam's "carrying out his own version of the final solution."[42] The Simon Wiesenthal Center charged that German firms had built "gas chambers" for the Iraqi dictator.[43] As in the case of Afghanistan, it was clearly geopolitical considerations, not concern over a new holocaust, that motivated Operation Desert Storm. Holocaust imagery may have contributed to building support for the operation in Congress and with the public, but its role seems to have been marginal.[44]

The one occasion when the United States did intervene to prevent mass death abroad, the famine in Somalia, was the one in which the Holocaust was invoked least — though it may be that, in a diffuse sense, all the talk of the world's indifference to the fate of the Jews during World War II played a role in persuading some segments of the public to support the U.S. military's Operation Restore Hope.[45] The denouement of the venture — the killing and humiliation of American troops at the hands of Somali warlords — convinced many Americans that the operative meaning of "Never again!" was that never again should American soldiers be put at risk in the absence of a clear threat to U.S. national interests. Consistent with the tragic lessons he'd drawn from the Holocaust, George Will expressed the hope that the Somalia experience would "inoculate America's body politic against the temptations of humanitarian interventionism."[46]

The other, much greater African catastrophe of recent years, the 1994 Rwandan genocide, *was* widely talked about as a holocaust, as well it might have been, since it met just about every imaginable criterion. But given the backlash from the Somali venture (yet almost certainly even without that), there was not the slightest will in American political circles for any U.S. intervention. Indeed, the principal action of the Clinton administration while the killing was going on was to issue a directive cutting back the American commitment to peacekeeping operations and stressing that there would be no U.S. involvement in such operations when our national security wasn't directly threatened.[47] Though few of those saying that something must be done about the Rwandan genocide had any clear idea of what the "something" was, to be on the safe side the administration instructed officials to avoid calling what was going on in Rwanda genocide.[48] (To acknowledge that it was genocide would, in principle, oblige the United States, along with other signers of the UN Genocide Convention, to take action.)

It is sometimes said that even if memories of the Holocaust have not induced the United States to intervene in recent cases of genocide, the memories of Jewish refugees desperately seeking asylum in the 1930s and 1940s have led America to take a more welcoming attitude toward those fleeing oppression. Thus, in the late 1970s, when large numbers of Vietnamese boat people were admitted to the United States, Rabbi Irving Greenberg claimed that this was clearly attributable to "the cumulative impact of raised consciousness of the Holocaust."[49] It is true that the precedent of Jewish refugees from Nazism was cited in appeals on behalf of the boat people, and it is conceivable that this played some role in the decision. But the welcome accorded the boat people was continuous with American refugee policy throughout the cold war, which made special provisions for those fleeing Communism (Hungarians, Cubans, etc.), and no others.[50] Appeals to the memory of those trying to escape the Holocaust — reminders of the fate of the SS *St. Louis* — were pressed equally hard in the early 1990s on behalf of Haitian refugees. The Haitians, however, had the misfortune to be fleeing a right-wing dictatorship, and the by then more elevated Holocaust consciousness cut no ice. Presidents Bush and Clinton delivered them back into the clutches of the thugs from whom they had sought to escape, with the predictable murderous consequences.[51]

The crisis in which the lessons of the Holocaust were most frequently and fervently invoked was the onslaught by Serbian forces against Bosnian Muslims from early 1992 on. By the summer of that year there were reports of Serbian atrocities that had a chillingly familiar ring.

> There are mounting indications that Omarska . . . houses a death camp where Serb authorities . . have taken thousands of Muslims. [A witness] quoted the camp commander as warning the inmates that they will never leave it alive. . . . Nearly every night someone is taken in for questioning and does not return. . . . "We all felt like Jews in the Third Reich," said [a Muslim student]. Women, children and old people rounded up by police from their villages . . . are packed like cattle into sealed boxcars and deported.[52]

"Fifty years after Adolf Hitler's stormtroopers packed millions of Jews, Gypsies and others into boxcars and sent them off to death camps," wrote one news magazine, "locked trains are once again carrying human cargoes across Europe. The West's response to this new holocaust has been as timid as its reaction to the beginnings of Hitler's genocide."[53] The reports from Bosnia often contained qualifying phrases, indicating that most of this information was secondhand and not independently verified, but there was verification of enough of it for the stories to be credible. And there were the photographs, which appeared on the covers of national magazines: emaciated Bosnians peering out from behind barbed wire, pictures that might have been captioned "Buchenwald, 1945." Early reports — also unverified, but widely believed — claimed that hundreds of thousands of Bosnian Muslim civilians had already been killed.

Soon after these first reports, Jewish organizations and individual Jewish leaders sounded the alarm. "Stop the Death Camps" was the headline of an advertisement placed in the *New York Times* by three important American Jewish organizations.

> To the blood-chilling names of Auschwitz, Treblinka, and other Nazi death camps there seem now to have been added the names of Omarska and Brcko. . . . Is it possible that fifty years after the Holocaust, the nations of the world, including our own, will stand by and do nothing, pretending we are helpless? . . . We must make it clear that we will take every necessary step, including the use of force, to put a stop to this madness and bloodshed.[54]

It was not only Jews who made the analogy and insisted on action. At the State Department, a desk officer for the area resigned to protest American inaction. "This may not be how the Holocaust ended," he said, "but it is how the Holocaust began. In 1945 we had the pictures and the evidence after it was over. In 1992 we know what is going on as it happens in Bosnia."[55] Campaigning for the presidency, Bill Clinton said that "if the horrors of the Holocaust taught us anything, it is the high cost of remaining silent and paralyzed in the face of genocide." He called on President Bush to "do whatever it takes," including armed intervention.[56] The Holocaust analogy was, of course, pushed hard by Bosnian representatives in the United States, and, in an interestingly circular fashion, the extent to which it had taken hold became evidence for its appropriateness. In response to a questioner on CNN's *Crossfire* who doubted that "genocide" was the right word for what was going on, the Bosnian ambassador to the United Nations replied:

> I think it's really quite unfortunate that you would question whether or not genocide occurs here when most of the Jewish community has been in uproar over what's going on in Bosnia, in fact has compared it to what happened during the Holocaust. Certainly the numbers are not comparable, but if the Jewish community says "Never again," I think, then, we have more than sufficient reason to come to the conclusion that there is genocide.[57]

Not everyone accepted the analogy. Comparing what was going on in Bosnia to the Holocaust, said *Washington Post* columnist Richard Cohen, was "like calling a traffic cop a Nazi for ticketing your car."[58] Andrew Greeley, along with many others, complained that the comparison "trivializes the Holocaust."[59] But the fact that the debate on American policy coincided with the opening of the Washington Holocaust Museum moved some to reflect bitterly on the alleged lessons of the Holocaust. Henry Siegman, the executive director of the American Jewish Congress and himself a Holocaust survivor, said that if the United States did not act decisively in Bosnia, the ceremonies opening the museum would be "worse than empty gestures. Not to act in Bosnia is to say that we have learned nothing from the Holocaust."[60] Mortimer Zuckerman, the publisher of *U.S. News & World Report*, echoed the view that in the absence of American intervention in Bosnia, the museum's opening would be "empty symbolism."[61]

Whether by coincidence or design, it was not until two weeks after the opening that the Clinton administration made clear that it had abandoned any Holocaust framework for the Bosnian events. What was involved there, Clinton's secretary of state, Warren Christopher, told a congressional committee, was a "morass" of "deep distrust and ancient hatreds"; "there were atrocities on all sides." Asked whether "ethnic cleansing" didn't amount to genocide, Christopher said, "I never heard of any genocide by the Jews against the German people."[62] With this clear signal from the administration, most of the steam went out of the debate over whether Bosnia was "a Holocaust." Had a forceful American response to ethnic cleansing in Bosnia — one based, even in part, on "the lessons of the Holocaust" — ever been seriously considered? It's impossible to be certain. But the arguments against it had always been formidable: the unlikelihood that anything short of placing American troops on the ground could reverse the Serbian victories; opposition to full-scale military engagement by America's allies in Europe; the unwillingness of the Congress, the public, and the Pentagon to countenance the deployment of American troops; the difficulty in defining an American national interest that would justify intervention. Hovering over everything were "the lessons of Vietnam," which easily trumped "the lessons of the Holocaust."

None of this refutes the claim that the Holocaust can "sensitize." Sometimes it does. Private relief efforts to aid victims in Biafra, Cambodia, and Somalia probably benefited from the invocation of the Holocaust. In the case of Bosnia, the Holocaust analogy roused some low-ranking officials, members of Congress, journalists, and private citizens to demand action, even if without success. Michael Berenbaum of the Washington Holocaust Museum said that though invoking the Holocaust failed to move the government to action, it created "conscience pangs . . . this generation feels guilty"; this, he said, was progress, albeit "very slight."[63]

Some might also call it progress that there was so much *talk* about Bosnia, that so many "bore witness" and "spoke out." If "Never again" means anything, said a leading Reform rabbi, "it means never again will good people stand by silently" — a sentiment echoed by many others.[64] In a parody of this injunction, President Clinton replied to a reporter's question as to whether his visit to the Holocaust museum influenced his decision-making on Bosnia: "I think the United States should always seek an opportunity to stand up against" — then he corrected himself — "at least to speak out against inhumanity."[65]

I am among that vast majority of Americans who don't know what American policy would have been in the best interests of the beleaguered Bosnian Muslims. I was unable (or unwilling) to invest the enormous amount of time and effort required to make an informed judgment. It was clear which was the virtuous *posture*; not so clear whether that coincided with the best, or least-bad, *outcome*. So I don't know how to evaluate the following argument, which David Rieff attributed to a number of UN officials. There was never the slightest possibility of Western military intervention, they said, but all the talk of such intervention (furthered by bringing up the lessons of the Holocaust) made it more difficult for the U.S. government to declare definitively that this was the case. As a result, the Bosnian Muslims lived on false hopes, prolonged the fighting, and increased their suffering. They finally had to settle for a peace settlement less favorable than that which they could have obtained earlier, had they accepted the inevitable.[66]

Even from the standpoint of those trying to mobilize support for action, it's not clear that invoking the Holocaust was, on balance, a rhetorical asset. For some, the association between Bosnia and the Nazi genocide was automatic and instantaneous — for them, the analogy clicked. "It is happening again," said a California rabbi. "The shock of recognition is overwhelming."[67] But for others the parallel was rejected out of hand. Erwin Knoll, editor of *The Progressive*, found the comparison "inappropriate and even offensive."[68] For anti-interventionists, it wasn't like the Holocaust at all; it was a matter of "age-old Balkan hatreds." To which interventionists like Susan Sontag replied: "It's as if the camera crews were inside the Warsaw Ghetto and people . . . said, 'Oh, that's just age-old European anti-Semitism, what can we do?'"[69] A battle of sound bites, but one not fought on a level field. The debate over Bosnia took place after years of insistence on the uniqueness and incomparability of the Holocaust and on the dangers of "trivializing it."[70] The rhetorical advantage was with those who would point out all the ways — they were numerous and important — in which what was happening in Bosnia was quite unlike the Holocaust. Anti-interventionists, like A. M. Rosenthal, agreed that "if Bosnia is the Holocaust again . . . there would be no decent course but for the West to go fully to war, ground troops and all." He had no difficulty in demonstrating, to his own satisfaction and that of many others, that it wasn't, which settled the question.[71] Apart from the Holocaust's alleged uniqueness, its extremity, which made it so potent a rhetorical weapon, also meant that compared to the Holocaust, anything else looked not so bad. The comparison, by raising the threshold of outrage, could easily desensitize.

Certainly desensitization hadn't been the intention of those who have talked about the lessons of the Holocaust — quite the reverse. But there is a curious anomaly in how Americans have responded to mass death abroad. And that anomaly makes one wonder whether desensitization may, in fact, have been an unintended consequence of our making the Holocaust our central symbol of atrocity.

No theme has been more prominent in talk of the Holocaust's lessons than "the crime of indifference." That bystanders, in both the United States and Europe, went about their business while millions went to their deaths remains a source of incredulity and outrage. Those working for American intervention against murderous atrocities abroad insisted that a repetition of wartime indifference in the face of events reminiscent of the Holocaust could not be tolerated. Those who opposed intervention in Bosnia agreed in principle that indifference in the face of "a holocaust" was intolerable; they insisted, however, that Bosnia wasn't reminiscent of the Holocaust. For both sides — and not just with respect to Bosnia — the Holocaust has become the emblematic horror against which all other horrors are measured. Do or do not the intentions and aspirations of the killers, or the means they employ, remind us of the Holocaust? Other horrors have a claim on our attention, and our resources, to the extent that they resemble this archetype of barbarism.

Among the most moving symbols of the atrocities that went on while others stood by is that more than a million children — always and everywhere the most innocent and helpless of victims — were among those consumed by the Holocaust. How could one have been indifferent to *that*? Nowadays, well over *ten times* that many children around the world die of malnutrition and preventable diseases *every year*.[72] They are not targeted for death by an identifiable villain — a Hitler or a Pol Pot. Their deaths are not the result of any satanic, genocidal impulse, nor even the result of hatred. They die for the banal reason that they lack the food and minimal medical facilities that would keep them alive. Their deaths are, that is to say, in no way "holocaustal."

The curious anomaly to which I referred a couple of paragraphs back is that all of the Holocaust-generated talk of the world's indifference, and how intolerable it is, rarely if ever extends to these children. The anomaly is the more curious not because of the ways in which their plight resembles that of children who died in the Holocaust, or in other genocidal crimes, but because of two important ways in which it differs.

How much the American government could have done during the Holocaust to save the million Jewish children, and all the other victims, is a question historians will continue to debate. Obviously it could have done more than it did, but the limitations on rescue possibilities were very real. It may be true that there was little or nothing that the U.S. government could have done in 1994 to prevent countless Tutsi children in Rwanda from being hacked to death by machetes. But the possibilities for rescuing millions of children around the world who die, no less horribly, from malnutrition and disease are readily available — and are largely ignored. The United States is, by a wide margin, the wealthiest country in the world. In the humanitarian assistance it offers to the poorest nations, as a percentage of gross national product, it ranks, also by a wide margin, last among the industrialized countries.[73] Every American president in recent years has had moving words to say about how shameful it was that the United States stood by as millions died. If one president has been moved by, or has noticed, America's standing on the list just mentioned, if he has expressed shame and mortification at that standing, it's escaped my research.

There is another difference between, on the one hand, the relationship of American bystanders to willful genocide and, on the other hand, their relationship to the tens of thousands of children now dying every day. Both in the face of the Holocaust and in the face of later genocidal atrocities, there were private individuals who urged our government to intervene for purposes of rescue — who were not indifferent. But when they failed, there was nothing they, as individuals, could do to stop the killing. That was something only governments could do. It is quite otherwise in our relationship to children dying today. Countless Americans, Jews and gentiles alike, have shaken their heads in sadness, or their fists in anger, at those who stood by while millions died in the Holocaust. They have nodded in profound agreement at the epigraph of *Schindler's List* — "Whoever saves one life saves the world entire." As concerns the children dying today, each of us individually (via OXFAM, UNICEF, or other agencies) can save not just one life but many, not in some one-time crisis, but every year. And doing so does not involve, as it did in occupied Europe, risking our own lives and the lives of others; at most it's a matter of forgoing some luxury we'd hardly miss.

By making the Holocaust the emblematic atrocity, have we made resemblance to it the criterion by which we decide what horrors command our attention? Is the (quite unintended) result that horrors which don't meet that criterion seem insufficiently dramatic, even a bit boring? I'm not sure of the answers to these questions. But the curious anomaly remains. For many years we've been talking about the culpability of bystanders and the crime of indifference. And over those years very few have thought that our standing by in the face of the preventable, if unholocaustal, deaths of millions of children annually has any connection to "the crime of indifference."

Probably the Holocaust both sensitizes and desensitizes, and there's no way to draw up a balance sheet. Nor is there any way to draw up an overall balance sheet of the impact on America of the lessons of the Holocaust. One part of the balance sheet is pretty clear. Only the most starry-eyed can believe that the universal version of "Never again" — never again will the United States tolerate genocidal atrocities — is a lesson American political leaders are willing to put into practice. Henceforth, wrote Leonard Fein, founding editor of the Jewish magazine *Moment*, "let us have the decency to refrain from ever saying 'Never again.' "[74] "Never again," said another disillusioned advocate of intervention in Bosnia, appeared to mean "Never again would Germans kill Jews in Europe in the 1940s." One might as well say, he added, referring to the thirteenth-century Crusades, "Never again the slaughter of the Albigensians."[75] Those people who continued to say "Never again" did so the way secular Jews, at the conclusion of a Seder, say "Next year in Jerusalem": not an expectation, not even an aspiration; rather, a ritualized reminder of expectations and aspirations now tacitly abandoned. It was not that events in Bosnia constituted "a Holocaust," which was clearly hyperbolic; rather, it was that the way in which American policy evolved, in this and other crises, revealed the hollowness of high-sounding phrases mouthed by political leaders — the ongoing reign of *Realpolitik*. There seems not the slightest likelihood that this will change in the foreseeable future.

On a different level, the lessons of the Holocaust continue to be zealously promoted. In state after state, legislation has mandated that all students be taught those lessons. But to the lessons of the Holocaust were quickly added, via the same sort of ethnic log-rolling that made the study of the Holocaust mandatory, the lessons of the Armenian genocide, the lessons of the Irish Potato Famine, and lots of other lessons — depending on local demography and configurations of power. In New Jersey, when proposed legislation mandating the teaching of the Holocaust hit a logjam because of competing ethnic demands for inclusion, it was decided to have a commission draw up a menu of "approved atrocities" from which local school boards could choose. The representative of the New Jersey School Boards Association said that "if a teacher in Paramus or Fort Lee, where there is a significant Southeast Asian student population, decided it is more relevant to discuss the story of journalist Dith Pran's experience in the killing fields of Cambodia . . . that teacher should have no pause in making that decision."[76]

The Jewish initiators of the legislative mandates were sometimes offended. "We don't want the Holocaust trivialized, and to include all these other instances of atrocities is ludicrous."[77] But most of the time they bowed to political realities. The chairman of the New Jersey Commission on Holocaust Education thought that the inclusion of teaching of the victimhood of Poles and Ukrainians would "dilute and even deny the uniqueness of the Holocaust." He was willing, however, to accept the inclusion of the Armenian genocide, which may not have been unconnected to the fact that the speaker of the state assembly was of Armenian descent.[78] Whatever other atrocities were included, the Holocaust almost always was the centerpiece: in part because it had been the focus of the original proposals; in part because of the much greater availability of historical and literary material on the subject (not least the Holocaust survivors, whose personal appearance before classes became a regular feature of many programs); in part because of all the external support that Holocaust programs received from American Jews — prepackaged curricula, fellowships for teachers to visit camp sites in Europe and Yad Vashem in Jerusalem, sponsored trips for both teachers and students to the Washington Holocaust Museum, the establishment of prizes for the best student essays or stories on the Holocaust.

In the end, it hardly seemed to matter whether one was learning the lessons of the Holocaust or the lessons of the Potato Famine, because the lessons were all pretty much the same: tolerance and diversity were good, hate was bad, the overall rubric was "man's inhumanity to man." There was, of course, enormous variety in what went on in the thousands of classrooms across the country in which these curricula were enacted.[79] Often mandating the teaching of the Holocaust was part of a larger initiative for civic and moral education in the schools, as in the Florida law that required the schools to teach "the traditional values of self-restraint, obedience to the law, sobriety, honesty, truthfulness, that working is better than not working, . . . the importance of children being born within a loving marital relationship, chastity, . . . respect for authority."[80]

Holocaust curricula were often expansive frameworks on which a host of such lessons were hung. But the lessons of the Holocaust contained in some curricula were anathema to conservative critics. Lucy Dawidowicz complained that one of the most widely used programs was "a vehicle for instructing thirteen-year-olds in civil disobedience and indoctrinating them with propaganda for nuclear disarmament." Do American children, she asked, "raised in unprecedented freedom and permissiveness, need to be instructed in the virtues of disobedience?" The only way to teach the real lessons of the Holocaust, she said, was to bring God back into the schools.[81] Like Dawidowicz, Deborah Lipstadt thought it pernicious that the Holocaust was being linked, however loosely, to Hiroshima and My Lai; like Dawidowicz, she deplored the way the uniqueness of the Holocaust was being implicitly questioned.[82]

Many teachers grumbled at the fact that legislators, not educators, were deciding what had to be taught, and treated teaching the Holocaust as an unwanted chore. Others threw themselves enthusiastically into the subject; like Elie Wiesel, they thought that taking a class on the Holocaust should be a "life-changing experience" for students.[83] I'm sure it sometimes is. Wonderful things can happen when the right teacher meets the right student in the right circumstances, whatever the subject. With ill-prepared teachers and indifferent students . . . ? I am skeptical about the understanding to be gained from such courses by that roughly half of American high school juniors who can't place World War II in the correct half century, but that may be a pedantic prejudice.[84] Though some Holocaust educators disapprove, role-playing games continue to be a feature of many Holocaust courses, and this certainly increases student interest.[85] A different kind of interest — often overwhelming the students — is generated by the frequent visits of survivors to classrooms. To be overwhelmed is clearly an appropriate response to this kind of vicarious encounter with the catastrophe. Whether it teaches lessons — whatever we mean by that — is another question. We don't know much about how moral education works; it's an open question how successful schools are in inculcating values or moral/political lessons of any kind. But it can't hurt to try, and if curricula on the Holocaust are a convenient framework, why not?

The push behind teaching the Holocaust in the schools is the conviction that an encounter with the Holocaust, particularly an emotional encounter, is bound to be productive of lessons. The same conviction was held by those who built the Washington Holocaust Museum. They assumed that a visit to the museum would produce a moral transformation, that visitors would be inspired to work for a "deepening of [the] quality of American civil and political life and a strengthening and enrichment of the moral fiber of this country."[86] Jeshajahu Weinberg, who oversaw the final design of the museum, spoke of his belief that it was through ensuring the emotional involvement of visitors that they would come to internalize the moral lessons embedded in its story. "Where 'normal' museums do not usually affect visitors emotionally, this museum not only does, but must."[87] On the other hand, he wrote,

> The museum . . . tries meticulously to refrain from any attempt at indoctrination, from any manipulation of impressions or emotions. . . . It restricts itself to the dissemination of knowledge; to presenting, dispassionately, the facts. . . . And while the factual story of the Holocaust is imbued with a multitude of moral lessons of enormous human importance, the museum leaves it to each visitor to draw his or her own conclusions, each according to individual background, upbringing, and personality.[88]

Indeed, visitors did draw their own conclusions, extract their own lessons. A "pro-life" visitor reported that the exhibits deepened her conviction that Americans who turn away from the awful reality of what happens in abortion clinics are just like the Germans who averted their eyes from the fate of the Jews. A teacher from an apostolic church school told the students she was shepherding through the museum that if the Jews of Europe had recognized Jesus as the Messiah, "the Lord could have heard their prayers a lot more."[89]

In their content these responses are far from typical, yet in another sense — that by and large people leave the museum with what they brought to it — they probably are typical. Typical is not the same thing as universal. There are surely those who are turned around by the experience, emerge with altered values or perspective, just as no doubt there are those who had this kind of experience with *Schindler's List*. But how many? It is difficult to imagine anyone leaving this magnificently designed museum less overwhelmed by the horror of the Holocaust, and, as with *Schindler's List*, it's usually the reverse. But to go from that to the notion that visitors are in any sense different after the encounter — that they have in any worthwhile sense "learned lessons" — seems to me to confuse an admirable aspiration with actual or attainable accomplishment.

I have, in this chapter, expressed doubts about the usefulness of the Holocaust as a bearer of lessons. In large part these doubts are based on the Holocaust's extremity, which on the one hand makes its practical lessons of little applicability to everyday life; on the other hand makes anything to which it is compared look "not so bad." But there's another dimension to this. Along with most historians, I'm skeptical about the so-called lessons of history. I'm especially skeptical about the sort of pithy lessons that fit on a bumper sticker. If there is, to use a pretentious word, any wisdom to be acquired from contemplating an historical event, I would think it would derive from confronting it in all its complexity and its contradictions; the ways in which it resembles other events to which it might be compared as well as the ways it differs from them. It is not — least of all when it comes to the Holocaust — a matter of approaching the past in a neutral or value-free fashion, or of abstaining from moral judgment. And it's not a matter of taking a disengaged academic stance. It is medical researchers' commitment to conquering diseases that makes researchers want to understand them in their messy complexity, to acknowledge things about them that violate their preconceptions. Expressions of moral outrage don't help. Talk of evil humors in the blood leads you to try bleeding as a remedy (it doesn't work). Talk of demonic possession leads you to try exorcism (which doesn't work either). If there *are* lessons to be extracted from encountering the past, that encounter has to be with the past in all its messiness; they're not likely to come from an encounter with a past that's been shaped and shaded so that inspiring lessons will emerge.

In early writings about the Holocaust — particularly in Israel but also in the United States — Jewish resistance was inflated for inspirational purposes. In much cold war writing in America responsibility for the Holocaust was transferred from Nazi Germany to "totalitarianism," so that the appropriate anti-Soviet lessons could be learned. More recently, the possibilities for rescue available to the Allies and to gentiles in Hitler's Europe have been exaggerated so as to teach lessons about indifference.

And, of course, these shapings and shadings to accommodate lessons are of crucial importance when lessons move to the top of the agenda. In the Bosnian debate, they served both sides. Those who were for intervention argued — sometimes explicitly, always implicitly — that the history of the Holocaust proved that rescue efforts like bombing Auschwitz could have saved countless lives then, and similar measures would save countless lives now.[90] Those against intervention repeatedly insisted that the Serbs' desire to live in a territory from which Bosnian Muslims had been "cleansed" was a rational, albeit deplorable, aspiration; not at all like Hitler's desire to eliminate Jews from a Europe under German domination.[91]

If, despite my skepticism, there are lessons to be learned from the Holocaust, they're not likely to be derived from lesson-driven versions of it. And there are perhaps a few modest lessons to be learned. As George Steiner pointed out some years ago:

> We who come after know that whatever the news is, it may be so. Whatever the massacre, the torture . . . it may be so. We no longer have that complex psychological blindness whereby many decent human beings, when the first reports leaked through . . . about railroads taking 9,000 people a day to a camp, could say: "This cannot be. . . . This is beyond human reason." We have no more such excuse.[92]

There was also a disposition, before the Holocaust, to think of the most barbarous deeds as being the work of the most barbarous folk — the least cultured, the least advanced. We've learned from the Holocaust that that's wrong. Perhaps there are other lessons, but nothing that will fit on a bumper sticker, and nothing to inspire. Awe and horror when confronting the Holocaust — for the first time or the thousandth time; then, now, and forever — are surely appropriate. Yet no matter how broadly we interpret the word "lesson," that's not a lesson — certainly not a useful one.

The desire to find and teach lessons of the Holocaust has various sources — different sources for different people, one supposes. Probably one of its principal sources is the hope of extracting from the Holocaust something that is, if not redemptive, at least useful. I doubt it can be done.

Part Five

FUTURE YEARS

"We Are Not Equipped to Answer"

W HAT OF THE FUTURE? Over the course of a generation the Holocaust has moved from the margins to the center of American Jewish consciousness; from an event that rarely appeared in American public discourse to one that is omnipresent. Will the Holocaust, one or two generations down the road, loom as large as it does now? Will its centrality prove short-lived? These aren't questions that anyone can answer with confidence, but looking at the idea of collective memory in general, and at what's happened so far with the memory of the Holocaust in particular, may offer a few clues.

Some collective memories are very long-lived — the Battle of Kosovo for Serbs, the expulsion of 1492 for Sephardic Jews. The reason that these memories endured for centuries is that the conditions they symbolized also endured: foreign oppression, foreign exile. Long-lived memories are most characteristic of stable, relatively unchanging societies. When we speak of collective memory, we often forget that we're employing a metaphor — an organic metaphor — that makes an analogy between the memory of an individual and that of a community. The metaphor works best when we're speaking of an organic (traditional, stable, homogeneous) community in which consciousness, like social reality, changes slowly. When Maurice Halbwachs first advanced the idea of collective memory in the 1920s, the great French medievalist Marc Bloch, who was suspicious of organic metaphors for society, nevertheless thought it might be usefully applied to such things as a peasant grandparent, grandchild on knee, passing on rural traditions.[1] A very organic image. How appropriate the metaphor is for the very inorganic societies of the late twentieth century (fragmented rather than homogeneous, rapidly changing rather than stable, the principal modes of communication electronic rather than face to face) seems to me questionable.

The life expectancy of memories in today's society appears greatly diminished. With the circumstances of our lives changing as rapidly as they do, it is the rare memory that can connect with an unchanging condition. Nowhere is this more true than in the United States, that notoriously most "now" and amnesiac of nations. Years ago, the Fourth of July was a day when the community gathered to hear patriotic speeches. When was the last time you went to a patriotic speech on the Fourth of July? When was the last time you even thought about the Declaration of Independence, which it commemorates, on that day? "The world will little note, nor long remember what we say here, but it can never forget what they did here." But of course Lincoln got it backward. His words at Gettysburg still (perhaps, sometimes) resonate; not one American in a hundred has the faintest notion of the significance of the Battle of Gettysburg, or who won it. November 11 used to be Armistice Day, on which we paid homage to a memory; now it's Veterans Day, on which we pay homage to an interest group.[2] Some of my colleagues continue to be shocked that incoming freshmen know nothing of such "ancient history" as the Vietnam War and Watergate. My colleagues acknowledge — grudgingly, because it makes them feel old — that these things happened before the students were born, but protest that the kids' *parents* lived through them; "they *must* have told them about it"! Maybe the parents did, but the kids didn't (as kids don't) listen. We're a long way from traditional notions of the transmission of collective memories, let alone the sort that endure for centuries.

Whether or not we want to call it memory, *consciousness* of the Holocaust has grown enormously over the last generation — most notably among American Jews, more diffusely among all Americans. What does the process by which that growth took place suggest about "the future of the Holocaust"?

Much of the original impetus behind the Jewish drive for centering the Holocaust is, if not spent, at least declining in power. Those who once complained, with justification, that the Holocaust had been neglected, and that it was necessary to counteract that neglect, have surely succeeded in their task, and the complaint no longer has any force. As we've seen, Holocaust awareness was promoted to mobilize support for a beleaguered Israel, pictured as being in a kind of pre-Holocaust danger. Such arguments are rarely heard anymore and would be unlikely to attract many adherents if they were heard. Though the chances for a mutually satisfactory accommodation between Israelis and Palestinians remain in doubt, it's hard to imagine the circumstances in which Israel's problems will summon up images of the Holocaust. In the early seventies there was a good deal of talk about a rampant "new anti-Semitism" in America, of the need to remind both Jews and gentiles of the Holocaust in order to combat it. I've argued that at the time claims about a new anti-Semitism were nonsense; certainly they're nonsense today. While anti-Semites will probably always be with us, their influence, insignificant twenty-five years ago, is even more insignificant now.

A number of those who took the lead in promoting Holocaust awareness were moved by the belief that it called for a reorientation of Jewish religious belief and practice. This view has failed to win much support, and its power seems to be waning. Rabbi Irving Greenberg was perhaps the single most influential figure in centering the Holocaust in Jewish and general American consciousness, through the private commemorative activities he sponsored and through his service as director of President Carter's Commission on the Holocaust. For Greenberg, as we've seen, the Holocaust was a "revelational event" on a par with receiving the Torah at Mount Sinai. As Jews ritually eat matzo to commemorate the Exodus, he urged them to ritually eat rotten potato peelings to commemorate the Holocaust. Greenberg argued that just as the destruction of the Temple brought forth the new institution of the synagogue, so the destruction of European Jewry was bringing forth another new religious institution, the Holocaust museum.[3] But most of the Jewish religious establishment has resisted the efforts of Greenberg, Emil Fackenheim, and others who sought to win for the Holocaust a major place in formal Jewish liturgy and theology. For Ismar Schorsch, head of the Jewish Theological Seminary (Conservative), the Holocaust was "a theological 'black hole' so dense that it fails to emit even a single ray of light. A collapsed star can never serve as a source of illumination."[4] Representatives of other segments of American Judaism have been equally opposed to seeing the Holocaust centered in Jewish religious belief, and nowadays there are few pressing this cause.[5] In a broad sense the Holocaust remains sacred in American "folk Judaism," especially among the less observant, and this is likely to continue in the short term. Whether this will endure without formal religious institutionalization is hard to say.

The argument for raising Holocaust consciousness that has been advanced with the greatest urgency is, by any sober evaluation, the most absurd: the alleged necessity of responding to the tiny band of cranks, kooks, and misfits who deny that the Holocaust took place. Concern about the "growing influence" of this corporal's guard was widespread for a time, but now seems to be abating.

The "star" of American Holocaust denial is Arthur Butz, an associate professor of electrical engineering at Northwestern University, who in 1976 arranged the private publication of *The Hoax of the Twentieth Century: The Case Against the Presumed Extermination of European Jewry*. A few years later the Institute for Historical Review was established in California; its principal activity was publishing the *Journal of Historical Review*, a slender quarterly devoted to exposing "the myth of the six million." The institute rented the mailing list of the unsuspecting Organization of American Historians, and sent sample copies of its journal to the organization's twelve thousand members, garnering some publicity from the resulting reaction. More publicity came when its offer of a $50,000 reward for anyone who could prove any Jews were gassed at Auschwitz was taken up by Mel Mermelstein, a survivor of that camp; after bringing a lawsuit, he collected. The deniers' most successful publicity coup was their clever idea of sending college newspapers advertisements calling for "open debate" on the Holocaust. A series of fusses were occasioned by several undergraduate editors' notion that rejecting the ads raised "First Amendment issues." This kept the pot boiling, though in no case known to me was the Holocaust itself ever debated on campuses; rather, it was a question of whether boycott or exposure was the best strategy for dealing with these screwballs. So far as one can tell, it was only fellow screwballs that they ever attracted: John Hinckley, who shot President Reagan, was a denier; so was Eric Rudolph, at this writing wanted for the murder of a guard at an abortion clinic; so was the crazed chess genius Bobby Fischer.[6]

The activities of these fruitcakes were irritating, indeed infuriating — especially, though not exclusively, to survivors. Some insisted that the deniers should be taken more seriously, but since there was no evidence that they'd had the slightest influence, it was hard to say *why* one should do so. Then seemingly powerful evidence of the deniers' influence was supplied by a public opinion poll conducted for the American Jewish Committee by the Roper Organization. Its results were announced on the eve of the opening of the Washington Holocaust Museum in 1993. Twenty-two percent of the public, according to the poll, doubted that the Holocaust had really occurred. "What have we done? Twenty-two percent . . . oh, my God," said Elie Wiesel — an understandable reaction to this astonishing statistic, and one echoed in the press across the country.[7] Coming on the eve of the museum opening, the poll finding was cited in newspaper editorials and other commentaries as the decisive argument for its indispensability, an unanswerable response to those who had doubted that such a museum belonged in the United States.[8] Deborah Lipstadt's *Denying the Holocaust: The Growing Assault on Truth and Memory* arrived in bookstores at the same time as the poll results were announced. It was the rare review of Lipstadt's book that didn't cite the poll as proof that the deniers had indeed had the success Lipstadt attributed to them.

For the next several months the growing menace of the deniers and the evidence of their astonishing influence offered by the Roper poll were repeatedly discussed. The poll results were said to underscore the importance not only of the Washington museum but of Spielberg's *Schindler's List* in checking the denier menace.[9] Steven Spielberg himself said that he had feared, during the making of the movie, that if he made any mistakes, it would help the deniers.[10] All of this coincided with the height of the onslaught against American universities as hotbeds of nihilism and relativism. Lipstadt, in her book, claimed that the willingness of campus editors to run deniers' advertisements was evidence of the strength of postmodernism and deconstructionism in the universities. This theme was eagerly picked up by conservative commentators — still another lesson, though this time not of the Holocaust but of its denial.[11] (In fact, the student editors in question had not been immersing themselves in Foucault and Derrida, but instead reading, somewhat carelessly, those "dead white males" Thomas Jefferson and John Stuart Mill, and concluding that their principles required making a place in the marketplace of ideas for the deniers.)

It was a different sort of marketplace that "deconstructed" the Roper poll results. Officials of the Gallup polling organization — Roper's main competitor — were struck by the fact that the question that produced the astonishing 22 percent who doubted the Holocaust had, against all the rules of survey research, been framed in an extraordinarily confusing way: "Does it seem possible or does it seem impossible to you that the Nazi extermination of the Jews never happened." Seizing this opportunity to show up a rival's incompetence, the Gallup people asked one sample group the original Roper question and presented another group with a straightforward version. The version containing the double negative again produced dramatically high results. When the question was put clearly — by Gallup, by a chastened Roper Organization, and by others — those who expressed doubt about the reality of the Holocaust shrank from 22 percent to between 1 and 2 percent, making plain just how inconsequential these nuts were after all.[12] As these results were assimilated, as the tiny denier camp was torn apart by schisms, as college editors came to realize that the ghost of Thomas Jefferson wasn't demanding that they run deniers' advertisements, Holocaust denial began to fall off the screen. Some continue to trumpet the threat of deniers. But it seems unlikely that the menace they pose will be as exaggerated in the future as it has been in the past, unlikely that Holocaust denial will continue to act as a spur to commemoration, as it has in earlier years.

Finally, there is the inevitable disappearance from the scene of the survivors. All but child survivors are now in their seventies or older, and so are less active than they had been. Many are already gone, and within a generation all but a few will be. How significant is this likely to be for how, and how much, the Holocaust is remembered in the future?

In the first postwar decades, when nobody besides survivors seemed much interested in the Holocaust, they were responsible for organizing commemorative events and the construction of some monuments. But their efforts didn't reach much beyond their own group, with even Jewish organizations distancing themselves from these ventures. The decision by Jewish agencies in the 1970s to initiate Holocaust programming seems to have been taken without much input from survivors. In the seventies and eighties, survivors — by now usually with the cooperation of other Jews — often took the lead in memorial projects at the local level. Survivors, however, played no role in the initiation of the largest museums — in Washington, where plans were set in motion by the Carter White House; in New York, where local politicians and real estate developers were in the forefront; in Los Angeles, where the Simon Wiesenthal Center was constructed in competition with a smaller, survivor-based museum. (Once the Washington museum project was under way, survivors, as we've seen, were an important voice in determining its direction.) In other realms as well, like lobbying for legislatively mandated Holocaust curricula and determining their content, the role of survivors was mostly marginal.

If, except sometimes at the local level, survivors played a relatively small role in initiating the major efforts at Holocaust remembrance, once those efforts bore fruit, their role thereafter was substantial. At museums, they often guide visitors or recount their experiences. In schools, classes on the Holocaust have frequently featured survivors as speakers. In community Holocaust observances, survivors have usually played a leading part. To speak of survivors in this global fashion is a bit misleading, because many survivors did not associate themselves with commemorative activity; indeed, they often avoided identifying themselves as survivors, preferring to put their past behind them.[13] The "survivor presence" was made up of those survivors who chose, or felt obliged, to assume that role. For some, serving as bearers and transmitters of memory has been cathartic, has brought some release from bottled-up pain. In those cases we're certainly glad that they've had the opportunity. In other cases — in ways reminiscent of Claude Lanzmann's treatment of the barber Abraham Bomba in the documentary film *Shoah* — they've been bullied or cajoled into reliving memories they would have preferred to let lie dormant.[14] (More broadly, it's clear that for many survivors all the attention paid to the Holocaust has been gratifying, and helped scars to heal; for others it has reopened old wounds and given rise to nightmares once quiescent. There is no possible way to know the relative proportions of the two groups.)[15]

It was the *symbol* of the survivor — the survivor as emblematic of Jewish suffering, Jewish memory, and Jewish endurance — rather than the highly diverse reality of survivors, that made the greatest contribution to Holocaust commemoration. And it had to be the *right* symbol. When a documentary on survivors was shown in Atlanta a few years ago, a poster was designed to advertise it. The face of a survivor was needed for the poster. There were many survivors in Atlanta, but none of them had the "survivor look," so a local Jewish man of the right age — he had spent World War II in the Pacific with the Army Air Corps — was recruited. His face, it was explained, would better "reflect the spirit of the show." *

Elie Wiesel, of course, became the emblematic survivor. His gaunt face, with its anguished expression, seemed to freeze time — to be staring out from a 1945 photograph of the liberation of the camps. Numerous Jewish critics — occasionally in print, more often in private — have been acerbic about what they see as Wiesel's carefully cultivated persona as symbol of suffering, as Christ figure.[17] Such criticism ignores the extent to which this stance is thoroughly authentic, reflects Wiesel's immersion, even before his Holocaust experiences, in the depths of Jewish mysticism and asceticism. His autobiography tells how, as an adolescent in Romania, he was jealous of the suffering of the poor — how, to paraphrase Sholem Aleichem, he "would have given anything for a tiny taste of misery." He describes his daily lessons from his master in Kabala: "ascetic exercises, feverish incantatory litanies, descent into the torments of the abyss in the hope of reascending toward dizzying heights." He recounts how in France, after the war, still in his teens, he picked up those studies, exploring

> the lure of and quest for suffering, the will to suffer so as to infuse one's own suffering and that of others with meaning. . . . The relation between suffering and truth, suffering and redemption, suffering and spiritual purity, suffering as a gateway to the sacred. . . . Was it necessary, even indispensable, to punish the body so as to allow the soul to soar to new heights?[18]

All of this was rooted in a tradition no less authentically Jewish for being quite distant from mainstream Jewish thought. But one can't avoid being struck by how much more powerfully it resonates with Christian doctrines. It is therefore not surprising that many of Wiesel's greatest admirers are to be found among devout Christians — especially Catholics, for whom there is a close link between suffering and redemption, and in whose tradition not just asceticism, but the deliberate mortification of the flesh, is highly valued.

For both Christians and Jews, Wiesel has been, and remains, not only the emblematic survivor but the most influential interpreter of the Holocaust as sacred mystery. The relationship between his eminence and the rise of Holocaust consciousness is clearly circular, with no way of distinguishing cause from effect. So far as the quality of American discourse about the Holocaust is concerned, it seems certain that the widespread inclination to speak of its uniqueness, its incomprehensibility, and its unrepresentability owes much to Wiesel's influence.[19] It seems likely that the absence in the future of authoritative voices insisting on that approach will lead to its decline.

It has been argued — though less now than formerly — that once the survivor-witnesses are gone, Holocaust deniers will flourish in the absence of those whose memories refute them.[20] More generally, it is held that survivors' memories are an indispensable historical source that must be preserved, and elaborate projects are under way to collect them. In fact, those memories are not a very useful historical source. Or, rather, some may be, but we don't know which ones. A few years ago the director of Yad Vashem's archive told a reporter that most of the twenty thousand testimonies it had collected were unreliable: "Many were never in the places where they claim to have witnessed atrocities, while others relied on secondhand information given them by friends or passing strangers."[21] Primo Levi, one of the most renowned of survivor-witnesses, has described this phenomenon:

> The greater part of the witnesses . . . have ever more blurred and stylized memories, often, unbeknownst to them, influenced by information gained from later readings or the stories of others. . . . A memory evoked too often, and expressed in the form of a story, tends to become fixed in a stereotype . . . crystallized, perfected, adorned, installing itself in the place of the raw memory and growing at its expense.[22]

To say that survivors' memories, or some unknown portion of them, are not a reliable historical source is not to say they haven't been, or won't continue to be, important in evoking the Holocaust experience. Videotaped reminiscences have been among the most emotionally powerful elements in Holocaust museums (this has been my own experience), and this, not their accuracy, is why they're used. To be moved by *All Quiet on the Western Front* — to feel, after reading it, that one has had a kind of access to the experience of trench warfare in World War I, and enhanced empathy with those who underwent the experience — is surely legitimate. (When evidence emerged that one Holocaust memoir, highly praised for its authenticity, might have been completely invented, Deborah Lipstadt, who used the memoir in her teaching of the Holocaust, acknowledged that if this turned out to be the case, it "might complicate matters somewhat," but insisted that it would still be "powerful" as a novel.)[23]

Through various initiatives, of which the largest is Steven Spielberg's $100 million project of collecting videotaped testimonies, survivors' evocative accounts will outlive them. The uses to which they'll be put in the future, and how much of an audience they'll command, we can't know.[24]

There are at least two ways in which the gradual departure of the survivors themselves from the scene seems likely to reduce the salience of the Holocaust. After having gone through thousands of newspaper stories on the Holocaust, I'm struck by how often the pathos of interviewing or quoting a local survivor was the peg on which such stories were hung. Absent this connection, coverage will probably not be as full. Within Jewish communities, and among American Jews in general, the physical presence of survivors has exercised tacit pressure for activities that pay tribute to their suffering and endurance. Here again — and again, it's hardly more than a guess — it seems unlikely that in their absence the same pressure will be felt.

We've been looking at various factors that may gradually reduce the level of attention now paid to the Holocaust — developments that in the aggregate may lower the ceiling of Holocaust memory. But there is one very large factor working in the other direction — which, at a minimum, sets a floor below which the level of Holocaust commemoration will not fall for the foreseeable future. That factor is the extent to which that commemoration has become institutionalized — literally set in stone.

Institutionalization might not be an effective force for the continuation of Holocaust memory if it was simply a matter of monuments. Every American city has its monuments to the dead of the Civil War, the Spanish-American War, the First World War. They attract more attention from pigeons than they do from human passersby. The same is true of some monuments to the Holocaust. A few years after its dedication, Denver's Babi Yar Memorial Park "seems all but forgotten by its community."[25] Baltimore's Holocaust memorial suffered from too many rather than too few visitors: located near the downtown "adult entertainment" block, it became a shooting gallery for drug addicts, a rendezvous for prostitutes and their clients, an outdoor dormitory for the homeless; after some years it had to be demolished.[26] Boston's Holocaust memorial is striking and centrally located, the result of years of dedicated labor. How long — if it hasn't happened already — before it becomes part of the tuned-out urban background?

But the institutionalization of Holocaust memory has, for the most part, taken less ignorable forms. Preeminently, there is the Washington Holocaust Museum, which receives each year tens of millions of dollars from the federal government. And there are the major museums in New York and Los Angeles, followed by numerous substantial museums in other cities (with others in the planning or construction stage).

All these institutions have active educational and outreach programs. Steven Spielberg's massive project of videotaping thousands of survivor testimonies is committed to their widest dissemination, in a variety of media. An equally important form of the institutionalization of Holocaust memory is the legislative mandate, in several states, that the Holocaust be taught in the schools. And a growing number of colleges and universities now have endowed chairs in Holocaust studies. Considering all the Holocaust institutions of one kind or another in the United States, there are by now thousands of full-time Holocaust professionals dedicated to keeping its memory alive.

Even if, as I've suggested, the original momentum behind the museums and the programs is likely to decrease, Holocaust institutions, like all institutions, generate their own momentum; at a minimum, are dedicated to their own continuation. The opening of these institutions required great effort and resources, but their establishment was generally uncontroversial. Imagine the controversy that would attend any initiative to *close* them, a legislative act to *cease* requiring the teaching of the Holocaust in the schools. The particular constellation of circumstances that led to the establishment of these institutions may no longer obtain, or no longer obtain in the future. The French, who have an aphorism for everything, say *"Rien dure que le provisoire"* — nothing lasts like the temporary. At least for the short term, the set-in-stone-ness of Holocaust commemoration is the guarantor of its continuation, places a floor below which it will not fall.

In my account of how the Holocaust came to become so central in American life, I have moved back and forth between, on the one hand, changing circumstances beyond the control of any individual, and, on the other hand, the choices that individuals have made within those circumstances. In this concluding chapter I've briefly reviewed the circumstantial factors that seem likely to influence "the future of the Holocaust." What of choices?

As concerns non-Jews, Elie Wiesel has recently made a prediction. Noting the current high level of attention paid to the Holocaust — stories about it every day in the *New York Times* — he thought that this was likely to decline substantially in the next few years.

> Good friends of ours will come and say, "Listen, you know we are with you. But it's enough. . . . Give us a chance now to breathe. Once a year we will come and cry with you on Yom Hashoah. . . . But we cannot take it every

day." . . . Good people will say, "Enough. There are . . . other issues, other obligations, other priorities. . . ." Because the moment you say "Holocaust" everything else fades away.

"And you know something?" he added. "We are not equipped to answer. What do you answer to that?"[27]

Wiesel wasn't really talking about the American public. The "good friends" to whom he referred are presumably those gentiles — often Christian clergy — who do cry on Yom Hashoah. There are such people — but not, I think, all that many. As I've indicated in an earlier chapter, it seems to me that for most Americans deploring the Holocaust is a rather ritualistic, albeit undoubtedly well-meant, gesture toward Jews who ask them to do so — a cost-free avowal that, as decent people, they are moved by the murder of European Jewry.

For all of the extent to which the Holocaust has reverberated throughout American society, it's not clear that the Holocaust is an American collective memory in any worthwhile sense. One way that an historical occurrence becomes deeply embedded in collective consciousness is when it serves to define the group, remind people of "who they are." The Holocaust is simply too remote from the experience of Americans for it to perform that function. And, as a result of demographic changes, it is becoming even more remote. James Rudin, the director of interreligious affairs for the American Jewish Committee, worried whether, in a society whose members were increasingly of non-European background, there would be the same level of interest in the Holocaust. "Will that . . . continue among Hispanics, blacks and Asians, who may not sense either guilt or responsibility for what white Christians did to Jews in the Europe of the 1930s and 1940s?"[28]

If the Holocaust does not speak to any consensual American identity, commemorating it is, at the same time, quite uncontroversial. Which points to the second sense in which it is not a significant American collective memory — because the other way in which a memory may continue to resonate in a society is when it is the framework for continuing conflict. In France, the Revolution was a living memory for so long not because the population agreed about it, but because for more than a hundred and fifty years the major political divisions in the country and the major political struggles seemed to date from the Revolution.[29] In Israel (though less now than formerly), the Holocaust has been both a source of collective identity and a framework within which partisan conflicts were played out. In Germany, attitudes toward the commemoration of the Holocaust have often been a reflection of political, ideological, and generational conflicts. In France, the Holocaust has become entangled with later struggles over racism and xenophobia. In Poland, it remains a touchstone of cultural conflict between the forces of clerical reaction and of liberal modernism.

The politicizing of the memory of the Holocaust is often deplored. But collective memory, when it is consequential, when it is worthy of the name, is characteristically an arena of political contestation in which competing narratives about central symbols in the collective past, and the collectivity's relationship to that past, are disputed and negotiated in the interest of redefining the collective present. In the United States, memory of the Holocaust is so banal, so inconsequential, not memory at all, precisely because it is so uncontroversial, so unrelated to real divisions in American society, so *apolitical*.

In any case, American gentiles have for the most part been consumers, not producers, of talk about the Holocaust. Indeed, the entry of the Holocaust into the American cultural arena has been largely a byproduct, or spillover effect, of its having become important to how American Jews understand and represent themselves. Short of some repudiation of the Holocaust as an honorary American memory — of which there seems not the slightest prospect — American gentiles aren't called upon to make any choices concerning Holocaust memory, except perhaps to consider whether they have allowed it to displace more disturbing ones, closer to home. As an American, the extent to which this displacement has occurred concerns me some. But it's a rather abstract concern, since realistically it's doubtful whether, absent the central place of the Holocaust in American historical consciousness, my fellow citizens would be any more inclined to address memories that would make serious demands on them. If memory of the Holocaust hasn't had that much real impact on Americans in general, the centering of the Holocaust in American Jewish consciousness has had a lot, often in ways that concern me a good deal as a Jew. And American Jews have now, as in the past, real choices to make in this regard. It is to those choices, and thus principally to my fellow Jews, that I'll address my final remarks.

The evolution of Holocaust memory in the United States has been, in the main, the result of a series of choices made by American Jewry about how to deal with that memory — in practice, usually choices made by Jewish leaders, tacitly ratified by their constituents. Those changing choices have reflected a changing American climate, changing assessments of the immediate needs of the Jewish community, changes in the values and styles of Jewish leadership. As we've seen, through the mid-1960s Jewish communal leaders downplayed the Holocaust, believing, for various reasons, that to center it wasn't in the best interests of American Jewry. In their emphasis on the future rather than the past, and in submerging rather than insisting upon ethnic difference, they reflected the dominant ethos. In those years, American Jewish leaders were, on the whole, more integrationist and more universalist in sensibility, less religious and less Israel-oriented, than most of those for whom they claimed to speak. Critics of the choice to remain relatively silent about the Holocaust in the first postwar years see an element of timidity, even of shame, in that choice — a dishonorable evasion of a past Jews were obliged to confront. There is surely something to that view.

Over the last quarter century, American Jewish leadership, in response to a perception that needs had changed, has chosen to center the Holocaust — to combat what they saw as a "new anti-Semitism"; in support of an embattled Israel; as the basis of revived ethnic consciousness. That choice was made in a culture that had come to celebrate rather than disparage ethnic difference and to elevate the status of victims. The Jewish leaders making the relevant decisions have been, overall, more particularist, more religious, and more Israel-oriented than their constituents. In recent years, critics of those leaders' choices have deplored what they have seen as a perverse sacralization of the Holocaust, and objected to the competition over "who suffered most," to the way in which Jews now often seemed almost proud of the Holocaust. As I've made clear, I am among those critics.

Whatever we think of past choices to marginalize or center the memory of the Holocaust, to use it for specific purposes, the making of such choices is inescapable. We can only hope that the choices we make will be as thoughtful as possible, made with careful attention to all the consequences, including long-term consequences, of those choices. Memories, once deployed for this or that immediate purpose, can become an enduring force for self-definition, telling us not just about the past, but about who we are now and what we can expect in the future. The most powerful collective memories are usually memories of deep grievances. For that reason, we cling to them, but as we grasp them tightly — or they grasp us — the results can be problematic. This is by no means a peculiarity of Jewish memory. Leon Wieseltier, discussing black Americans' memory of oppression, and its consequences, but also with an eye to the Jewish experience, has written about how a memory of this kind

> instructs the individual and the group about what to expect of the world, imparts an isolating sense of . . . apartness. . . . It transforms experiences into traditions, as the sons learn to see themselves in the fathers. Because it abolishes time and dissolves place, collective memory . . . leaves the individual and the group too skeptical about change; does not ready them for discontinuity. . . . Don't be fooled, it teaches, there is only repetition. The collective memory of an oppressed group . . . robs people who have been delivered from the *Judengasse* and Jim Crow of the resources they require for problems that are not like the *Judengasse* or Jim Crow.
>
> In the memory of oppression, oppression outlives itself. The scar does the work of the wound. . . . Injustice retains the power to distort long after it has ceased to be real. It is a posthumous victory for the oppressors, when pain becomes a tradition.[30]

Whether the memory is of slavery, the Holocaust, or any of the other terrible events of human history whose scars do the work of the wound, the role of that memory in group consciousness has to be carefully considered. There is a sense in which Emil Fackenheim was right to say that for Jews to forget Hitler's victims would be to grant him a "posthumous victory." But it would be an even greater posthumous victory for Hitler were we to tacitly endorse his definition of ourselves as despised pariahs by making the Holocaust the emblematic Jewish experience.

In the future, as in the past, changing circumstances will influence the choices we make about remembering the Holocaust. But while circumstances will influence our choices, we ourselves are ultimately responsible for those choices — with all their consequences, intended and unintended. It is in the hope of making those choices more informed and more thoughtful that I have written this book.

NOTES

ACKNOWLEDGMENTS

INDEX

Notes

A Note on the Notes

The archival collections cited in the notes were, at the time that I used them, at the following locations. Since then, the collections at the American Jewish Historical Society and at YIVO have been moved to the new Center for Jewish History in New York City.

American Jewish Committee. Files. Offices of the American Jewish Committee, New York, N.Y.

American Jewish Committee. Papers. YIVO: The Yiddish Scientific Organization, New York, N.Y.

American Jewish Congress. Papers. American Jewish Historical Society, Brandeis University, Waltham, Mass.

Anti-Defamation League. Microfilms. Offices of the Anti-Defamation League, New York, N.Y.

Arendt, Hannah. Papers. Manuscript Division, Library of Congress, Washington, D.C.

Boston Jewish Community Relations Council (JCRC). Papers. American Jewish Historical Society, Brandeis University, Waltham, Mass.

Carter, Jimmy. Papers. Carter Presidential Library, Atlanta, Ga.

Cincinnati Jewish Community Relations Council (JCRC). Papers. American Jewish Archives, Cincinnati, Ohio.

Cohen, Oscar. Papers. American Jewish Archives, Cincinnati, Ohio.

Fineberg, S. Andhil. Papers. American Jewish Archives, Cincinnati, Ohio.

Haber, William. Papers. University of Michigan Library, Ann Arbor, Mich.

Jewish Defense League (JDL). File. American Jewish Historical Society, Brandeis University, Waltham, Mass.

Kallen, Horace. Papers. American Jewish Historical Society, Brandeis University, Waltham, Mass.

Lemkin, Raphael. Papers. American Jewish Archives, Cincinnati, Ohio.

National Community Relations Advisory Council (NCRAC) [After name change, National Jewish Community Relations Advisory Council (NJCRAC)]. Papers. YIVO: The Yiddish Scientific Organization, New York, N.Y.

Near East Crisis Collection. American Jewish Historical Society, Brandeis University, Waltham, Mass.

Polier, Shad. Papers. American Jewish Historical Society, Brandeis University, Waltham, Mass.

Wise, Stephen. Papers. American Jewish Historical Society, Brandeis University, Waltham, Mass.

World Jewish Congress. Papers. American Jewish Archives, Cincinnati, Ohio.

In the notes that follow, I have abbreviated American Jewish Committee as AJCommittee, American Jewish Congress as AJCongress, Anti-Defamation League as ADL, National Community Relations Advisory Council as NCRAC (after name change, National Jewish Community Relations Advisory Council as NJCRAC), and World Jewish Congress as WJC.

Introduction

1. J. Laplanche and J.-B. Pontalis, *The Language of Psychoanalysis* (New York, 1973), 465, 398.
2. A good introduction to Halbwachs's thought is Lewis A. Coser, ed., *Maurice Halbwachs on Collective Memory* (Chicago, 1992).
3. Cindy Loose, "Marking a Rite for Those Denied the Chance," *Washington Post*, 27 September 1993, A1; Stuart Vincent, "Good Deed for Lost 'Twin,' " *Newsday*, 28 May 1994, A6; Kendall Anderson, "Committed to Memory," *Dallas Morning News*, 22 April 1995, 1G.
4. See, e.g., Pamela Selbert, "Grim Lesson," *St. Louis Post-Dispatch*, 6 June 1994, West Zone sec., 2.
5. Charles S. Maier, "A Surfeit of Memory? Reflections on History, Melancholy and Denial," *History & Memory* 5 (Fall-Winter 1993): 147.
6. French Jewish filmmaker Marcel Ophuls observed that "New York Jews who never got any closer than Rumpelmayer's to the Warsaw ghetto claim the uniqueness of their suffering." (Joan Dupont, "Marcel Ophuls: Seeking Truth in an Uneasy Present," *International Herald Tribune*, 15 November 1994.)
7. "ADL Says Ted Turner's Reported 'Fuhrer' Comment Disturbing," U.S. Newswire, 30 September 1996; "Once Again, Turner Makes Offensive 'Nazi' Comments — and Then Apologizes to ADL," ibid., 25 October 1996.
8. Michael Berenbaum, "The Nativization of the Holocaust," *Judaism* 35 (1986): 454.
9. Cynthia Ozick, "All the World Wants the Jews Dead," *Esquire* 82 (November 1974): 103ff.
10. Yosef Hayim Yerushalmi, *Zakhor: Jewish History and Jewish Memory* (Seattle, 1982), 5.
11. There are exceptions. See Raphael Patai, "Memory in Religion," *Midstream* 29 (December 1983).
12. As a secularist, I'm not entitled to object to all of this on religious grounds, but it grates on me all the same, just as, without observing the laws of *kashrut*, I'm put off by the idea of butter on a meat sandwich.
13. "On Murder Considered as One of the Fine Arts," Second Paper, in David Masson, ed., *The Collected Writings of Thomas De Quincey* (Edinburgh, 1890), XIII, 56.
14. See Eric Stein, "History Against Free Speech: The New German Law Against the 'Auschwitz' — and Other — 'Lies,' " *Michigan Law Review* 85 (1986); Robert G. Moeller, "War Stories: The Search for a Usable Past in the Federal Republic of Germany," *American Historical Review* 101 (October 1996).

1. "We Knew in a General Way"

1. In the aftermath of Kristallnacht, the German ambassador in Washington reported to Berlin that "without exception" the American public was "incensed against Germany." (Cited in Kenneth S. Davis, *FDR: Into the Storm, 1937–1940* [New York, 1993], 365.)
2. In late 1939 there was an attempt to interest the publisher Henry Holt & Co. in a manuscript on the plight of German Jews. A representative of the firm replied that "the outbreak of the war has changed conditions considerably and . . . interest in books dealing with Jewish persecution in Germany has been side-tracked." (Jonathan D. Sarna, *JPS: The Americanization of Jewish Culture, 1888–1988* [Philadelphia, 1989], 186.)
3. Alex Grobman, "What Did They Know? The American Jewish Press and the Holocaust, 1 September 1939–17 December 1942," *American Jewish History* 68 (March 1979): 331.
4. "While the Jews Die," *New Republic* 108 (8 March 1943): 303–4; "The Jews of Europe," *Nation* 158 (13 March 1943): 355–56, cited in John M. Muresianu, *War of Ideas: American Intellectuals and the World Crisis, 1938–1945* (New York, 1988), 225.
5. W. H. Lawrence, "50,000 Kiev Jews Reported Killed," *New York Times,* 29 November 1943.
6. "Enclosure No. 1 to Dispatch No. 44 (memorandum) dated September 28, 1942, from Paul C. Squire, American Consul at Geneva, Switzerland, on the subject of Jewish Persecutions," in David S. Wyman, ed., *America and the Holocaust,* vol. 1: *Confirming the News of Extermination* (New York, 1990), 205; R. Borden Reams to Edward R. Stettinius, 8 October 1943, ibid., vol. 2: *The Struggle for Rescue Action* (New York, 1990), 269.
7. Victor Cavendish-Bentinck, of the British Foreign Office, quoted in Tom Bower, *The Pledge Betrayed* (Garden City, N.Y., 1982), 23.
8. Letters from Henry Fachter and Walter Laqueur, *Commentary* 69 (April 1980): 20. The French diplomatic historian Étienne Mantoux, then resident at the Institute for Advanced Study in Princeton, wrote Morris Waldman of the American Jewish Committee suggesting that it was a bad idea to circulate the "soap" story. It might, Mantoux thought, be Nazi disinformation, spread to "sow the seeds of disbelief" about the larger truth of the Holocaust. But even if, as Mantoux thought quite possible, the story was true, it didn't add much to the horrors of what was going on and might "have the effect of detracting from it in so many minds who are always ready to disbelieve 'propaganda.' . . . Whether or not true, it cannot, at the present juncture, do any good to the cause of the persecuted Jews of Europe, and may very well do it much harm." (Mantoux to Waldman, 2 December 1942, in AJCommittee Papers, FAD-1, Box 24, Germany, Nazism, Atrocities, 1938–59.) A few days earlier, representatives of the American Jewish Committee and of B'nai B'rith had pressed Stephen Wise of the American Jewish Congress as to whether the State Department vouched for the veracity of the "soap" story, and wished it disseminated. Wise assured them — falsely — that this was the case. (M. Gottschalk to Mr. Waldman, 27 November 1942, in AJCommittee Papers, FAD-1, Box 36, Germany, 1942–43, Nazism–Jewish Agencies.) An editorial in *The Christian Century,* 5 December 1942, "Horror Stories from Poland," based its skepticism about the scale of the atrocities reported by Wise in part on the "soap" story — "unpleasantly reminiscent of the 'cadaver factory' lie which was one of the propaganda triumphs of the First World War."

9. For survey data, see Charles Herbert Stember et al., *Jews in the Mind of America* (New York, 1966), 141.
10. William Casey, *The Secret War Against Hitler* (Washington, D.C., 1988), 218.
11. William L. Shirer, *A Native's Return: 1945–1988* (Boston, 1990), 26–27.
12. Letter from Marion R. Lieder, *Life* 18 (4 June 1945): 2.
13. Curtis E. LeMay with MacKinley Kantor, *Mission with LeMay: My Story* (Garden City, N.Y., 1965), 425.
14. Christopher Browning, *Fateful Months: Essays on the Emergence of the Final Solution*, rev. ed. (New York, 1991), 6.
15. Quoted in Paul Fussell, *Wartime* (New York, 1989), 137–38.
16. Quoted in Deborah Lipstadt, *Beyond Belief: The American Press and the Coming of the Holocaust, 1933–1945* (New York, 1986), 255.
17. Lester Cole, *Hollywood Red* (Palo Alto, Cal., 1981), 204; Bernard F. Dick, *The Star-Spangled Screen: The American World War II Film* (Lexington, Ky., 1985), 207–8.
18. World Jewish Congress, "Meeting of the Planning Committee, December 17, 1942, Joint Report by Wise, Goldmann, and Shulman on Their Trip to Washington," in David S. Wyman, ed., *America and the Holocaust*, vol. 2 (New York, 1990), 23. Harold Ickes, one of the most philo-Semitic members of Roosevelt's cabinet, responded in parallel fashion to a suggestion that a volume be published on Hitler's crimes against Jews. (Diary entry of 2 December 1944, in ibid., 215.)
19. Virginia M. Mannon to John Pehle, 16 November 1944, in Wyman, ed., *America and the Holocaust*, vol. 13: Responsibility for America's Failure (New York, 1991), 108.
20. Walter Laqueur has suggested the possibility — it is no more than that — that some Germans who passed on the news of the Final Solution to Swiss acquaintances were doing so to further a Nazi propaganda stratagem. They may have wanted to increase Allied commitment on behalf of Jews, which would, in their view, sow discord in the Allied camp. (*The Terrible Secret* [Boston, 1980], 211–12.)
21. Quoted in David Brody, "American Jewry, the Refugees and Immigration Restriction, 1932–1942," *American Jewish Historical Quarterly* 45 (1956): 235.
22. Richard Breitman and Alan M. Kraut, *American Refugee Policy and European Jewry, 1933–1945* (Bloomington, Ind., 1987), 241.
23. Among those summoned was Darryl Zanuck, one of the few leading Hollywood executives who wasn't Jewish. He began his testimony by noting that all four of his grandparents were born in the United States, and, along with his parents, "were regular attendants and life long members of the Methodist Church." (Judith E. Doneson, *The Holocaust in American Film* [Philadelphia, 1987], 42–43.)
24. Quoted in ibid., 44.
25. K. R. M. Short, "Hollywood Fights Anti-Semitism," in Short, ed., *Film and Radio Propaganda in World War II* (Knoxville, Tenn., 1983), 159.
26. For this fascinating phenomenon, see Mark Silk, "Notes on the Judeo-Christian Tradition in America," *American Quarterly* 36 (1984).
27. See, e.g., "The First to Suffer," editorial, *New York Times*, 2 December 1942, 24; "The Threat to European Jewry," *Bulletin of the World Jewish Congress* 1 (October 1942): 2.

2. "If Our Brothers Had Shown More Compassion"

1. Rafael Medoff, *The Deafening Silence: American Jewish Leaders and the Holocaust* (New York, 1987); Haskel Lookstein, *Were We Our Brothers' Keepers? The Public Response of American Jews to the Holocaust, 1938–1944* (New York, 1985).
2. Elie Wiesel, "A Plea for the Survivors," in his *A Jew Today* (New York, 1978), 191–92.

3. Lookstein, *Brothers' Keepers*, 216.
4. The counterposing of ties to the Jewish people and an abstract, meretricious, and usually leftist universalism has been a standard device of neo-conservative critics who thus simultaneously avoid the uncomfortable issue of "dual loyalty" and cast doubt on the American loyalty of those so charged. See, e.g., Midge Decter, "Socialism and Its Irresponsibilities: The Case of Irving Howe," *Commentary* 74 (December 1982); Lucy S. Dawidowicz, "Indicting American Jews," *Commentary* 75 (June 1983).
5. Philip Roth, *The Facts* (New York, 1988), 122–23. For a report that parallels Roth's, see Joseph Epstein, "Our Debt to I. B. Singer," *Commentary* 92 (November 1991): 32.
6. Quoted in David Brody, "American Jewry, the Refugees and Immigration Restriction, 1932–1942," *American Jewish Historical Quarterly* 45 (1956): 240.
7. Shlomo Katz, "What Should We Write?" *Jewish Frontier* 7 (May 1940): 16.
8. Quoted in Henry L. Feingold, *A Time for Searching* (Baltimore, 1992), 219.
9. Virginia Anderson, "Holocaust Victims Remembered," *Atlanta Journal and Constitution*, 15 April 1996.
10. On this subject, vital in my view to understanding American Jewish consciousness, see the rich and suggestive essays collected in Philip Gleason's *Speaking of Diversity: Language and Ethnicity in Twentieth-Century America* (Baltimore, 1992), especially "Americans All" and "Hansen, Herberg, and American Religion."
11. Yehuda Bauer, *Jewish Reactions to the Holocaust* (Tel Aviv, 1989), 199.
12. Dina Porat, *The Blue and the Yellow Stars of David: The Zionist Leadership in Palestine and the Holocaust, 1939–1945* (1986; English trans., Cambridge, Mass., 1990), 41–42, 54–55, 62–63.
13. Leo Bogart, "The Response of Jews in America to the European Jewish Catastrophe, 1941–45," University of Chicago master's thesis in sociology, 1948, 89.
14. Eli Ginzberg, *My Brother's Keeper* (New Brunswick, N.J., 1989), 61–62.
15. Lewis Weinstein, "The Liberation of the Death Camps," *Midstream* 32 (April 1986): 21.
16. Solomon Grayzel, quoted in Jonathan D. Sarna, *JPS: The Americanization of Jewish Culture, 1888–1988* (Philadelphia, 1989), 186–87. Grayzel and the publication committee preferred a story about the capture and liberation of fifteenth-century Spanish Jewish children imprisoned by pirates, as "a ray of hope to those of our faith who saw nothing but darkness ahead."
17. Shad Polier to Justine Wise Polier, 16 November 1938, Shad Polier Papers, American Jewish Historical Society, Box 15.
18. Shlomo Katz, "Shall We Forget?" *Jewish Frontier* 11 (January 1944): 21.
19. Memo from NB (probably Nathan/Norton Belth) to Frank N. Trager, 26 March 1942, AJCommittee Papers, GS 10, Box 244, Minorities, 1937–48.
20. Editorial, *Menorah Journal* 31 (Winter 1943): i.
21. Stephen S. Wise, "Hitlerism — and Beyond," in Wise, ed., *Never Again! Ten Years of Hitler* (New York, 1945), 9.
22. An example will illustrate the problem. In her memoir of the war years, Lucy Dawidowicz reports what was surely a common emotion: her "unquenchable passion for revenge"; her wish to see Germany's population "ravaged with fire and sword"; how she rejoiced when she heard that thousands of German civilians had been killed in air raids. (Lucy S. Dawidowicz, *From That Place and Time: A Memoir, 1938–1947* [New York, 1989], 230, 246.) At this time, Jewish spokesmen were consistently making distinctions between Nazi leaders and the German people and repudiating any thought of "Old Testament vengeance."

23. Abraham Karp, *Haven and Home: A History of the Jews in America* (New York, 1985), 298–99.

24. Michael Sheridan, "Israel 'Shocked' by Bush's Stand," *Independent*, 14 September 1991. Addressing leaders of American Jewish organizations, Israeli cabinet minister Ariel Sharon demanded that they atone for American Jewish inaction during the Holocaust by organizing a mass demonstration protesting the American government's opposition to West Bank settlements. (Bernard Wasserstein, "The Myth of 'Jewish Silence,' " *Midstream* 26 [August-September 1980]: 10.)

25. Letter written by Pollard to an unnamed rabbi and presented in Pollard's defense by Rabbi Joseph B. Glaser, executive vice president of the Central Conference of American Rabbis (Reform), as a sidebar to Samuel Rabinove, "Pollard's Gamble," *Reform Judaism* 21 (Winter 1992): 32.

26. Weill quoted in Stephen J. Whitfield, "The Politics of Pageantry, 1936–1946," *American Jewish History* 84 (September 1996): 244.

27. This explanation is especially favored by Israelis, who frequently "know" (deductively, from Zionist ideology) that Jews in the Diaspora are craven and unassertive. See, e.g., Yoav Gelber, "Moralist and Realistic Approaches to the Study of the Allied Attitude to the Holocaust," in Asher Cohen et al., eds., *Comprehending the Holocaust* (Frankfurt, 1988), 119–20; Yehuda Bauer, "When Did They Know?" *Midstream* 14 (April 1968): 56; David Vital, "Power, Powerlessness and the Jews," *Commentary* 89 (January 1990): 25.

28. Paul Jacobs, *Is Curly Jewish?* (New York, 1965), 15.

29. Richard E. Gutstadt, "Memorandum in re the Future Program of the Anti-Defamation League, December, 1941," copy in AJCommittee Papers, EXO-29 (Waldman), Box 3, Folder 60.

30. Medoff, *Deafening Silence*, 108. Medoff reports the secondhand assertion that Joseph Proskauer of the American Jewish Committee said that "such an anti-Christian attitude could well bring on Jewish pogroms in the U.S.A."

31. To say this is *not* to say that the Bergsonites were in any sense insincere in their zeal to promote rescue. There is no reason to think this is so, and much reason to believe the contrary.

32. Many young American Jews were, of course, in the armed forces. It is possible that given the frequency of charges of Jewish draft dodging, those who weren't in uniform were hesitant to call attention to themselves.

33. Rabbi Howard Singer, quoted in Leon Weliczker Wells, *Who Speaks for the Vanquished?* (New York, 1987), 247. Incidentally, it is very unlikely that, after FDR became president, Wise ever did call him Franklin. And since Singer's recollection (recorded in 1971) came after there had been a good deal of published discussion of this issue, it may be that his memory is unreliable.

34. Steven Fraser, *Labor Will Rule: Sidney Hillman and the Rise of American Labor* (New York, 1991), 528.

35. Shabtai Teveth, *Ben-Gurion: The Burning Ground, 1886–1948* (Boston, 1987), 847–48.

36. Tom Segev, *The Seventh Million* (New York, 1993), 102.

37. David S. Wyman, introduction to Wyman, ed., *America and the Holocaust*, vol. 5: *American Jewish Disunity* (New York, 1990), viii–ix. The quotation is Wyman's paraphrase of a document he was denied permission to reproduce.

38. Ibid., 351–52. Also Wyman's paraphrases.

39. Aaron Berman, *Nazism, the Jews and American Zionism: 1933–1948* (Detroit, 1990), 98–99.

40. Minutes of WJC Advisory Council on European Jewish Affairs, 28 October 1942

(mistakenly dated 1943 in printed volume), and 10 May 1943, in Henry Friedlander and Sybil Milton, eds., *Archives of the Holocaust*, vol. 8 (New York, 1990), 320–28, 266–72. In both cases, the quoted words are a paraphrase by the person taking minutes.

41. At Lidice the Germans had murdered hundreds of Czechs in retaliation for the assassination of Nazi leader Reinhard Heydrich. "Minutes of Meeting of Sub-Committee of Special Conference on European Affairs, Held at the Office of the American Jewish Congress, Monday, November 30, 1942," in Wyman, ed., *America and the Holocaust*, vol. 2: The Struggle for Rescue Action (New York, 1990), 41.

42. Dawidowicz, *From That Place*, 236–37.

43. Both editorials cited in Lookstein, *Brothers' Keepers*, 124–25.

3. "The Abandonment of the Jews"

1. David S. Wyman, *The Abandonment of the Jews* (New York, 1984); Herbert Druks, *The Failure to Rescue* (New York, 1977); Arthur D. Morse, *While Six Million Died* (New York, 1967); Saul Friedman, *No Haven for the Oppressed* (Detroit, 1973); Monty Penkower, *The Jews Were Expendable* (Urbana, Ill., 1983).

2. Josef Goebbels's diary entry of 13 December 1942 is frequently cited: "The question of Jewish persecution in Europe is being given top news priority by the English and the Americans. . . . At bottom, however, I believe both the English and the Americans are happy that we are exterminating the Jewish riff-raff." (Louis P. Lochner, ed., *The Goebbels Diaries: 1942–1943* [Garden City, N.Y., 1948], 241. What is usually not noted is that this entry was written just four days before the Allied declaration promising retribution for those guilty of the murder of Jews. Wyman, for example, citing Goebbels's diary entry, but without mentioning the 17 December declaration, says that if, in addition to offering asylum, Roosevelt and Churchill had threatened punishment, "the Nazis at least would have ceased to believe that the West did not care what they were doing to the Jews. That might possibly have slowed the killing." (*Abandonment*, 334.)

3. Deborah Lipstadt, "Witness to the Persecution: The Allies and the Holocaust," *Modern Judaism* 3 (October 1983): 323, 329.

4. Wyman, *Abandonment*, 3–0.

5. See David Friedman, "4,000 at Holocaust Memorial Meeting," *Jewish Telegraphic Agency Daily Bulletin*, 18 April 1977, reporting the remarks of Gideon Hausner, minister without portfolio, who had been the prosecutor at the Eichmann trial.

6. Shultz, speech at Yad Vashem, Jerusalem, 10 May 1985; Bush, speech to Thirtieth Anniversary Convocation of Bar-Ilan University, 5 June 1985 — both reprinted in Ilya Levkov, ed., *Bitburg and Beyond* (New York, 1987), quoted remarks on 212 and 216, respectively; "Remarks at the Dedication of the U.S. Holocaust Memorial Museum, 22 April 1993," *Public Papers of the Presidents of the United States: William J. Clinton, 1993* (Washington, D.C., 1994), 479.

7. Helen Fagin on ABC *World News Tonight*, 21 April 1993.

8. Henry L. Feingold, review of Richard Breitman and Alan M. Kraut, *American Refugee Policy and European Jewry, 1933–1945* (Bloomington, Ind., 1987), *Moment* 17 (April 1992): 61–62.

9. For Lucy Dawidowicz, see "Could America Have Rescued Europe's Jews?" in her *What Is the Use of Jewish History?* (New York, 1992), quoted phrase on 160; for Martin Gilbert, see his remarks in interview on National Public Radio's *All Things Considered*, 22 April 1993 for Henry Feingold, see his "Stephen Wise and the Holocaust," *Midstream* 29 (January 1983): 46. The most systematic critique of

Wyman's *Abandonment* is Frank W. Brecher, "David Wyman and the Historiography of America's Response to the Holocaust: Counter-Considerations," *Holocaust and Genocide Studies* 5 (1990). (Wyman refused to respond to Brecher's article.) For an overview of professional historians' judgments on the issue, see "Transcript of the Summary of the Conference on 'Policies and Responses of the American Government Toward the Holocaust,' 11–12 November 1993," in Verne W. Newton, ed., *FDR and the Holocaust* (New York, 1996), 3–28. A recent book by William D. Rubinstein (*The Myth of Rescue: Why the Democracies Could Not Have Saved More Jews from the Nazis* [London, 1997]) seems to me — and to most other scholars — to be as tendentious in one direction as Wyman is in the other. Rubinstein asserts that nothing could have been done, where Wyman asserts that a lot could have been done.

10. David Brody, "American Jewry, the Refugees and Immigration Restriction, 1932–1942," *American Jewish Historical Quarterly* 45 (1956): 220.

11. David S. Wyman, *Paper Walls: America and the Refugee Crisis, 1938–1941* (New York, 1968), 4–5.

12. Howard M. Sachar, *A History of the Jews in America* (New York, 1992), 476. There was, in the prewar and wartime State Department, a pervasive sense that in the long run it was Communism, rather than fascism, that was the main threat to the United States, and a diffuse sense in which Jews were associated with Communism.

13. Ben-Gurion in a meeting at Mapai Center, 7 December 1938, quoted in Hava Wagman Eshkoli, "Three Attitudes Toward the Holocaust Within Mapai, 1933–1945," *Studies in Zionism* 14 (1993): 79.

14. Though it hardly gets the American government off the hook, the State Department was in fact active in unsuccessfully lobbying the Cuban government to reverse its decision, and later in inducing European governments to take in the passengers. (See Irwin F. Gellman, "The *St. Louis* Tragedy," *American Jewish Historical Quarterly* 61 (December 1971).

15. Yoav Gelber, *A New Homeland* (Jerusalem, 1990), 136, cited in Tom Segev, *The Seventh Million* (New York, 1993), 44.

16. Wyman, *Paper Walls*, 4–7.

17. Ibid., 24, 67–71, 93, 210–12. Some have suggested that there were more self-regarding motives for Jewish failure to press for liberalized immigration legislation: wealthy Jews fearing a greater philanthropic burden; working Jews fearing economic competition; timorous Jews fearing that the attempt, particularly if successful, would exacerbate anti-Semitism. (For an exposition of these suggestions, see Brody, "American Jewry.") No doubt there were American Jews moved to inaction by such considerations. Among the soundest of historical maxims is "If you can imagine it, someone will do it." But there's no reason to believe that such motives were common. Self-regarding motives could at least as plausibly be attributed to those who did press for changing the quota system, among them Rep. Emanuel Celler and Rep. Samuel Dickstein of New York. Were their initiatives serious, or were they grandstanding for their largely Jewish constituencies?

18. As Kristallnacht coincided with Democratic losses in 1938, the confirmation of the news of full-scale mass murder in 1942 coincided with losses in that year's elections. Republicans came within eight votes of capturing the House of Representatives, and isolationists in both parties grew stronger. The House Ways and Means Committee, dominated by Republicans and southern Democrats, turned down Roosevelt's request for broader wartime powers, which included the right to suspend federal statutes "affecting movement of war goods, information and

persons into or out of the United States." (See Leonard Dinnerstein, "What Should American Jews Have Done to Rescue Their European Brethren?" *Simon Wiesenthal Center Annua* 3 [1986]: 281.) As in 1938, it is unlikely that things would have been different in the absence of these political setbacks, but they serve as a reminder of the constraints under which the administration operated.

19. Frank W. Brecher writes "Of the some half-million Jews who managed to find refuge outside of German-dominated Europe, nearly one-half found it in the United States. . . . In percentage terms, during the late 1930s and early 1940s, Jews accounted for over half of all immigrants into the country, whereas, even during the historical heights of Jewish immigration into America, 1890–1910, they accounted for less than 15 percent. In a word, as short of the actual need for refuge as it was, the American immigration record during the Hitlerian period is not that of a country that was, from the humanitarian point of view, indifferent to the Nazi atrocities." (*Reluctant Ally* [New York, 1991], 88.)

20. "20,000 Plead: 'Act Now to Rescue Jews,' " *Chicago Daily Tribune*, 15 April 1943.

21. Thus Walter Laqueur has criticized Nahum Goldmann for disparaging negotiation initiatives out of the mistaken belief that Germany's allies were mere "puppet dependencies" of the Nazis. (*The Terrible Secret* [Boston, 1980], 159.)

22. See Ephraim Ophir, "Was the Transnistria Rescue Plan Achievable?" *Holocaust and Genocide Studies* 6 (1991).

23. The most up-to-date scholarly account of this initiative is Richard Breitman and Shlomo Aronson, "The End of the 'Final Solution'?: Nazi Plans to Ransom Jews in 1944," *Central European History* 25 (1992).

24. For this problem, see Yoav Gelber, "Moralist and Realistic Approaches in the Study of the Allies' Attitude to the Holocaust," in Asher Cohen et al., eds., *Comprehending the Holocaust* (Frankfurt, 1988), 114.

25. Martin Gilbert, *Auschwitz and the Allies* (New York, 1981). 310, 316. But cf. ibid., 330, 334–35, for later, somewhat more optimistic estimates of the damage inflicted.

26. See Richard Foregger, "Technical Analysis of Methods to Bomb the Gas Chambers at Auschwitz," *Holocaust and Genocide Studies* 5 (1990); James H. Kitchens III, "The Bombing of Auschwitz Reexamined," in Newton, *FDR and the Holocaust*, 183–217. Cf. Richard H. Levy, "The Bombing of Auschwitz Revisited: A Critical Analysis," in ibid. 218–72.

27. Dawidowicz, "Could America," 172.

28. David Wyman, "Why Auschwitz Was Never Bombed," *Commentary* 65 (May 1978): 43, 44; cf. his letter *Commentary* 66 (July 1978): 11. In the same spirit, Kai Bird, biographer of John J. McCloy, writes: "Even if the bombing had failed to take out a single gas chamber–crematoria unit, and even if thousands of lives had been lost, the attempt would have been justified." ("Bombing Auschwitz Was Feasible," *Washington Jewish Week*, 10 June 1993, 15–16.) Max Weber might have been writing about Wyman and Bird when he discussed the "ethic of ultimate ends," which he contrasted with the "ethic of responsibility." "If an action of good intent leads to bad results, then, in the actor's eyes, not he but the world, or the stupidity of other men, or God's will who made them thus, is responsible for the evil. . . . The believer in an ethic of ultimate ends feels 'responsible' only for seeing to it that the flame of pure intentions is not quelched." (Weber, "Politics as a Vocation" [1919], in Hans Gerth and C. Wright Mills, eds., *From Max Weber* [New York, 1958], 121.)

29. For an example of the claim that prisoners desired bombing, see, e.g., the testimony of Daniel Haroch, a twelve-year-old prisoner at Auschwitz, on the occasion

of a mock trial, held in Israel, of the Allies for not bombing the camp. (Victor Perry, "In the Skies over Auschwitz," *Jerusalem Post*, 3 August 1990, 10.) Cf. the testimony of Louis Micheels, a Dutch physician imprisoned at Auschwitz, who believes that those who so report have forgotten the "fear and agony" when bombs accidentally hit the camp, and the pervasive "urge to live." (*Doctor 117641: A Holocaust Memoir* [New Haven, 1989], 181–82.)

30. Foregger, "Technical Analysis," 403. There was, in addition, another gas chamber, not then in operation, at Auschwitz-I. Cf. Frantiszek Piper, "Gas Chambers and Crematoria," in Yisrael Gutman and Michael Berenbaum, eds., *Anatomy of the Auschwitz Death Camp* (Bloomington, Ind., 1994), 173–74.

31. See John S. Conway, "The Holocaust in Hungary: Recent Controversies and Reconsiderations," in Randolph L. Braham, ed., *The Tragedy of Hungarian Jewry* (New York, 1986), 14; Piper, "Gas Chambers."

32. Gilbert, *Auschwitz and the Allies*, 256; Herbert Druks, "The Allies and Jewish Leadership on the Question of Bombing Auschwitz," *Tradition* 19 (1981), and "Why the Death Camps Were Not Bombed," *American Zionist* 67 (December 1976).

33. Eliahu Matz, "Britain and the Holocaust," *Midstream* 28 (April 1982): 59; Levy, "Bombing Revisited," 219–20, 271–72.

34. "Proceedings of World Conference," *Congress Weekly* 11 (1 December 1944): 15–16, cited in Rafael Medoff, *The Deafening Silence* (New York, 1987), 160.

35. Gilbert, *Auschwitz and the Allies*, 279.

36. Wyman, "Why Auschwitz Was Never Bombed," 40–41.

37. McCloy has been so demonized that it is risky to suggest that he may possibly have possessed moral merits. Primarily he was a servant of the officially defined national interest. When, as U.S. high commissioner in Germany after the war, his mission of furthering German integration into the Western alliance required him to grant amnesty to Nazi war criminals, outraging Jews, he did so; when it required him to press Konrad Adenauer to be generous in reparations to Israel, pleasing Jews, he did that. His actions with respect to bombing Auschwitz have been entered in red ink in the Jewish ledger, but as I have suggested, this may well be an error. It is interesting that, about a year before the Auschwitz affair, he argued, against a reluctant Office of War Information, for making army films attacking Nazi anti-Semitism available to civilians: "If the men come into the Army with these prejudices, it is going to be hard to eradicate them." (See Richard Breitman, "The Allied War Effort and the Jews, 1942–1943," *Journal of Contemporary History* 20 [1985]: 140.)

4. "The DP Camps Have Served Their Historic Purpose"

1. "Freeing the Survivors," *U.S. News & World Report* 118 (3 April 1995): 63.

2. Jeshajahu Weinberg and Rina Elieli, *The Holocaust Museum in Washington* (New York, 1995), 76.

3. Susan Sontag, *On Photography* (New York, 1977), 19–20.

4. The full text of Murrow's broadcast is in Edward Bliss, Jr., *In Search of Light: The Broadcasts of Edward R. Murrow, 1938–1971* (New York, 1967), 90–95. Cf. Margaret Bourke-White, *Dear Fatherland, Rest Quietly* (New York, 1946).

5. Cable from Eisenhower to General Marshall, cited in *Report to the Senate and House of Representatives of the Joint Committee Representing the Two Houses Named to Investigate Atrocities and Other Conditions in Concentration Camps in*

Germany, as Requested by Gen. Dwight D. Eisenhower Through the Chief of Staff, Gen. George C. Marshall, reprinted in *Cong. Rec.,* 79th Cong., 1st sess., 1945, 91, pt. 4:4577–8; House, Rep. Luther A. Johnson of Texas speaking on the "Editors' Report on German Atrocities," 79th Cong., 1st sess., *Cong. Rec. Appendix* (15 May 1945) 91, pt. 11:A2307.

6. Sidney Olson, "Defeated Land," *Life* 18 (14 May 1945): 103–4; Ben Hibbs, "Journey to a Shattered World," *Saturday Evening Post* 217 (9 June 1945): 84.

7. Deborah E. Lipstadt, *Beyond Belief: The American Press and the Coming of the Holocaust, 1933–1945* (New York, 1986), 254, 256.

8. For an overall estimate, see Henry Friedlander, "Darkness and Dawn in 1945: The Nazis, the Allies, and the Survivors," in United States Holocaust Memorial Museum, *1945: The Year of Liberation* (Washington, D.C., 1995), 24; for Buchenwald, Yehoshua R. Büchler, "Buchenwald," *Encyclopedia of the Holocaust* (New York, 1990), 1:254–56; for Dachau, calculation based on Barbara Distel, "Dachau," ibid., 1:343.

9. There is another reason why the Jewish presence in the liberated camps may have been downplayed, but it is not one that reflects discredit on the correspondents. They would frequently refer to a French Jew as a Frenchman rather than as a Jew, a Czech Jew as Czech rather than Jewish, etc. It is quite true that most often they were there as Jews. But in the early forties, to refer to a French Jew as a Jew rather than as a Frenchman seemed to be buying into Hitler's categories. It was the Nazis who denied that a French Jew could be a real Frenchman, etc. American correspondents' usage was "anti-fascist."

10. Quoted in Moshe Kohn, "Biting and Clipping," *Jerusalem Post,* 4 January 1991.

11. Friendly's letter reprinted in *Federation Voice* (Providence, R.I.), November 1987, 2–3.

12. Werner Weinberg, *Self-Portrait of a Holocaust Survivor* (Jefferson, N.C., 1985), 150–52.

13. Ibid. Weinberg went on to note the danger that "a survivor, officially so classified, is more readily inclined to exploit that survivorship in order to attract interest, pity, awe. . . . A survivor easily falls into the trap of looking upon himself the way compassionate and charitable people see him or her. This may lead to the fallacy of using one's survivorship as an excuse for any and all inadequacies and failures, for inherited or normally acquired frailty and shortcomings both physical and psychological."

14. All figures given here are rough estimates. Reputable scholarly sources differ widely with respect to all aspects of postwar Jewish population movements.

15. Leo W. Schwarz, "The Survivors and Israel," *Jewish Frontier* 33 (October 1966): 11.

16. Ibid., 8.

17. Samuel Lubell, "The Second Exodus of the Jews," *Saturday Evening Post* 219 (5 October 1946): 16–17, 86.

18. Ralph Segalman, "The Psychology of Jewish Displaced Persons," *Jewish Social Service Quarterly* 23 (September 1947): 362.

19. Morris Waldman to John Slawson, undated, but received 26 August 1946, AJCommittee Papers, FAD-1, Box 80, Israel/Palestine Partition, AJC, 1937–48.

20. Moshe Tabenkin, quoted in Yoav Gelber, "Zionist Policy and the Fate of European Jewry, 1943–1944," *Studies in Zionism* 7 (Spring 1983): 141.

21. Quoted in Zahava Solomon, "From Denial to Recognition: Attitudes Toward Holocaust Survivors from World War II to the Present," *Journal of Traumatic Stress* 8 (1995): 218.

22. Quoted in Tom Segev, *1949: The First Israelis* (New York, 1986), 138.

23. Reproduced in Henry Friedlander and Sybil Milton, eds., *Archives of the Holocaust: Central Zionist Archives, Jerusalem* (New York, 1990), 380–86.

24. Letter to Meyer Weisgal, quoted in Aaron Berman, *Nazism, the Jews and American Zionism, 1933–1948* (Detroit, 1990), 107–8.

25. Shabtai Teveth, *Ben-Gurion: The Burning Ground, 1886–1948* (Boston, 1987), 854, 860. Cf. Dina Porat, "Ben-Gurion and the Holocaust," in Ronald Zweig, ed., *David Ben-Gurion: Politics and Leadership in Israel* (London, 1991), 161.

26. Evyatar Friesel, "The Holocaust and the Birth of Israel," *Wiener Library Bulletin* 32 (1979): 59.

27. Tad Szulc, *Then and Now: How the World Has Changed Since World War II* (New York, 1990), 63.

28. Eric Alterman, "West Bank Story," *Present Tense* 16 (March-April 1989): 19.

29. David Horowitz, *Holocaust and Rebirth: Lectures Delivered at a Symposium Sponsored by Yad Vashem — April 1973* (Jerusalem, 1974), 157.

30. Dan Raviv and Yossi Melman, *Friends in Deed: Inside the U.S.-Israel Alliance* (New York, 1994), 22. For other examples of this ubiquitous assertion, see Jack Zipes, "The Paradox of New Anti-Semitism in Emancipated Europe," *Hungry Mind Review*, Summer 1991, 16; Rabbi Seymour Siegel in American Histadrut Cultural Exchange Institute, *The Impact of Israel on American Jewry: 20 Years Later* (New York, 1969), 23; Abraham R. Besdin, "Reflections on the Agony and the Ecstasy," *Tradition* 11 (Spring 1971): 66.

31. Friesel, "Holocaust and Birth of Israel," 55, 58. Friesel's arguments about the disjunction between the Holocaust and the birth of Israel appear to be gaining support among Israeli historians. See Dan Michman, "She'erit Hapletah, 1944–1948: Rehabilitation and Political Struggle," *Holocaust and Genocide Studies* 7 (Spring 1993). David Vital, one of the leading historians of Zionism, denounces as "absurd" the notion that "modern Israel resulted from, was, so to speak, born of, the Holocaust — perhaps as a bone thrown to the unfortunates by belatedly and guiltily benevolent powers as compensation for miseries suffered. Nothing could be further from the truth, as even a superficial examination of British and American policy in the immediate postwar period will show." ("After the Catastrophe: Aspects of Contemporary Jewry," in Peter Hayes, ed., *Lessons and Legacies: The Meaning of the Holocaust in a Changing World* [Evanston, Ill., 1991], 348 n1.) Some rejections of a link between the Holocaust and the birth of Israel have an ideological dimension. Thus Shmuel Katz, an Irgun veteran and adviser to Prime Minister Menachem Begin, found linking the two a "travesty," devaluing "fifty years of political history, and the rivers of sweat and blood and sacrifice which nourished [Israel's] roots." Moreover, the linkage "harmonizes with one of the persistent themes of Arab propaganda, that Israel "was inflicted on the Arabs by the Western powers as an act of compensation for the crime of the European Holocaust; that the Arabs are thus being made to pay for the 'imperialists' ' crimes against the Jews." ("The Holocaust and Israel," *Jerusalem Post*, 16 March 1979.) Cf. Benjamin Netanyahu, *A Place among the Nations: Israel and the World* (New York, 1993), 29–30.

32. Federal Council of Churches statement, March 1946, quoted in Lawrence S. Wittner, *Rebels Against War: The American Peace Movement, 1933–1983* (Philadelphia, 1984), 126–27. See also Paul Boyer, *By the Bomb's Early Light: American Thought and Culture at the Dawn of the Atomic Age* (New York, 1985).

33. See Hertzel Fishman, *American Protestantism and a Jewish State* (Detroit, 1973).

34. See Esther Yolles Feldbam, *The American Catholic Press and the Jewish State, 1917–1959* (New York, 197), 55.
35. Stephen Wise frequently sounded this note. See his "United Nations vs. Mass Murder," *Opinion* 13 (January 1943): 5; New Year's Message, in Business and Professional Associates of the American Jewish Congress *Newsletter*, 29 September 1944; speech to the Consultative Conference of the World Jewish Congress, *Opinion* 15 (September 1945) 74; statement to the Anglo-American Committee of Inquiry, *Congress Weekly* 1 (25 January 1946): 11–12; "Our People's Future," *Opinion* 18 (August 1948). Cf. Israel Goldstein, "A Time for Penitence," in Stephen S. Wise, ed., *Never Again! Ten Years of Hitler* (New York, 1943), 81. One partial and somewhat ambiguous exception to the generalization that no agitational use was made of American "complicity" was a minor initiative by some Jewish newspapers following *Collier's* publication in October 1947 of an excerpt from Henry Morgenthau's diaries that noted State Department obstruction of rescue efforts. (See Bruce J. Evensen, *Truman, Palestine, and the Press: Shaping Conventional Wisdom at the Beginning of the Cold War* [New York, 1992], 113.) But there is no evidence in Morgenthau's article that he intended this use to be made of it, and in any case, nothing came of it.
36. Dorothy Thompson, "Why the Zionists Are Right," *Palestine* 2 (February 1945), as cited in Louis L. Gerson, *The Hyphenate in Recent American Politics and Diplomacy* (Lawrence, Kans., 1964), 154; Peter Kurth, *American Cassandra: The Life of Dorothy Thompson* (Boston, 1990), 382–84, 422–29.
37. In this respect, the response paralleled that of European socialist and trade-union leaders lobbied by their Jewish comrades abroad. Emanuel Muravchik of the Jewish Labor Committee said they "got the impression that they said, 'O.K., why not? We have nothing against it, so we'll vote for it [at the UN],' without . . . having deep feelings about the issue." Quoted in Menahem Kaufman, *An Ambiguous Partnership: Non-Zionists and Zionists in America, 1939–1945* (Jerusalem, 1991), 271.
38. House, remarks of Rep. Matthew M. Neely of West Virginia, 79th Cong., 1st sess., *Cong. Rec.* (10 December 1945) 91, pt. 9:11743–46.
39. House, Rep. Melvin Price of Illinois speaking on "Hebrews in Germany," 79th Cong., 1st sess., *Cong. Rec. Appendix* (18 September 1945) 91, pt. 12:A3924.
40. Dr. Henry A. Atkinson, quoted in House, Rep. Helen Gahagan Douglas of California speaking on "Palestine," 79th Cong., 1st Sess., *Cong. Rec. Appendix* (4 October 1945) 91, pt. 12:A418.
41. Senate, Sen. Brian McMahon of Connecticut speaking on "The Jewish-Palestinian Issue," 79th Cong., 1st sess., *Cong. Rec.* (28 September 1945) 91, pt. 7:9244–45.
42. Frank Buxton, a member of the Anglo-American Committee of Inquiry, quoted in Leonard Dinnerstein, *America and the Survivors of the Holocaust* (New York, 1982), 96.
43. See Ilan Pappé, *The Making of the Arab-Israeli Conflict: 1947–1951* (London, 1994), 28.
44. Yehuda Bauer, *The Jewish Emergence from Powerlessness* (Toronto, 1979), 68.
45. Writing in 1991, Clark Clifford described a key meeting at the White House where he argued for prompt american recognition of Israel on the grounds, among others, that we should "atone" for the crimes of the Holocaust. ("Serving the President: The Truman Years–1," *New Yorker* 67 [25 March 1991]: 63.) But the contemporary record, including Clifford's own carefully prepared notes of his pre-

sentation, includes no mention at all of the Holocaust, let alone "atonement." (*Foreign Relations of the United States, 1945* [Washington, D.C., 1967], V:972–78.)

46. See Truman's letter to Sen. Walter George, quoted in Robert J. Donovan, *Conflict and Crisis* (New York, 1977), 321–22.

47. A few days after drafting this paragraph, I received a membership solicitation letter from the American Israel Public Affairs Committee (AIPAC). "For Americans of conscience, Israel is a solemn pledge to six million Jews who perished in the Holocaust. It is why America was the first country to recognize Israel in 1948 . . . and why we have been her strongest ally ever since. *Defending Israel is a matter of honor and responsibility.*" (Italics in original.)

48. Edward Shapiro, *A Time for Healing* (Baltimore, 1992), 62.

49. Kaufman, *Ambiguous Partnership*, 208.

50. "This Is Our Home: America and Israel — Public Opinion Studies," 16 May 1951, AJCommittee Papers, Box 252, Political Philosophy, 1949–58, This Is Our Home.

51. Remarks of Isidore Sobeloff, executive director, Detroit Welfare Federation, in Martin M. Cohen, ed., "Notes on Fund Raising," *Jewish Social Service Quarterly* 22 (December 1945): 177.

52. Arthur Hertzberg, "Speaking the Reader's Language: How a Yiddish Magazine Has Stayed Alive," *New York Times Book Review*, 20 December 1992, 14–15.

53. Kaufman, *Ambiguous Partnership*, 243, 252–53.

54. Menachem Friedman, "The State of Israel as a Theological Dilemma," in Baruch Kimmerling, ed., *The Israeli State and Society: Boundaries and Frontiers* (Albany, 1989), 184.

55. Milton Himmelfarb to members of Staff Committee on Palestine and AJC Programs, "AJC Position on the Jewish State," 31 December 1947, AJCommittee Papers, FAD-1, Box 78, Staff Meetings, 1947–48.

56. Shabtai Teveth, *Ben-Gurion: The Burning Ground, 1886–1948* (Boston, 1987), 850.

57. Ibid., 853.

58. Aaron Berman, "Rescue in the Opening Rounds of the American Jewish Conference," *Holocaust Studies Annual* 1 (1983): 138.

59. Yehiam Weitz, "The Positions of David Ben-Gurion and Yitzhak Tabenkin vis-à-vis the Holocaust of European Jewry," *Holocaust and Genocide Studies* 5 (1990): 1995. In 1944 a Mossad agent in Constantinople warned that it was an illusion to count on survivor support after the war unless rescue efforts were stepped up. Otherwise, "their accusation will rankle so poisonously that the Yishuv will never be able to free itself of it." (Quoted in Dalia Ofer, *Escaping the Holocaust: Illegal Immigration to the Land of Israel, 1939–1945* [New York, 1990], 205.)

60. Quoted in Leo W. Schwarz, *The Redeemers: A Saga of the Years 1945–1952* (New York, 1953), 51.

61. Anita Shapira, "The Holocaust and World War II as Elements of the Yishuv Psyche until 1958," in Alvin H. Rosenfeld, ed., *Thinking about the Holocaust* (Bloomington, Ind., 1997), 76.

62. Michael J. Cohen, *Palestine and the Great Powers: 1945–1948* (Princeton, 1982), 254.

63. Ibid., 101–2; Lubell, "Second Exodus," 86.

64. A number of the DP leaders who proclaimed that it was "Palestine or nothing" themselves chose the United States. (See Abraham S. Hyman, *The Undefeated* [Jerusalem, 1993], 378.)

65. Pappé, *Arab-Israeli Conflict*, 27; Zeev Tzahor, "Holocaust Survivors as a Political Factor," *Middle Eastern Studies* 24 (1988): 442.

66. Letter to the editor, *Commentary* 34 (August 1962): 168.

67. The director of the Joint Distribution Committee in Bavaria is reported to have

spoken of "terrorism," to have said, presumably hyperbolically, that it was worth a Jewish DP's life to say he didn't want to go to Palestine. (Pierce Williams to Harold Glasser, 27 July 1948, AJCommittee Papers, GS 10, Box 133, Immigration, 1948–49, DPs, Screening. Williams was reporting a conversation with Samuel Haber.) William Haber, official Jewish adviser to the American Military Government, reported to Jewish organizations at home that when an American general had protested heavy-handed recruitment methods, he assured him that the reports were "probably exaggerated." He went on to say, "Fortunately, General Harrold was not aware of all the methods being employed." ("Summary of Conversations with . . . General Harrold on April 13 and 20 [1948]," in Haber Papers, Box 51, Reports of Adviser.) In another report, Haber said that at least initially, the pressure was "crude, often reflecting techniques which the people had learned from their own oppressors." (Report of 10 June 1948, AJCommittee Papers, FAD-1, Box 33, Germany, West, 1949, Haber Reports.) American Displaced Persons Commissioner Ugo Carusi complained that "the Zionists had sent in scandalous, untrue stories about men of military age who sought to go to the United States rather than Palestine because it was hoped that rejection by the United States would result in their going to Palestine instead." ("Notes on Telephone Conversation with Ugo Carusi — September 21, 1948," attached to Max Isenbergh to Joel D. Wolfsohn, 21 September 1948, AJCommittee Papers, GS 10, Box 124, Immigration, September 1948.)

68. Yehuda Bauer, "Jewish Survivors in DP Camps and *She'erith Hapletah*," in *The Nazi Concentration Camps: Proceedings of the Fourth Yad Vashem International Historical Conference* (Jerusalem, 1980), 503. Cf. Bauer, *Jewish Emergence*, 66–67.

69. Summary of report by Abraham Klausner, 2 May 1948, AJCommittee Papers, GS 10, Box 125, 1948, May-June.

70. "Meeting of the Jewish Co-operating Organizations on Rabbi Abraham Klausner's Suggestions Respecting the DP Situation (May 4, 1948)," ibid. Stephen Wise dissociated himself from Goldmann's recommendation, particularly that DPs enter the German economy.

71. Letter to Meir Grossman of American Jewish Conference, 10 June 1948, in Abraham J. Peck, ed., *The Papers of the World Jewish Congress, 1945–1950* (vol. 9 of *Archives of the Holocaust*, New York, 1990), 326.

72. "Statement of the Jewish DP Problem in Europe and an Outline of Its Liquidation," undated, but from internal evidence shortly after state established, in Haber Papers, Box 54, Germany, Reports of Advisers to Gen. Clay.

73. Notably in Leonard Dinnerstein, *America and the Survivors of the Holocaust* (New York, 1982). Unless otherwise noted, information in this section comes from Dinnerstein's exhaustive work.

74. See, e.g., Theodore N. Lewis, "Men and Events," *Opinion* 16 (February 1946): 14.

75. Selma Hirsh to Louis Neikrug, 26 April 1946, AJCommittee Papers, GS 10, Box 148, Refugees, 1945–50.

76. Leo J. Margolin to George Hexter, 16 April 1947, AJCommittee Papers, GS 12, Box 29. The picture in question appeared in the *New York Daily News* of 2 April 1947.

77. Sen. Alexander Wiley, quoted in Dinnerstein, *Survivors*, 147.

78. Israel Gutman, "Remarks on the Literature of the Holocaust," *In the Dispersion* 5/6 (Spring 1966): 127.

79. Quoted in William B. Helmreich, *Against All Odds: Holocaust Survivors and the Successful Lives They Made in America* (New York, 1992), 38.

80. Ibid., 49.

81. Adolph Held, "Community Relations Aspects of the DP Problem," address to

March 1947 plenary session of National Community Relations Advisory Council, NCRAC Papers, Box 2, Plenary Sessions, 1947.

5. "That Is Past, and We Must Deal With the Facts Today"

1. Quoted in Robert H. Abzug, *Inside the Vicious Heart: Americans and the Liberation of Nazi Concentration Camps* (New York, 1985), 30.
2. For a full and semi-official statement of the theory, see Carl Friedrich and Zbigniew Brzezinski, *Totalitarian Dictatorship and Autocracy* (Cambridge, Mass., 1956). The best history of the doctrine is Abbott Gleason, *Totalitarianism: The Inner History of the Cold War* (New York, 1995). See also Herbert J. Spiro and Benjamin R. Barber, "Counter-Ideological Uses of 'Totalitarianism,' " *Politics and Society* 1 (November 1970), and Les K. Adler and Thomas G. Patterson, "Red Fascism: The Merger of Nazi Germany and Soviet Russia in the American Image of Totalitarianism, 1930s–1950s," *American Historical Review* 75 (April 1970). In the academic world, the explanatory power of the theory came to be increasingly discounted after the mid-1950s. Revolutionary upsurges in the Eastern European satellites and limited but nonetheless real scaling back of terror in the Soviet Union (both quite impossible in terms of the theory) produced among scholars increased skepticism about totalitarianism as an analytic category. In the years that followed, historians of the Third Reich more and more came to question whether Nazi Germany had been as tightly organized from the top down as the theory had asserted. By the 1980s and 1990s the theory, and the Nazi-Soviet equation that went along with it, was at a discount in the university.
3. "The End of Belsen?" *Time* 46 (11 June 1945): 36.
4. "Speech of the Honorable A. A. Berle, Jr., Assistant Secretary of State, at a Mass Meeting to Protest Against the Inhuman Treatment of Civilians by the Germans in the German-Occupied Europe, Particularly of the Jews, Held in the Boston Garden, Sunday, May 2, 1943, 3 P.M. (Delivered by Mr. Robert G. Hooker, Jr., Executive Assistant to Mr. Berle, on Behalf of Mr. Berle, Whose Illness Prevented Him from Attending.)" Carbon-copy typescript in Boston Jewish Community Relations Council Papers, Box 207, World War II — Miscellany.
5. Friedrich and Brzezinski, quoted in Spiro and Barber, "Uses of 'Totalitarianism,' " 132, 137.
6. The understanding attitude that the theory of totalitarianism suggested toward active or passive participants in Nazi criminality contributed to the theory's great popularity in postwar Germany. The theory, and the cold war mobilization it sustained, had the added benefit of giving a measure of retroactive legitimacy to Nazi Germany's war on the eastern front. Not, perhaps, a struggle conducted under the best auspices, but one whose target was now acknowledged to have been the right one. Small wonder that the theory of totalitarianism became, as one German historian wrote in the 1970s, "the quasi official ideology of the West German state." (Wolfgang Wipperman, quoted in Gleason, *Totalitarianism*, 157.) See also the remarks of Eberhard Jäckel in Gina Thomas, ed., *The Unresolved Past: A Debate in German History* (New York, 1990), 84–85.
7. See editorial, *Christian Century* 64 (23 April 1947): 515; Haim Genizi, *America's Fair Share: The Admission and Resettlement of Displaced Persons, 1945–1952* (Detroit, 1993), 74, 76, 77–78.
8. George Hexter to John Slawson, 2 October 1946, AJCommittee Papers, GS 10, Box 126A, Immigration, September-October 1946.

9. Unnamed IRO official quoted in David W. Nussbaum, "Pro-Nazis Entering US Under DP Law That Keeps Out Jews," *New York Post*, 19 November 1948, 2.
10. There were calls in the Jewish press for tougher screening of DPs, but some Jewish leaders were ambivalent about this. They pointed out that the screening was likely to be carried out by unsympathetic army personnel, and that in any case, "the Jewish DPs are in as vulnerable a position . . . as the non-Jews, since they either have no documents at all or fraudulent documents." In addition, they feared the impression that "the Jews are concerned only about their own unfortunate brethren, and want to keep out all non-Jewish DPs, to a point of seeking permission to set up a Jewish Gestapo." (Sidney Lisofsky to John Slawson, 6 January 1949, in AJCommittee Papers, GS 10, Box 124, Immigration, January-February 1949.)
11. David Martin, "Jews, Christians — and 'Collaborators,'" *America* 80 (1 January 1949): 344–45.
12. Genizi, *America's Fair Share*, 93–94.
13. NCRAC Committee on Immigration, 19 June 1950, AJCommittee Papers, GS 10, Box 121, Immigration, June-December 1950.
14. Lisofsky to Slawson, 6 January 1949.
15. Eugene Hevesi, "Political Considerations Involved in the Problem of Admission of German Expellees to the United States," memorandum, 23 February 1950, AJCommittee Papers, GS 10, Box 134, German Expellees, 1950, sec. 12.
16. For a discussion of this case, see "Summary of Discussions at Luncheon Meeting Re: Amnesty of Nazi War Criminals," 13 March 1951, NCRAC Papers, Box 68.
17. David Bernstein to John Slawson, 11 December 1947, AJCommittee Papers, FAD-1, Box 23A, Germany, May-December 1947.
18. Memorandum, Eugene Hevesi to John Slawson, 16 November 1949, AJCommittee Papers, FAD-1, Box 25, Germany, West, 1949–51.
19. Henry Morgenthau III, *Mostly Morgenthaus: A Family History* (New York, 1991), 363, 372, 388–90.
20. William Henry Chamberlin, "Vengeance Not Justice," *Human Events* 6 (18 May 1949); reprinted in *Cong. Rec. Appendix*, 1949, A3434–35.
21. Jay Mathews, "'48 Nazi Hunt Barred Jews," *Washington Post*, 21 July 1985, A6. The directive, quoted in this article, excluded those with less than ten years of U.S. citizenship, but in practice this meant, in almost every case, Jewish refugees.
22. Editorial in issue of 25 November 1950, reprinted in *Cong. Rec.*, Senate, 1950, 15777. The editorial went on to say that calling for halting the trials "does not imply any revision of our attitude toward nazism . . . but rather a better understanding of the facts of international life."
23. Minutes of NCRAC Committee on Overt Anti-Semitism, 24 June 1949 (AJCommittee Papers, GS 10, Box 8, Anti-Semitism, 1946–50, NCRAC Committee on Overt Anti-Semitism, Minutes); Minutes of Executive Committee of NCRAC, 29 June 1950 (NCRAC Papers, Box 32); Minutes of NCRAC Committee on Germany, 16 March 1951 (NCRAC Papers, Box 68).
24. Jewish organizations were prominent in supporting special fund appeals to aid the Russians. Stephen Wise noted that in defending their homeland the Soviet armies also "defended millions of Jews against a ruthless enemy who has singled out the Jewish people for extermination. . . . As Americans, we owe a great debt to the Soviet Army and peoples. As Jews we are under special obligation to them and it should be a special privilege for us to repay it even in part." (Press release of the United Jewish War Effort, 28 September 1942, AJCongress Papers, Box 67, United

Jewish War Effort/AJC.) One local Jewish leader observed that while special Jewish efforts of this kind were worthwhile, they "may embarrass us sometime in the future." (Henry W. Levy to Louis E. Kirstein et al., 9 May 1942, Boston Jewish Community Relations Council Papers, Box 26, AJC, 1939–42.)

25. Lucy Dawidowicz to John Slawson, 1 May 1953, AJCommittee Papers, GS 12, Box 173, HUAC, 1953–60; Dawidowicz, "Report on Jews and Non-Jews in the Press Re Communism," 12 June 1953, AJCommittee Papers, GS 10, Box 246, Communism, 1951–53; Dawidowicz to Slawson, 15 June 1954, AJCommittee Papers, GS 10, Box 249, Jews–Communism, 1950–59.

26. "Jewish Involvement in CP-Controlled Groups," p. 4, AJCommittee Papers, GS 10, Box 249, Jews–Communism, 1948–49; S. Andhil Fineberg to members of Committee on Communism, 21 November 1952, AJCommittee Papers, Box 246, Communism, 1941–53. A bit later, another member of the Committee staff estimated that two-thirds of party members were Jews. (Joseph Gordon to Morris Fine, 25 January 1954, AJCommittee Papers, GS 10, Box 253, Political Philosophy, 1947–61, Totalitarianism.) The best scholarly treatment of Jews in the Communist Party of which I am aware is Nathan Glazer, *The Social Basis of American Communism* (New York, 1961). Jews were often even more overrepresented in highly visible roles in the Communist Party, and among those charged with being Communists. (Gentile members of the party were more likely to be rank-and-file trade unionists.) The memorandum on "Jewish Involvement," just cited, noted that the editor and three of the four other members of the editorial board of the Communist magazine *Political Affairs* were Jewish, as were four of the five Americans who wrote for the current issue. The memo also noted that of eight names on the letterhead of the party's youth affiliate, American Youth for Democracy, "four are almost certainly Jewish and three seem likely to be" (pp. 10, 5). In New York, all eight of the schoolteachers fired for refusing to say whether they were Communists were Jewish. (S. Andhil Fineberg to Charles Y. Lazarus, 4 April 1952, AJCommittee Papers, GS 10, Box 249, Jews–Communism, 1950–59.) In an investigation by the House Un-American Activities Committee of Communists in the Philadelphia school system, "nearly 100%" of those called had "Jewish-sounding names." (Edwin J. Lukas to Ben Herzberg, 7 May 1954, AJCommittee Papers, GS 112, Box 180, US Govt Loyalty & Security, 1954.) In a Miami investigation, 135 of 138 people named as Communists "had Jewish names." (Manheim S. Shapiro to A. Harold Murray, 8 November 1954, AJCommittee Papers, GS 10, Box 246, Communism, 1954–57.)

27. Quoted in Arthur Liebman, "The Ties That Bind: Jewish Support for the Left in the United States," in Ezra Mendelsohn, ed., *Essential Papers on Jews and the Left* (New York, 1997), 341.

28. Copy of leaflet in possession of the author.

29. Morris U. Schappes, "Resistance Is the Lesson," *Jewish Life* 15 (April 1948): 14.

30. House of Representatives, *Communist Methods of Infiltration* (Education, Part 6): *Hearings before the Committee on Un-American Activities* (29 June 1953), 83rd Cong., 1st sess. (Washington, D.C., 1953), 1900.

31. Arthur D. Kahn, "Letter to Roy M. Cohn," *Jewish Life* 19 (July 1952): 8.

32. *Party Voice* (bulletin of the New York Communist Party), January 1955, quoted in "Memorandum on Communist Propaganda Plans to Exploit the Issue of Rearming West Germany," 28 February 1955, AJCommittee Papers, FAD-1, Box 39, West Germany Rearmament, 1950–60.

33. Quoted by Julius Rosenberg in his 28 November 1952 letter to Emmanuel Bloch, in Robert and Michael Meeropol, *We Are Your Sons: The Legacy of Ethel and Julius*

Rosenberg (Boston, 1975), 159. The Rosenbergs' letters appear to have been written with an eye to publication; in any case, they were published. But in this respect at least there is no reason to doubt Julius's sincerity. His wartime Soviet handler reported years later that he frequently discussed Hitler's persecution of Jews and "wanted to do everything he could to fight against Fascism." (Michael Dobbs, "Julius Rosenberg Spied, Russian Says," *Washington Post*, 16 March 1997, A01.)

34. Letter of 12 February 1953 in *Death House Letters of Ethel and Julius Rosenberg* (New York, 1953), 134.

35. Quoted in "The Defense of Ethel and Julius Rosenberg: A Communist Attempt to Inject the Jewish Issue," March 1952, AJCommittee Papers, GS 12, Box 139.

36. Letter of 16 June 1953, in Meeropol, *We Are Your Sons*, 225.

37. Report No. 2 from Hollywood representative, 15 October 1948, NCRAC Papers, Box 51.

38. Report No. 8, 4 March 1949, NCRAC Papers, Box 51.

39. Report No. 10, 23 May 1949, NCRAC Papers, Box 51.

40. Report No. 41, 25 February 1952, NCRAC Papers, Box 51.

41. Report No. 31, 11 June 1951, NCRAC Papers, Box 51. NCRAC also kept track of foreign films. Reporting to member agencies on the Polish film *The Last Stop*, which dealt with Auschwitz, Jules Cohen, national coordinator of NCRAC, was enthusiastic. "We believe that if this picture could be seen periodically, it might serve to arouse the conscience of mankind so that such atrocities might never again be permitted to be visited upon civilization." But he added a word of caution: while the film's representation of the camp's having been liberated by the Red Army was, he conceded, historically accurate, "these scenes could be interpreted as pro-Russian propaganda. In view of present East-West relationships, it is suggested that consideration be given locally to the implications of any action by the Jewish community relations agency designed to stimulate attendance at local showings of this film." (Jules Cohen to NCRAC Member Agencies, 22 March 1949, AJCommittee Papers, GS 10, Box 228, Films-Movies [L–O].)

42. Minutes of the NCRAC Executive Committee, 10 October 1950, p. 11, NCRAC Papers, Box 32; Isaac Toubin to Officers of Congress, 19 July 1950, AJCongress Papers, Box 3.

43. Marcus Cohen to John Slawson, undated memorandum reporting on a meeting of representatives of the Committee, the ADL, and the Jewish War Veterans with representatives of HUAC, 2 July 1953, AJCommittee Papers, GS 12, Box 173, HUAC, 1946–55.

44. Norman Podhoretz, *Making It* (New York, 1967), 101.

45. Solomon Andhil Fineberg Papers, 1/1 (Files on Communism); Fineberg Papers, 1/7 (American Jewish Committee [Committee on Communism], 1947–64); Fineberg to John Slawson, 6 October 1950, AJCommittee Papers, GS 10, Box 248, Communism/Program Activities, 50–55.

46. Edwin J. Lukas to John Slawson, 2 May 1950, AJCommittee Papers, GS 12, Box 4, All-American Conference to Combat Communism; John Slawson to Nathan E. Cohen, 10 May 1951, GS 12, Box 4. The conference's national director, Robert W. Hansen, virtually extorted money from the American Jewish Committee, noting that without the Committee's participation and contributions the All-American Conference "might easily have become a very fascist slanted and dangerous group." (Hansen to "Dear Joe" [probably Joseph J. Woolfson], 26 June 1951, AJCommittee Papers, GS 12, Box 3, All-American Conference to Combat Communism. Cf. Edwin J. Lukas to Walter Mendelsohn, 28 June 1955, AJCommittee Papers, GS 12, Box 3, All-American Conference to Combat Communism.

47. Lukas to John Slawson, 24 April 1951, AJCommittee Papers, GS 12, Box 182, US Govt, Loyalty Security, 1944–54.
48. "The Rosenberg Case: 'Hate-America' Weapon," *New Leader* 35 (22 December 1952): 13.
49. Minutes of the NCRAC Committee on Overt Anti-Semitism, 18 March 1949, AJCommittee Papers, FAD-1, Box 23A, Germany, January-April 1949; Mordecai Kosover to Simon Segal, 24 February 1949, AJCommittee Papers, FAD-1, Box 35, Germany/West, Industrial Exhibition, 1949–51. It required a special plea from former New York governor Herbert Lehman to get the Jewish War Veterans — something of a loose cannon among national Jewish organizations — to abandon the idea of picketing. An American Jewish Committee staffer noted that the fair was scheduled for the same time as the anniversary of the Warsaw Ghetto Uprising, and this "undoubtedly will be used as a slogan for public demonstrations by various Jewish organizations in New York." (Kosover to Segal, 7 March 1949, FAD-1, Box 35.
50. Minutes of the NCRAC Committee on Overt Anti-Semitism, 18 March 1949, AJCommittee Papers, GS 10, Box 6, Anti-Semitism, 1946–50.
51. Ibid., 6 April 1949.
52. Ibid.
53. Minutes of the NCRAC Executive Committee, 21 March 1949, NCRAC Papers, Box 32.
54. NCRAC press release, 7 April 1949, AJCommittee Papers, FAD-1, Box 35, West Germany, Industrial Exhib., Organizations, 1949. As Jewish organizations debated what course to follow, they learned what the public relations firm hired by the fair intended to do if there was non-Communist picketing. They planned to contact young Communists on the campuses of NYU, CCNY, and Columbia who would be "needled into picketing," carrying signs that the firm would provide. The signs would depict "fat German capitalists with swastikas linking hands with fat American capitalists to build up new war industries for war profits at the expense of the people." At the same time, a newspaper reporter would maneuver one of the defendants in the ongoing trial of Communist Party leaders into attacking the German fair. The firm's overall strategy was "playing up Communist opposition to the Exhibition . . . newspapers would pick the Communist opposition angle, and . . . opposition by non-Communist groups, especially Jews, because of their fear of being identified with Communists would probably be killed off." (Selma Hirsh to Murray Gurfein, 1 April 1949, AJCommittee Papers, FAD-1, Box 35, Germany/West, Industrial Exhibition, 1949–51.) In a letter to John Slawson, on 21 April 1949, Hirsh wrote: "At one time we had considered the possibility of an exposé of this, but as events have developed there would seem little to be gained by such publicity at this moment. . . . Actually there has been no violence at the Exhibit and negligible picketing, most of it identifiable as Communists (much to the satisfaction of the Fair administrators)." (AJCommittee Papers, FAD-1, Box 35, Germany/West, Industrial Exhibition, 1949–51.)
55. Minutes of NCRAC Committee on Germany, 16 March 1951, AJCommittee Papers, FAD-1, Box 42, West Germany, Re-Education, NCRAC, 1949–51.
56. Ibid.
57. "The German Problem: Background Memorandum for the Executive Committee Meeting: 6 May 1951," AJCommittee Papers, FAD-1, Box 26, Germany, Lay Committee, 1949–52.
58. Minutes of NCRAC Committee on Germany, 16 March 1951.

59. Minutes of Staff Policy Committee, 21 March 1951, AJCommittee Files. There were differences in style. The American Jewish Committee, with a more established constituency and a tradition of quiet diplomacy with government officials, was the most concerned with "controlling emotionalism." The American Jewish Congress, whose rank and file were more often of recent immigrant background, and which was usually more confrontational, was in theory less concerned, but in practice not that different. The Anti-Defamation League of B'nai B'rith was somewhere between the two. The strongly anti-Communist Jewish Labor Committee was aligned with the American Jewish Committee on the issue.

60. G. George Freedman to S. Andhil Fineberg, 16 February 1950, AJCommittee Papers, GS 12, Box 3, All-American Conference to Combat Communism. Freedman was an official of the Jewish War Veterans and a veterans' affairs consultant to the American Jewish Committee.

61. "AJC Program to Combat Soviet Anti-Semitism: Objectives and Themes," 29 May 1952, Solomon Andhil Fineberg Papers, 1/7, American Jewish Committee [Committee on Communism], 1947–64.

62. Joseph Gordon to Staff Committee on Communism, 24 November 1952, ibid.

63. Minutes of the Staff Committee on the Communist Problem, 25 November 1952, ibid.

64. Elliot Cohen to John Slawson, 12 December 1952, ibid. At the American Jewish Committee there was some hesitation before embarking on a campaign on the issue of Soviet-bloc anti-Semitism. Samuel H. Flowerman worried that "people might say that even in so terrible a place as Russia, Jews are not tolerated." (Flowerman to John Slawson, 31 July 1950, AJCommittee Papers, GS 12, Box 181, US Govt Loyalty & Security, 1950.) In the case of the Slansky trial, another staffer warned of the danger of "making it seem as if we are trying to defend Slansky as a good Communist." (Minutes of Staff Policy Committee, 4 December 1952, AJCommittee Files.) Another staffer questioned a Committee pamphlet that spoke of "eleven Jews killed" in Czechoslovakia. "Perhaps," he said, "it would be more advisable to describe them as Communists who were once Jews." (Philip Jacobson to Ethel Phillips, 26 March 1953, AJCommittee Papers, GS 10, Box 224, Book Reviews, 1951–61.) While in the early 1950s these reservations were overcome, they apparently grew in the late fifties the Committee, on these grounds, suspended publicity on Soviet-bloc anti-Semitism for three years. (Minutes of Special Projects Committee, 1 March 1962, AJCommittee Papers, GS 10, Box 248, Committee/Staff/Special Projects.)

65. Peter Meyer, "Stalin Plans Genocide," *New Leader* 35 (15 December 1952): 5.

66. "A Time for Protest," *New Leader* 35 (22 December 1952): 31.

67. Bela Fabian, "Hungary's Jewry Faces Liquidation," *Commentary* 12 (October 1951): 330, 334.

68. Press release, 27 January 1953, AJCommittee Papers, FAD-1, Box 25, Germany, East, 1951–53.

69. Joseph Roos to Jules Cohen, 9 July 1951, NCRAC Papers, Box 21 (press release attached).

70. Irving M. Engel, 21 March 1956, accompanying Léon Poliakov and Josef Wulf, eds., *Das Dritte Reich und die Juden*, AJCommittee Papers, FAD-1, Box 24, Nazism–Germany, 1954–56.

71. Stan Wexler to CRCs, 20 July 1961, AJCommittee Papers, GS 10, Box 252, Political Philosophy, Nazism, 1945–50–61.

72. For reasons that need not concern us here — principally, intransigent opposition

by conservative senators — the United States did not ratify the Genocide Convention until 1986. For an overview of the whole subject, see Lawrence J. LeBlanc, *The United States and the Genocide Convention* (Durham, N.C., 1991).

73. See "Genocide (The Newest Soviet Crime) as Discussed by Professor Raphael Lemkin, Author of the Genocide Pact, and Mr. Joseph P. Burns, Moderator, 'WNHC-TV College Roundtable,' 30 January 1953," copy in Cincinnati Jewish Community Relations Council Papers, 67/7.

74. Raphael Lemkin, "Genocide," *American Scholar* 15 (March 1946): 227.

75. For financial relations between these groups and Lemkin, see Lev E. Dobriansky (Ukrainian Congress Committee of America) to Lemkin, 23 June 1954, Lemkin Papers, American Jewish Archives, 1/4; Pius Grigaitis (Lithuanian American Council) to Lemkin, 16 May 1952, 10 November 1953, 22 September 1954, Lemkin Papers, 1/7.

76. Lemkin to George Eberle, 8 November 1951, Lemkin Papers, 2/1; Lemkin to Hans Steinitz, 18 April 1957, Lemkin Papers, 2/5.

77. When American Jewish groups participated in the campaign for ratification of the Genocide Convention, they were careful to point out that this was in no sense a parochial Jewish issue: the Nazi slaughter of "almost nine million civilians" [*sic*] was, they said, unique only in its magnitude. (NCRAC Legislative Information Memorandum, 3 February 1950, copy in Cincinnati Jewish Community Relations Council Papers, 67/6. Cf. Herman L. Weisman, memorandum to NCRAC Membership, 30 March 1953, Cincinnati JCRC Papers, 67/6.) Contemporary examples of the phenomenon were "Greek Reds kidnap[ping] 28,000 Greek children and . . . tak[ing] them behind the Iron Curtain solely because of their nationality"; "Chinese Reds and North Koreans . . . slaughter[ing] whole groups of clergymen and children because of their religion." (Draft text of American Jewish Committee genocide pamphlet attached to 27 December 1951 memorandum from Ralph Bass to Edwin Lukas, AJCommittee Papers, GS 10, Box 93, Genocide Convention, AJC Membership Education, 1947–61.) Failure to ratify the Genocide Convention, said the Jewish agencies, deprived the United States of "a potentially effective instrumentality for formally branding Communist persecution of minorities before the bar of world opinion." (Herman L. Weisman, memorandum to NCRAC Membership, 30 March 1953, Cincinnati JCRC Papers, 67/6.)

78. Crister S. and Stephen A. Garrett, "Death and Politics: The Katyn Forest Massacre and American Foreign Policy," *East European Quarterly* 20 (January 1987): 437–41.

79. *New York Times*, 2 May 1943, and *New York Herald Tribune*, 27 April 1943, respectively, as cited in David G. Januszewski, "The Case for the Polish Exile Government in the American Press, 1939–1945," *Polish-American Studies* 43 (1986): 62.

80. "Good for Goebbels," *Time* 41 (26 April 1943): 32.

81. Robert Szymczak, "A Matter of Honor: Polonia and the Congressional Investigation of the Katyn Forest Massacre," *Polish-American Studies* 41 (1984): 33.

6. "Not in the Best Interests of Jewry"

1. Another exception was John Hersey's 1950 novel *The Wall*, a fictionalized version of Emmanuel Ringelblum's Warsaw diary, which sold well, perhaps in part due to the reputation of the author: a few years earlier, Hersey's *A Bell for Adano* had won the Pulitzer Prize, and his *Hiroshima* had been a major cultural event. The American Jewish Committee promoted *The Wall*, and sponsored a radio play based on it, which aired in 1950. A movie sale fell through. The Broadway version (dramatization by Millard Lampell) was to have closed after 119 performances but

got a temporary reprieve as a result of a fund-raising effort by the wife of the violinist Isaac Stern. Morton Wishengrad attributed the failure of the play to its being "silently boycotted by Jewish theater parties . . . instead they were patronizing *Irma La Douce* and *Under the Yum Yum Tree.*" (Letter to *Commentary* 31 [April 1961]: 364.) A similar explanation for the play's failure at the box office is offered by David Boroff ("The Living Arts," *American Judaism* 9 [Passover 1961]: 15; 9 [Purim 1961]: 13).

2. See Gerd Korman, "Silence in the American Textbooks," *Yad Vashem Studies* 8 (1970): 183–202.

3. See Charles K. Krantz, "Alain Resnais' *Nuit et Brouillard*: A Historical and Cultural Analysis," *Holocaust Studies Annual* 3 (1985): 107–20. In fact, the word "Jew" appeared once, in passing, in the French voice-over, but not in the English subtitles. The author of the script, Jean Cayrol, was a *résistant* who had been sent to Mauthausen.

4. Jewish Film Advisory Committee, October-November 1962 Report, NCRAC Papers, Box 51; Report 27, February 1969, NCRAC Papers, Box 52. For the sake of completeness, it should be noted that the Holocaust makes a brief appearance at the end of *The Young Lions* (1958) and is briefly talked about in *The Caine Mutiny* (1954) and *Exodus* (1960).

5. The pseudonymous Rufus Learsi (Israel spelled backward) led a campaign for including mention of the Holocaust in Passover observance in the home, which attracted a fair amount of support and also some critics. The papers of Learsi's Seder Ritual Committee are on deposit in the American Jewish Historical Society.

6. Note by Isaac Schwarzbart, 1 November 1952 (World Jewish Congress Papers, F20, Tenth Anniversary); Rabbi Aaron Gewirtz to Schwarzbart, 22 June 1956 (WJC Papers, F22, April 1956—USA); Schwarzbart memorandum "re Warsaw Ghetto Uprising Commemoration" (WJC Papers, F23, Fifteenth Anniversary); note by Schwarzbart on memorancum from Julius Schatz of AJCongress to Schwarzbart, 9 May 1952 (WJC Papers, F19). In 1951 Schwarzbart wrote to David Petegorsky of the AJCongress: "Needless to say . . . our affiliates will be somewhat astonished to hear that the largest Jewish community, with millions of Jews of European extraction, has forgotten the Warsaw Ghetto Uprising." (WJC Papers, F19, Eighth Anniversary.)

7. Nathan Glazer, *American Judaism* (Chicago, 1957), 114–15. This is also the conclusion of Lothar Kahn in his "Another Decade: The American Jew in the Sixties," *Judaism* 10 (Spring 1961).

8. Norman Podhoretz, "The Intellectual and Jewish Fate," *Midstream* 3 (Winter 1957).

9. Leo Bogart, "The Response of Jews in America to the European Catastrophe, 1941–45," University of Chicago master's thesis, 1948, 4.

10. Ibid., 216, 146. Though it is not, strictly speaking, a contemporary report, one might add sociologist Herbert Gans's recollection that when he studied the Jews of Park Forest in 1949–50, the Holocaust "was almost never mentioned, and its memory played no part whatsoever in the creation of a Jewish community there." (Gans, "Symbolic Ethnicity: The Future of Ethnic Groups and Cultures in America," in Gans et al., eds., *On the Making of Americans: Essays in Honor of David Riesman* [Philadelphia, 1979], 207.)

11. The series began in the issue of 11 March 1957 and concluded in the issue of 22 July 1957.

12. *Commentary* 31 (April 1961): 306–59. Two other contributors' remarks were ambiguous on this score.

13. *Judaism* 10 (Fall 1961): 291–352.

14. Alan Dershowitz, *The Best Defense* (New York, 1982), 10.

15. Daniel J. Elazar, "Detroit, the Early 1950s: 'Habonim Was Looked At as a Bit Wild,' " in J. J. Goldberg and Elliot King, eds., *Builders and Dreamers: Habonim Labor Zionist Youth in North America* (New York, 1993), 173.

16. I am not counting his remark that while taking basic training at Fort Dix, in 1953, he was overwhelmed with a sense of its resemblance to "the Nazi camps as Hannah Arendt had described them in *The Origins of Totalitarianism.*" (Norman Podhoretz, *Making It* [New York, 1967], 134.)

17. Todd Gitlin, *The Sixties* (New York, 1987), 25–26.

18. Daphne Merkin, *Dreaming of Hitler* (New York, 1997); Meredith Tax, "Speak, Memory: Primo Levi's Living History," *Voice Literary Supplement,* March 1986, 12.

19. Otto Friedrich, *City of Nets: A Portrait of Hollywood in the 1940s* (New York, 1986), 179.

20. Allen Rivkin, October-November 1962 Report, and Report 27, February 1969, NCRAC Papers, Box 51. Not only American consumer preferences were involved; Germany was a significant segment of Hollywood's overseas market. (See "Films' New Nice-Nasty Nazis," *Variety,* 16 April 1958.)

21. "A Trumpet for All Israel," *Time* 58 (15 October 1951): 52.

22. Emil Fackenheim, who later became an important "Holocaust theologian," recalled his earlier avoidance of the issue. "One does not have to be either an enemy of Jews or an indifferent Jew in order to change the subject when the Holocaust comes up. . . . I once did the same thing. . . . The cause was a hidden fear that if a Jew faced up to the scandal truly, fully, honestly, the result would be despair of Judaism." (Fackenheim, "Jew of Fidelity," in Harry James Cargas, ed., *Telling the Tale: A Tribute to Elie Wiesel* (St. Louis, 1993), 114.

23. Eugene Borowitz, "Rethinking Our Holocaust Consciousness," *Judaism* 40 (Fall 1991): 390.

24. Quoted in Edward T. Linenthal, *Preserving Memory: The Struggle to Create America's Holocaust Museum* (New York, 1995), 6.

25. In the late 1940s Jewish picketing forced the abandonment of a Carnegie Hall concert by Walter Gieseking (and his departure from the country), and leading Jewish musicians, threatening a boycott, succeeded in securing the cancellation of a contract between the Chicago Symphony Orchestra and the conductor Wilhelm Furtwängler. There were also protests against appearances by the Norwegian singer Kirsten Flagstad on the basis of her husband's alleged Nazi Party membership. In the 1950s there were protests against appearances by the conductor Herbert von Karajan and the soprano Elizabeth Schwarzkopf, both of whom had been Nazi Party members.

26. Lothar Kahn, "Another Decade: The American Jew in the Sixties," *Judaism* 10 (Spring 1961): 10.

27. Lloyd P. Gartner, "Jewish Historiography in the United States and Britain," in A. Rapoport-Albert and S. J. Zipperstein, eds., *Jewish History: Essays in Honour of Chimen Abramsky* (London, 1988), 227. Gartner added: "It was also felt that intensive research and exposure might hinder the mental rehabilitation of the survivors."

28. Statement of Federal Council of Churches, Commission on the Relation of the Church to the War in the Light of the Christian Faith, March 1946, quoted in Mark Silk, *Spiritual Politics* (New York, 1988), 25. The members of the commission

included, besides Niebuhr, John Bennett and Henry P. Van Dusen, all of whom had been and were anti-pacifist interventionists.

29. Sermon reprinted in Harry Emerson Fosdick, *On Being Fit to Live With: Essays on Post-War Christianity* (New York, 1946), 76–77.

30. Quoted in Donald Porter Geddes et al., *The Atomic Age Opens* (New York, 1945), 58.

31. Lewis Mumford, "The Morals of Extermination," *Atlantic Monthly* 204 (October 1959): 39.

32. Robert Lane Fenrich, "Imagining Holocaust: Mass Death and American Consciousness at the End of the Second World War," Northwestern University Ph.D. diss., 1992, 96–98; "The Thirty-six Hour War," *Life* 19 (19 November 1945): 27–35.

33. Ruth Benedict, "The Past and the Future" (review of John Hersey's *Hiroshima*), *The Nation* 163 (7 December 1946): 656.

34. Stuart Chase, *For This We Fought: Guide Lines to America's Future as Reported to the Twentieth Century Fund* (New York, 1946), 119–20.

35. Henry Seidel Canby, "Mass Death in Miniature," *Saturday Review of Literature* 28 (8 September 1945): 18.

36. Cited in Robert Jay Lifton and Eric Markusen, *The Genocidal Mentality: Nazi Holocaust and Nuclear Threat* (New York, 1990), 9.

37. Bernard Rosenberg, "Balance Sheet of Madness," *Jewish Frontier* 12 (June 1955): 6–7; A. Alvarez, "The Literature of the Holocaust," *Commentary* 38 (November 1964): 65.

38. Herbert Gold, *The Age of Happy Problems* (New York, 1962), 4.

39. Marshall Sklare to John Slawson, 20 October 1958, AJCommittee Papers, GS 10, Box 8, Anti-Semitism, 1942–58. For a useful compendium of poll results, see Charles Herbert Stember et al., *Jews in the Mind of America* (New York, 1966). In 1946, 64 percent of those surveyed reported having heard anti-Semitic remarks in the past six months. By 1959, this had declined to 12 percent, with most of the drop taking place before 1951. (Leonard Dinnerstein, *Anti-Semitism in America* [New York, 1994], 151.)

40. The exceptions were few and mostly unimportant. A handful of social clubs, vacation resorts, and wealthy neighborhoods were the last holdouts. As of the sixties, it was said that executive suites in some industries were not fully open to Jews, but whatever barriers existed there were soon to tumble.

41. Both the rhythm of the decline and the simultaneous drop in other ethnic antipathies suggest that factors other than the Holocaust were at work. No scholar has yet addressed this phenomenon in a systematic way, but there is an interesting discussion in Stember et al., *Mind of America*, esp. 142–44, 216, 265–69, 290–97, 377–99.

42. Philip Roth, *The Facts* (New York, 1988), 123.

43. Edward Shapiro, *A Time for Healing: American Jewry Since World War II* (Baltimore, 1992), 8–15.

44. Interview with Selma Hirsh, 5 January 1987, Oral History Collection, AJCommittee, 16–17.

45. Daniel Boorstin, Louis Hartz, and Richard Hofstadter (who was half Jewish).

46. WJC, "Is the Commemoration of the Warsaw Ghetto Uprising Going to Remain a Permanent National Memorial Day?" (1954), WJC Papers, Box F21.

47. I. Schwarzbart, "The Lasting Significance of the Warsaw Ghetto Uprising," 9 April 1951, WJC Papers, Box F19, Eighth Anniversary.

48. Gertrude Samuels, "Five Who Came Out of the Terror," *New York Times Magazine*, 3 August 1952, 52.

49. Peter Hellman, *The Auschwitz Album: A Book Based Upon an Album Discovered by a Concentration Camp Survivor, Lili Meier* (New York, 1981), xxiii.
50. Jeffrey Shandler, " 'This Is Your Life': Telling a Holocaust Survivor's Life Story on Early American Television," *Journal of Narrative and Life History* 4 (1994): 50–51. During the fifties and early sixties there were five other similar episodes on the program.
51. R. C. Rothschild to Charles Einfeld, 14 March 1947, AJCommittee Papers, GS 10, Box 227, Mass Media, Films-Movies (A–K).
52. "Radio Broadcast for Rochester," 15 December 1948, AJCongress Papers, Box 49, Community Service Bureau.
53. "Summary of the Proceedings of the Meeting of the NY Area Members of the [ADL] National Program Committee," 19 December 1961, AJCommittee Papers, GS 12, Box 16, ADL Activities, 1945–61.
54. Stuart W. Cook to David Petegorsky, 21 February 1949, AJCongress Papers, Box 19. There is a good deal of information on the postwar orientation of Jewish defense agencies in Stuart Svonkin, *Jews Against Prejudice: American Jews and the Fight for Civil Liberties* (New York, 1997).
55. Jules Cohen to Membership, 6 April 1959, AJCommittee Papers, GS 10, Box 229, Films/Reviews, NCRAC, 1951–61.
56. For a (far from exhaustive) sampling of this discourse, see Edward Alexander, *The Holocaust and the War of Ideas* (New Brunswick, N.J., 1994); Ilan Avisar, *Screening the Holocaust* (Bloomington, Ind., 1988); Judith E. Doneson, *The Holocaust in American Film* (Philadelphia, 1987); Sidra Ezrahi, *By Words Alone: The Holocaust in Literature* (Chicago, 1980); Lawrence L. Langer, "The Americanization of the Holocaust on Stage and Screen," in Sarah Blacher Cohen, ed., *From Hester Street to Hollywood* (Bloomington, Ind., 1983); Deborah E. Lipstadt, "America and the Memory of the Holocaust, 1950–1965," *Modern Judaism* 16 (October 1996); Alvin H. Rosenfeld, "Popularization and Memory: The Case of Anne Frank," in Peter Hayes, ed., *Lessons and Legacies: The Meaning of the Holocaust in a Changing World* (Evanston, Ill., 1991); Stephen J. Whitfield, "Value Added; Jews in Postwar American Culture," *Studies in Contemporary Jewry* 8 (1992).
57. Cynthia Ozick, "Who Owns Anne Frank?" *New Yorker* 73 (6 October 1997): 87.
58. "Still Young in Spirit," *Newsweek* 53 (30 March 1959): 98.
59. *The Diary of Anne Frank,* dramatized by Frances Goodrich and Albert Hackett (New York, 1956), 168, 174; Kanin quoted in Lawrence Graver, *An Obsession with Anne Frank: Meyer Levin and the* Diary (Berkeley, 1995), 89.
60. Meyer Levin to Otto Frank, 25 December 1952, quoted in Graver, *Obsession,* 52.
61. Meyer Levin, "The Child Behind the Secret Door," *New York Times Book Review,* 15 June 1952, 1, 22.
62. Meyer Levin, "A Classic Human Document," *Congress Weekly* 19 (16 June 1952): 13.
63. The only expression of (qualified) public support for Levin that I have found in the 1950s was by a Chicago rabbi: Jacob J. Weinstein, "Betrayal of Anne Frank," *Congress Weekly* 24 (13 May 1957): 5–7. Once the Hacketts' adaptation had been produced, Levin's crusade focused on the right to produce his version. Many endorsed this "civil libertarian" appeal without expressing a preference for Levin's script, which few if any had seen. From the 1970s on, by which time Levin had become the hero of "anti-universalists," he had much more support. While I disagree with some of Lawrence Graver's judgments, his book, *An Obsession with Anne Frank,* is a reliable chronicle. The same cannot be said of Ralph Melnick's *The Stolen Legacy of Anne Frank: Meyer Levin, Lillian Hellman, and the Staging of*

the Diary (New Haven, 1997). Melnick not only embraces all of Levin's paranoid fantasies, but adds new ones of his own. (See, e.g., Melnick, 208.)

64. Robert Alter, "The View from the Attic," *New Republic* 213 (4 December 1995): 41–42. Another scholar of Holocaust literature who has distanced himself from the notion of a very Jewish Anne, maliciously de-Judaized, is James E. Young. He writes of Anne that "even though she felt the sufferings of millions [Young is here quoting from the *Diary*], in the context of her assimilated world view, it seems to have been as an extremely sensitive and intelligent member of the human community, and not as one who identified herself as part of a collective Jewish tragedy." (*Writing and Rewriting the Holocaust* [Bloomington, Ind., 1988], 27–28.)

65. Review by Leo W. Schwarz, *Jewish Social Studies* 14 (1952): 379. In the last sentence, I have substituted "might," which is what Schwarz clearly meant, for his word "may."

66. Israel Gutman, "Remarks on the Literature of the Holocaust," *In the Dispersion* 5/6 (Spring 1966): 123.

67. Lawrence Langer, "The Uses — and Misuses — of a Young Girl's Diary," *Forward*, 17 March 1995, 5; "A Playwright's Obsession with the Story of Anne Frank," *Forward*, 19 September 1997, 14.

68. Henry Popkin, "The Diary of Anne Frank," *Jewish Frontier* 23 (January 1956): 30–31; William Schack, "Diary into Drama," *Midstream* 2 (Spring 1956): 2–4.

69. Edward Alexander, "Stealing the Holocaust," *Midstream* 26 (November 1980): 48.

70. Netherlands State Institute for War Documentation, *The Diary of Anne Frank: The Critical Edition* (New York, 1989), 636–37, 601. These entries date from shortly before the *Diary* was terminated by Anne's capture. At the very beginning of the *Diary*, before the family entered the secret annex, Anne reports that at the age of twelve she had begun attending meetings of a Zionist club, but was quitting. (Ibid., 201.)

71. If the fact that Anne resembled an American teenager made it possible for American gentiles to think of her as being like their own children, this was no less true for American Jews.

72. Andrew Kopkind, quoted in Shapiro, *Time for Healing*, 15.

73. "Scientific Research on Anti-Semitism: Paper Delivered by John Slawson, Executive Vice-President [of AJCommittee], at NCRAC, September 11, 1944," in AJCommittee Papers, GS 10, Box 9, Anti-Semitism, 1938–60, Speeches, 7, 9, 13, 14. Slawson was oversimplifying the more nuanced and qualified views of the social scientists. (Cf. the stenographic report of the conference, AJCommittee Files.)

74. Minutes of the Defense Policy Committee, 16 May 1945, AJCommittee Files. Cf. the retrospective account in minutes of Mass Media Education Committee, 1 December 1960, AJCommittee Papers, GS 12, Box 40.

75. Elliot Cohen, "Letters," *Commentary* 4 (October 1947): 348.

76. Ethel C. Phillips to Isaiah Terman, 6 August 1958, AJCommittee Papers, GS 10, Box 228, Films-Movies (L–O).

77. Marie Jahoda to Dorothy M. Nathan, 29 June 1945, AJCommittee Papers, GS 10, Box 7, Anti-Semitism, 1944–45, Mass Media, Films, "Tomorrow the World." Various other reasons were offered for downplaying the Holocaust. Eugene Hevesi, the AJCommittee's foreign policy expert, was consulted in 1951 about a proposed scholarly investigation of the causes of the Jewish catastrophe. He pointed to what he considered a danger in undertaking such a study. "The position of the Jews today," he began, "is a morally strong one and we are 'living off' the martyrdom of the six million exterminated Jews. [A study] might find that the Jews in

truth held considerable economic power in certain countries. . . . To open up this entire question . . . would be to jeopardize the favorable moral position of the Jews and therefore Dr. Hevesi questioned the wisdom of going through with this suggestion. Such an investigation might provide the facts which could be interpreted as justification for the catastrophe itself." (Morroe Berger to John Slawson, 10 April 1951, AJCommittee Papers, GS 10, Box 92, AJC-CCJO, Genocide Convention, 1947–52. Berger was summarizing the views of participants in meetings held to discuss the proposal.)

78. Jules Cohen of NCRAC, summarizing objections raised by the various Jewish agencies, in "Minutes of a meeting of an ad hoc committee with representatives of the American Memorial for the Six Million Jews of Europe, Inc., held at the offices of the NCRAC, September 10, 1947," AJCommittee Papers, GS 12, Box 15; "Memorandum on Memorial to Six Million Jews in Europe, Inc.: History of NCRAC Consideration of This Subject," 10 May 1948, NCRAC Papers, Box 32. The avoidance of the victim image was consistently advanced as the principal objection, but there were others: that it would represent a diversion of resources from other projects; that such a memorial properly belonged in Europe. At a 1947 meeting of AJCongress staffers to discuss the proposed memorial, it was the consensus that "in general, attention should be concentrated on assistance to the Jews who are living rather than commemorating those who are dead." (Minutes of [AJCongress] Office Committee Meeting, 22 July 1947, WJC Papers, A76/5.)

79. Thus, for example, when the idea of a memorial in New York was revived in the late fifties, Israel Goldstein of the American Jewish Congress wrote in a memorandum that he didn't think it a good idea. "There is Yad Vashem in Israel. There is an impressive monument in Paris. Such a monument makes sense in Israel. It also makes sense in Paris, because the tragedy took place on the soil of Europe. It does not seem to me to be as important to have such a monument in New York. . . . It is the kind of thing in which we ought to let well enough alone." (Goldstein to Isaac Toubin, 10 February 1958, WJC Papers, F23, Fifteenth Anniversary.)

7. "Self-Hating Jewess Writes Pro-Eichmann Series"

1. "Kennedy, Praising Anne Frank, Warns of New Nazi-like Peril," *New York Times,* 20 September 1961, 5.
2. See Gavriel D. Rosenfeld, "The Reception of William L. Shirer's *The Rise and Fall of the Third Reich* in the United States and West Germany, 1960–62," *Journal of Contemporary History* 29 (1994).
3. David Danzig to John Slawson, 4 March 1960, AJCommittee Papers, FAD-1, Box 25, Germany–West, 1959–61; Samuel Kaminsky to Area Directors, 21 June 1960, AJCommittee Papers, GS 10, Box 253, Political Philosophy, Nazism, 1960.
4. Address of Dr. Israel Goldstein, 28 May 1960, AJCongress Papers, Box 13.
5. Estimate in "The Impact of the Eichmann Trial," (ADL) *Facts* 14 (August-September 1961): 203.
6. "Israel and the Law," *New Republic* 142 (20 June 1951): 5.
7. Telford Taylor, "Large Questions in the Eichmann Case," *New York Times Magazine,* 22 January 1961.
8. Quoted in Embassy of Israel, "Analysis of U.S. Editorial . . . Comment on Israel and the Middle East," 8–14 April 1961, AJCommittee Papers, GS 12, Box 40.
9. "In the Case of Eichmann vs. Humanity," *New York Post,* 2 June 1960.
10. Oscar Handlin, "The Ethics of the Eichmann Case," *Issues* 15 (Winter 1961);

Wechsler quoted in Pnina Lahav, "The Eichmann Trial, the Jewish Question, and the American-Jewish Intellectual," *Boston University Law Review* 72 (May 1992).

11. Quoted in American Jewish Congress, "The Opening of the Eichmann Trial: A Study of Press Reaction," 12. (AJCongress Papers, Box 26.)

12. Paul E. Killinger, "Mercy for Mass Murder," *Unitarian Register* 139 (October 1960): 6.

13. Rev. Charles E. Curley in *The Tablet*, quoted in "The Impact of the Eichmann Trial," 207. *The Tablet*, the newspaper of the Roman Catholic Diocese of Brooklyn, was notoriously thuggish and not representative of mainstream Catholic journalism. More typical in tone were editorials in the Jesuit periodical *America*. "It is now time to close the books on this tragic and dismal chapter in the history of the human race. A sound and healthy world community cannot rest solidly on fear and the spirit of vengeance." ("Trial of a Nazi," *America* 105 [29 July 1961]: 564.) "Is it good psychology or good mental health to exhume, in all their sordid, criminal and tragic detail, the experiences of world Jewry at the hands of the Nazis? Can good understanding between Christian and Jew be built on such a foundation? History can teach its lessons better than through the incessant reliving and re-enacting, often verging on the morbid, of the past." ("Eichmann the 'Christian'?" *America* 106 [24 March 1962]: 814.)

14. "Where Is Israel?" *National Review* 8 (4 June 1960): 352.

15. "The Law and the Eichmann Case," *National Review* 8 (18 June 1960): 382. Shortly thereafter, another editorial insisted that "the Jewish community is not lawmaker for the world." ("Israel Against the Jews," *National Review* 8 [2 July 1960]: 415.)

16. W. H. von Dreele, "The Gold Problem," *National Review* 10 (14 January 1961): 17. A few weeks later, it carried an item about the fact that a New York broadcasting company, which had contracted with the Israeli government to distribute films of the trial, had lowered its prices to the networks. Not very newsworthy, one would think, but it gave the magazine the chance to observe, "They must have known a chap who could get it for them wholesale." (*National Review* 10 [11 March 1961]: 134.)

17. "Let's All Hate Germany, Comrade," *National Review* 10 (25 March 1961): 172. This theme was reiterated three weeks later, when the magazine's newsletter bemoaned how "the fire of anti-Germanism [was] fanned by the Eichmann case." (*National Review Bulletin* 10 [15 April 1961]: 2.)

18. "Thoughts on Eichmann," *National Review* 10 (22 April 1961): 238–39.

19. "Propagandists of the World, Arise!" *National Review* 10 (6 May 1961): 271. If there were subsequent comments in the magazine, I missed them. At about the time of Eichmann's capture, it was editorially critical of "a mob of Jews" who "hurled insults" at American Nazi leader George Lincoln Rockwell. ("Let Us Try, at Least, to Understand," *National Review* 10 [3 June 1961]: 338.) The following year, it explained that contrary to Rockwell's claim, he had not exactly been "employed" by the *National Review*; it had given him an advance to promote the magazine, which, when he failed to deliver, he "promptly and amiably" returned. ("Notes and Asides," *National Review* 11 [18 November 1961]: 331.)

20. Grossman's remarks paraphrased in *Jerusalem Post*, 31 March 1961, 5.

21. Michael Keren, "Ben-Gurion's Theory of Sovereignty: The Trial of Adolf Eichmann," in Ronald W. Zweig, ed., *David Ben-Gurion: Politics and Leadership in Israel* (London, 1991), 45.

22. American Jewish Congress, "Opening of the Eichmann Trial," 1, 2.

23. Arnold Forster to ADL Regional Offices, memorandum, 7 March 1961, ADL microfilms, "–1974," Eichmann.

24. "Notes on the Adolf Eichmann Trial," 13 February 1961, ADL microfilms, "–1974," Eichmann.

25. Rabbi Samson R. Weiss, paraphrased in "Summary of Minutes of NCRAC Committee on the Community Relations Aspects of Developments in the Middle East, July 18, 1960," in ADL microfilms, "–1974," Eichmann.

26. Robert Disraeli to John Slawson, 1 November 1960, AJCommittee Papers, GS 12, Box 41.

27. S. Andhil Fineberg, "Capital Punishment and the Eichmann Case," 18 December 1961, AJCommittee Scientific Research Department Files, Box 6, Eichmann Trial, Clippings/Publicity.

28. Minutes of meetings of Mass Media Education Committee, 20 October and 1 December 1960, AJCommittee Papers, GS 12, Box 40.

29. Arnold Forster, "The Eichmann Case," *ADL Bulletin,* March 1961, 1–2.

30. Isaiah Terman to Area Directors and Executive Assistants, 24 March 1961, AJCommittee Papers, GS 12, Box 40.

31. For an example of the ideological critique of "holocaust," see Zev Garber and Bruce Zuckerman, *Modern Judaism* 9 (May 1989) For the religious connotations of "*shoah*," see Uriel Tal, "Excursus on the Term: Shoah," *Shoah* 1:4 (1979): 10–11; Dalia Ofer, "Linguistic Conceptualization of the Holocaust in Palestine and Israel, 1942–1953," *Journal of Contemporary History* 31 (1996).

32. "Proclamation of Independence," *Palestine Year Book* 4 (5709): 66.

33. "Eichmann and Jewish Identity," *New Leader* 44 (3 July 1961): 13.

34. George Salomon, "The End of Eichmann: America's Response," *American Jewish Yearbook* 64 (1963); American Jewish Committee, *The Eichmann Case in the American Press* (New York, n.d.).

35. Midge Decter, "Study of Press Reactions to the Eichmann Case," AJCommittee, Scientific Research Department Files, Box 6, Study: Eichmann Trial, Press Reaction, Midge Decter Memo.

36. Arendt was best known for her 1951 book, *The Origins of Totalitarianism.* She had been arrested by the Nazis in the early days of the regime for illegal Zionist activity. After her release she fled to France, where she worked for Youth Aliyah. Interned during the war at Gurs, in Vichy France, she escaped and made her way to the United States, where she again worked for Jewish organizations, eventually breaking with mainstream Zionism. For her life, including much detail about the controversy over *Eichmann in Jerusalem,* see Elisabeth Young-Bruehl, *Hannah Arendt: For Love of the World* (New Haven, 1982).

37. *Intermountain Jewish News,* 19 April 1963, 4.

38. Arnold Forster to ADL Regional Offices, 27 March 1963, Hannah Arendt Papers, Box 47, Corres. Jewish Orgs.

39. Jacob Robinson, *And the Crooked Shall Be Made Straight: The Eichmann Trial, the Jewish Catastrophe, and Hannah Arendt's Narrative* (Philadelphia, 1965).

40. Joachim Prinz, *Arendt Nonsense* (New York, 1963), pamphlet distributed by AJCongress.

41. Leo Mindlin, "During the Week," *Jewish Floridian,* 15 March 1963. (Copy attached to Forster memorandum of 27 March 1963.)

42. Barbara Tuchman, "The Final Solution," *New York Times Book Review,* 29 May 1966, 3, 12.

43. The phrase "banality of evil" did not appear in the *New Yorker* articles; in the book, it was used only once, at the very end, where it was not explicated. I have here woven together Arendt's remarks in "Thinking and Moral Considera-

tions," *Social Research* 38 (Fall 1971): 417, and from her notes for a lecture. ("Columbia/Jewish Students/ Eichmann/July 23, 1963," in Hannah Arendt Papers, Box 49, Private Reply to Jewish Critics, 1963.) I have corrected her punctuation in the case of the lecture notes.

44. "Notes on the Adolf Eichmann Trial," 13 February 1961, memorandum distributed to ADL affiliates, ADL microfilms, "–1974," Eichmann.

45. Norman Podhoretz, "Hannah Arendt on Eichmann: A Study in the Perversity of Brilliance," *Commentary* 36 (September 1963): 206.

46. Ibid., 201.

47. Constantine Fitzgibbon, "Again the Issue of German Guilt," *New York Times Magazine,* 18 August 1963, 17.

48. The most accessible account of the experiment is Stanley Milgram, *Obedience to Authority: An Experimental View* (New York, 1974).

49. Ibid., 54.

50. There are those who reject the implications that Milgram and others have drawn from his findings. See Arthur G. Miller, *The Obedience Experiments: A Case Study of Controversy in Social Science* (New York, 1986).

51. Yehuda Bauer, "Reflections Concerning Holocaust History," in Louis Greenspan and Graeme Nicholson, eds., *Fackenheim: German Philosophy and Jewish Thought* (Toronto, 1992), 166–67, 169.

52. Daniel Jonah Goldhagen, *Hitler's Willing Executioners: Ordinary Germans and the Holocaust* (New York, 1996).

53. Quoted in Young-Bruehl, *Hannah Arendt,* 349.

54. Minutes of NCRAC special committee meeting, 23 April 1963, ADL microfilms, "–1974," Eichmann.

55. Julius Schatz to Phil Jacobson, 27 May 1963, NCRAC Papers, Box 50.

56. *Encylopædia Judaica* (Jerusalem, 1971), 3:406.

57. Hannah Arendt, *Eichmann in Jerusalem* (New York, 1963), 201, 108.

58. The use of the phrase in this context originated with the Jewish resistance leader and poet Abba Kovner.

59. Arnold Forster, 10 May 1961 report from Jerusalem, quoted in his *Square One* (New York, 1988), 228.

60. Bruno Bettelheim, "The Ignored Lesson of Anne Frank," *Harper's Magazine* 221 (November 1960): 46. Cf. his *The Informed Heart* (Glencoe, Ill., 1960), and "Freedom from Ghetto Thinking," *Midstream* 8 (Spring 1962), in which this argument was extended.

61. Letter to *Midstream* 8 (September 1962): 86.

62. In a 20 April 1964 letter to Karl Jaspers, Arendt wrote: "I haven't heard anything about Hilberg's coming out on my side. He's talking some nonsense now about the 'death wish' of the Jews. His book is really excellent, but only because he just reports facts in it. His introductory chapter that deals with general and historical matters wouldn't pass muster in a pigpen." (Lotte Kohler and Hans Saner, eds., *Hannah Arendt–Karl Jaspers Correspondence: 1926–1969* [1985; English trans., New York, 1992], 550.)

63. Arendt, *Eichmann in Jerusalem,* 104, 111.

64. This was a distinction that Hilberg had refused to make: for him, the leaders "represented the essence of a time-honored Jewish reaction to danger." (Raul Hilberg, *The Politics of Memory: The Journey of a Holocaust Historian* [Chicago, 1996], 150–51.)

65. W. Z. Laqueur, "The Kastner Case," *Commentary* 20 (December 1955): 509.

66. Hanna Yablonka, "The Formation of Holocaust Consciousness in the State of Israel: The Early Days," in Efraim Sicher, ed., *Breaking Crystal: Writing and Memory after Auschwitz* (Urbana, Ill., 1997).

67. *"Judenrat"* continued to be used this way in internal Jewish communications. In 1971 the president of the Anti-Defamation League was defending his organization against criticism for having given information to the FBI on the Jewish Defense League. "To charge that the ADL or any other Jewish agency, in making information available to a government bureau, is acting as did the 'judenrat' traitors in Europe during the Nazi period, is to suggest that there is a similarity between the American government and the Nazi regime. All of us reject any such comparison out of hand." (Seymour Graubard's statement to NJCRAC Plenum, 25 June 1971, copy in JDL files of American Jewish Historical Society.)

68. Loudon Wainwright, " 'You Are the Man Who Killed My Brother,' " *Life* 29 (11 December 1950). The hearing ended inconclusively because of insufficient evidence. The full text of the judgment was printed in *Congress Weekly* 17 (11 December 1950).

69. Hilberg, *Politics of Memory*, 66.

70. Mosez Torcyzner in *The American Zionist*, quoted in Richard I. Cohen, "Breaking the Code: Hannah Arendt's *Eichmann in Jerusalem* and the Public Polemic: Myth, Memory and Historical Imagination," *Michael: On the History of the Jews in the Diaspora* 13 (1993): 68.

71. Arnold Forster to ADL Regional Offices, 11 March 1963, NCRAC Papers, Box 67.

72. Minutes of NCRAC special committee meeting, 23 April 1963, ADL microfilms, "–1974," Eichmann.

73. Primo Levi, *The Drowned and the Saved* (New York, 1988), 40, 43.

75. Yehuda Bauer and Nathan Rotenstreich, eds., *The Holocaust as Historical Experience* (New York, 1981), 237.

75. The title was variously rendered as *The Vicar* or *The Representative*, which are translations of the original German *Der Stellvertreter*, referring to the pope's official role as Christ's vicar on Earth. Hochhuth's text was published as *The Representative* (London, 1963).

76. Jules Cohen to Phil Jacobson et al., 20 June 1963, AJCommittee Files, IAD, 1963–64, "The Deputy," Corres., A–Z; Judith Hershcopf, "The Church and the Jews: The Struggle at Vatican Council II," *American Jewish Yearbook* 66 (1965): 115.

77. See "Eisenhower Airs Grief of Nation," *New York Times*, 9 October 1958, 24; "Sorrow Is Voiced by Public Figures," *New York Times*, 10 October 1958, 12. As far as I know, the only comment on Pius's silence during the Holocaust that was made at the time of his death came from a writer for the French Communist newspaper *L'Humanité*. ("Dulles to Attend Rites for Pontiff," *New York Times*, 11 October 1958, 11.)

78. John Slawson to Irving Salomon, 20 November 1963, Isaiah Terman to CAD Professional Staff, 21 February 1964, both in AJCommittee Files, Vatican/Der Stellvertreter/Interreligious Catholic-Jewish/1963–65.

79. Preliminary draft, ibid.; final statement in AJCommittee Files, DOM 1963–64, "The Deputy."

80. Joseph Lichten, *A Question of Judgment: Pius XII and the Jews* (Washington, D.C., 1963), 4.

81. Quoted in "Der Stellvertreter — (God's) Deputy: Background Memorandum for Domestic Affairs Committee Meeting, January 20, 1964," AJCommittee Files, DOM, 1963–64, "The Deputy."

82. These included Rabbi Theodore Friedman, president of the Rabbinical Assembly,

and Rabbi Jay Kaufman, a vice president of the Union of American Hebrew Congregations. (Robert C. Doty, " 'The Deputy' Is Here," *New York Times*, 23 February 1964, 3.) Kaufman circulated a letter to colleagues urging them to arrange theater parties "so the house will be filled in the early weeks." (Kaufman to "Colleagues," 28 January 1964, AJCommittee Files, IAD, 1963–64, "The Deputy," Corres., A–Z.)

83. These included *Commentary, Congress Bi-Weekly, Jewish Frontier*, and *Midstream*.

84. Alfred Kazin, "The Vicar of Christ," in Eric Bentley, ed., *The Storm over the Deputy* (New York, 1964), 103.

8. "A Bill Submitted 'for Sufferings Rendered' "

1. For this process, see Melvin I. Urofsky, "A Cause in Search of Itself: American Zionism after the State," *American Jewish History* 69 (September 1979).

2. Nathan Perlmutter, *A Bias of Reflections* (New Rochelle, N.Y., 1972), 73–74.

3. Lucy Dawidowicz, review of Joseph B. Schechtman, *The Arab Refugee Problem, New Leader* 36 (19 January 1953): 23–24.

4. Joachim Prinz, "Beyond the Zionist Dream," *Congress Bi-Weekly* 28 (16 January 1961): 6.

5. Isaac Alteras, "Eisenhower, American Jewry, and Israel," *American Jewish Archives* 37 (November 1985); William Schneider et al., "Bloc Voting Reconsidered," *Ethnicity* 1 (1974): 356.

6. Marshall Sklare and Joseph Greenbaum, *Jewish Identity on the Suburban Frontier* (New York, 1967), 322–24 Of the respondents, 47 percent thought supporting Israel was "desirable"; 32 percent thought it made no difference in judging whether one was a good Jew. For "helping the underprivileged," the respective figures were 37 percent and 5 percent.

7. The plan was not instituted for several decades, as a result of opposition from American non-Zionists. Though Yad Vashem, for understandable reasons, seeks to disguise the fact, half of its budget came from German reparations. This portion of reparations was administered by the Conference on Jewish Material Claims Against Germany, an international body, one of the senior officers of which was Jacob Blaustein of the American Jewish Committee. Blaustein objected on ideological grounds to this Israeli assertion of hegemony over the Holocaust, and refused to authorize funds for the citizenship project. It was agreed that posthumous citizenship would be granted only on an individual basis, when a relative or close friend of the victim made special application. In 1985, by which time the original objections were forgotten, blanket posthumous citizenship was granted. (See Ronald W. Zweig, "Politics of Commemoration," *Jewish Social Studies* 49 [Spring 1987]; "Holocaust Victims Given Posthumous Citizenship by Israel," *Los Angeles Times*, 9 May 1985, 1:26. For details of the original conflict, see AJCommittee Papers, FAD-1, Box 285.)

8. Ben-Gurion quoted in Tom Segev, *The Seventh Million* (New York, 1993), 330.

9. All Israeli scholars agree that until the 1960s, and in some respects until the 1970s, the Holocaust played a relatively minor role in Israelis' self-understanding and self-representation — at least in public discourse. See, e.g., Eliezer Don-Yehiya, "Memory and Political Culture: Israeli Society and the Holocaust," *Studies in Contemporary Jewry* 9 (1993).

10. The ambiguities of the dominant representation could be found in what was undoubtedly the most influential work shaping American Jewish images of Israel: the movie version of Leon Uris's *Exodus*. The Holocaust connection was present in the psychologically maimed camp-survivor-turned-terrorist, Dov Landau (Sal

Mineo). The most positive characters were the stalwart native-born Israelis, whose struggle for a state long predated the Holocaust — epitomized by Ari Ben Canaan (Paul Newman). It seems a fair guess that fewer American Jews identified Israel with the short, dark, and damaged Mineo than with the tall, self-confident, and blue-eyed Newman.

11. Quoted in Lucy Dawidowicz, "American Public Opinion," *American Jewish Yearbook* 69 (1968): 204.

12. Robert S. McNamara, *In Retrospect: The Tragedy and Lessons of Vietnam* (New York, 1995), 278.

13. "Surprisingly few" reflects my own surprise when I went through the Near East Crisis Collection at the American Jewish Historical Society. The society's then director, Bernard Wax, was aware that an historic moment was at hand, and collected twenty boxes of materials on Jewish reactions to the crisis across the country. When I began looking at the collection, I had expected to find hundreds of invocations of the Holocaust, but while there were some — in synagogue bulletins, student leaflets, this or that speech — there were far fewer than I'd anticipated. A subjective judgment, but one that I think would be shared by most people going through the thousands of documents in the collection.

14. Oscar Cohen to Philip Perlmutter, 28 June 1978, Oscar Cohen Papers, 2/6/O–Q. Cohen added: "I often wonder why the poll response to the question 'Are Jews more loyal to Israel than the United States' is not higher than it is."

15. Charles S. Leibman and Steven M. Cohen, *Two Worlds of Judaism: The Israeli and American Experiences* (New Haven, 1990), 83.

16. Alan L. Berger, *Crisis and Covenant: The Holocaust in American Jewish Fiction* (Albany, 1985), 213 n33.

17. Jacob Neusner, *Death and Birth of Judaism: The Impact of Christianity, Secularism and the Holocaust on Jewish Faith* (New York, 1987), 268–69, 279.

18. American Histadrut Cultural Exchange Institute, *The Impact of Israel on American Jewry: 20 Years Later* (New York, 1969), 12.

19. *Hester panim* has been an attractive notion because it avoids making the Holocaust a *willed* act of God, occasioned by Jewish sin. But it is not a very satisfactory solution, because the Torah (Deuteronomy 31:17) makes quite clear that God's hiding of His face is a result of His anger with the Jews, and that as a result of His withdrawal "they shall be devoured and many evils and distress shall befall them." There is a large literature on the subject; a good introduction is David Wolpe, "*Hester Panim* in Modern Jewish Thought," *Modern Judaism* 17 (1997).

20. Neusner, *Death and Birth of Judaism,* 269.

21. It was in 1974 that the body that coordinated the work of various Jewish organizations, the National Jewish Community Relations Advisory Council, asked member agencies to sponsor Holocaust Day observances around the country, promote teaching of the Holocaust in schools, and include the Holocaust as a priority item in Jewish-Christian dialogue. (J. J. Goldberg, *Jewish Power: Inside the American Jewish Establishment* [Reading, Mass., 1996], 191.)

22. Leonard Fein, "Right in the First Place," *Moment* 1 (September 1975): 28.

23. Arnold Forster and Benjamin R. Epstein, *The New Anti-Semitism* (New York, 1974), 1–2, 3, 13–14, 309, 16.

24. See Arthur Hertzberg, *Jewish Polemics* (New York, 1992), 30.

25. Golda Meir, "Who Can Blame Israel?" *Times* (London), 15 June 1969, 12.

26. Undated memorandum by Sidney Wallach, attached to 17 May 1974 memorandum from Nathan Perlmutter to Oscar Cohen, ADL microfilms, roll 228, The Holocaust, 1971–74.

27. David Singer review of Deborah Lipstadt, *Denying the Holocaust, New Leader* 76 (17–31 May 1993): 19.
28. "Stealing the Holocaust," *Midstream* 26 (November 1980): 47.
29. David Twersky wrote of a Palestinian attempt to "kidnap . . . the moral capital Jews derive from the Holocaust." ("Palestinian Tactics, Palestinian Goals," *Partisan Review* 55 [Summer 1988]: 452–53.) Frederick Krantz said the principal problem was not Holocaust denial but "appropriation of its moral capital." ("The 'Holocaust Analogy' and the Media: The Lebanon War and Today," *Midstream* 34 [February-March 1988]: 22.)
30. Judy Balint, national director of Amcha: The Coalition for Jewish Concerns, quoted in Lee Moriwaki, "Crosses at Death Camps Anger Jews," *Seattle Times,* 17 September 1994, A10.
31. "Book by Green Seen as Help to Israel's Lobby," *American Examiner–Jewish Week,* 30 April 1978.
32. Oscar Cohen to David Hyatt, 4 September 1980, Oscar Cohen Papers, 1:18/H.
33. Wolf Blitzer, *Between Washington and Jerusalem* (New York, 1985), 9–10.
34. Hyman Bookbinder to Michael Berenbaum, 16 March 1979, AJCommittee Papers, Washington Subject Files 1967–86, Box 11, Chron. Corres.
35. Bookbinder to Ambassador Peter Hermes, 22 January 1981, ibid. The arms sale did not go through, but the chances that Bookbinder's threat had anything to do with this are near zero.
36. Bernice S. Tannenbaum, president of Hadassah, letter to *New York Times,* 29 April 1979, 18E.
37. I. L. Kenen, "Twisted Comparison Cheapens Memory of Holocaust," *Near East Report* 22 (3 May 1978).
38. Leon Wieseltier, "Palestinian Perversion of the Holocaust," *New York Times,* 12 June 1988, 27.
39. For the postwar campaign against the Mufti, see Aaron Berman, *Nazism, the Jews and American Zionism, 1933–1948* (Detroit, 1990), 161–62. For examples of the continuing effort to connect Palestinians with the Holocaust via the Mufti, see, e.g., Saul S. Friedman, "Arab Complicity in the Holocaust," *Jewish Frontier* 42 (April 1975); Elliot A. Green, "Arabs and Nazis — Can It Be True?" *Midstream* 40 (October 1994). On the career of the Mufti, see Philip Mattar, *The Mufti of Jerusalem: Al-Haj Amin al-Husayni and the Palestinian National Movement* (New York, 1966).
40. For examples of this internal discourse, see Joseph Tennenbaum, "They Might Have Been Rescued," *Congress Weekly* 20 (2 February 1953): 5–7; "Eichmann," *Jewish Frontier* 32 (July 1960): 3; Herbert B. Ehrmann, Presidential Address, 29 April 1961, AJCommittee Papers, GS 12, Box 41.
41. Undated leaflet in Near East Crisis Collection, American Jewish Historical Society, Box 4.
42. See Sol I. Littman to ADL Regional Offices, "Guidelines for Discussion with the Christian Religious Community on the Middle East Crisis," 29 June 1967, Near East Crisis Collection, American Jewish Historical Society, Box 3; Marc H. Tannenbaum, "Israel's Hour of Need and the Jewish-Christian Dialogue," *Conservative Judaism* 23 (Winter 1968).
43. See Dawidowicz, "American Public Opinion"; Marshall Sklare, "Lakeville and Israel: The Six-Day War and Its Aftermath," in his *Observing American Jews* (Hanover, N.H., 1993).
44. Elie Wiesel, "Ominous Signs and Unspeakable Thoughts," *New York Times,* 28 December 1974, 23.

45. Martin Peretz, "A Cold Compress of Sympathy," *New Republic* 178 (29 April 1978): 46.
46. David Wyman, "Why Auschwitz Was Never Bombed," *Commentary* 65 (May 1978): 46.
47. "Papal Profanity," *New Republic* 187 (4 October 1982): 12.
48. Milton Himmelfarb, " 'Never Again!' " *Commentary* 52 (August 1971): 73.
49. This concern is presumably the reason for the quite false claim at the Washington Holocaust Museum that American Jewish organizations had pressed for the bombing of Auschwitz. See Chapter 3, pp. 56–57.
50. Carl Schrag, "Can You Appreciate Israel If You Haven't Seen Auschwitz?" *Baltimore Jewish Times,* 6 April 1990.
51. Tom Hundley, "Two Views of Horror," *Chicago Tribune,* 9 May 1993, 1.
52. Kevin Griffin, "Haunted Look at Unforgettable Horror," *Vancouver Sun,* 19 May 1994, B7.
53. Pham-Duy Nguyen, "Shocking Memories," *St. Petersburg Times,* 20 July 1992, 1D.
54. Quoted in Hundley, "Two Views of Horror."
55. Rebekah Denn, "Marching in the Steps of the Dead," *Jerusalem Post,* 4 May 1990.
56. Sandi Dolbee, "Days of Remembering," *San Diego Union-Tribune,* 13 May 1994, E1.
57. Tom Sawicki, "6,000 Witnesses," *Jerusalem Report* 4 (5 May 1994): 33.
58. Yossi Klein Halevi, "Who Owns the Memory?" *Jerusalem Report* 3 (25 February 1993): 31.
59. Survey by Prof. William Helmreich, reported in Sawicki, "6,000 Witnesses," 33. (March participants may have been more likely than other young Jews to *say* they were considering immigration to Israel, but there's no evidence that they in fact followed through.) The March of the Living is not the only venture in Holocaust-to-redemption theater. For some years before it was begun, a similar itinerary was organized for the "young leadership" cadres of the United Jewish Appeal. Another version was a simulated trip of Jewish DPs to Haifa for Jewish teenagers, replicating the voyage of the *Exodus.* One sour Israeli commentator suggested that "it's a shame that we don't take full advantage of our potential. Around Masada, for example, we can develop a great attraction with 'the Romans,' the 'rebels,' and a mass suicide that will save these kids' parents the price of a return ticket." (Meier Shalev, quoted in Allison Kaplan Sommer, " 'Two-Four-Six-Eight, We Deserve a Jewish State,' " *Jerusalem Post,* 15 July 1994.)
60. Richard Wagner, "Reflections on the March of the Living," *Jewish Education* 56 (Summer 1988): 41.
61. "Sounding Off with a Vengeance," *Time* 117 (18 May 1981): 37.
62. William E. Farrell, "Israel Affirms Conditions on West Bank Talks," *New York Times,* 20 August 1981, A15.
63. Ilan Peleg, *Begin's Foreign Policy, 1977–1983* (New York, 1987), 67.
64. Ze'ev Mankowitz, "Beirut Is Not Berlin," *Jerusalem Post,* 4 August 1982, 8.
65. Roger Rosenblatt, "How Much Past Is Enough?" *Time* 120 (20 September 1982): 42. Cf. Richard Cohen, "When Jews Lose Their Tolerance for Dissent," *Washington Post,* 26 September 1982, B1.
66. David Shipler, "Anguish over the Moral Questions," *New York Times,* 24 September 1982, A1.
67. "The alibi of not knowing," wrote Mary McGrory, "comes gratingly from Jewish lips. It was an alibi they heard during their own holocaust." ("After the Massacre, the See-No-Evil, Hear-No-Evil Excuses," *Washington Post,* 23 September

1982, A3.) *Newsweek* thought it "an ugly irony" that the massacre "made the army of Israel a collaborator in the sort of atrocity that history has too often inflicted on Jews." (Tom Mathews, "The Troubled Soul of Israel," *Newsweek* 100 [4 October 1982]: 30.)

68. Thomas A. Sancton, "Israel: Crisis of Conscience," *Time* 131 (8 February 1988): 39.

69. Judea B. Miller, "How Normal Should a Jewish State Be?" *Jewish Frontier* 57 (May-June 1988): 9. Cf. Rabbi Stanley M. Kessler, "Conflict Colors a Rabbi's Affection for Israel," *Bergen* (N.J.) *Record*, 12 February 1988, B11; Ellen Kamp (the daughter of survivors), "Israel: How Could It Do This?" *Newsday*, 12 February 1988, 90; A. Robert Kaufman, "A Jew Reflects," *Louisville Courier-Journal*, 2 April 1989, 3D; Irena Klepflsz (a child survivor), "Yom Hashoah, Yom Yerushelayim," *Genesis* 2 (Spring 1989).

70. Ari Shavit, "On Gaza Beach," *New York Review of Books* 38 (18 July 1991): 3–4. Another Israeli, responding at a symposium to an American Jewish academic who was defending Israel's actions in putting down the *intifada*: "It's American Jews like you that are precisely the problem. Nazi things are being done in Israel. Who are you to tell me that my daughter should go into the Army and beat up children in the West Bank?" (Benjamin Harshev, responding to Ruth Wisse, quoted in Rick Hornung, "Family Feud: Israeli and American Jewish Writers Mix It Up," *Village Voice*, 7 February 1989, 26.)

71. Cited in *American Jewish Yearbook* 80 (1980): 105.

72. Norman Podhoretz, "The State of the Jews," *Commentary* 76 (December 1983): 45. See also his letter in response to critics, *Commentary* 77 (March 1984): 16.

73. Richard Rubenstein, "Attacking the Jews," *Commentary* 89 (March 1990): 71.

74. A. M. Rosenthal, "Dancing with Wolves," *New York Times*, 15 September 1992, A27; Siegman letter to *New York Times*, 27 September 1992, 16E.

75. *All Things Considered*, National Public Radio, 25 February 1994, Transcript 1404–10.

76. Gustav Niebuhr, "Peace Effort in Israel Sparks War of Words," *New York Times* (national edition), 23 September 1995, 7. Foxman resigned from the congregation.

77. A volunteer at the "Yigal Amir Defense Line" in New York told a reporter that "it was the equivalent to somebody killing Adolf Hitler before the Holocaust." (Jonathan Sapers, "Where the Killer Is a Hero," *U.S. News & World Report* 119 [20 November 1995]: 74.)

78. Amos Oz, "Amalek Week," *Davar*, 13 April 1987, reprinted in his *The Slopes of Lebanon* (San Diego, 1989), 123.

79. *Ha'aretz*, 2 March 1988; English trans. provided by Prof. E.kana.

80. Charles Liebman, "What Should Have Been Done?" *Jerusalem Report* 2 (9 January 1992): 37.

81. Ze'ev Chafets, "Benjy and Baruch," *Jerusalem Report* 4 (24 March 1994): 26.

82. Advertisement in *Forward*, 17 November 1995, 8.

83. For the elaboration of this argument, see Steven L. Spiegel, *The Other Arab-Israeli Conflict: Making America's Middle East Policy from Truman to Reagan* (Chicago, 1985); A. F. K. Organski, *The $36 Billion Bargain: Strategy and Politics in U.S. Assistance to Israel* (New York, 1990). For a brief summary of this analysis, see Charles Lipson, "American Support for Israel: History, Sources, Limits," in Gabriel Sheffer, ed., *U.S.-Israeli Relations at the Crossroads* (London, 1997).

84. Lloyd Grove, "On the March for Israel," *Washington Post*, 13 June 1991.

85. The policy was modified in early 1995.

86. Elli Wohlgelernter, "Interactive Remembrance," *Jerusalem Post*, 16 April 1993.

87. UPI dispatch by Andrea Hertzberg, 29 April 1984.

88. Lawrence Weinbaum, "Is This 'Third Temple' Really Necessary?" *Jerusalem Post*, 4 August 1991.

89. Rabbi Arnold Jacob Wolf, of Congregation KAM–Isaiah Israel, in a discussion at the University of Chicago Hillel chapter.

9. "Would They Hide My Children?"

1. Benjamin R. Epstein, "American Jewry in the Mid-1970s: Security, Problems and Strategies," in National Jewish Community Relations Advisory Council, *Papers from the 1974 Plenary Session*, NCRAC Papers, Box 12, Plenary Sessions, 1974, 4, 5, 16.

2. Norman Podhoretz interview with Oscar Cohen, 12 April 1978, Oscar Cohen Papers, 21:1.

3. Earl Raab, "The Deadly Innocence of American Jews," *Commentary* 50 (December 1970): 31.

4. Henry Siegman in "Should We Be Afraid? Symposium on American Anti-Semitism Today," *Moment* 3 (July-August 1978): 22.

5. Henry Raymond, "Crisis-Level Anti-Semitism Found Here by B'nai B'rith," *New York Times*, 23 September 1969, 1.

6. American Histadrut Cultural Exchange Institute, *The Impact of Israel on American Jewry: 20 Years Later* (New York, 1969), 14–15.

7. Address by Norman Podhoretz to Sixty-fifth Annual Meeting of American Jewish Committee, 16 May 1971, copy in Hannah Arendt Papers, Box 16, AJCommittee, 1954–73.

8. Some Jewish organizations had joined with black groups in legislative and legal campaigns against housing and employment discrimination that disadvantaged both blacks and Jews. They had, together with other sections of the Democratic Party coalition, supported the civil rights and voting rights bills pressed by President Johnson in 1964 and 1965. But the two largest Jewish "defense organizations," the American Jewish Committee and the Anti-Defamation League, had distanced themselves from the struggle against segregation in the South, largely in response to the pleas of their southern members. The organizations urged "moderation" and support for "the forces of law and order." (For the American Jewish Committee, see the minutes of its Domestic Affairs Committee, 20 March 1956, in AJCommittee Papers, GS 10, Box 153, Integration, 1954–62. For the Anti-Defamation League, see Samuel Lubin to A. Harold Murray, Report of ADL Southwide Meeting, 11 May 1958, AJCommittee Papers, GS 10, Box 303, Community Relations Orgs., South, 1958.) The American Jewish Congress, with hardly any southern constituency, was more outspoken, and critical of the American Jewish Committee and the ADL for their silence. (See AJCongress press release, 22 May 1956, in AJCommittee Papers, GS 10, Box 153, AJC-ADL Integration, 1956, AJCongress Attack.) Edwin J. Lukas of the AJCommittee staff suggested applying pressure on local Jewish Federations to cut allocations to the American Jewish Congress in order to restrain it from making further statements on desegregation. (Lukas to John Slawson, 3 June 1957, AJCommittee Papers, GS 10, Box 153.) In 1964 Martin Luther King's Southern Christian Leadership Conference asked Henry Schwartzschild, a New York ADL staff member (and a refugee from Nazi Germany), to help out in Birmingham, Alabama, over a weekend. The top executives of the ADL told him that if he went, he needn't bother coming back. Schwartzschild

went to Birmingham, and left the ADL. (Murray Friedman, *What Went Wrong? The Creation and Collapse of the Black-Jewish Alliance* [New York, 1995], 287.)

9. In 1963 Rabbi Joachim Prinz, president of the American Jewish Congress, who had participated in Martin Luther King's March on Washington and had been profoundly moved by it, told a meeting of the Congress's Governing Council that in his opinion, American Jewry, "at the grassroots," did not support the civil rights struggle. (Minutes of the AJCongress Governing Council Meeting, 7–8 September 1963, AJCongress Papers, Box 9, Governing Council Meetings.) A 1964 study of Jewish attitudes toward blacks found a level of prejudice not much different from that of other white Americans. (Donald J. Bogue and Jan E. Dizzard, "Race, Ethnic Prejudice, and Discrimination as Viewed by Subordinate and Superordinate Groups," Community and Family Study Center, 16 April 1964, cited in B. Z. Sobel and May L. Sobel, "Negroes and Jews: American Minority Groups in Conflict," *Judaism* 15 [1956]: 15.) In the same year, another survey asked white New Yorkers whether the civil rights movement was moving too fast or too slow. By a three-to-one margin, New York Jews said "too fast." (Fred Powledge, "Poll Shows Whites in City Resent Civil Rights Drive," *New York Times,* 21 September 1964, 1, 26.) Among Protestants the ratio was two to one, among Catholics ten to one.

10. Shlomo M. Russ, "The 'Zionist Hooligans': The Jewish Defense League," City University of New York Ph.D. diss. in sociology, 1981, 1:85.

11. Perlmutter's remarks in Synagogue Council of America, *The Negro Revolution and the Jewish Community* (New York, 1969), 18.

12. "The Profile of the American Jewish Congress Member" (no date, but c. 1970), Horace Kallen Papers, 37/2.

13. Deborah Lipstadt, "The Holocaust: Symbol and 'Myth' in American Jewish Life," *Forum on the Jewish People, Zionism, and Israel* 40 (Winter 1980–81): 82.

14. John Leo, "Black Anti-Semitism," *Commonweal* 89 (14 February 1969). Leo concluded his article by observing: "This is not Weimar Germany, and it is no disrespect to the six million to say so. The insecurity of New York Jews, as revealed in the current furor, bears no relation to their social or economic status today. . . . As a friend said recently, 'I never thought I'd live to see New York Jews running around in circles like a bunch of *Brooklyn Tablet* Catholics.' "

15. Hertzberg quoted in Stephen D. Isaacs, *Jews and American Politics* (Garden City, N.Y., 1974), 166.

16. Ibid., 15.

17. Jonathan Sarna, "Anti-Semitism and American History," *Commentary* 71 (March 1981): 45.

18. Jerome A. Chanes, "Interpreting the Data: Antisemitism and Jewish Security in the United States," *Patterns of Prejudice* 28 (1994): 88. Because the wording of the question and the sampling method varied somewhat, it's difficult to measure the precise dimensions of the changing perceptions, but the upward trend is clear. It's also hard to know just what respondents meant when they called anti-Semitism a "serious problem."

19. In 1974 the leaders of the ADL argued that one of the things that made anti-Semitic black demagogues a more significant threat than they'd previously been was the media exposure they received. "A street-corner haranguer in Harlem once had a limited audience. Today, via local and national radio and television and more comprehensive newspaper coverage of the black community, his audience can be vast, his imitators many; in the late sixties, if you were a black and seek-

ing some degree of instant celebrity, it paid to be anti-Jewish — the TV cameras were there in a flash. The potential for damage against the Jewish community is significantly multiplied." (Arnold Forster and Benjamin R. Epstein, *The New Anti-Semitism* [New York, 1974], 177.) In recent years, the ADL itself has been the primary catalyst of the attention black hustlers have received — and thus the dispenser of rewards for anti-Semitic trash talk.

20. Epstein, "American Jewry," 7.
21. Podhoretz interview with Cohen.
22. Berenbaum quoted in Michael Kernan, "The Specter of Anti-Semitism," *Washington Post,* 1 December 1982, C1.
23. Foxman quoted in Herb Keinon, "Antisemitism Now 'Respectable' in the U.S., ADL Head Reports," *Jerusalem Post,* 14 April 1992.
24. Jack Newfield, *The Education of Jack Newfield* (New York, 1984), 30.
25. Jonathan Rieder, *Canarsie: The Jews and Italians of Brooklyn Against Liberalism* (Cambridge, Mass., 1985), 206–7.
26. Roberta Strauss Feuerlicht, *The Fate of the Jews* (New York, 1983), 208–9.
27. "Excerpts from Address by Rabbi Marc H. Tannenbaum . . . ," AJCommittee Papers, FAD-1A, Box 140, Negro-Jewish Relations, 1968.
28. J. J. Goldberg, "Scaring the Jews: Hyping Anti-Semitism," *New Republic* 208 (17 May 1993): 24. In 1989 the comedian Jackie Mason was dismissed from Rudolph Giuliani's mayoral campaign in New York when he made egregiously racist jokes about Giuliani's opponent, David Dinkins. Mason made a formal apology "for my insensitivity." He added: "They say my jokes aren't funny offstage, but why doesn't a comedian have freedom of speech? Anyway, Jews should never stay silent — look what happened to them when they were." (Glenn Collins, "Mason Takes Stock after the Political Storm," *New York Times,* 5 October 1989, C21.)
29. Jewish agencies sometimes maintained that it was not affirmative action they opposed, but quotas. "We lived through a Hitler period which set up quotas," said Benjamin Epstein of the ADL. (Epstein, "Myths and Realities in Black-Jewish Relations," 23 April 1979 speech, Oscar Cohen Papers, 25:11.) But even the smallest gestures to tilt hiring toward excluded minorities came under Jewish fire. When, in 1971, the New York City Department of Health announced job openings, and said "we are particularly anxious to get qualified Black or Puerto Rican staff," the American Jewish Congress went on the attack, and the notice was withdrawn. (*American Jewish Yearbook* 73 [1972]: 112.) In 1994 a banner headline in the *Forward* read, "Clinton Health Plan Means Quotas for Jewish Doctors, Critics Warn." The occasion for this was a provision in the plan that would have offered hospitals incentives to provide residency slots for members of racial minorities. (*Forward,* 18 February 1994, 1, 4.) The article quoted Irving Kristol as saying that he "regard[ed] it as certain that the authorities would see that no Jewish male would be able to enter a medical specialty for two generations."
30. Forster and Epstein, *New Anti-Semitism,* 5, 324.
31. The term derives from a rabbinic maxim, whose canonical form comes from the writings of Maimonides, in the twelfth century: "Righteous gentiles have a place in the world to come." Maimonides endorsed the traditional view that all Jews, except those guilty of the most grievous sins, had a place in the world to come; only a tiny minority of gentiles might qualify. All of this was natural enough during the centuries when mutual disdain and hostility marked virtually all relations between Jews and Christians — when each viewed the other with wary suspicion. With the Enlightenment, and Jewish emancipation, the doctrine became ana-

thema to those, like Moses Mendelssohn, who looked forward to cordial interactions between Jews and gentiles, and whose notion of those with "a place in the world to come" included all who behaved decently. Except among the ultra-Orthodox, the traditional, highly restrictive definition of "Righteous Gentile" became an embarrassment. (See Eugene Korn, "Gentiles, the World to Come, and Judaism: The Odyssey of a Rabbinic Text," *Modern Judaism* 14 [1994]: 271.)

32. For an elaboration of this point, see Berel Lang, "For and Against the 'Righteous Gentiles,' " *Judaism* 46 (Winter 1997).

33. Moshe Bejski, "Righteous among the Nations," *Encyclopedia of the Holocaust* (New York, 1990), 3:1280–81.

34. Ibid., 1279.

35. Mordechai Paldiel, "Righteous Gentiles Vindicated Humanity," *Jerusalem Post*, 31 July 1990.

36. Abraham Foxman, letter to *New York Times Book Review*, 31 July 1994, 31, apropos Eva Fogelman's *Conscience and Courage*.

37. Andrea Herzberg, "Regional News" (reporting Meed's remarks at Yom Hashoah commemoration), UPI dispatch, 29 April 1984, AM cycle.

38. Lawrence Baron, "Restoring Faith in Humankind," *Sh'ma* 14:276 (7 September 1984): 126–27.

39. See, e.g., Diana Jean Schemo, "Good Germans: Honoring the Heroes, Hiding the Holocaust," *New York Times*, 12 June 1994, 4:1; Marvin Hier, "Lessons of the Holocaust," *USA Today Magazine*, September 1995; Judith E. Doneson, "The Image Lingers," in Yosefa Loshitzky, ed., *Spielberg's Holocaust* (Bloomington, Ind., 1997), 140.

40. Howard I. Friedman to Bertram H. Gold, 16 May 1979, AJCommittee Files, Holocaust/BGX, 1979.

41. Vanessa L. Ochs, "Not in My Backyard," *Tikkun* 8 (July-August 1993): 55.

42. Aviva Cantor, *Jewish Women/Jewish Men* (San Francisco, 1995): 390.

43. Leslie Brody, introduction to Brody, ed., *Daughters of Kings: Growing Up as a Jewish Woman in America* (Boston, 1997), 17. Cf. Rabbi Arthur Hertzberg, who writes of "the question I ask myself in my darkest thoughts about each of those friends who are not Jews: Who among them would risk his life . . . to hide my grandchildren." ("A Lifelong Quarrel with God," *New York Times Book Review*, 6 May 1990, 40.)

44. Samuel Heilman, *Jewish Unity and Diversity: A Survey of American Rabbis and Rabbinical Students* (New York, 1991), 37.

45. Nathan Perlmutter interview with Oscar Cohen, 2 November 1979, Oscar Cohen Papers, 21:1, 25–26, 23. Earlier, Perlmutter had written that while his "cerebral self" recognized that blacks were "underdogs," his "visceral self" saw them as "overdogs." (Perlmutter, *A Bias of Reflections* [New Rochelle, N.Y., 1972], 93.)

46. For a case study, see Charles S. Liebman, "Leadership and Decision-making in a Jewish Federation: The New York Federation of Jewish Philanthropies," *American Jewish Yearbook* 79 (1979).

47. See the tabulation of resolutions of the UAHC's Social Action Commission before and after 1970 in Simeon J. Maslin, "The Language of Survival: Social Action," *CCAR Journal* 24 (Summer 1977).

48. Ibid., 32.

49. Abraham Foxman reports that when he first went to work for the ADL in the mid-sixties it "was not a Jewish organization"; rather, it was "an organization that sometimes worked for Jews. . . . I had to negotiate to go home early on Friday. . . .

Today, we're much more Jewish. We have people with yarmulkes here." (Quoted in William B. Helmreich, *Against All Odds: Holocaust Survivors and the Successful Lives They Made in America* [New York, 1992], 206.)

50. This is the version (variously translated, but always with reference to Jews) in standard editions of the Mishna and of the Babylonian Talmud. The words "of Israel" are omitted in the Jerusalem Talmud, but, for the observant, it is the text of the Babylonian Talmud that is definitive, and that is taught and studied. (See Maslin, "Language of Survival," 35; *The Mishnah,* trans. Herbert Danby [London, 1933], 388; Jacob Shachter, *Hebrew-English Edition of the Babylonian Talmud: Sanhedrin* [London, 1969], 37a; Jacob Neusner, *The Talmud of Babylonia: An American Translation* [Chico, Cal., 1984], XXIIIB, Bavli Sanhedrin, chap. 4, 37a.) For the version in the Jerusalem Talmud, see Jacob Neusner, *The Talmud of the Land of Israel,* vol. 31: *Sanhedrin and Makkot* (Chicago, 1984), 146. So far as I know, the only critic of *Schindler's List* to note the discrepancy was Philip Gourevitch, but his remark on it was so elliptical — he referred, without elaboration, to the text's being "slightly mangled" — that it amounted to an inside joke. ("A Dissent on 'Schindler's List,' " *Commentary* 97 [February 1994]: 51.)

51. Remarks in "10th American-Israeli Dialogue," *Congress Bi-Weekly* 40 (13 April 1973): 19.

52. Lucy Dawidowicz, "State of World Jewry," 2 December 1984 lecture at 92nd Street YM-YWHA, quoted in Charles E. Silberman, *A Certain People* (New York, 1985), 346.

53. Nathan Perlmutter in Oscar Cohen and Stanley Wexler, eds., *"Not the Work of a Day": Anti-Defamation League of B'nai B'rith Oral Memoirs* (New York, 1987), 1:84–85.

54. *Commentary* took such a hard right-wing line that the American Jewish Committee, for a time, tried to balance it with a more liberal journal, *Present Tense.* But when the Committee's budget got tight, *Present Tense* was dropped. The leading Jewish weekly, the *Forward,* also shifted sharply to the right, its new editor having moved over from the *Wall Street Journal.* The same rightward turn could be seen in magazines that were de facto, though not de jure, Jewish, like *The Public Interest* and *Partisan Review.*

55. It's hard to say how "Jewish" Jewish voters' continuing tilt toward the Democratic Party was. Conservatives were surely right when they disputed the claim of liberals that they represented authentic Jewish tradition. If that were so, it ought to have been the most traditional Jews who were the most liberal, which was clearly not the case. Several hypotheses are plausible. Among the best predictors of conservative voting is general "religiosity." Overall, Jews are, by any measure, much less religious than Protestants and Catholics — and this, of course, was of greater importance as conservatism was more and more defined in terms of "lifestyle" issues. Another excellent predictor of voting is how one's parents voted: here, the earlier Jewish tilt toward the Democratic Party undoubtedly played a role. And despite the efforts of Jewish neo-conservatives to convince Jews that Christian fundamentalists were really their allies, the increasingly prominent presence of the Christian right in the Republican Party almost certainly gave many Jews bad vibes.

56. Charles S. Liebman and Steven M. Cohen, "Jewish Liberalism Revisited," *Commentary* 102 (November 1976): 51–53.

57. Saul Bellow, *Mr. Sammler's Planet* (New York, 1970), 231.

58. Michael Lerner, *The Socialism of Fools* (Oakland, Cal., 1992), 20; Cantor, *Jewish Women/Jewish Men,* 377. Jewish leftists, along with many others, repeatedly invoked the Holocaust in anti–Vietnam War protests.

59. Weiss, to be sure, is no leftist, but his is very much a "sixties style." For a fascinating and insightful account of the playing out of the confrontational style around a Holocaust issue, see David Biale and Fred Rosenbaum, "The Pope Comes to San Francisco: An Anatomy of Jewish Communal Response to a Political Crisis," in Seymour Martin Lipset, ed., *American Pluralism and the Jewish Community* (New Brunswick, N.J., 1990).

60. Insert in *Tikkun* 4 (March-April 1989). I don't pretend to be an expert in this realm, but the popular notion that the repeated venting of rage frees one from it seems to me naïve. I find much more persuasive the view, supported by a good deal of research, that instead, repeatedly talking about one's anger rehearses it. (See Carol Tavris, *Anger: The Misunderstood Emotion*, rev. ed. [New York, 1989], and the research cited there.) For another example of the ideology of "letting it all hang out," see Cherie Brown, "Beyond Internalized Anti-Semitism: Healing the Collective Scars of the Past," *Tikkun* 10 (March-April 1995): 46, where she proposes establishing "ongoing support groups for Jews in which they can acknowledge . . . the fear and pain from the past. Participants would be helped to release the grief from the stories about the Holocaust they'd listened to."

61. Richard M. Joel, quoted in Victor Volland, "Jewish Students Finding Solace," *St. Louis Post-Dispatch*, 1 April 1996, 1B.

62. See, e.g., David Gibson, "For Non-Orthodox, an Uphill Battle," *Bergen* (N.J.) *Record*, 15 December 1995; David R. Mark, "On TV, Even Jewish Characters Don't Recognize Jewish Holidays," *Asbury Park* (N.J.) *Press*, 30 December 1996; Sheldon Engelmayer, "A Spiritual Holocaust," *Washington Jewish Week*, 13 June 1991, 20.

63. Norman Lamm, "Schools and Graves," in Ivan L. Tillem, ed., *The 1987–88 Jewish Almanac* (New York, 1987), 111.

64. Thomas B. Morgan, "The Vanishing American Jew," *Look* 28 (5 May 1964): 43ff. For the early stages of "survival anxiety" among American Jews, see Samuel C. Heilman, *Portrait of American Jews* (Seattle, 1995); Edward S. Shapiro, *A Time for Healing* (Baltimore, 1992). For a brief overview, see Steven M. Cohen and Leonard J. Fein, "From Integration to Survival: American Jewish Anxieties in Transition," *Annals* 480 (July 1985). Rabbi Arthur Hertzberg said at this time that "an unillusioned look" at the evidence indicated that American Jewry would not survive. ("The Present Casts a Dark Shadow," *Jewish Heritage* 6 [Winter 1963–64], reprinted in his *Being Jewish in America* [New York, 1979], 82.)

65. Heilman, *Portrait*, 59.

66. Council of Jewish Federations, *Highlights of the CJF 1990 National Jewish Population Survey* (New York, 1991), 14, 16.

67. The third-generation phenomenon was suggested by historian Marcus Lee Hansen in a 1937 essay, "The Problem of the Third Generation Immigrant," reprinted in *Commentary* 14 (November 1952). (For critical commentary, see Peter Kivisto and Dag Blanck, eds., *American Immigrants and Their Generations: Studies and Commentaries on the Hansen Thesis after Fifty Years* [Urbana, Ill., 1990]). *The Rise of the Unmeltable Ethnics* is the title of a 1972 book by Michael Novak. Some years earlier, Nathan Glazer and Daniel Patrick Moynihan confidently asserted that "the point about the melting pot is that it did not happen." (*Beyond the Melting Pot* [Cambridge, Mass., 1963], v.) Nowadays, it would be hard to find an historian who takes any of this seriously.

68. Probably the best overall survey is Richard D. Alba, *Ethnic Identity: The Transformation of White America* (New Haven, 1990).

69. The notion of symbolic ethnicity was developed by Herbert J. Gans, in his "Sym-

bolic Ethnicity: The Future of Ethnic Groups and Cultures in America," in Gans et al, eds., *On the Making of Americans* (Philadelphia, 1979).

70. Address at the National Biennial Convention, 27 April–1 May 1966, AJCongress Papers, Box 16, Convention Speeches.

71. Gold quoted in Linda Charlton, "Jews Fear Anti-Zionism of New Left," *New York Times*, 14 August 1970.

72. Irving Spiegel, "Reform Leaders Concerned over the Lack of Awareness by American Jewish Youth of the Nazi Holocaust," *New York Times*, 8 November 1971.

73. David S. Landes, "How to Make the Children Understand," *Congress Bi-Weekly* 39 (10 March 1972): 54.

74. North American Jewish Students' Network, "Report on the Albuquerque Conference," February 1972, Boston JCC Papers, Box 108, Holocaust General Files, 1972.

75. Report of discussion in *Workshop Reports: Papers from the Plenary Session, June 28–July 2, 1972*, 8, NCRAC Papers, Box 12, Plenary Sessions, 1972.

76. Ellen K. Coughlin, "On University Campuses, Interest in the Holocaust Started Long Ago," *Chronicle of Higher Education*, 1 May 1978. Others have presented lower estimates, but all agree that the number of such courses increased greatly during the 1970s, and increased even more thereafter.

77. Samuel Belzberg, quoted in James E. Young, *The Texture of Memory* (New Haven, 1993), 306. While American Jews have donated hundreds of millions of dollars to institutions devoted to detailing the death of Jews in Europe, institutions like YIVO, which have studied and celebrated Jewish life in Europe, have led a hand-to-mouth existence.

78. Greenberg quoted in Paula E. Hyman, "New Debate on the Holocaust," *New York Times Magazine*, 14 September 1980, 109.

79. Benedict Anderson, *Imagined Communities* (London, 1983; rev. ed., 1991).

80. Jonathan S. Woocher, *Sacred Survival: The Civil Religion of American Jews* (Bloomington, Ind., 1986), 111.

81. Blacks — or rather, some blacks — had been in the vanguard of the new particularism. More than members of any other group, they were often disillusioned (usually for good reasons) with the promise of equality through integration. It was among blacks, albeit only a minority of blacks, that an ideology of withdrawal and separation from the larger society was most fully articulated. Afros and dashikis paved the way for yarmulkes on campuses and on city streets. Insistence on the distinctiveness of black culture and the black experience — and the institutionalization of this insistence in black studies programs — set the precedent for similar institutionalized claims on the part of women, Spanish-speakers, Jews, and others.

82. Examples could be multiplied. In Hollywood, the story of American westward expansion came to focus less on the heroism of the Seventh Cavalry and more on their victims (*Little Big Man, Dances with Wolves*).

83. Appelfeld quoted in Charles S. Liebman and Steven M. Cohen, *Two Worlds of Judaism* (New Haven, 1990), 31.

84. *Every Day Remembrance Day: A Chronicle of Jewish Martyrdom* (New York, 1986). Thus I can celebrate my birthday (and my Jewish identity) by learning that on that date in 1298 nineteen Jews were killed in Krautheim, Germany; in 1648 Chmielnicki's men massacred 600 Jews in Ostrog, Ukraine; in 1941 the SS killed 250 in Brianska Gora, Belorussian SSR.

85. Willis quoted in Liebman and Cohen, *Two Worlds of Judaism*, 46.

86. Epstein, "American Jewry in the Mid-1970s," 7.

87. Jeffrey C. Alexander and Chaim Seidler-Feller, "False Distinctions and Double

Standards: The Anatomy of Antisemitism at UCLA," *Tikkun* 7 (January-February 1992): 14. Cf. "Jewish Students Are Under Siege," *Forward*, 31 January 1992.

88. "Farrakhan's Jewish Problem," *Tikkun* 9 (March–April 1994): 10.

89. Clara Spotted Elk, "Skeletons in the Attic," *New York Times*, 8 March 1989, A31.

90. Steven T. Katz, "The Pequot War Reconsidered," *New England Quarterly* 64 (June 1991): 223.

91. David E. Stannard, *American Holocaust: The Conquest of the New World* (New York, 1992), 318.

92. Pierre Papazian, "A 'Unique Uniqueness'?" and "Was the Holocaust Unique? Responses to Pierre Papazian," *Midstream* 30 (April 1984), 20, et passim.

93. Edward T. Linenthal, *Preserving Memory: The Struggle to Create America's Holocaust Museum* (New York, 1995), 228–40. In this case, and in the incidents recounted later in this paragraph, there were sometimes hints that Turkish Jews would suffer if Jews, in either Israel or the Diaspora, cooperated with Armenians in memorializing the 1915 genocide. This may have had some influence, but most did not take the suggestion seriously, and, throughout, Israeli diplomatic concerns seem to have been paramount. (See Brant Coopersmith to Abe Karlikow, 25 April 1979, AJCommittee Files, Holocaust Commission, 1979; Abraham S. Karlikow to Bertram H. Gold and Marc Tannenbaum, 9 September 1981 [and attached correspondence], AJCommittee Files, "Foreign Countries, A–Z, BGX, 1981; George E. Gruen, file memorandum, "Off-the-record Meeting with Turkish Officials on April 2, 1982," AJCommittee Files Turkey, FAD, 1982, Meeting with Turkish Government Officials; Nives Fox to Foreign Affairs Department, 6 July 1982, AJCommittee Files, Foreign Countries, A–Z, BGX, 1982.)

94. The fullest account is Israel W. Charny, "The Conference Crisis: The Turks, Armenians and the Jews," in *International Conference on the Holocaust and Genocide, Tel Aviv, June 20–24, 1982, Book One: The Conference Program and Crisis* (Tel Aviv, 1983).

95. Wolf Blitzer, "Turkey Seeks Help of Israel and U.S. Jews to Fight U.S. Senate Resolution Marking Armenian Genocide," *Jerusalem Post*, 24 October 1989. See also Jon Greene, "Armenian Genocide Bill Creates Conflict for Jews," *Washington Jewish Week*, 26 October 1989 6, 40; Hugh Orgel and Gil Sedan, "Israelis Said to Spur Lobbying Against Armenian Memorial," (Boston) *Jewish Advocate*, 26 October 1989.

96. Mark Epstein (former head of the Union of Councils for Soviet Jews), letter to *Washington Jewish Week*, 7 December 1989, 13. In a debate on an earlier version of the resolution, Stephen Solarz, a prominent Jewish congressman and member of the council overseeing construction of the Washington Holocaust museum, said that his opposition to a resolution denouncing the genocide of Armenians was based on considerations of "linguistic accuracy": "mass killings . . . have gone on since the beginning of time"; the Turks weren't trying to kill *all* Armenians. (*Cong. Rec.*, 99th Cong., 2d sess., 1985, 131, pt. 29:36155.) Turkish spokesmen repeatedly voiced great solicitude about keeping the memory of the Holocaust "unique." The Turkish ambassador to Washington insisted that calling the "events of 1915" genocide "dilutes the moral force that recollection of the Holocaust should generate for us all." (Letter to *Washington Post*, 26 April 1983, A18.) The Turkish chargé d'affaires in Tel Aviv said that "the Holocaust stands as a unique tragedy of the Jewish people, with no other parallel in the history of mankind." (Ekrem Guvendiren, "The Events of 1915," *Jerusalem Post*, 31 January 1989.)

97. The Union of American Hebrew Congregations went on record in support of the resolution. *Washington Jewish Week* commented on Jewish lobbying efforts

against the resolution in an editorial entitled "Shameful" (2 November 1989, 12.) See also Gershom Greenberg, "Israel Demeans Itself in an Affront to Armenians," *Los Angeles Times*, 30 October 1989.

98. Penelope McMillan and Cathleen Decker, "Israel a 'Wicked Hypocrisy' — Farrakhan," *Los Angeles Times*, 15 September 1985.

99. Suzanne Fields, "To the Defenders of Free Speech," *Washington Times*, 2 May 1994.

100. It is pedantry run amok to critically examine a novelist's sources, but for the record, Morrison says that she consulted historians about the figure. In one interview she says, "Some historians told me 200 million died. The smallest number I got from anybody was 60 million." (Bonnie Angelo, "The Pain of Being Black," *Time* 133 [22 May 1989]: 120.) She told another interviewer that "some people told me 40 million, but I also heard 60 million, and I didn't want to leave anybody out." (Elizabeth Kastor, "Toni Morrison's 'Beloved' Country," *Washington Post*, 5 October 1987, B1.) The most recent scholarly estimates with which I am familiar are that about twelve million African slaves were shipped to the Western Hemisphere, of whom perhaps two million died during the Middle Passage. Nobody has any idea how many enslaved Africans died before undertaking the voyage, but forty to sixty million is off the wall. (See Hugh Thomas, *The Slave Trade* [New York, 1997], 861–62; Paul E. Lovejoy, *Transformations in Slavery* [Cambridge, Eng., 1983], 61.) The black critic Stanley Crouch — unfairly, in my view — describes *Beloved* as a "blackface holocaust novel [that] seems to have been written in order to enter American slavery into the big-time martyr ratings contest, a contest usually won by references to, and works about, the experience of Jews at the hands of Nazis." ("Beloved," *New Republic* 197 [19 October 1987]: 40.)

101. The exception that tests the rule is Jesse Jackson's 1979 remark — made privately, but then leaked to the press — that he was "sick and tired of hearing about the Holocaust. . . . The Jews do not have a monopoly on suffering." (Rick Atkinson, "Peace with American Jews Eludes Jackson," *Washington Post*, 13 February 1984, A1.) Jackson at first denied, then later apologized for, making the remark.

102. James Baldwin, "Negroes Are Anti-Semitic Because They're Anti-White," *New York Times Magazine*, 9 April 1967, 135, 136, 137.

103. For the fate of these proposals, see Faith Davis Ruffins, "Culture Wars Won and Lost, Part II: The National African-American Museum Project," *Radical History Review* 70 (Winter 1998). The only black historical project that has received significant public funds is in 80 percent–black Detroit, where the city government supported the Museum of African-American History.

104. The Jewish historian David Biale noted this with chagrin. See his "The Melting Pot and Beyond," in Biale et al., eds., *Insider/Outsider: American Jews and Multiculturalism* (Berkeley, 1998), 28. Melvin Bukiet, an editor of *Tikkun* and the son of a Holocaust survivor, noted it with satisfaction. He describes the Washington Holocaust Museum as "a statement of raw power, and that's the only thing I like about it. . . . It's not Jewish tragedy that's remembered on the Mall . . . ; it's Jewish power to which homage is paid." (Bukiet, "The Museum vs. Memory: The Taming of the Holocaust," *Washington Post*, 18 April 1993, C3.) Cf. Matthew 25:29.

105. Wiesel quoted in Hyman, "New Debate," 82.

106. Bukiet, "Museum vs. Memory"; Edward Alexander, "Stealing the Holocaust," *Midstream* 26 (November 1980): 48. Cf. Deborah Lipstadt, "Invoking the Holocaust," *Judaism* 30 (1981): 341. Of course, there was neither barbed wire nor guard towers in the medieval Italian cities from which the term derives. The word "ghetto" has been used since the late nineteenth century to describe black slums.

107. Deborah Lipstadt says that denial of the uniqueness of the Holocaust is "far more

insidious than outright denial. It nurtures and is nurtured by Holocaust-denial."
(Lipstadt, "Holocaust-Denial and the Compelling Force of Reason," *Patterns of
Prejudice* 26:1/2 [1992]: 72–73.) In the first sentence of the article on "Holocaust
Denial" in the *Encyclopedia of the Holocaust* (3:681–2), Israel Gutman includes un-
der that designation "tendentious and trivializing claims that the Holocaust was
not unique and that there had been precedents."

108. For surveys of grounds on which the Holocaust is said to be unique, see Alan
Rosenberg and Evelyn Silverman, "The Issue of the Holocaust as a Unique Event,"
in Michael N. Dobkowski and Isidor Wallimann, eds., *Genocide in Our Time* (Ann
Arbor, 1992); Alan S. Rosenbaum, ed., *Is the Holocaust Unique?* (Boulder, Colo.,
1996); and the early chapters of Steven T. Katz, *The Holocaust in Historical Context,* vol. 1.

109. Judith Weinraub, "The Philosopher's Dilemma: New Holocaust Museum Chief
Faces Hard Choices," *Washington Post,* 4 January 1995, B1. In the event, Katz re-
signed before taking office as a result of revelations that he had been censured at
Cornell University for various academic improprieties. (Judith Weinraub, "New
Holocaust Museum Chief Was Censured," *Washington Post,* 23 February 1995, C1;
Judith Weinraub, "Holocaust Museum Chief Forced Out Before Starting," *Wash-
ington Post,* 4 March 1995, A1.)

110. Katz, *Holocaust in Historical Context,* 28.

111. See reviews by Mark Levene (*Patterns of Prejudice* 29:2/3 [1995]) and David Biale
(*Tikkun* 10 [January 1995]).

112. Katz, *Holocaust in Historical Context,* 13–14.

113. This interpretation is buttressed by another acknowledgment by Katz, buried in a
footnote: "I recognize that different scholars, like different groups, have different
agendas. . . . Thus, Armenian scholars and Gypsy scholars . . . come to the Sho'ah
seeking to analogize, to compare. . . . This approach might be called . . . a paradigm of similarity; mine, in contrast, is a paradigm of distinctiveness. The incom-
mensurability between the two approaches is not settled simply by an appeal to
empirical evidence." (Ibid., 47 n96.)

114. Berel Lang, review of *The Holocaust in Historical Context, History and Theory* 35
(1996): 378, 383.

115. Hilberg quoted in Linenthal, *Preserving Memory,* 11; Berenbaum quoted in
Jonathan Tilove, "African-American Museum Debated in D.C.," *Cleveland Plain
Dealer,* 26 June 1994, 9A.

116. Howard Singer, "Forget the Holocaust?" *New York Times,* 6 April 1981, A15.

117. A certain selective prosecution can be observed: nothing could be more over the
top than Steven Katz's assertion that the declining Jewish birth rate is a "silent,
self-inflicted Holocaust," but to the best of my knowledge, the Anti-Defamation
League and the Simon Wiesenthal Center didn't land on him like a ton of bricks
for this speech crime. (Gillmon, "Jewish Community Faces Challenge," *San Diego
Union-Tribune,* 2 December 1989, B10.)

118. Ismar Schorsch, "The Holocaust and Jewish Survival," *Midstream* 27 (January
1981): 39.

119. Jacob Neusner, *The Public Side of Learning* (Chico, Cal., 1985), 128.

120. Arthur Hertzberg, "How Jews Use Antisemitism," in Jerome A. Chanes, ed., *Anti-
semitism in America Today* (New York, 1995), 341–42.

121. Of course, fierce insistence on the uniqueness of an event need not be religiously
grounded, unless we define "religion" more broadly. Thus when, some years ago,
a few historians began to treat the French Revolution as part of an "Atlantic Revolution" of the eighteenth century, or as a key event in "the Age of the Democratic

Revolutions," there were outraged protests from the French about the insidious "universalizers" who were "stealing" or "trivializing" their *unique* revolution, the only *real* revolution — the event that, for many secular Frenchmen, constituted their "civil religion," defined their identity. (See Robert R. Palmer, *"The Age of the Democratic Revolution,"* in L. P. Curtis, Jr., ed., *The Historian's Workshop* [New York, 1970].) But there seems to me to be a strong correlation between a religious framing of the Holocaust and the strength of insistence on its uniqueness. The dedicated secularist Yehuda Bauer also claims that the Holocaust is unique, but his arguments on this point are much more nuanced and qualified than the arguments of those who, like those just mentioned, or like Steven Katz, are observant Jews. Thus Bauer has recently written that "never before . . . has a well-organized state, representing a social consensus, tried to murder, globally, every single member of an ethnic or ethno-religious group . . . for purely ideological reasons that bore not the slightest relation to reality." (Bauer, "A Past That Will Not Go Away," in Michael Berenbaum and Abraham J. Peck, eds., *The Holocaust and History* [Bloomington, Ind., 1998], 16.)

122. Abraham Foxman, *"Schindler's List* — The Meaning of Spielberg's Film," *Front-line* (ADL newsletter) 4 (January 1994): 2.

123. Emil Fackenheim in symposium, "Jewish Values in the Post-Holocaust Future," *Judaism* 16 (Summer 1967): 272–73. Fackenheim was at this time a Canadian citizen (he has since immigrated to Israel), but his principal audience was American.

124. See Greenberg's "Clouds of Smoke, Pillar of Fire," in Eva Fleischner, ed., *Auschwitz: Beginning of a New Era?* (New York, 1977); and *The Jewish Way* (New York, 1988), chap. 10.

125. Greenberg quoted in Kenneth L. Woodward, "Debate over the Holocaust," *Newsweek* 95 (10 March 1980): 97; Greenberg, *Jewish Way,* 365.

126. Greenberg quoted in Linenthal, *Preserving Memory,* 55.

127. Michael Wyschogrod, "Faith and the Holocaust," *Judaism* 20 (1971): 294.

128. Linenthal, *Preserving Memory,* 2.

129. Wieseltier quoted in Judith Miller, *One, by One, by One: Facing the Holocaust* (New York, 1990), 231. In Wieseltier's view, the Holocaust has become, for American Jews, "virtually a cult of death."

130. Elie Wiesel, "Words from a Witness," *Conservative Judaism* 21 (Spring 1967): 43; "Art and the Holocaust: Trivializing Memory," *New York Times,* 11 June 1989, 2:1; "Holocaust Survivor Elie Wiesel Decries a Rising Tide of Anti-Semitism at Home and Abroad," *People* 18 (29 November 1982): 75.

131. Harry J. Cargas, "An Interview with Elie Wiesel," *Holocaust and Genocide Studies* 1 (1986): 5.

132. Shalmi Barmore, quoted in Amy Dockser Marcus, "Trading with the Germans," *Wall Street Journal,* 31 March 1993.

133. It remains true that for all Jews, including the marginally observant and even the quite unobservant, the Passover Seder is still the most frequently observed religious ritual, combining as it does an affirmation of familialism ("the Jewish Thanksgiving") and the recital of what traditionally has been the defining myth for Jews — the story of the Exodus.

134. I am grateful to the American Jewish Committee for making available to me the results of the study, unpublished as of this writing.

135. "Rabbi's Message," *News from the* (Detroit) *Holocaust Memorial Center* 1 (May-June 1988).

136. Esther Polen, of the Philadelphia Jewish Community Relations Council, explaining the functions of the Philadelphia Holocaust Memorial in "Workshop on

Holocaust Memorial Sites as Focal Points for Community Action and Interpretation," in National Jewish Community Relations Advisory Council, *Workshop Reports* (1978), Cincinnati JCRC Papers, 91, Memorials–1; Alvin Rogal, chairman, (Cincinnati) Holocaust Memorial Committee, explaining the functions of proposed memorial in memorandum to UJF board of directors, 22 April 1980, Cincinnati JCRC Papers, Memorials 1983–1. Other goals of the Cincinnati memorial were to "enhance and support Jewish consciousness and Jewish identity" and "expand allegiance of our young."

10. "To Bigotry No Sanction"

1. For discussions of the phenomenon, see Stephen J. Whitfield, *American Space, Jewish Time* (Armonk, N.Y., 1988), chap. 7; J. J. Goldberg, *Jewish Power* (Reading, Mass., 1996), chap. 11.
2. Blu Greenberg, "Talking to Kids about the Holocaust," in Roselyn Bell, *The Hadassah Magazine Jewish Parenting Book* (New York, 1989), 247.
3. Michael Berenbaum, "The Nativization of the Holocaust," *Judaism* 35 (1986): 457.
4. Paul Mendes-Flohr and Jehuda Reinharz, eds., *The Jew in the Modern World*, 2nd ed. (New York, 1995), 457–59.
5. There are various estimates of the viewership, ranging downward from 120 million. See Sander A. Diamond, " 'Holocaust' Film's Impact on Americans," *Patterns of Prejudice* 12 (July-August 1978): 1; Jerome Bakst to Arnold Forster (both of ADL), 27 April 1978, Oscar Cohen Papers, 8:6.
6. For a survey of these activities, see Diamond, " 'Holocaust' Impact," 4; for contemporary documentation on the efforts of various Jewish organizations on behalf of the series, see AJCommittee Files, Holocaust/January-April/BGX, 1978 and May-December/BGX, 1978; Oscar Cohen Papers, 8:6.
7. "Watching Holocaust," *Moment* 3 (April 1978): 34.
8. Barbara Stern Burstin, "The 'Holocaust' Reverberates in Pittsburgh," *International Journal of Political Education* 4 (1981): 22.
9. National Jewish Interagency Project, *"Holocaust" Study Guide* (New York, 1978), booklet two, p. 3; booklet four, p. 2; booklet five, p. 7. All of the major Jewish agencies, except for the ADL, which ran a separate operation, participated in this project. (Copies in AJCommittee Papers, Washington Subject Files, Box 6, 1964–86, Holocaust.)
10. There was, e.g., the scene at Auschwitz in which Eichmann, dining with colleagues, sniffs the air and remarks disgustedly that the stench of the chimneys is keeping him from enjoying his meal. "We cut then to a Lysol commercial in which a woman character named 'Snoopy Sniffer' arrives at a housewife's kitchen and informs her that she has house odors. From her ovens?" (Diamond, " 'Holocaust' Impact," 5.)
11. Marc Tannenbaum quoted in Tom Shales, "NBC's Powerful 'Holocaust,' " *Washington Post*, 12 April 1978, B2.
12. Elie Wiesel, "Trivializing the Holocaust," *New York Times*, 16 April 1978, 2:1.
13. Raul Hilberg, "I Was Not There," in Berel Lang, ed., *Writing and the Holocaust* (New York, 1988), 17. That the experiences of Holocaust victims is uniquely unrepresentable carries with it a corollary, doubtless often unintended by those who make the claim: whereas the terror and horror of a Tutsi mother seeing her child hacked to pieces with machetes is representable, that of a Jewish mother in analogous circumstances is not.
14. Molly Haskell, "A Failure to Connect," *New York* 11 (15 May 1978): 79.

15. Peter Sourian, "Television," *Nation* 226 (24 June 1978): 773.
16. All quotations in this paragraph are from Jeffrey Herf, "The 'Holocaust' Reception in West Germany," in Anson Rabinbach and Jack Zipes, eds., *Germans and Jews Since the Holocaust: The Changing Situation in West Germany* (New York, 1986), 214.
17. Scriptwriter Gerald Green later said that he wanted his contribution to the continuing prosecution of war criminals engraved on his tombstone. "That's not a bad accomplishment," he said. (Steve Weinstein, " 'Holocaust': Keeping the Truth Alive," *Los Angeles Times,* 8 April 1994, F14.)
18. Heinz Höhne in *Der Spiegel,* quoted in Herf, " 'Holocaust' Reception," 217.
19. For a comprehensive and insightful account of the Holocaust on American television, see Jeffrey Shandler, *While America Watches: Televising the Holocaust* (New York, 1999).
20. Winfrey quoted in Yosefa Loshitzky, introduction to Loshitzky, ed., *Spielberg's Holocaust: Critical Perspectives on* Schindler's List (Bloomington, Ind., 1997), 15.
21. Philip Gourevitch in *Commentary* 97 (February 1994); Jason Epstein in the *New York Review of Books* 41 (21 April 1994).
22. Jim Hoberman, quoted in Peter Rainer, "Why the 'Schindler's List' Backlash?" *Los Angeles Times,* 30 January 1994, 21.
23. The first postwar estimates of the Jewish death toll — hardly more than educated guesses, based on very incomplete information — were that it was something under six million, usually rounded to six. This has remained the most-cited figure, and it is endorsed by most historians. (See "Estimated Jewish Losses in the Holocaust," app. 6 of the *Encyclopedia of the Holocaust.*) The principal dissenter is Raul Hilberg, whose calculations lead him to conclude that the correct figure is approximately 5,100,000. (*The Destruction of the European Jews,* rev. ed. [New York, 1985], vol. 3, app. B: "Statistics of Jewish Dead.") The problems of estimation are daunting, and we are unlikely ever to know for sure. While of course one wants to get it right, no important historical, let alone moral, questions depend on whether the toll was five, or six, or more.
24. Yehuda Bauer, "Don't Resist: A Critique of Phillip Lopate," *Tikkun* 4 (May-June 1989): 67.
25. Michael Getler, "The Hunter's Remembrance," *Washington Post,* 1 April 1979, H1.
26. Michael Berenbaum — quite unfairly, in my view — speculates that Wiesenthal's insistence on always speaking of non-Jewish as well as Jewish victims may reflect "his present status as a European Jew: he belongs to a demoralized community that may be psychologically incapable of taking a Judeo-centric perspective in the public domain, preferring instead the aphorism of Judah Leib Gordon to 'be a Jew in your own home and a man in the street.' " Wiesenthal's postwar career hardly suggests someone fleeing public Jewish identification. (Berenbaum, *After Tragedy and Triumph* [Cambridge, Eng., 1990], 18–19.)
27. For the establishment of the Wiesenthal Center, see Gary Rosenblatt, "The Simon Wiesenthal Center," *Baltimore Jewish Times,* 14 September 1984; Sheldon Teitelbaum and Tom Waldman, "The Unorthodox Rabbi," *Los Angeles Times,* 15 July 1990; Judith Miller, *One, by One, by One: Facing the Holocaust* (New York, 1990).
28. In a 1980 speech to an organization of children of survivors, Wiesenthal said that he had lent his name only on the condition "that this center will be for the memory of the Eleven Million, among them six million Jews." ("Simon Wiesenthal Speaks," *The Generation After* 1 [Summer 1980]: 2.)
29. Rosenblatt, "Wiesenthal Center," 66; Wiesenthal Center fund-raising letter, cited in Seymour Bolton to Ed Sanders, 28 November 1979, Carter Papers, Special

Adviser to the President—Moses, Box 7, Holocaust Memorial Council, 11/2/79–9/2/80.

30. *Public Papers of the Presidents of the United States: Jimmy Carter, 1978* (Washington, D.C., 1979), 813.

31. For the political background to the venture, see Edward T. Linenthal, *Preserving Memory: The Struggle to Create America's Holocaust Museum* (New York, 1995). In what follows, I have relied heavily on Linenthal's extraordinarily detailed and insightful book. The previous year, 1977, one White House staffer had urged that Carter might visit a Holocaust center in Brooklyn in order to "begin to heal the rift between himself and the Jewish population," and there began to be preliminary explorations by Jewish members of the White House staff of some administration initiatives with respect to Holocaust commemoration. (Linenthal, *Preserving Memory,* 18.) As the crisis deepened in early 1978, Carter's Jewish affairs adviser resigned because he could no longer defend the president's Middle Eastern policy before Jewish audiences.

32. J. J. Goldberg agrees with most other accounts in reporting that "Jewish money" comprises about half the funding of the Democratic National Committee and of Democratic presidential campaign funds. (*Jewish Power* [Reading, Mass., 1996], 276.)

33. Thus Stuart Eizenstadt, head of the White House domestic policy staff, and the leading promoter of the memorial initiative in the administration, was on the board of directors of Rabbi Irving Greenberg's National Jewish Conference Center, the organization that, more than any other, pressed such activities. The staff memoranda about the project, deposited in the Carter Library, suggest that Eizenstadt was far from the only one whose concern with the initiative was more than political.

34. Memorandum by Bert Carp (Eizenstadt's deputy), 26 April 1978; reply attached, of uncertain authorship, Carter Papers, Domestic Policy Staff, Box 216, Holocaust Commission (O/A 6242:1).

35. Ellen Goldstein to Stuart Eizenstadt, 2 May 1978, Carter Papers, Staff Offices, ibid.

36. *Cong. Rec.,* 95th Cong., 2nd sess., 27 April 1978, 124, pt. 9:11799–11800.

37. If there was any pattern to the choice, it was too subtle for me to detect.

38. Quoted in Linenthal, *Preserving Memory,* 40–41.

39. Aloysius Mazewski to Irving Greenberg (director of the commission), 12 April 1979, Carter Papers, FG 316, 1977–79, Box FG-225.

40. B. A. Michalski to President Carter, 20 April 1979, ibid.

41. The "Days of Remembrance" were proposed by Senator John Danforth, independent of Carter's commission. In urging Carter to sign a proclamation for the "Days of Remembrance," Eizenstadt noted "the Resolution's importance to its sponsor, Senator Danforth, and his undecided position on the gas bill." (Eizenstadt to the President, 15 September 1978, Carter Papers, FG 316, 1977–79, Box FG-225.

42. President's Commission on the Holocaust, *Report to the President* (Washington, D.C., 1979), app. C and D, 26, 28.

43. Ibid., 3, 10, iii. Michael Berenbaum was deputy director of the commission and the principal author of the report. Shortly after his departure from that position, he wrote that not only were Poles, Gypsies, Ukrainians, and other European ethnics not "victims of the Holocaust," but that (for reasons he failed to specify) he wasn't even sure that they deserved to be called "victims of Nazism." (Berenbaum, "On the Politics of Public Commemoration of the Holocaust," *Shoah* 2 [Fall-Winter 1981–82]: 8, 9.)

44. Seymour Bolton, quoted in Linenthal, *Preserving Memory*, 43.
45. Eizenstadt to Carter, 25 October 1979, quoted in ibid., 41.
46. Seymour Bolton to Ed Sanders, 28 November 1979, Carter Papers, Special Adviser to the President — Moses, Box 7, Holocaust Memorial Council, 11/2/79–9/2/80.
47. David Rubenstein to the President, 21 March 1980, Carter Papers, FG 352, 1977–81, WHCF, FG-231. Freedman warned that he and Wiesel would regard failure to accept the change as "a betrayal of a fundamental nature." (Freedman quoted in Linenthal, *Preserving Memory*, 50.)
48. Eizenstadt's views as paraphrased in the Rubenstein memo. Rubenstein recommended to the president that if he wanted to stick with the original wording, the executive order should be postponed until after the New York presidential primary — in which, as it turned out, Jewish voters chose Edward Kennedy over Carter by a margin of four to one. (Linenthal, *Preserving Memory*, 48.)
49. Strochlitz speech inserted by Rep. Christopher J. Dodd in *Cong. Rec.*, 96th Cong., 2nd sess., 2 July 1980, 126, pt. 14:18630.
50. Sultanik (vice president of the World Jewish Congress) quoted in Linenthal, *Preserving Memory*, 81.
51. Henryk Grynberg, "Appropriating the Holocaust," *Commentary* 74 (November 1982): 56. In another article, Grynberg also attacked the museum's "universalization" of the Holocaust on the grounds that it deprived Jews of a moral asset: "Sharing the Holocaust . . . deprives the Jews of that protective shield for which they paid." (Grynberg, "Don't Universalize the Holocaust Memorial!" *Midstream* 32 [April 1986]: 7.)
52. Leon Wieseltier, "At Auschwitz Decency Dies Again," *New York Times*, 3 September 1989, 4:13.
53. Melvin Jules Bukiet, "The Museum vs. Memory: The Taming of the Holocaust," *Washington Post*, 18 April 1993, C3. The assertion that Jews and gentiles, shot or gassed by the Nazi regime, died "different deaths" recurs frequently. The director of the Chicago office of the ADL, responding to the claim that various victims "died the same horrible deaths," insisted that this wasn't so: "they did not all die the same kinds of deaths, for the same reasons." (Michael C. Kotzin, letter to *Chicago Sun-Times*, 2 December 1987, 60.) Miles Lerman, a survivor, and later chair of the council of the Washington Holocaust Museum, likewise insisted that Poles murdered at Auschwitz "died different deaths and they died for different reasons." (Lerman quoted in Dan Stets, "Fixing the Numbers at Auschwitz," *Chicago Tribune*, 7 May 1992, 8.)
54. Yehuda Bauer, "Whose Holocaust?" *Midstream* 26 (November 1980): 45. Some years later, Bauer was outraged by what he saw as a similar tendency to dilute the Jewish specificity of the Holocaust in the plans for a museum being built under exclusively Jewish auspices: New York's Museum of Jewish Heritage. He wrote its director: "I am absolutely appalled at the program and its basic concepts. . . . I must also warn you that I shall take every opportunity . . . to attack this outrageous design from every public platform I have." (Bauer to David Altshuler, 29 July 1987, quoted in Rochelle G. Saidel, *Never Too Late to Remember* [New York, 1996], 212.)
55. For the process by which the permanent exhibition was designed, see Linenthal, *Preserving Memory*. "Other victims" received greater attention in temporary exhibits, various publications of the museum, and conferences run by the museum's research institute. It was the permanent exhibition that was most closely monitored by those who wished to limit commemoration of non-Jewish victims; their

inclusion in other museum activities often represented a desire by museum staffers to define its mandate more broadly.

56. Hyman Bookbinder to Elie Wiesel, 23 August 1983, AJCommittee Papers, Washington Subject Files, 1964–86, Box 13, Chronological Corres.

57. As an example of this ambiguity, see the museum's "Guidelines for Teaching About the Holocaust," on its Web site (in August 1998). Near the beginning, there is a paragraph headed "Define what you mean by 'Holocaust.'" The first sentence reads: "The Holocaust refers to a specific event in 20th century history: The systematic, bureaucratic annihilation of six million Jews by the Nazi regime and their collaborators as a central act of state during World War II." (This comes straight out of Wiesel's presidential commission report of 1979, intended to counter Carter's "eleven million.") But four-fifths of the remainder of this defining paragraph is then devoted to Gypsies, the disabled, Soviet POWs, Poles and other Slavs, homosexuals, and political dissidents.

58. There is no contemporary record of Niemöller's first (oral) delivery of this recital in the late forties or early fifties, but the list of those included, and the order — which corresponds to the order in which the Nazi regime rounded up its enemies — is well established. The version in the text, authorized by Niemöller's widow, is from Ruth Zerner, "Martin Niemöller, Activist as Bystander: The Oft-Quoted Reflection," in Marvin Perry and Frederick M. Schweitzer, eds., *Jewish-Christian Encounters over the Centuries* (New York, 1994). See also Martin Marty, "Oral Confession," *Christian Century* 111 (14 December 1994).

59. Stefan Kanfer, "Writing about the Unspeakable," *Time* 117 (2 March 1981): 89; U.S. Newswire, "Text of Vice President's Speech at Capital Ceremony ['Days of Remembrance']," 7 April 1994; "Remarks by Mary Fisher," *Washington Post*, 25 August 1992; Lionel Kochan, "Martin Niemöller," *Encyclopedia of the Holocaust* (New York, 1990), 3:1061.

60. Quoted in descriptive brochure (n.p., n.d.) of the New England Holocaust Memorial, in possession of the author.

61. Jeshajahu Weinberg and Rina Elieli, *The Holocaust Museum in Washington* (New York, 1995), 163.

62. James B. Nelson, letter to the editor, *Minneapolis Star Tribune*, 23 December 1993, 12A. Marvin Liebman, a gay conservative, invoking Niemöller's remark in defense of gay rights, omitted Communists and Social Democrats and added "industrialists" to "unionists." (Liebman, "Perspectives on Gay Rights," *Los Angeles Times*, 15 October 1992, B7.)

63. Murray Greenfield offered this analogy: "First they asked for Gaza/Jericho. I didn't live there, so I agreed. Then they asked for Judea/Samaria. . . ." (Quoted in Moshe Kohn, "Whose Statute of Limitations?" *Jerusalem Post*, 7 October 1994, 5B.) The Massachusetts Association of Life Underwriters updated the quotation this way: "They came first for the disability market and I didn't speak up because I didn't sell disability insurance. Then they came for the nongroup health insurance market. . . ." (Quoted in Joan Vennochi, "Rewriting History," *Boston Globe*, 26 July 1996, E1.) Rep. John Lewis of Georgia, after quoting the original, said: "Read the Republican contract. They are coming for the children. They are coming for the poor. . . ." (Quoted in William Raspberry, "Civil Discourse — or Scoring Points?" *Washington Post*, 28 April 1995, A27.) An anti-abortion activist, after quoting a version of the original, added: "Each of us must speak up for the baby in the womb." (Patricia B. McCarthy, letter to the editor, *Indianapolis Star*, 28 March 1995, A09.) The lawyer for a Teamsters Union official under government

investigation for corruption offered a version that began, "First they came for the trade unionists. . . ." (UPI dispatch, 20 March 1990, BC cycle.) Hugh Hefner invoked the Niemöller quotation as a warning that the banning of *Playboy* from 7-Eleven stores was the first step in the destruction of the First Amendment. (Hefner, "The Blacklist," *Playboy* 33 [July 1986].)

64. It's like engaging in an endless, highly charged dispute over who is really a New Yorker, while at the same time coyly refusing to say whether you're talking about a resident of New York County (Manhattan), New York City (the five boroughs), the New York metropolitan area, or New York State. As one who grew up across the Hudson River in Jersey City, and yearned for inclusion, then lived for many years in Manhattan, scorning the pretension of "bridge and tunnel people" who called themselves New Yorkers, I've been on both sides of this.

65. Ernest Tucker, "Hyde Likens Abortion to Holocaust's Horrors," *Chicago Sun-Times*, 10 April 1998, 10.

66. Kate Folmar, "Events Planned to Remember Holocaust," *Los Angeles Times*, 13 April 1996, B2.

67. Joan Jacobson, "Holocaust Memorial Leaving for Redesign," *Baltimore Sun*, 18 May 1996, 1C.

68. Holocaust Memorial Center brochure, in possession of the author.

69. Waveney Ann Moore, "Never Forget, Wiesel Urges as Holocaust Museum Opens," *St. Petersburg Times*, 22 February 1998, 1A.

70. We often speak much too glibly about "the survivors' point of view," thus homogenizing what is a highly diverse group.

71. Elie Wiesel, "Eichmann's Victims and the Unheard Testimony," *Commentary* 32 (December 1961): 511. For another, similar assertion, among many others, see Richard Cohen, "The Site of Auschwitz Was No Accident," *Washington Post*, 18 August 1989, A23.

72. For the figure of 700,000 to one million, see remarks of Miriam Ben-Shalom, quoted in UPI dispatch, 18 June 1983, AM cycle. Frank Rector, in *The Nazi Extermination of Homosexuals* (New York, 1981), 116, suggests that 500,000 may be too conservative a figure. San Francisco Supervisor Harvey Milk said it was 300,000. (Pamela Brunger, "An Interview with Harvey Milk," *San Francisco Examiner*, 29 November 1978, as cited in an unpublished paper by David Ari Bianco: "Pink Triangles in America: The Holocaust and Gay and Lesbian Identity, 1950–1994." I am grateful to Mr. Bianco for making this paper available to me.) Ira Glasser, executive director of the New York Civil Liberties Union, said that nearly a quarter of a million homosexuals were executed by the Third Reich. (Glasser, "The Yellow Star and the Pink Triangle," *New York Times*, 10 September 1975, 45.)

73. All figures are estimates, based on the number of homosexuals sent to concentration camps (5,000–15,000) and a death rate of about 60 percent. For a review of recent scholarly literature, see Günter Grau, "Final Solution of the Homosexual Question?" and Rüdiger Lautmann, "The Pink Triangle," both in Michael Berenbaum and Abraham J. Peck, eds., *The Holocaust and History* (Bloomington, Ind., 1998).

74. *New England Holocaust Memorial Newsletter*, Fall 1993. The newsletter reports that the text was reviewed, "to ensure accuracy and appropriateness," by a group of scholars that included Jehuda Reinharz (president of Brandeis University) and Michael Berenbaum of the Washington Holocaust Museum.

75. Mike Harden, "Pop Tabs Take Flight in Artwork Honoring Saviors of Jews," *Columbus Dispatch*, 20 April 1998, 1B.

76. *Cong. Rec.*, 96th Cong., 2nd sess., 8 December 1980, 126, pt. 25:32895.
77. *Cong. Rec.*, 97th Cong., 1st sess., 28 September 1981, 127, pt. 17:22266–67. James Young, in connection with research for his study of Holocaust memorials, was in Denver when the decision was being made. "They asked me what I thought the inscription should be, and I suggested: 'To the memory of the 33,000 Jews murdered at Babi Yar, and to the Ukrainians who killed them.' I thought that covered the bases properly." (Young quoted in S. T. Meravi, "Remembrance of Things Past," *Jerusalem Post*, 2 June 1989.) Cf. Young, *The Texture of Memory* (New Haven, 1993), 294–96.
78. John Murray Cuddihy, *No Offense: Civil Religion and Protestant Taste* (New York, 1978).
79. Wiesel quoted in Linenthal, *Preserving Memory*, 53.
80. There was the predictable division between the minority who thought the First Amendment meant what it said and the majority who thought it shouldn't apply in the case of the most objectionable speech. The question divided Jews as well as gentiles. The constitutional issue pitted the Anti-Defamation League against the (largely Jewish) leadership of the American Civil Liberties Union. Indeed, in a way it was a three-way (or rather, two-and-a-half-way) Jewish dispute: the leader of the local Nazis, Frank Collin, was half Jewish — the son of a refugee from Germany. (Jonathan Miller, "Frank Collin's Roots," *New Republic* 179 [1 July 1978]: 9–10.)
81. Adam Clymer, "Public Is Split on Bitburg, Poll Finds," *New York Times*, 8 May 1985, A12.
82. Barry Sussman, "Majority Opposes Cemetery Visit," *Washington Post*, 24 April 1985, A29. As the headline indicates, this poll, conducted two weeks earlier than the one cited in the previous note, found a majority opposed to the visit.
83. Ibid.
84. Milton Himmelfarb to David Gordis, "Roper Report on Opinion about Bitburg," 15 October 1985, AJCommittee Papers, Washington Subject Files, 1964–86, Box 13, Chronological Corres.
85. My guess is that some part of the 40 percent reflected resentment at the embarrassment recently visited on a popular president.
86. William F. Buckley's *National Review* squirmed: an editorial referred to Cardinal Glemp's remarks "which in their English translation [!] seem to echo old themes of anti-Semitism." ("Whose Auschwitz?" *National Review* 41 [29 September 1989]: 18.) Shortly thereafter Buckley felt obliged to acknowledge that "as a Catholic, I am bound to admit that my leaders have made a most awful botch of the Auschwitz business." (*National Review* 41 [13 October 1989]: 63.)
87. Discussing criticism of a 1998 Vatican declaration, which spoke of the failings of "sons and daughters of the Church," Father Richard Neuhaus wrote: "The criticism that this falls short of a confession that *the Church* has sinned fails to understand Catholic ecclesiology, which holds that, while members of the Church are sinners, the Church herself is sinless, as exemplified by the Blessed Virgin, the icon of the Church." (Neuhaus, "The Public Square," *First Things* 84 [June–July 1998]: 73.)
88. Eli Rosenbaum, quoted in Peter S. Canellos, "A Third Reich Dilemma," *Boston Globe*, 21 September 1997, A1.
89. One early case that attracted a great deal of attention in Chicago was that of Frank Walus, a Polish immigrant accused of having been a Gestapo agent in Poland during the war, responsible for many atrocious murders. Several survivors

who identified Walus (some flown in from Israel) gave vivid testimony about his sadism at his denaturalization hearing, testimony that received detailed coverage in the local press. After his denaturalization, it became clear that what Walus had claimed all along — that he had spent the war as a conscripted farm laborer in Germany — was true, and the court decision was vacated. Announcing that there would be no further prosecution, Allan Ryan, head of the Justice Department's Office of Special Investigations, explained that the Supreme Court required "clear and convincing evidence" for denaturalization and that the evidence in the Walus case fell short of that standard. Ryan apparently couldn't bring himself to say "we got the wrong guy." For Ryan's account, see his *Quiet Neighbors* (San Diego, 1984), 210–17. Cf. Flora Johnson, "The Nazi Who Never Was," *Chicago Tribune*, 10 May 1981, B1ff.; Michael Arndt, "The Wrong Man," *Chicago Tribune*, 10 May 1981, 15ff. In the light of later developments in the Demjanjuk case, it's interesting to note the response of an American Jewish Committee staff member after a conversation with Ryan about how the OSI would proceed with the Walus matter. "One of our greatest concerns regarding the development in this case is that the fact of having 12 witnesses proved wrong will have a very negative spill-over effect on the credibility of such witnesses in similar cases." (David Geller to Abe Karlikow, 19 February 1980, AJCommittee Files, BGX, 1980, Nazis.)

90. Himmelfarb to Gordis, "Roper Report."

91. Eban quoted in Peter Grose, "Anti-Eban Moves in the Knesset Fail Despite Criticism of Views on Nazis," *New York Times,* 21 November 1971, 24; Lipstadt quoted in Andrea Stone, "The Nation's Top Nazi Hunter Refuses to Fade into History," *USA Today,* 18 August 1993, 7A. As early as 1978, Hyman Bookbinder of the American Jewish Committee expressed the view that "a campaign of seeking out and punishing these criminals smacks too much of harassment, revenge, bitterness, etc." (Bookbinder to Murray Friedman, 12 September 1978, AJCommittee Files, BGX 78, Nazis.) Ephraim Zuroff, the Simon Wiesenthal Center's representative in Israel, reported a 1986 conversation with the political adviser to Prime Minister Shimon Peres. The adviser was opposed to further trials; in Zuroff's paraphrase, he thought "such trials would strengthen extremism . . . reinforce 'the entire world is against us' mentality of certain sectors of the population." (Zuroff, *Occupation: Nazi Hunter* [Hoboken, N.J., 1994], 197–98.)

92. Wiesel quoted in Janny Scott, "Jews Tell of Lost Holocaust Deposits," *New York Times,* 17 October 1996, B5.

93. Congressional Press Releases, 1 April 1998: "Senator Moseley-Braun Proposes Holocaust Assets Commission."

94. Todd S. Purdum, "Dinkins Says Germany, Yes; Free Trip, No," *New York Times,* 2 November 1991, 25.

95. " 'Shooters' Crew Filmed Bush in Israel," Reuters dispatch, 5 August 1986, BC cycle.

96. Murray Wass, "Media Specter," *New Republic* 193 (30 September 1985): 13.

97. Matthew Fleischer, "Slaying the Christ Killer: Ralph Reed Woos Jews in Jersey," *Village Voice,* 26 December 1995, 27.

98. Al Gore, "An Ecological Kristallnacht. Listen.," *New York Times,* 19 March 1989, E27.

99. Rachel L. Swarns, "A Debate over Definitions: 'Cuban Holocaust' Memorial Dismays Many Jews," *Miami Herald,* 6 November 1994, 1A.

100. Randy Alfred, "Fighting for Our Lives . . . and Others," *San Francisco Sentinel,* 8 April 1977, 6, as quoted in Bianco, "Pink Triangles," 8.

101. Phil McCombs, "Watt's Own 'Persecution' Brings Support for Memorial," *Washington Post*, 13 April 1983, A15.
102. Bakker quoted in David Crook, "Morning Report," *Los Angeles Times*, 3 January 1989, 6:2.
103. Allen quoted in Dennis Hamill, "Woody's Ordeal," *St. Louis Post-Dispatch*, 26 March 1993, 1G.
104. Tom W. Smith, "World War II and the Lessons of History," *Public Perspective* 6 (August-September 1995): 52. Smith here presents a compilation of several polls, and for that reason the responses may not be strictly comparable.
105. "Key Findings from a Nationwide Study of Knowledge and Attitudes among the American Public" (a 1998 study conducted for the U.S. Holocaust Memorial Museum by Peter D. Hart Research Associates), 20. I am grateful to Hart Associates for making this unpublished poll available to me.
106. Sarah Bloomfield quoted in "Poll: Most Americans Want to Learn about Holocaust," *Jerusalem Post*, 24 April 1998, 3.
107. "American Public Awareness of and Attitudes Toward the Holocaust, Part I: A Case for Further Education" (a 1990 study conducted for the U.S. Holocaust Memorial Museum and the ADL by Yankelovich, Skelly & White), 18. I am grateful to the U.S. Holocaust Memorial Museum for making this unpublished poll available to me.
108. Jennifer Golub and Renae Cohen, *What Do Americans Know about the Holocaust?* (reporting on a 1992 poll conducted by the Roper Organization for the American Jewish Committee) (New York, 1993), 6; Yankelovich poll, "American Public Awareness," 38.
109. Yankelovich poll, "American Public Awareness," 26.
110. Robert Wuthnow, *Meaning and Moral Order: Explorations in Cultural Analysis* (Berkeley, 1987), 124–44.
111. Ibid., 128.
112. Ibid., 130–31. Wuthnow surveyed clergymen (of various denominations) and schoolteachers, and while this is a limitation of his study, I don't think it seriously vitiates the general implications of his findings.
113. Michael Berenbaum, "United States Holocaust Memorial Museum," *Sh'ma* 23:452 (16 April 1993); Sarah Bloomfield, quoted in Linenthal, *Preserving Memory*, 65.
114. John Aloysius Farrell, "Why Do They Come? American Innocence Confronts the Holocaust Museum," *Boston Globe*, 11 September 1994, 24.
115. This argument has been developed by Richard D. Logan, "The Concerned Onlooker and the Holocaust," *Midstream* 38 (April 1992).
116. Linenthal, *Preserving Memory*, 187.
117. Epstein, "A Dissent on *Schindler's List*," *New York Review of Books* 41 (21 April 1994).
118. Phillip Lopate, "Resistance to the Holocaust," *Tikkun* 4 (May-June 1989): 58.
119. See p. 118.
120. Green quoted in Frank Rich, "Reliving the Nazi Nightmare," *Time* 111 (17 April 1978): 61. In *Playing for Time* and *Triumph of the Spirit*, the Jewish protagonists had the very American occupations of nightclub singer and prizefighter. The emblematic Jewish victim in *War and Remembrance* was a famous writer.
121. Rt. Rev. Paul Moore, Jr. "Welcome," in Eva Fleischner, ed., *Auschwitz: Beginning of a New Era?* (New York, 1977), xvii.
122. Martin S. Jaffee, "The Victim-Community in Myth and History," *Journal of Ecumenical Studies* 28 (Spring 1991): 227–28. Prof. Jaffee goes on to discuss the religious

significance of such rituals for Jews in ways that are interesting but do not concern us here. For a journalistic description of one such ritual, see Frank P. L. Somerville, "A Christian Search for 'Costly Grace,'" *Baltimore Sun*, 10 April 1995, 1B.

123. See Linenthal, *Preserving Memory*, 224–28.

124. For a brief introduction to these figures, and the response they've met, see Stephen R. Haynes, "Christian Holocaust Theology: A Critical Reassessment," *Journal of the American Academy of Religion* 62 (1994).

11. "Never Again the Slaughter of the Albigensians"

1. Elie Wiesel quoted in Walter Goodman, "Israeli Clashes with American Jew about Persecution Past and Present," *New York Times*, 9 September 1984, 1:46.

2. George Will, "Holocaust Museum: Antidote for Innocence," *Washington Post*, 10 March 1983, A19. Cf. his "The Stones of Treblinka Cry Out," *Washington Post*, 10 September 1989, C7.

3. Vice President Bush, remarks at groundbreaking of Washington Holocaust Museum, quoted in "Ground Broken for Holocaust Museum," *New York Times*, 1 May 1984, A16.

4. Ronald Aronson, "The Holocaust and Human Progress," in Alan Rosenberg and Gerald E. Myers, eds., *Echoes from the Holocaust: Philosophical Reflections on a Dark Time* (Philadelphia, 1988), 224.

5. George Will, "Remembering Buchenwald," *Washington Post*, 8 April 1975, A19.

6. For an example of this argument, see George Kren and Leon Rappaport, "The Holocaust and the Human Condition," in Roger S. Gottlieb, ed., *Thinking the Unthinkable: Meanings of the Holocaust* (New York, 1990).

7. The most influential statement of this view is Zygmunt Bauman, *Modernity and the Holocaust* (Ithaca, N.Y., 1989). Despite my reservations about some of the more far-reaching claims about the connection between the Holocaust and modernity, I find Bauman's work to be filled with interesting and provocative suggestions.

8. Is it, in any case, useful (as many seem to believe) to talk of a *thing* called evil — a noun rather than an adjective? A philosophical (or religious) question we can sidestep.

9. This is even truer of the cosmic pessimism expressed in this not untypical "lesson": "What died at Auschwitz was the promise and hope embodied in Western civilization." (Henry Feingold, "Four Days in April," *Sh'ma* 1 [n.d.]: 16.) What do we do with *that* lesson?

10. Michael Berenbaum, quoted in Philip Gourevitch, "Behold Now Behemoth," *Harper's Magazine* 287 (July 1993): 56.

11. Those living in major metropolitan areas are often unaware of how commonly vivid Holocaust imagery is employed in "pro-life" campaigns in middle America. For an example, see the Web page of "The American Holocaust Memorial" (http://user.mc.net/dougp/ahm), which juxtaposes photographs of stacked-up bodies at liberated camps and of heaps of discarded aborted fetuses from "unliberated" clinics.

12. C. Everett Koop, "The Sanctity of Life," *Journal of the Medical Society of New Jersey* 75 (June 1978): 62. For those who find it not a matter of progression but of equation, there's an obvious lesson: "Would it have been wrong to go into Auschwitz in the middle of the night and burn the building down knowing they were ready to bring in the next group of Jews in the morning? . . . No, it wouldn't be wrong. . . .

Or to shoot the guards when they came to work to do the killing." (Roy McMillan, an anti-abortion activist, quoted in Lisa Belkin, "Kill for Life?" *New York Times Magazine,* 30 October 1994, 62.) A Texas sheriff who said he wouldn't answer calls to halt protesters at abortion clinics argued that if law officers in Germany had done as he was doing the Nazis would never have taken power. (Sheriff James Hickey, quoted in James C. Harrington, "Abortion Battle Leads Sheriff to Shirk Duties," *Texas Lawyer,* 19 February 1990.) Morley Jefferson has made the ingenious argument that the fact that most "pro-life" activists don't endorse bombing clinics proves that they don't take their Holocaust analogy seriously. ("Right-to-Life Porn," *New Republic* 192 [25 March 1985].) Maybe — but this "inconsistency" could also be attributed to timidity.

13. Sylvia Neil, acting chair of the Illinois Jewish Alliance for choice, quoted in "Jews Rally to Support Legalized Abortion," UPI dispatch, 9 August 1989, BC cycle. The *real* lesson of the Holocaust on this issue, said the Midwest director of the ADL, is as a "chilling example of the drastic consequences of government power over reproductive matters." (Barry Morrison, "Wrong to Link Holocaust and Abortion," *Chicago Tribune,* 11 November 1992, 20.) An official of the American Civil Liberties Union wrote that "if Hitler were alive today he would sympathize with the antichoice view that women should not have a free choice in making decisions that concern their bodies." (Colleen Connell, "Exploiting Nazism in Abortion Debate," *Chicago Tribune,* 10 July 1987, 18.) Cf. the remarks of Henry Siegman, executive director of the AJCongress, quoted in Michael Briggs, "300,000 in March for a 'Choice,' " *Chicago Sun-Times,* 10 April 1989, 4.

14. For "patriarchal values," see Aviva Cantor, quoted in Judy Chicago, *Holocaust Project* (New York, 1993), 13. Deborah Dwork and Robert Jan van Pelt, in their extraordinarily rich and informative *Auschwitz: 1270 to the Present* (New York, 1996), twice point out (12, 277) that its planners and operators were "mostly men." Gender-oriented writing on the Holocaust has mainly focused on differences between the experiences of Jewish men and women caught in its jaws — differences that are obviously real and worth investigating. As in all fields, particularly new fields, much of the work merits criticism. But some who write disparagingly of those who explore gender divisions in the Holocaust seem mostly interested in bashing feminism and appear to be moved as well by communal considerations. "What can be the object of such exercises," writes Gabriel Schoenfeld, "if not to sever Jewish women, in their own minds, from their families as well as from the larger Jewish community?" ("Auschwitz and the Professors," *Commentary* 105 [June 1998]: 45.)

15. Rep. Mickey Edwards, *Cong. Rec.,* 95th Cong., 2nd sess., 1978, 124, pt. 9:10988.

16. Andrew Silow Carroll, "Animals Rights . . . and Wrongs," *Washington Jewish Week,* 7 June 1990, 15–16.

17. Vivian Berger, "A Holocaust Parallel Close to Home," *Los Angeles Times,* 23 August 1992, M5.

18. Geoffrey Cowley, "How the Mind Was Designed," *Newsweek* 113 (13 March 1989): 5.

19. David I. Caplan, "The Warsaw Ghetto: Ten Handguns Against Tyranny," *American Rifleman* 136 (February 1988): 31, 75.

20. Gingrich quoted in Richard Stengel, "Newt Scoot," *New Republic* 213 (3 July 1995): 10.

21. Robert Lane Fenrich, "Imagining Holocaust: Mass Death and American Consciousness at the End of the Second World War," Northwestern University Ph.D

diss., 1992, 181–82. Cf. Larry Kramer, *Reports from the Holocaust: The Making of an AIDS Activist* (New York, 1989); Douglas Crimp, ed., *AIDS: Cultural Analysis/Cultural Activism* (Cambridge, Mass., 1988).

22. David P. Gushee, "Why They Helped the Jews," *Christianity Today* 18 (24 October 1994): 34. His argument is not self-congratulatory: "How encouraging it would be for Christians if it could be reported that rescuers were . . . committed Christians, or evangelicals, and nonrescuers not. But research shows that rescuers do not appear to have differed on any test of religiosity."

23. Social circumstances as well as the Zeitgeist influence whether one accepts that the Holocaust teaches bleak lessons. When a sample group were asked whether they agreed that one of its lessons was "There is no hope for the human race," there was no difference in the responses of the educated and the uneducated, but many more blacks than whites, and many more poor people than rich people, agreed. (Jennifer Golub and Renae Cohen, *What Do Americans Know about the Holocaust?* [New York, 1993], 44.)

24. Quoted in Berger, "Holocaust Parallel."

25. Hershaft quoted in Andrew Silow Carroll, "Seeking Justice, a Survivor Turns to the Treatment of Farm Animals," *Washington Jewish Week*, 7 June 1990, 15.

26. See pp. 136–37.

27. The experiment was designed so that it appeared to be a matter of chance whether the naïve subject was a "teacher" or a "learner."

28. Jeshajahu Weinberg, "A Narrative History Museum," *Curator* 37 (December 1994); 231.

29. A. M. Rosenthal, *Thirty-eight Witnesses* (New York, 1964), 37.

30. A. M. Rosenthal, in his account of the *New York Times* coverage of the Genovese case, writes of the follow-up story the paper ran, in which expert opinions were solicited. "My own favorite comment came from the theologian who said that he could not understand it, that perhaps 'depersonalizing' in New York had gone farther than he thought. Then he added, in monumental, total unconsciousness of irony: 'Don't quote me.' Ever and ever, I shall treasure that theologian." (Ibid., 50.)

31. Dr. Herman Middlekoop, of Church World Service, cited in Karen Rothmyer, "What Really Happened in Biafra?" *Columbia Journalism Review* 9 (Fall 1970): 43.

32. Father Fintan Kilbride quoted in Marc H. Tannenbaum, "Biafran Tragedy Accelerates Christian-Jewish Cooperation," *Religious News Service*, 14 August 1968, 4.

33. Paul E. Onu, quoted in John J. Stremlau, *The International Politics of the Nigerian Civil War* (Princeton, 1977), 113.

34. William Shawcross, *The Quality of Mercy: Cambodia, Holocaust and Modern Conscience* (New York, 1984), 421–22. Shawcross points out that for all the Nazi imagery, Tuol Sleng more closely resembled Moscow's Lubyanka prison: those killed in Tuol Sleng were mostly members of the Khmer Rouge (or their families) who had fallen out of favor; they were required to draft elaborate confessions before being executed.

35. "Aid for Kampucheans," 24 October 1979, *Public Papers of the Presidents of the United States: Jimmy Carter, 1979* (Washington, D.C., 1980), 2011–12.

36. Brzezinski quoted in Strobe Talbott, "America Abroad: Defanging the Beast," *Time* 133 (6 February 1989): 40. The policy of ambiguous support for the Khmer Rouge against the Vietnamese continued during the Reagan and Bush administrations.

37. Leaflet quoted in Ann Cooper, "Third World Insurgent Groups Learning to Play the Washington Lobbying Game," *National Journal*, 8 February 1986, 329. The Soviet invasion was described as a holocaust by CIA Director William Casey, as well

as by Brzezinski. (Philip Geyelin, "Casey and the 'Focus of Evil,'" *Washington Post* 17 June 1985, A11; Zbigniew Brzezinski, "Linking Two Crises," *New York Times,* 6 October 1985, 21.) Cf. John F. Di Leo, "Afghan 'Holocaust,'" *Chicago Tribune,* 29 December 1986, 12; Rosanne T. Klass, "The New Holocaust," *National Review* 37 (4 October 1985): 28.

38. A dozen years later, the United States was pursuing one of its associates in this venture, Osama bin Laden for having bombed American embassies in Africa; and was attacking with rockets his presumed headquarters at one of the bases the CIA had earlier set up for the rebels.

39. "Remarks at a Republican Fundraising Breakfast in Burlington, Massachusetts," 1 November 1990, *Public Papers of the Presidents of the United States, George Bush 1990* (Washington, D.C., 1991), 1509; "The President's News Conference in Orlando, Florida," 1 November 1990, ibid., 1514–15, 1518.

40. For comparisons by columnists, see remarks of George Will and Charles Krauthammer, quoted in Marjorie Williams, "Monster in the Making," *Washington Post,* 9 August 1990, D1.

41. Testimony about babies torn from incubators was arranged by the public relations firm hired by Kuwait's Washington embassy, and may have been invented. The matter is in dispute.

42. A. M. Rosenthal, "America at the Vistula," *New York Times,* 5 April 1991, A25.

43. Dail Willis, "Germans Built Gas Chambers for Iraq, Wiesenthal [Center] Says," *Forward,* 15 February 1991, 20. The alleged parallels were extended in other ways. Rep. Stephen Solarz told a congressional committee that while it was true that in bombing Kuwait the United States would be "killing the very people we presumably want to save," the example of the attitude of prisoners at Auschwitz convinced him that Kuwaiti civilians were prepared to "pay any price to see that they are liberated" and would die gladly so long as their oppressors died with them. (Federal News Service, "Capitol Hill Hearing about the Middle East," 8 January 1991.) On the occasion of a Warsaw Ghetto Uprising commemoration after the operation in the Gulf was over, Solarz said that although there were differences between the uprising and Desert Storm, "the similarities . . . are ultimately far more significant." ("Address by Rep. Stephen J. Solarz, Warsaw Ghetto Uprising Anniversary, April 7, 1991," *Cong. Rec.,* 102nd Cong., 1st sess., 1991, 137, pt. 57:E1303.

44. In a tribute to the presumed power of this kind of imagery, a group of right-wingers opposed to American military intervention organized the Committee to Avert a Mideast Holocaust. (Federal News Service, "Press Conference of a Coalition Opposing U.S. Intervention in the Persian Gulf Crisis," 4 September 1990.)

45. A statement on Somalia by all the leading Jewish organizations was headed: "This Is Not the First Time the World Ignored a Cry for Help." (Advertisement in *New York Times,* 4 October 1992, 18.) Holocaust survivors were quoted on how viewing photographs of skeletal Somalis summoned up memories of their own ordeal.

46. George Will, "America's Inoculation by Somalia," *Newsweek* 122 (6 September 1993): 62.

47. Alain Destexhe, "The Third Genocide," *Foreign Policy* 97 (Winter 1994–95): 10.

48. Douglas Jehl, "Officials Told to Avoid Calling Rwanda Killings 'Genocide,'" *New York Times,* 10 June 1994, A8.

49. Irving Greenberg, "The Challenge of Teaching about the Holocaust," in Mary T. Glynn et al., *American Youth and the Holocaust* (New York, 1982), xx.

50. See Gil Loescher and John A. Scanlan, *Calculated Kindness: Refugees and America's Half-Open Door, 1945 to the Present* (New York, 1986).

51. It's worth noting that in the case of the *St. Louis*, the American government made an effort — which appeared successful at the time — to see to it that the fleeing Jews were not returned to Germany. Haitian refugees dropped on the docks of Port-au-Prince by the U.S. Coast Guard were sometimes immediately scooped up by the secret police, never to be seen again. (Howard W. French, "A Rising Tide of Political Terror Leaves Hundreds Dead in Haiti," *New York Times* [national edition], 2 April 1994, 1–2.)

52. Roy Gutman, " 'There Is No Food, There Is No Air,' " *New York Newsday*, 19 July 1992, 39; "If Only They Could Flee," *New York Newsday*, 26 July 1992. Gutman won a Pulitzer Prize for his reporting from Bosnia.

53. Louise Lief et al., "Europe's Trail of Tears," *U.S. News & World Report* 113 (27 July 1992): 41.

54. *New York Times*, 5 August 1992, A14. The sponsors of the ad were the American Jewish Committee, the American Jewish Congress, and the Anti-Defamation League.

55. George Kenney, "Yugoslav Policy: A Return to Isolationism," *Christian Science Monitor*, September 1992, 19.

56. Clinton quoted in Clifford Krauss, "U.S. Backs Away from Charge of Atrocities in Bosnia Camps," *New York Times*, 5 August 1992, A12, and in Carl M. Cannon, "Turning Point for President: The Holocaust," *Baltimore Sun*, 9 May 1993 (reporting a 5 August 1992 statement by Clinton). "We stood by once before when this happened," said Clinton's running mate, Al Gore. "The world should have learned a lesson from that." (Gore quoted in Scot Lehigh, "Clinton Backs Military Action in Bosnia over Genocide," *Boston Globe*, 6 August 1992, 11.)

57. Ambassador Mohammed Sacirbey on CNN, *Crossfire*, 17 December 1992, transcript 726 (Nexis). Cf. "Remarks by Ambassador Mohammed Sacirbey . . . to the American Jewish Committee Ambassador's Forum Luncheon," Federal News Service, 22 October 1992.

58. Richard Cohen, "Nothing New Here," *Washington Post*, 22 April 1993, A23.

59. Andrew Greeley, "Bosnia Mission Is Moral — but Also Impossible," *Chicago Sun-Times*, 16 May 1993, 44.

60. Henry Siegman, quoted in "Jewish Leaders Link Bosnia to Holocaust in Open Letter to President Clinton," PR Newswire, 19 April 1993.

61. Mortimer Zuckerman, "The Tough Options in Bosnia," *U.S. News & World Report* 114 (3 May 1993): 84.

62. Warren Christopher, quoted in Elaine Sciolino, "U.S. Goals on Bosnia," *New York Times*, 19 May 1993, A10.

63. Berenbaum quoted in Norman Oder, "Are Pangs of Conscience Progress?" *New York Newsday*, 9 June 1974, A37.

64. David Saperstein, quoted in "Groups Join in Urging Tougher U.S. Action on Bosnia," Reuter Library Report, 6 January 1993.

65. "Exchange with Reporters Prior to Discussions with President Václav Havel of the Czech Republic," *Public Papers of the Presidents of the United States: William J. Clinton, 1993* (Washington, D.C., 1994), 465.

66. David Rieff, "Bosnia's Fall, Our Failure," *Harper's Magazine* 290 (February 1995): 13.

67. Harold M. Schulweis, quoted in Nancy Hill-Holtzman, "Images of Atrocities in Bosnia Stir Protest," *Los Angeles Times*, 8 August 1992, B1.

68. Erwin Knoll, "The Uses of the Holocaust," *Progressive* 57 (July 1993): 16.

69. Sontag quoted in Carla Anne Robbins, "Americans' Inaction Stirs Critics to Debate and Despair," *Wall Street Journal*, 18 March 1994, A1.

70. Serbian spokesmen were particularly insistent that the Holocaust not be "trivialized" by comparing it to events in Bosnia. (See Steven A. Holmes, "Photographs of Balkans Draw Fire," *New York Times*, 24 September 1992, 1:6.) One should also note those Holocaust survivors for whom the relevant Holocaust memory ("lesson") was that during World War II Serbs, like Jews, had been victims of Croats and Muslims allied with the Axis. (See the remarks of Louis de Groot, president of the Holocaust Center of Northern California, quoted in Leslie Katz, "Holocaust Survivors in Conflict over Bosnia War," *Jewish Bulletin of Northern California*, 21 July 1995; advertisement by Survivors of the Buchenwald Concentration Camp, USA, in *New York Times*, 29 April 1993, A14.)

71. A. M. Rosenthal, "Bosnia and the Holocaust," New York Times, 26 April 1994, A23.

72. It is distasteful to justify such comparisons statistically, but the reader is entitled to know the number's source. Michael Berenbaum estimates the number of Jewish children under the age of fifteen killed in the Holocaust as "more than a million." (*The World Must Know* [Boston, 1993], 192.) Others say a million and a half. The United Nations Children's Fund estimates, as of 1998, that more than twelve million children under the age of five die preventable deaths every year. (UNICEF Web page: http://www.unicef.org/.) Taking account of the different definitions of "children," "well over ten times" seems a very conservative figure.

73. United Nations, *Statistical Yearbook 1994* (New York, 1996), 843. Figures are for 1994, the last year for which data are available. The United States was ranked twenty-first among the twenty-one countries listed.

74. Leonard Fein, "Never Again?" *Forward*, 2 April 1993, 7.

75. David Rieff, *Slaughterhouse: Bosnia and the Failure of the West* (New York, 1995), 27.

76. John Henderson, quoted in Mary McGrath, "Measure Requiring Holocaust Studies Clears Committee," *Bergen* (N.J.) *Record*, 7 December 1993, A1. Noting that the proposed curriculum included a tribute to Jewish resistance during the Holocaust, he asked: "What about the . . . no less heroic level of resistance of the Ibo tribesmen to the Nigerian majority during the time of the short-lived Biafra state?"

77. Alan Steinberg, senior policy adviser in the New Jersey Assembly's Majority Office, quoted in David Twersky, "Holocaust Bill Begets Mayhem in New Jersey," *Forward*, 21 January 1994.

78. Ibid. In California, where the governor was of Armenian descent, the Armenian genocide was also included. Turkish groups, predictably, campaigned against this: it was "hate provoking"; they urged Californians not to make the schools a "place to settle the scores of the Old World." (Robert Marquand, "A Context for Democracy," *Christian Science Monitor*, 4 December 1987, 19.)

79. For a brief survey of some of the states' curricula, see Samuel Totten and William S. Parsons, "State-Developed Teacher Guides and Curricula on Genocide and/or the Holocaust," *Inquiry in Social Studies* 28 (Spring 1992).

80. Curtis Krueger, "Senate Bill Requires Lessons in Morality," *St. Petersburg Times*, 17 March 1994, 5B. But the content of some Holocaust curricula could bring them into conflict with other legislative enactments: material on Nazi repression of gays used in a Salt Lake City classroom ran afoul of a Utah law that forbade teaching "acceptance of or advocacy of homosexuality as a desirable or acceptable sexual adjustment or lifestyle." ("Material on Holocaust Raises Concern in Utah," *New York Times* [national edition], 15 March 1990, A17.)

81. Lucy Dawidowicz, "How They Teach the Holocaust" (1990), reprinted in her *What Is the Use of Jewish History?* (New York, 1992), 66, 79, 80 Dawidowicz's stric-

tures were endorsed by the heads of the ADL's Center for Holocaust Studies. (Letter from Nat Kemeny and Dennis B. Klein, *Commentary* 91 [March 1991]: 2.)

82. Deborah Lipstadt, "Not Facing History," *New Republic* 212 (6 March 1995). For a defense of the Holocaust curriculum that was the principal target of Dawidowicz and Lipstadt, Facing History and Ourselves, see Melinda Fine, *Habits of Mind* (San Francisco, 1995).

83. Wiesel quoted in William H. Honan, "Holocaust Teaching Gaining a Niche, but Method Is Disputed," *New York Times*, 12 April 1995, B11.

84. Tom W. Smith, "Remembering the War," *Public Perspective* 6 (August-September 1995): 51.

85. Antonio Olivo, "Just a Number," *Los Angeles Times*, 1 June 1995, B1; Christine Wolff, "Feeling Pain of Prejudice," *Cincinnati Enquirer*, 26 March 1996, B01; Lewis W. Diuguid, "Learning to Confront Prejudice," *Kansas City Star*, 25 May 1996, C1; Bill Teeter, "8th Graders Learn about Holocaust in Unique Lesson," *Fort Worth Star-Telegram*, 4 October 1997, 10. In the 1980s the ADL distributed a curriculum that included the role-playing games "Gestapo" and "Judenrat," but this may have been discontinued. (Totten and Parsons, "Teacher Guides," 28–29.)

86. Transcript of the President's Commission on the Holocaust, 15 February 1979, 20, cited in Edward T. Linenthal, *Preserving Memory: The Struggle to Create America's Holocaust Museum* (New York, 1995), 112.

87. Weinberg, "Narrative History Museum," 231.

88. Ibid., 232.

89. Both quoted in Philip Gourevitch, "What They Saw at the Holocaust Museum," *New York Times Magazine*, 12 February 1995, 45.

90. Henry Siegman said in a speech: "Don't we who are survivors of the Holocaust see through the hollowness and dishonesty of the claims of statesmen that nothing can be done to end or even slow the carnage? Does anyone today believe that the railroad tracks to the concentration camps could not have been bombed by the Allies during World War II?" ("American Jewish Leader Decries European and American Inaction in Bosnia-Herzegovina," PR Newswire, 14 October 1992.) Siegman slightly misspoke: it was not a question of whether railroad tracks could be bombed, but whether it would have done any good. The larger question, however, is how much authority such "lessons" should have. In an earlier chapter, I suggested that the bombing of Auschwitz would not have substantially helped halt the murder program. If I'm right, that doesn't lead to the conclusion that analogous action in Bosnia *wouldn't* have helped. And if I'm wrong, and it would have helped in the case of the Holocaust, that doesn't demonstrate that it would have in Bosnia.

91. In an attempt to underline its uniqueness, and to establish it as the archetype of evil, Hitler's onslaught against European Jewry is often described as "evil for its own sake," *purposeless* mass killing — presumably a greater crime than if it had served some end, however depraved. While the means that Hitler employed, the ruthlessness with which he employed those means, and the vast scope of his genocidal ambition may be without equal, the end was, in principle, a familiar one. He believed, as did others before and since, that there was no room in the sort of society he envisioned for this alien element; if the Jews could not be expelled, they had to be destroyed. The point is not the "equivalence" (whatever that means) between Hitler's beliefs and Pol Pot's belief that there was no room in his rural socialist utopia for urban intellectuals, or white Australians' belief that there was no place in the society they envisioned for the aboriginal population. And the point is certainly not that the Holocaust was "merely" or "essentially" an exercise

in ethnic cleansing — it was clearly much more. Rather it is that if we are sincerely interested in understanding the Holocaust, we have to look at it from multiple perspectives, and one of the most useful perspectives is to consider the extent to which it was *zweckrational* ("instrumentally rational") for the creation of Hitler's racial utopia. For an exposition of this perspective, see Richard L. Rubenstein, "Modernization and the Politics of Extermination," in Michael Berenbaum, ed., *A Mosaic of Victims* (New York, 1990). Those who read German may consult Götz Aly, *Endlösung: Völkerverschiebung und der Mord an den europäischen Juden* (Frankfurt, 1995). In a complementary fashion, the assertion that Hitler gave a high priority to the murder of European Jewry, which is true enough, is "sharpened" by claiming that military requirements were routinely sacrificed to this end; that trains needed to bring munitions to the front were diverted to transport Jews to their deaths; that even in the final days of the Nazi regime, everything took second place to continuing the murder process. In fact, while in the administrative chaos that was the Third Reich it sometimes happened that those pursuing murder won out in the battle of priorities over those pursuing military victory, this was not the rule. Although we are (properly) impressed by the image of thousands of boxcars taking Jews to their doom, as a percentage of total railroad usage in the Third Reich, these trains took up some tiny fraction of 1 percent. (There is no quantitative study of this issue, but Raul Hilberg, who has made a specialty of investigating the use of railroads in the Final Solution, has confirmed to me, in private conversation, that this was the case. And while some of the Nazis' murderous work went on to the bitter end, when German industry was collapsing in the final months of the war, Hitler himself authorized diverting Hungarian Jews from the gas chambers of Auschwitz to work camps inside Germany. (Raul Hilberg, *The Destruction of the European Jews*, rev. ed., [New York, 1985], 3:1132. See also Henry Friedlander, "The Camp Setting," in Esther Katz and Joan Miriam Ringelheim, eds., *Proceedings of the Conference on Women Surviving the Holocaust* [New York, 1983], 113; Ulrich Herbert, "Labour and Extermination: Economic Interest and the Primacy of *Weltanschauung* in National Socialism," *Past and Present* 138 [February 1993].) Does the fact that sometimes killing Jews took second place to military requirements make the Holocaust less evil? Do we understand the Holocaust better if we ignore these things?

92. Steiner in "Jewish Values in the Post-Holocaust Future: A Symposium," *Judaism* 16 (Summer 1967): 285–86. Steiner's point remains valid despite the fact that one consequence of the Holocaust is that we're now often inclined — as in the case of Bosnia — to belive reports that *are* exaggerated.

12. "We Are Not Equipped to Answer"

1. Marc Bloch, "Mémoire collective, tradition et coutume," *Revue de synthèse historique* 40 (1925).
2. This last observation is not mine, but I've forgotten where I read it. I apologize to its author.
3. Irving Greenberg, *Living in the Image of God* (Northvale, N.J., 1998), 231.
4. Ismar Schorsch, "The Holocaust and Jewish Survival," *Midstream* 27 (January 1981): 40.
5. See, e.g., Norman Lamm (president of Yeshiva University), "The Face of God: Thoughts on the Holocaust," in Bernhard H. Rosenberg and Fred Heuman, eds., *Theological and Halakhic Reflections on the Holocaust* (Hoboken, N.J., 1992); Michael Goldberg (a Reform rabbi), *Why Should Jews Survive?* (New York, 1995). For

a brief overview of the issue, see Arnold Eisen, "Jewish Theology in North America: Notes on Two Decades," *American Jewish Yearbook* 91 (1991).

6. For Hinckley, see "Reagan Assailant Hinckley Tried Suicide in 1983, Doctor Says," Reuters dispatch, 25 September 1989, AM cycle; for Rudolph, see Ron Martz and John Harmon, "Fugitive Was Known as Anti-Government," *Atlanta Journal and Constitution*, 17 February 1998, 3A; for Fischer, see William Nack, "Bobby Fischer," *Sports Illustrated* 63 (29 July 1985): 78.

7. Wiesel quoted in "1 in 5 Polled Voice Doubts on Holocaust," *New York Times* (national edition), 20 April 1993, A10. For detailed results of the survey, see Jennifer Golub and Renae Cohen, *What Do Americans Know about the Holocaust?* (New York, 1993).

8. See, e.g., editorials in *New York Times*, 23 April 1993, A34; *Christian Science Monitor*, 22 April 1993, 20; *Los Angeles Times*, 22 April 1993, B6; *USA Today*, 22 April 1993, 10A; *Dallas Morning News*, 24 April 1993, 28A.

9. See, e.g., Jonathan Alter, "After the Survivors," *Newsweek* 122 (20 December 1993): 116.

10. Jill Vejnoska, "Spielberg: 'I Thought I Knew What War Was,' " *Atlanta Journal and Constitution*, 19 July 1998, 10L.

11. See, e.g., Michiko Kakutani, "When History Is a Casualty," *New York Times*, 30 April 1993, C1; David Singer, review of *Denying the Holocaust*, *New Leader* 76 (17 May 1993): 19. For other associations of Holocaust denial with postmodernism and deconstructionism, see Edward Norden, "Yes and No to the Holocaust Museum," *Commentary* 96 (August 1993): 29–30; Gertrude Himmelfarb, *On Looking into the Abyss* (New York, 1994).

12. Michael R. Kagay, "Poll on Doubt of Holocaust Is Corrected," *New York Times*, 8 July 1994, A10; Everett Carll Ladd, "The Holocaust Poll Error: A Modern Cautionary Tale," *Public Perspective* 5 (July-August 1994): 3. For the fullest discussion, see Tom W. Smith, *Holocaust Denial: What the Survey Data Reveal* (New York, 1994).

13. There is something of a status hierarchy among survivors. "Treblinka survivors feel superior to the ones who were in Terezin [Theresienstadt] — a summer camp in comparison — who are above those in labor camps, who supersede the escapees to Sweden, Russia, and South America. . . . The more dire the circumstances, the more family murdered, the greater the starvation and disease, the higher the rung in this social register." (Sonia Pilcer, the daughter of survivors, quoted in William B. Helmreich, *Against All Odds: Holocaust Survivors and the Successful Lives They Made in America* [New York, 1992], 173–74.) One result of this system of invidious ranking is that those lower down on the scale are less likely to identify themselves as survivors and less likely to tell their stories. This is particularly true of what is probably the largest single group of survivors: Polish Jews who found themselves in, or made their way to, the part of Poland occupied by the Soviets in 1939, and who spent the war years in the USSR.

14. The reference is to the scene in Lanzmann's documentary in which a disraught Bomba, a survivor of Treblinka, begs the filmmaker not to force him to relive his most painful memories, to which Lanzmann replies "We have to do it. . . . We must go on." (The text of the scene — though not Bomba's tearful desperation — is in Lanzmann, *Shoah* [New York, 1985], 117.) Though there are examples of this sort of thing in American projects collecting survivor testimony, much more common is cajolery: survivors being told that even if they'd prefer not to summon up these memories, it is their duty "to history," or that their testimony is necessary to "refute deniers."

15. William Helmreich notes that the great majority of the research on how survivors

deal with the memory of their experiences is based on that relatively small portion who have been in psychotherapy — not a representative sample. (Helmreich, *Against All Odds*, 221.) He also reports that a number of survivors "attributed an increase in nightmares to having read books and seen films on the Holocaust when the topic became very popular in recent years." (Ibid., 224.) It may be that on balance survivors have benefited from all the recent attention to the Holocaust; we simply don't know. But I am struck by the one-size-fits-all assumption behind confident assertions that increased attention to the Holocaust is beneficial to "the [i.e., all] survivors."

16. A. Scott Walton, "WWII Veteran Is on Poster for TBS Film," *Atlanta Journal and Constitution*, 7 December 1995, 2E.

17. For a sampling of these criticisms, see Theodore Frankel, "Out of Auschwitz — Balm?" *Midstream* 10 (December 1964); Michael Brown, "On Crucifying the Jews," *Judaism* 27 (Winter 1978); David Roskies, *Against the Apocalypse* (Cambridge, Mass., 1983), 262–63, 301–2; Alan Mintz, "Echoes of the 'Event,' " *Jerusalem Report* 1 (25 October 1990); Matti Golan, *With Friends Like You* (New York, 1992), xi, 183–84. For the widespread criticisms of Wiesel that don't "go public," see Samuel G. Freedman, "Bearing Witness," *New York Times Magazine*, 23 October 1983, 32ff.; Berenbaum, *After Tragedy and Triumph*, 119.

18. Elie Wiesel, *All Rivers Run to the Sea: Memoirs* (New York, 1995), 4–5, 37, 150.

19. Another unanswerable question: What would talk of the Holocaust be like in America if a skeptical rationalist like Primo Levi, rather then a religious mystic like Wiesel, had been its principal interpreter?

20. See, e.g., Deborah Lipstadt, "A Clear and Future Danger: Denial of the Holocaust," *Tikkun* 10 (May 1995): 17.

21. Shmuel Krakowski, quoted in Barbara Amouyal, "Doubts over Evidence of Camp Survivors," *Jerusalem Post*, 17 August 1986, 1.

22. Primo Levi, *The Drowned and the Saved* (1986; English trans., New York, 1988), 19, 24. This is not a peculiarity of Holocaust survivors' memories; it is in the nature of memory. In 1825, on the occasion of the fiftieth anniversary of the Battle of Bunker Hill, depositions were collected from veterans and presented to the Massachusetts Historical Society. A committee of the society reported that they were historically useless; many of the testimonies were "inconsistent and utterly untrue mixtures of old men's broken memories and fond imaginings.... They had got so used to telling the story for the wonderment of village listeners as grandfathers' tales and . . . representatives of 'the spirit of '76' that they did not distinguish between what they had seen and done and what they had read, heard, or dreamed." (Committee report quoted in Richard M. Ketchum, "Memory as History," *American Heritage* 42 [November 1991]: 141–43.)

23. Lipstadt quoted in Blake Eskin, "Wilkomirski's New Identity Crisis," *Forward*, 18 September 1998, 12.

24. Early indications suggest that the way in which the testimonies have been collected and presented by Spielberg's Survivors of the Shoah Foundation will result in a meretricious, Hollywood-to-the-max sort of evocation. Most interviewers have only the sketchiest knowledge of the Holocaust. The format of the interviews (at Spielberg's insistence) manipulates them in a "redemptive" direction, with all narratives ending with the survivor surrounded by his or her family. The way in which the material is being presented to the public also bodes ill. The foundation's first educational CD-ROM is narrated by teenage sex idol Leonardo DiCaprio. For critical accounts of the venture, see Adam Shatz and Alisa Quart, "Spielberg's List," *Village Voice*, 9 January 1996, 31ff.; Jory Farr, "Apocalypse Then,"

Riverside (Cal.) *Press-Enterprise*, 2 June 1996, E1; Marc Fisher, "Fragments of Memory," *Washington Post*, 7 April 1998. For a positive account, see Mark Goldberg, "An Interview with Michael Berenbaum," *Phi Delta Kappan* 79 (December 1997); and Berenbaum's letter to the *Jerusalem Post*, 6 May 1998, 10. See also "Shoah Foundation Releases First Educational CD-ROM," Business Wire, 8 September 1998.

25. James E. Young, *The Texture of Memory* (New Haven, 1993), 296.
26. JoAnna Daemmrich, "Profaned Holocaust Memorial to Be Razed; Jewish Council Tires of Desecration by Addicts, Prostitutes," *Baltimore Sun*, 28 November 1995, 1A. A redesigned monument was built elsewhere. The director of the Baltimore Jewish Council thought that when families drove by it and saw the words "Holocaust Memorial," "more often than not [a child] will ask the parent, 'What was the Holocaust'?" ("Baltimore to Tear Down Memorial to Holocaust Victims," NPR, *Morning Edition*, 8 January 1996, transcript 1776–7.)
27. Wiesel quoted in Elli Wohlgelernter, "Fears for the Future," *Jerusalem Post*, 16 May 1997. I have slightly rearranged the order of Wiesel's remarks, but without altering their sense.
28. James Rudin, "Will Non-Europeans Remember the Holocaust?" *Washington Jewish Week*, 2 May 1991, 19–20.
29. This is not eternal. By the time of the bicentennial of the Revolution, in 1989, many in France agreed with my late colleague François Furet that "the Revolution is over."
30. Leon Wieseltier, "Scar Tissue," *New Republic* 200 (5 June 1989): 20.

Acknowledgments

Work on this project was supported by fellowships from the National Endowment for the Humanities and the Center for Advanced Study in the Behavioral Sciences.

I am grateful to the following institutions for invitations to present portions of this book — particularly grateful for useful criticism I received on those occasions: Association for Jewish Studies, Australian National University, Cornell University, Hebrew Union College, Indiana University, Jewish Museum of New York, Northwestern University, Princeton University, Rutgers University, Stanford University, Tel Aviv University, University of Amsterdam, University of California at Berkeley, University of Michigan, University of Pennsylvania, University of Texas at El Paso, U.S. Holocaust Memorial Museum.

My work in archival collections was made much easier by the help I received from Bernie Wax and Nathan Kaganoff at the American Jewish Historical Society; Abe Peck at the American Jewish Archives; Helen Ritter and Cyma Horowitz at the American Jewish Committee; Sam Norich, Zach Baker, and Marek Web at YIVO.

Over the years I've worked on this project I've been very fortunate in my research assistants at the University of Chicago: Danny Greene, Elizabeth Mizrahi, André Wakefield, and William Whitehurst.

My thanks to Steve Fraser for first signing me up with Houghton Mifflin, and to Janet Silver, Eric Chinski, and Larry Cooper, who (along with others at the firm) facilitated the transition from manuscript to book.

The list of friends and colleagues who have supplied information, on whom I have tried out various ideas, or who have helped me in various ways, large and small, is too long to present here. I thank them all. Special thanks to three friends who read and criticized the entire manuscript: David Abraham, Gulie Arad, and Steve Zipperstein.

Index

cide, 100; world's inability to rescue Jews from, 44–46. *See also* Concentration camps; De-Nazification; Hitler, Adolf; Holocaust; Kristallnacht; Nuremberg Laws; Victims; War criminals

NBC. *See Holocaust* (miniseries)

NCRAC. *See* National Community Relations Advisory Council

Neely, Matthew M., 297n.38

Negotiation efforts (to save European Jews), 48, 52–54

Neil, Sylvia, 343n.13

Neo-conservatism, 183, 289n.4, 326n.55

Neuhaus, Richard, 339n.87

Neumann, Emmanuel, 43–44

Neumann, Franz, 141

Neusner, Jacob, 150, 151, 198

"Never again" slogan: American politicians' use of, 48, 253–54; in campaigns for Soviet Jewry, 39; in Eichmann trial, 132; as Jewish Defense League's motto, 173; Jews' use of, 158–59; as lesson of Holocaust, 199, 232, 253–57

"New Americans," 67, 84

New England Holocaust Memorial (Boston), 207, 221, 224, 276

New Jersey Commission on Holocaust Education, 258

New Jersey School Boards Association, 258

New Leader, The, 24, 96, 99, 105–6

New Palestine, 45

New Republic, The, 22, 129, 159

New York City: efforts to build Holocaust memorial in, 123, 168, 202, 272, 276, 312n.79, 336n.54; Holocaust survivors in, 83; school strike in, 172, 173, 177, 178–79

New York Daily News, 82

New York Herald Tribune, 111, 306n.79

New York magazine, 212

New York Post, 89, 129

New York Times, 197, 249, 277, 306n.79; on Babi Yar, 22; on *Holocaust* miniseries, 211; Kristallnacht reported in, 21, 41; on Palestinian massacres, 162; on Serbian death camps, 251–52

New York Times Book Review, 118

New York Times Magazine, 115, 136

New Yorker, The, 117, 134, 139

Nicaragua, 183

Niebuhr, Reinhold, 110

Niemöller, Martin, 221

Nigeria, 247–48, 347n.76. *See also* Biafra

Night (Wiesel), 11

Nixon, Richard, 166

No Haven for the Oppressed (Friedman), 47

None Shall Escape (movie), 27

Non-Sectarian Committee for German Refugee Children, 51–52

Nordhausen concentration camp, 55

North American Jewish Students' Network, 187

Nuclear weapons, 12, 66, 72, 73, 232; concern about, 110–12; opposition to, 106, 127

Nuit et brouillard (Resnais), 103

Numbers (involved in Holocaust), 20, 36, 334n.23, 338n.72, 347n.72

Nuremberg Laws (Nazi Germany), 21, 209

Nuremberg Trials (Germany), 129

Nye, Gerald, 28

Objective, Burma! (movie), 33

Ochs, Vanessa L., 325n.41

Odessa File, The (Forsyth), 157

Office of Strategic Services (U.S.), 24. *See also* Central Intelligence Agency

Office of War Information (U.S.), 23, 27, 101, 294n.37

Okinawa, 66

Olson, Sidney, 295n.6

On the Beach (movie), 112

Operation Desert Storm, 249

Operation Restore Hope, 249

Ophuls, Marcel, 286n.6

Organization of American Historians, 270

Oxford English Dictionary, 133

Oz, Amos, 164

Ozick, Cynthia, 10, 117, 152

Pacific conflict (in World War II), 26, 27, 66

Paldiel, Mordechai, 325n.35

Palestine. *See* Arab nations; Israel; Middle East; Palestine Liberation Organization; Yishuv; Zionism

Palestine Liberation Organization (PLO), 161, 183

Palestine Post, 35–36

Papazian, Pierre, 329n.92

Paris, 312n.79

Particularism (Identity politics; Separatism): emphasis on, in America, 5, 6–7, 171–91, 280; and victimhood, 8–10, 214–26

Partisan Review, 24, 326n.54

Passover, 257, 332n.133; Holocaust references in rituals of, 104, 184, 307n.5; not observed by Anne Frank, 119–20

Past. *See* History